Cyril of Alexandria's Refutations
By Cyril of Alexandria
This Edition Edited by Anthony Uyl

Cyril of Alexandria's Refutations
By Cyril of Alexandria
This Edition Edited by Anthony Uyl

The text of Cyril of Alexandria's Refutations is all in the Public Domain. The title, covers, background, layout and Devoted Publishing logo are Copyright ©2018 Devoted Publishing. This edition is published by Devoted Publishing a division of 2165467 Ontario Inc.

**What kind of philosophies do you have?
Let us know!**

Visit our webpage: www.devotedpublishing.com
Contact us at: devotedpub@hotmail.com
Visit our shop on Facebook: Devoted Publishing

Published in Ingersoll, Ontario, Canada 2018.

For bulk educational rates, please contact us at the above email address.

ISBN: 978-1-77356-283-4

Table of Contents

Cyril of Alexandria: Five Tomes Against Nestorius 4
PREFACE 5
    THE 12 CHAPTERS 6
    Footnotes: 48
Cyril of Alexandria, Five Tomes Against Nestorius - Book 1 58
    Footnotes: 77
Cyril of Alexandria, Five Tomes Against Nestorius - Book 2 84
    Footnotes: 105
Cyril of Alexandria, Five Tomes Against Nestorius - Book 3 114
    Footnotes: 137
Cyril of Alexandria, Five Tomes Against Nestorius - Book 4 140
    Footnotes: 155
Cyril of Alexandria, Five Tomes Against Nestorius - Book 5 160
    Footnotes: 176
Against Diodore of Tarsus and Theodore of Mospuestia 178
CYRIL FROM HIS TREATISE AGAINST DIODORE BISHOP OF TARSUS [1] 179
    Footnotes: 186
CYRIL OF ALEXANDRIA FROM HIS SECOND BOOK AGAINST THE WORDS OF THEODORE [1] 191
    Footnotes: 197
CYRIL OF ALEXANDRIA FROM THE THIRD BOOK AGAINST THEODORE BISHOP OF MOPSUESTIA 201
    Footnotes: 207
Against Julian 210
Book 1 Prefatory Address 211
Book 2 (beginning) 214
Book 3 THE CREATION OF THE WORLD 220
Cyril of Alexandria: Against the Synousiasts 234
CYRIL OF ALEXANDRIA FROM HIS TREATISE [1] AGAINST THE SYNOUSIASTS [2] 235
    Footnotes: 242

Cyril of Alexandria: Five Tomes Against Nestorius

By Cyril of Alexandria

PREFACE

On the death of Theophilus, Archbishop of Alexandria, in A.D. 412, his nephew and successor, S. Cyril, comes suddenly before us. For of S. Cyril's previous life we have only a few scattered notices. We do not know in what year he was born, nor any thing of his parents, nor where he was brought up. That S. Cyril had received a thoroughly good education, is abundantly clear; not only from his very extensive reading, which a mind of such large grasp as S. Cyril's would ever provide for itself, but that his reading being so well digested implies good early training. The great accuracy of his Theology implies a most accurate Theological education. That education included a large range of secular study as well as of Divinity, and probably comprised a good deal of learning by heart, not only of the holy Scriptures but also of profane authors, as witness a line of Antipater Sidonius quoted in his Commentary on Zechariah. He quotes too Josephus on the Jewish war. On Hab. iii. 2, he mentions interpretations of that verse of two different kinds: on Hosea he gives a long extract from a writer whom we do not apparently possess. Tillemont remarks, that " [1] his books against Julian shew that he had a large acquaintance with secular writers."

We may infer that S. Cyril was brought up at some monastery, as a place of Christian education, and from the great reverence which he ever paid to S. Isidore, Abbot of Pelusium, it seems not unlikely that S. Isidore was his instructor during some part of his early life. S. Isidore alludes to some especial tie, in one of his brief letters to S. Cyril, when Archbishop. Near the beginning, S. Isidore says, " [2] If I be your father as you say I be,.....or if I be your son as I know I am, seeing that you hold the chair of S. Mark &c." The large number of Platonic words in S. Isidore's letters seem to indicate that he too had extensive reading of Plato, and S. Cyril may have acquired from him some of his knowledge of Aristotle.

But a mind of S. Cyril's grasp would feel itself lost in the desert, yearning for its own calling, and another Letter [3] of the same S.Isidore to S.Cyril, reproaching him with his heart being in the world, may belong to this period. His uncle Archbishop Theophilus had him to live with him and, we may infer, ordained him priest and made him one of his Clergy. In a very long letter which S. Cyril wrote about A.D. 432 to the aged Acacius, Bishop of Beroea, he incidentally mentions the fact that he was at the synod of the Oak, in A.D. 403, where S. Chrysostom's troubles began. S. Cyril would of course be there, as a portion of Archbishop Theophilus' official attendance. S. Cyril says, " [4] [When your holy Synod was gathered at great Constantinople .... and I was one of those standing by, I know that I heard your holiness saying thus.----"

S. Cyril's accession to the Archiepiscopal Throne of Alexandria brought him at once into a position of great power in Alexandria; and brought too, in the early part of it, trials in regard of the disunion between him and Orestes the Governor resulting from the Jewish insurrection against the Christians. To this succeeded some years of great quiet, during which S. Cyril seems to have been very little heard of, outside his Great Diocese. The Archbishops of Alexandria, even in the very stillest times, were brought into yearly contact with the Churches every where by the annual Letter which they wrote to announce the day on which Easter would fall. S. Cyril's letters were evidently intended primarily for his own Egypt [5]. Thus in his seventh Paschal homily A.D. 419, he speaks very strongly about deeds of violence in Egypt and mentions the famine there. S. Cyril introduces the subject with, " [6] And these things we now say to you most especially, who inhabit Egyptian territory," shewing that the Letters themselves had a larger scope. I do not know at what time the Letter was sent out, so as to reach the distant churches of Rome and Constantinople and Antioch in good time to announce when Lent would begin. But although S. Cyril became Archbishop in October A.D. 412, his first Letter was for 414, in the early part of which (as Tillemont points out) S. Cyril speaks of having succeeded his Uncle. He introduces the subject by mentioning the natural dread of those of old, of " [7] [the greatness of the Divine Ministry," and speaking of Moses and Jeremiah as instances of this, adds, that "since the garb of the priesthood calls to preach, in fear of the words, Speak and hold not thy peace, I come of necessity to write thus."

Much of these quiet years S. Cyril probably employed on his earlier writings: of these, two were on select passages of the Pentateuch; one volume being allotted to those which S. Cyril thought could in any way be adapted as types of our Lord, the other to the rest, as being types of the church. The commentaries on Isaiah and the Minor Prophets and the Books against the Emperor Julian probably belong to this period. Besides these S. Cyril, following the example of his great predecessor S. Athanasius, wrote two Books against the Arians: first, the Thesaurus, in which S. Cyril brought to bear his knowledge of Aristotle; then the de Trinitate, which was written, though not published till later, before A.D. 424. In his Paschal homily for that year A.D. 424, S. Cyril also speaks of the Eternal Generation of the Son, and towards the close of the homily [8] he opposes the Arian terms "Generate," "Ingenerate."

A. D. 429, the circulation of tracts of Nestorius in Egypt occasioned him first to write on the heresy of Nestorius. There can be little doubt that the powerful mind of S. Leo, who was the soul of the Council of Chalcedon, was, in his young days when S. Celestine's Archdeacon in 429, taught through those writings; as S. Cyril himself had been taught by the writings of S. Athanasius.

The 12 Chapters, appended to his last letter to Nestorius, were made a trouble to S. Cyril at a later period of his Episcopate, so that it may be well to give them in full. They were framed to preclude any evasion of that letter.

THE 12 CHAPTERS

1. If any one confess not, that Emmanuel is in truth God, and that the holy Virgin is therefore Mother of God, for she hath borne after the flesh the Word out of God made Flesh, be he anathema.

2. If any one confess not, that the Word out of God the Father hath been personally united to Flesh, and that He is One Christ with His own Flesh, the Same (that is) God alike and Man, be he anathema.

3. If any one sever the Hypostases of the One Christ after the Union, connecting them with only a connection of dignity or authority or sway, and not rather with a concurrence unto Unity of Nature, be he anathema.

4. If any one allot to two Persons or Hypostases the words in the Gospels and Apostolic writings, said either of Christ by the saints or by Him of Himself, and ascribe some to a man conceived of by himself apart from the Word That is out of God, others as God-befitting to the Word alone That is out of God the Father, be he anathema.

5. If any one dare to say, that Christ is a God-clad man, and not rather that He is God in truth as being the One Son, and That by Nature, in that the Word hath been made Flesh, and hath shared like us in blood and flesh, be he anathema.

6. If any one dare to say that the Word That is out of God the Father is God or Lord of Christ and do not rather confess that the Same is God alike and Man, in that the Word hath been made Flesh, according to the Scriptures, be he anathema.

7. [9] If any one say that Jesus hath been in-wrought-in as man by God the Word, and that the Glory of the Only-Begotten hath been put about Him, as being another than He, be he anathema.

8. If any one shall dare to say that the man that was assumed ought to be co-worshipped with God the Word and co-glorified and co-named God as one in another (for the co-, ever appended, compels us thus to deem) and does not rather honour Emmanuel with one worship, and send up to Him One Doxology, inasmuch as the Word has been made Flesh, be he anathema.

9. If any one say that the One Lord Jesus Christ hath been glorified by the Spirit, using His Power as though it were Another's, and from Him receiving the power of working against unclean spirits and of accomplishing Divine signs towards men, and does not rather say that His own is the Spirit, through Whom also He wrought the Divine signs, be he anathema.

10. The Divine Scripture says that Christ hath been made the Sigh Priest and Apostle of our Confession and that He offered Himself for us for an odour of a sweet smell to God the Father. If any one therefore say that, not the Very Word out of God was made our High Priest and Apostle when He was made Flesh and man as we, but that man of a woman apart by himself as other than He, was [so made]: or if any one say that in His own behalf also He offered the Sacrifice and not rather for us alone (for He needed not offering Who knoweth not sin), be he anathema.

11. If any one confess not, that the Flesh of the Lord is Life-giving and that it is the own Flesh of the Word Himself That is out of God the Father, but says that it belongs to another than He, connected with Him by dignity or as possessed of Divine Indwelling only, and not rather that it is Life-giving (as we said) because it hath been made the own Flesh of the Word Who is mighty to quicken all things, be he anathema.

12. If any one confess not that the Word of God suffered in the Flesh and hath been crucified in the Flesh and tasted death in the Flesh and hath been made First-born of the Dead, inasmuch as He is both Life and Life-giving as God, be he anathema.

The Great Diocese of Antioch, barely rallying from its terrible devastation by Arian wickedness oppression and misbelief, had been in close quarters with Apollinarianism, a misbelief that the Only-Begotten Son took flesh only without a reasonable soul, and that His mind-less Body was somehow immingled with the Godhead. S. Athanasius and others add, among the forms of the misbelief, that some Apollinarians thought that our Lord's Body was consubstantial with His Godhead. S. Cyril in his Dialogue [10] speaks of the great fear prevalent among some, that if One Incarnate Nature were holden, the Body must be believed to be consubstantial with the Godhead. Successus, Bishop of Diocaesarea, at almost the extreme west boundary of that great Diocese or Province of Antioch, sent to S. Cyril a question to the same effect. Theodore of Mopsuestia, who had died only about two years before these Chapters were issued, had held that the Manhood of the Only-Begotten was a man distinct, having some undefined connection with God the Son, and this had appeared in his writings; and so great was Theodore's reputation and the dread of the Apollinarian heresy, that there seems to have been an unconscious vagueness in the minds of some of the Eastern Bishops. [Nestorius had dexterously sent the Chapters to John of Antioch apart from the Epistle to himself [11], which would have made misinterpretation impossible. He sent them as 'propositions circulated in the royal city to the injury of the common Church.'] John of Antioch, who at that time believed Nestorius to be orthodox, pronounced them at once (thus unexplained) to be Apollinarian; applied in an Encyclical letter [12] to the Bishops of his Patriarchate to have them 'disclaimed, but without naming the author,' whom John did not believe to be S. Cyril, and asked two of the Bishops of his Province, Andrew Bishop of Samosata, and Theodoret, to reply to them. Theodoret's reply shews that he read the Chapters with the conviction that they were Apollinarian, and he accordingly replies, not to the Chapters themselves but to the sense which he himself imagined that they contained. His reply is in the main orthodox, though it looks in one or two places as if his belief was rather vague [13], but he twists S. Cyril's words so as to mean 'mixture,' and so replies [14]. Theodoret seems never to have got over his misapprehension. For in his long Letter [15] to the Monks of his Province, Euphratesia, Osroene, Syria, Phoenicia, Cilicia, he still speaks of Chapter 1 as teaching that God the Word was changed into flesh; of chapters 2 and 3 as bringing in the terms, Personal Union and Natural Union, "teaching through these names a mixture and confusion of the Divine Nature and the bondman's form: this is the offspring of Apollinarius' heretical innovation." And after speaking of Chapter 4, he sums up, "These are the Egyptian's brood, the truly more wicked descendants of a wicked parent." In his letter [16] to John Bishop of Germanicia, written after the Robbers' council in 449, Theodoret says of it, "Let them deny now the chapters which they many times condemned, but have in Ephesus now confirmed."

Andrew of Samosata, on the other hand, seems to have been decidedly more definite in his belief on the Incarnation, and to have thought that some of S. Cyril's chapters were Apollinarian without objecting to all. Thus Andrew's chief objection to chapter 1 appears to have been that he mistook the words "for she hath borne after the flesh (sarkikos)" to mean that the Birth was entirely in the order of nature and so not of a Virgin [17] . Andrew passes over chapter 2, as though the term, "Personal Union," had not even struck him as a difficulty. In chapter 3, Andrew thinks that phusike, Natural Union, or Unity of Nature is an inadmissible expression, as to what is above our nature. In chapter 4, Andrew thinks that because the words are not to be apportioned to distinct Persons, therefore S. Cyril meant, that they are not to be apportioned at all, either to the Godhead or to the Manhood in the One Person of the Incarnate God. S. Cyril had all his life said that they were to be so apportioned, but Andrew had of course not read S. Cyril's writings. Andrew shews his own definite belief by the expression he akra henosis, entire union, here; and, ['we confess the union entire (ten henosin akran) and Divine and incomprehensible to us,' are the closing words of his reply to chapter 11. These are almost identical with S. Cyril's expressions, "we shall not take away the unlike by nature through wholly uniting them (dia to eis akron henoun) [18]," and in his reply to Andrew, diaten eis akron henosin.

Andrew says nothing on chapters 5 and 6, nor is there anything in them which one would expect him not to accept. With chapter 7 he agrees, merely saying that in rejecting what S. Cyril rejects, we must not reject the Apostolic words which speak of Him in His human nature. "With chapter 8 too Andrew agrees, but does not quite understand the co. In chapter 9, he overlooks the words, "as though it were Another's:" in chapter 10, Andrew thinks that " the Yery Word out of God was made our High-Priest and Apostle" means 'the Godhead apart by Itself was so made.'

[We see in our own times, how prejudice can distort the meaning of words in themselves perfectly intelligible; else it seems inconceivable that language so clear as that of the Anathematisms, if read with a view to understand their author's meaning, could be misunderstood as it was by John of Antioch, Theodoret, and Andrew. Much unhallowed dissension would have been saved, if John, instead of asking Theodoret and Andrew to reply to them, had sought an explanation from S. Cyril himself. S. Cyril, in clear consciousness of his own meaning, would, of course, have given the explanation which afterwards satisfied John of Antioch, Acacius of Beroea, and Paul of Emesa.

S. Cyril's anathematisms have been weighed by Petavius with his usual solidity, as compared with the counter-anathematisms of Nestorius, the criticisms of the Orientals and of Theodoret, and S. Cyril's answers. His summary is, 'There is nothing in S. Cyril's Anathematisms not right and in harmony with the Catholic rule, nor did those who detract from or oppose them maintain their ground against him except through cavils and foolish calumnies.' De Incarn. L. vi. c. xvii. They have also been carefully compared in English in Dr. Bright's Later Treatises of S. Athanasius, pp. 149-170.]

Though Apollinarianism in its early form, ere its great spread as Eutychianism, seems to have chiefly troubled Asia rather than Egypt, S. Cyril always writes with full knowledge of it. In his Thesaurus, he distinctly mentions and repudiates Apollinarian errors and denies the [19] ouk en anthropo gegone, "made man, came not into a man like as He was in the Prophets." S. Cyril's tenth Paschal homily for A.D. 420, in its most carefully weighed language, contradicts both Apollinarianism and Nestorianism, not less than what S. Cyril wrote when the Nestorian troubles had begun. On Habaccuc [20] S. Cyril affirms, as he does through his whole life, that our Lord was not worsened by the Incarnation; "Yet even though He has been made flesh and hath been set forth by the Father as a propitiation, He hath not cast away what He was, i.e., the being God, but is even thus in God-befitting authority and glory."

In A.D. 428, Nestorius was brought from Antioch to be Archbishop of Constantinople. From the circumstance that S. Cyril's celebrated Paschal homily for the next year, A.D. 429, was on the subject of the Incarnation, it has been supposed that rumours of the denial of that Faith in Constantinople had already reached him. But the Paschal homilies for A.D. 420 and 423, shew that the Incarnation, the foundation and stay of our souls, was a subject, which S. Cyril loved to dwell on. In the course of the year 429, however, even Egypt was troubled by the false teaching of Nestorius. Some of Nestorius' sermons [21] passed into Egypt, and were read and pondered over in the Monasteries. This occasioned so much disturbance in the minds [22] of some of the Monks, that S. Cyril wrote a Letter to them, pointing out that the Incarnation means, that God the Son united to Him His own human nature which He took, as completely as soul and body are united in each of us, and in this way His Passion and Death were His own, though He, as God, could not suffer. This Letter had an extended circulation and reached Constantinople. It vexed [23] Nestorius. There was still a traditional soreness towards Alexandria, from the behaviour of Theophilus to S. Chrysostom [24]. Besides this, the Catholic doctrine of the Incarnation, the manhood united by God the Son to His own self, was to Nestorius, Apollinarianism or mixture. Nestorius says so [25]. In his letter to S. Celestine he tells of the 'corruption of orthodoxy among some' and thus describes it,

> 'It is a sickness not small, but akin to the putrid sore of Apollinarius and Arius. For they mingle the Lord's union in man to a confusion of some sort of mixture, insomuch that even certain clerks among us, of whom some from lack of understanding, some from heretical guile of old time concealed within them .. are sick as heretics, and openly blaspheme God the Word Consubstantial with the Father, as though He had taken beginning of His Being of the Virgin mother of Christ, and had been built up with His Temple and buried with His flesh, and say that the flesh after the resurrection did not remain [miscuisse seems an error for mansisse] flesh but passed into the Nature of Godhead, and they refer the Godhead of the Only-Begotten to the beginning of the flesh which was connected with It, and they put It to death with the flesh, and blasphemously say that the flesh connected with Godhead passed into Godhead, using the very word deifying, which is nothing else than to corrupt both [26].'

Nestorius repeats the same in his second letter to S. Celestine [27]. S. Cyril having in his first Ecumenical Letter to Nestorius put forth clearly the mode of the Union in these words, Nestorius does not understand the language and says thus of it,

> 'I come now to the second chapter of your Love, wherein I begin to praise the parting of the natures in regard to Godhead and Manhood and their connection into one Person, and that we must not say that God the Word needed a second generation out of a woman, and must confess that the Godhead is unrecipient of suffering. For such statements are truly orthodox and counter to the ill-reputes of all the heresies, as to the Lord's natures. As to the rest, whether they bring to the ears of the readers some hidden incomprehensible wisdom, pertains to your accuracy to know; to me they seem

to overturn what preceded. For Him Who in the preceding is proclaimed Impassible and non-recipient of a second birth, they introduce as somehow passible and new-created, as though the qualities by nature adherent in God the Word were corrupted by connection with the Temple &c. [28']

And yet S. Cyril's language is so carefully guarded, that no one who believed in True Union of Godhead and Manhood in the Incarnate Son would mistake it.

Nestorius does not appear to have taken any notice of S. Cyril's Paschal Homily, but he preached against the Letter to the Monks more than once, as we see from the extracts of such of his sermons as S. Cyril had access to. The passages of the Letter to the Monks referred to by Nestorius are;

[29] *These letters were directed by me against the Egyptian .... He, omitting to tell me by letter whether any thing appeared to him to need marking as blasphemous or wicked, moved by fear of proofs and looking out therefore for disturbances which should aid him, turns him to Celestine of Rome, as one too simple to fathom the force of the doctrines. And finding the simplicity of the man in regard to this matter, he in childish fashion circumvents his ears with crafty letters, long ago sending him my writings, as a proof which might not be gainsaid, as though I were making Christ out to be a mere man, I who at the very beginning of my consecration obtained a Law against those who say that Christ is a mere man and against other heresies.*

'But he compiled writings, interweaving extracts of my sermons, in order that the slander put on me by the piecing of extracts might not be found out. And some things he added to my sermons, he broke off bits of others and pieced what I had said of the Lord's Incarnation as though I had said them of a mere man. Things again which I had said in praise of the Godhead he cut entirely away from the context, leaving some out of their proper place, and thus made out a plausible misleading. And to publish his wickedness in a few instances such as it is in the rest, I said somewhere, speaking against the heathen who say that we preach that the Essence of God has been newly created from a Virgin, 'Mary, my friends, bare not the Godhead; she bare a man the inseparable instrument of Godhead.' But he changing the word, Godhead, made it, 'Mary, my friends, bare not God.' Here to say God, and to say the Godhead, makes very much difference. For the one signifies the Divine and unembodied Essence, but does not mean the flesh. For flesh is compound and created. But the word God belongs to the temple also of the Godhead, which obtains the dignity by union with the Divine Essence of God, yet is not changed into that Divine Essence.

'Again in another place I spoke against those who, hearing the like name, are offended as though like honour were also given. And when I say, Mother of Christ, they shudder as though the Godhead of the Lord Christ were denied by this name, seeing that many have been similarly called by this name in the Old Testament. And hence they think that we are calling Him Christ like these. Against these people therefore (as I said) I said in church-sermons, that equality of honour does not follow likeness of name. And this is what I said, 'Or if the Temple of Godhead, wo say that the descent of the Holy Ghost is not the same as was wrought on the Prophets, not the same as was celebrated on the Apostles, nor yet the same as takes place in regard to the Angels who are

strengthened unto the Divine Mysteries. For the Lord Christ is Lord of all, as to the body too. As therefore we say that God is the Creator of all things, yet does the Scripture call Moses too god, for it says, I have made thee a god to Pharoah, and yet we by no means attach equal honour to that word, so neither, because the word is common by which we say, Christ and Son, ought we to stumble at the likeness of expression. For as Israel is named son, for He says, Israel is My first-born son, and the Lord again Son, for He says, This is My Beloved Son, yet not, as the expression is one, is the meaning also one. And as Saul is called christ and David christ and again Cyrus christ and, besides, the Babylonian, albeit they were surely not equal in piety to David; so we call the Lord too Christ or Son, yet the community of names does not makes an equality of dignity.' From this which I said, he every where subtracting the last words, i.e. 'Christ,' and, 'we say, that not the same is the indwelling as was wrought on the prophets, not the same as was wrought on the Apostles,' and, ' we by no means allot like honour by like words,' and, 'yet the community of names does not make equality of dignity; ' cutting out all these expressions with the teeth of slander, he flings in the ears of men what precedes these words: i.e., ' [30] We call the Creator of all God, yet does the Scripture also call Moses god:, and, 'Israel is called God's son, Son too is the Lord called;' and, 'Saul is called christ and David christ yea and the Babylonian; thus then do we call Christ the Lord also christ.' He therefore thus piecing these things and chipping them off from the rest (as we said), made up here by his slander like as if from Paul's words by which he contests writing, If ye be circumcised Christ shall profit you nothing, one were to rend off what he says first, If ye be circumcised, and accuse Paul as though he preached, Christ shall profit you nothing. And why need we prolong our recital by going through each instance? In short Cyril using many such robberies and additions as pleased him, soon not others only but Celestine also were led away by his misleadings.'

    Much about this time S. Cyril probably wrote his Scholia on the Incarnation [31]. The treatise is very simple and almost uncontroversial, illustrating the Incarnation by simple analogies and Bible-types [32]. It contains one of S. Cyril's most careful statements of the doctrine, excluding Apollinarianism [33]. In the concluding sections [34], which may have been written at the very beginning of the controversy with Nestorius, are striking and simple statements, how God the Son's Passion is His, though Godhead cannot suffer.

    Soon after this S. Cyril wrote his first extant letter to Nestorius, a short letter, saying that he hears that Nestorius was very angry at S. Cyril's letter to the Monks, yet that since 'expositions,' whether Nestorius' or not, had been brought to Egypt and had gravely misled many, it became a duty to God to put forth the right doctrine. S. Cyril also says that S. Celestine and the Bishops with him had asked whether those 'expositions' which had come thither were Nestorius' or not. S. Cyril did not know. Finally, S. Cyril asked him to heal the confusion by the use of the one word Theotocos, of the Holy Virgin. For fear of misapprehension he mentions also a book, which he had written in the Episcopate of Atticus of blessed memory, on the Holy and Consnbstantial Trinity, in which he had interwoven some things on the Incarnation, like what he had now written.

    We do not know what time intervened between this and the second Letter which S. Cyril wrote in Synod to Nestorius, containing an exposition of the

Incarnation, which, from its acceptance by the Council of Ephesus and the whole Church subsequently, has Ecumenical authority [35]. It was probably written before the close of A.D. 429 and is the Letter quoted above [36], which Nestorius' reply shewed that he could not understand. It has been supposed that it was in consequence of Nestorius' allusion to the Imperial Court in the close of his reply, that S. Cyril wrote his Three Treatises de recta fide; whereof the first is to the Emperor Theodosius; the other two to the Emperor's Queen and Sisters. John Bishop of Caesarea in Palestine, in the century following S. Cyril, quotes from both among his extracts in defence of the Council of Chalcedon[37]. From the title with which he introduces his extracts, we learn that the longer Treatise was addressed to the Emperor's two younger sisters, the Princesses Marina and Arcadia, and the last of the Three to the Two Augusta's, Theodosius' Empress Eudocia, and his eldest sister Pulcheria who had the title of Augusta, from having been Regent for the Emperor in his minority. S. Cyril afterwards recast his Treatise to the Emperor in the form of a Dialogue, omitting what was specially addressed to the Emperor, and giving little touches here and there to the language. Thus the expression "[38] neither do we say Two christs, even though we believe that the Temple united to the Word has been ensouled with rational soul," becomes in the Dialogue, "[39] neither do we say Two christs, even though we believe that out of perfect man and out of God the Word has been wrought the concurrence unto unity of Emmanuel." A little further on, "[40] we say that the whole Word out of Grod has been co-united with the whole manhood that is of us," becomes, "[41] we say therefore that the whole Word has been united to whole man." This Dialogue was probably appended by S. Cyril to his older Dialogues de Trinitate. It is quoted as the seventh of those Dialogues. The other two treatises are chiefly made up of expositions of texts to prove that Christ is God and Man. Near the beginning of that to the Augusta's, S. Cyril alludes to his former treatise.

> "In my treatise to the holy Virgins [i. e. the Princesses Marina and Arcadia who had embraced the virgin estate] I made a very large provision of more obvious sayings which had nothing hard to understand; but in this I have made mention of the obscurer. For your Pious Authority ought both to know these and not to be ignorant of the other, in order that by means of both, perfection in knowledge, like a light, may dwell in your most pure understanding [42]"

Bishop Hefele [43] thinks that there are indications that the two Princesses had, in contrast with the Emperor, spoken for Cyril and against Nestorius.

Of the five sermons of Nestorius on the Incarnation which Marius Mercator translated into Latin, S. Cyril has cited copiously from the second: the fourth and fifth of Mercator's collection belong to the close of A.D. 430; for the fourth is dated the eighth of the Ides of December (Dec. 6), the Saturday after Nestorius had received S. Cyril's four Bishops with S. Celestine's Letter and S. Cyril's with the 12 Chapters. In it Nestorius recapitulates some of the teaching which S. Cyril had quoted from an earlier sermon, i.e. on God sending forth His Son. Of that earlier sermon we have only fragments, but it was preached against S. Cyril's letter to the Monks [44]. Nestorius speaks of S. Cyril as the "wrangler[45], "the heretic [46]," and he apostrophises S. Cyril or S. Proclus, "O heretic in clerical form [47]."

The last of that series in Mercator's collection was preached on Sunday Dec. 7.

Count Irenaeus has also preserved it; the compiler of the Synodicon gives it in another translation [48].

***

One of the interests and employments of the Bishops during their first days at Ephesus will have been the becoming acquainted with some whom they had never before seen. This time was probably the beginning of a lasting friendship between S. Cyril and Acacius the metropolitan of Melitene, on the borders of Armenia towards Cappadocia: the long letter which he wrote to Valerian Bishop of Iconium points at S. Cyril's having readied some degree of intimacy with him; he wrote too to Donatus, Bishop of Nicopolis, on the west of Greece, and no doubt there were other friendships too as the fruit of the long sojourn at Ephesus. Some of S. Cyril's letters shew how warm-hearted and sensitive he was, notwithstanding his mighty will and unswerving purpose.

But there were other sadder things belonging to that summer at Ephesus, sickness and death, the sickness probably the fever so prevalent now along all that poisonous coast, and passing in many cases into dysentery. "We do not know what Bishops the Council lost; for our knowledge of those who composed it is derived from the lists of names at the opening of the first and sixth session and the signatures to those two sessions. But the fact is mentioned several times: S. Cyril in the first session of the Council says,

"some have fallen into sickness and some are dead;"

the Council in its Relatio to the Emperors, says,

"and some of the holy Bishops weighed down by age did not endure their stay in a strange place; some were imperilled in weakness; some have even undergone the close of their life in the Capital of the Ephesians;"

in its account to S. Celestine,

"although many both Bishops and Clergy were both pressed by sickness and oppressed by expense and some had even deceased."

After waiting a fortnight, during which time, if all had been there, the business might have been completed and the Bishops dismissed, S. Cyril wrote to John Archbishop of Antioch. John, in his Relatio to the Emperors, says,

"and Cyril himself of Alexandria sent to me of Antioch two days before the assembly made by them [the Council], that the whole Synod is awaiting my presence [49]*."*

S. Cyril too alludes to the Letter. He says of John,

"he who was ever friendly and dear, who never at any time found fault with my words, who wrote kindly and received letters from me [50]*."*

While this letter was on its way, some of the Bishops of John's party arrived, and with them a letter to S. Cyril in which John spoke of being only about four days off. The Bishops of John's party were Alexander Metropolitan of Apamea and Alexander Metropolitan of Hierapolis; and, to all appearance, though we are not told so, Theodoret and Meletius bishop of Neocaesarea. The Council, speaking of the arrival in their Eelatio to S. Celestine, says,

" [51] Nevertheless after the sixteenth day there preceded him some of the Bishops who were with him, two Metropolitans, Alexander of Apamea and another Alexander of Hierapolis; and when we complained of the tardy arrival of the most reverend Bishop John, they said not once but over and over, 'he bid us tell your Reverence that, if he should even yet loiter, the synod was not to be put off, but rather to do what was meet.' "

S. Cyril says nearly the same in his Apology to the Emperor [52]. Nevertheless it is plain that John meant the words, 'if I yet loiter,' to be taken in connection with his own letter to S. Cyril that he was but 5 or 6 days off, and so that he should have that interval allowed him.

The Council however, in the distress of many of its members, determined to assemble the next day. Nestorius' friends headed by Tranquillinus, Bishop of Antioch in Pisidia, got up a memorial to the Council that they should wait for John of Antioch, "who is himself now at the door, as he has intimated by his Letters," and for some Western Bishops. The document further speaks of the unlawfulness of excommunicated or deposed Bishops being admitted into the Council and ends with the threatening words [53],

"And let your Reverence know, that all that shall be done in an abrupt way by daring men will be turned back against the daring of them who so presume, both by Christ the Lord and by the Divine Canons."

There follow 68 signatures, 16 of the Province of Antioch including the two newly-arrived Alexanders (an indication that they, while they delivered John's message, did not consider it as precluding four days' delay) about 30 other friends of Nestorius. They procured also about 23 other signatures. These 23 however joined the Council next day as a matter of course, and signed the deposition of Nestorius. Among the signatures is that of Euprepius Bishop of Byza who signs for himself and for his Nestorian Metropolitan Fritilas of Heraclea. But Euprepius did not remain with his Metropolitan. I do not see his name on the entry-roll of the Council at its opening session; but he signs the deposition of Nestorius. His name is among the last signatures, as though he had come in late.

No deliberative body whatever would accept such an insulting memorial as this of the friends of Nestorius, and of course it does not appear in the Acts of the Council. Count Irenaeus, the friend of Nestorius, afterwards Bishop of Tyre, has preserved it to us with other curious documents of his party.

Christian Lupus at the end of the 17th century transcribed the greater part of an unique manuscript in the Monastery Library of Monte Cassino [54]. The compiler is thought to be an African; he was a contemporary of Facundus, Bishop of Hermaeum, and just as Facundus wrote very eagerly in behalf of Theodore of Mopsuestia, this compiler wrote very strongly in defence of Theodoret. His principal material was a curious and extensive collection of documents and Letters made by Count Irenaeus, Bishop of Tyre, after the

Council of Ephesus; it contains Letters that passed between the different Bishops in the Province of Antioch about Nestorius and S. Cyril, and their views as to reconciliation with S. Cyril, and one sees how eagerly the principal Bishops got hold of a copy of any fresh letter which S. Cyril wrote. This collection alone preserves S. Cyril's great Letter to Acacius Bishop of Beroea, in reply to the first demand of the Eastern Bishops that the Nicene Creed was enough and that S. Cyril should burn all else which he had written on dogma. S. Cyril alludes to this Letter of his in his letter to his Proctors at Constantinople[55] and a fragment of it is preserved by John Archbishop of Caesarea in Palestine in his Thesaurus of extracts of S. Cyril in Defence of the Council of Chalcedon, and two or three fragments of it by John's opponent, Severus of Antioch, both belonging to the earlier half of the sixth century.

Irenaeus being a contemporary of the Council of Ephesus, all the letters and documents collected by him seem to have been accepted without any doubt as to their genuineness. We also possess several from other sources. But the Compiler, who made use of Count Irenaeus' collection, has also inserted towards the end of his compilation, some documents from other MSS. to which he had access: one of these is absolutely worthless, viz. a confession of faith, purporting to be that of Acacius Bishop of Beroea, but evidently of later date.

Irenaeus' compilation is called a Tragedy [56]. Renaudot, in his history, has pointed out that Ebed-jesu of Soba, who lived in the end of the 12th century, has mentioned the work in his catalogue of Ecclesiastical writers [57]. Ebedjesu says [58], "Irenaeus of Tyre compiled five Ecclesiastica on the persecution of Nestorius and all that happened at that time [59]." Two or three pages before[60], Ebedjesu, in his catalogue of Nestorius' writings, gives also, "A Book of a Tragedy."

The little treatise or rather Confession of S. Athanasius from which S. Cyril cites in his Book against Theodore [61] is put by Montfaucon, S. Athanasius' Editor, among the dubia. Montfaucon's grounds for doing so are twofold; 1, that the very famous expression, One Incarnate Nature of the Word [62], seems to contradict what S. Athanasius says in other writings; 2, that the treatise was objected to by Leontius of Byzantium, at the beginning of the seventh Century.

Of the first ground of doubt, no one but a student of S. Athanasius has any right to speak. The second dwindles to nothing. Leontius says,

"They [the party of Severus, the great Monophysite Bishop of Antioch] put forward another passage as S. Athanasius', from his treatise on the Incarnation. It is on this wise, 'And that the Same is Son of God after the Spirit, Son of man after the flesh; not that the one Son is two natures, the one to be worshipped, the other not to be worshipped, but One Nature Incarnate of God the Word.' To this we say, that first it in no wise opposes us, for neither do we hold two natures, one to be worshipped, the other not, but we hold One Nature Incarnate of God the Word. Next it is not S. Athanasius'. For when they are asked by us, where it is, and cannot easily shew it, in their perplexity they put forward some small treatise, about two leaves, in which this passage is: but it is evident to all, that all S. Athanasius' writings are very large.

"But what can we say, when they put forward blessed Cyril, citing this against Theodore, as being S. Athanasius?' To this we say, that it does indeed lie in the blessed Cyril's utterings against Theodore, yet it is an old error. For

Dioscorus succeeding blessed Cyril, and finding his works, would perchance not have minded adding what he pleased: we might even conjecture that the blessed Cyril did not cite it against Theodore; and that it is so, is clear from this. For Theodoret speaking in behalf of Theodore, overturning all the passages which blessed Cyril cited against him from the holy Fathers, has no where mentioned this. To this they say that Theodoret passed it over craftily: for not able to answer it as patent, he of purpose passed it by. To this we say that so far from passing it by if it had been there, when S. Cyril said elsewhere, One Nature Incarnate of God the Word, if he had known that this passage had been put by blessed Cyril as cited from S. Athanasius, he would not so unlearnedly have said, 'Who of the Fathers said, the One Nature Incarnate of God the Word?' But they say again that he knew so certainly that it was said by S. Athanasius that he said, 'As the Fathers have said.' To this we say that every one is anxious to shew that the Fathers said what he says, if not word for word, yet in sense [63]*."*

It is clear that no serious objection could be founded on a treatise or Confession of Faith being short, and that the fact of one's opponent passing over an objection would be no proof that the objection, which is confessedly there, was not made. The remainder of Leontius' objection lies in the, " perhaps Dioscorus added something."

This confession was very well known by S. Cyril; for besides citing it here, he cites (as Montfaucon observes) almost the whole of it in the beginning of his Treatise de recta Fide to the Princesses Arcadia and Marina, to shew that S. Athanasius used the term, Mother of God; S. Cyril also cited two pieces of it, to shew that in his eighth chapter in which he says, that 'Emmanuel must be worshipped with one worship, he had but said what S. Athanasius too had said [64]. In all three citations occur the words, One Nature Incarnate of the Word, and in the case of S. Cyril's defence of his eighth chapter, the whole passage is extant in the latin translation (believed to be by S. Cyril's contemporary, Marius Mercator) which leaves no room for possible monophysite insertion: besides that the citation forms an integral part of S. Cyril's Defence of his chapter.

It is then proved that the words were cited as S. Athanasius' by S. Cyril, the same S. Cyril who had had his own mind moulded and taught by the writings of S. Athanasius, and who in A. D. 431, produced from the archives, probably of his own Church of S. Mark, an authentic copy of S. Athanasius' Letter to Epictetus.

If this Confession is not genuine, it is but an illustration of how, being but men, we make mistakes in what we know best.

Montfaucon sums up, "I would not venture to say whether the extracts were added in the writings of Cyril after his decease or whether before Cyril a little book of this sort was made up and ascribed to Athanasius."

***

THE special form of the disease, to which the name of Nestorius became attached, was hereditary in the great Province of Antioch. It is the sadder, because it came to him, lurking in the writings of men of even great name, commentators on large parts of Holy Scripture, who seem to have inherited it unawares; Diodore of Tarsus, and Theodore of Mopsuestia. Both had fallen asleep in the peace of the Church. Diodore, of the very highest reputation, had shared in the persecution of S. Meletius by the Arians, had been one of the Bishops of the Second General Council, and had helped to form the mind of S. Chrysostom [65]. Theodore, in whom the heresy appears more copiously yet incidentally, had, during the thirty-eight years of his Episcopate, written against other heretics, Arians, Eunomians, Origen, Apollinarius, and was intimate with S. Chrysostom and with S. Gregory of Nazianzus. The way of truth as well as the way of life is narrow.

It appears to have been a tradition of heresy over against the tradition of faith. Of the last two stages of the heretical tradition there is no doubt. Of both it is clear from the fragments of their writings still extant. S. Cyril speaks fully as to Diodore of Tarsus [66], 'by whose books,' he says, 'the mind of Nestorius was darkened.' Leontius says [67], that 'Diodorus had been to Theodorus the author and leader and father of those evils and impieties.' In the 9th century the Nestorians counted Diodorus, Theodorus and Nestorius their 'three fathers.' A Nestorian Patriarch elect promised, ' [68] that he would adhere to the true [Nestorian] faith, and the Synods of East and West, and the three fathers, Diodorus, Theodorus, Nestorius.' An eminent Syrian writer in the century after S. Cyril, Simeon Bishop of Beth-arsham (who had the title of honour of, 'the Persian Preacher or Philosopher ') says, that Paul of Samosata derived his heresy through Artemon from Ebion; that Diodore derived his from Paul, and Theodore from Diodore and Paul [69]. Theodore held the true faith of the Holy Trinity, which Paul did not; but the heresy on the Incarnation was in much alike.

In an Adjuration publicly put forth by the Clergy of Constantinople at the beginning of the Nestorian heresy and published in a Church, a parellel was drawn between the teaching of Nestorius and that of Paul of Samosata on the doctrine of the Incarnation. The parallel ran [70];

Paul said, 'Mary did not hear the Word;' Nestorius, in harmony, said, 'Mary, my good man, did not bear the Godhead;' [the Anathema approved by Nestorius denied that 'Mary bare God' not 'the Godhead.'] Paul, 'For he was not before ages.' Nestorius,---- 'And he assigns a temporal Mother to the Godhead, the Creator of times.' Paul, 'Mary received the Word and is not older than the Word.' 'Nestorius, 'How then did Mary bear Him Who is older than herself?' Paul, 'Mary bore a man like unto us.' Nestorius, 'He Who was born of the Virgin is man.' Paul,---- 'but a man in all things superior, since He is from the Holy Ghost, and from the promises, and from the Scripture is the grace upon Him.' Nestorius said, 'It saith, "I saw the Spirit descending like a dove upon Him and abiding on Him," which bestowed upon Him the Ascension. "Commanding, it saith, the Apostles whom He had chosen He was taken up through the Holy Ghost." This then it was, which conferred on Christ such glory.' Paul said, 'that neither He Who is of David having been anointed be alien from Wisdom, nor that Wisdom should dwell in any other in like way, for it was in the Prophets and yet more in Moses and in many Saints, and yet more in Christ as in the Temple of God.' And elsewhere he says, that 'other is Jesus Christ and other the Word.' Nestorius said, 'That it was not possible that He Who was born before all ages should anew be born, and that, according to the Godhead.' See, the transgressor is made manifest, saying, that He Who was begotten of the Father was not born of Mary. See, he agrees with the heretic

Paul of Samosata who says that 'Other is the Word and other Jesus Christ' and is not one, as the right Faith teaches.

The heresy stumbled at man's wonted stumbling-block, the love of God in the Incarnation, "when Thou tookest upon Thee to deliver man, Thou didst not abhor the Virgin's womb." Theodore held it to be [71] madness to say that God was born of a Virgin; he held that the man who was so born was united to God only by grace [72], that he was a son only by adoption [73].

This and other false doctrines had probably escaped notice, because they were scattered up and down in controversial writings against the Apollinarians, or in interpretations of Holy Scripture. They were brought out by the vanity of Nestorius.

Born of low parentage at least [74], he had the perilous gift of great fluency of extempore preaching and 'a very beautiful and powerful voice.' He was moreover accounted an ascetic. S. Cyril said to the Emperor,

'[75] he was chosen as one practised in the doctrines of the Gospels and the Apostles, trained in godliness, and holding the right faith, altogether blamelessly. Your Pious Majesty longed to have such a man, and all who were set over the holy Churches, and I myself also. And indeed when the letters of the most pious Bishops about his consecration were sent round by those who advanced him thereto, I wrote back without delay, rejoicing, praising, praying that by the decree from above all choicest good should come to our brother and fellow-minister.'

S. Celestine wrote to Nestorius himself, that he had been anxious as to the Bishops successively appointed to his see,

'[76] because good is apt not to be lasting, and what joy he had had in the successor of the blessed John [Chrysostom], Atticus of blessed memory, the teacher of the Catholic faith; then in the holy Sisinnius, who was so soon to leave us, for his simple piety and pious simplicity; and when he was removed, the relation of the messenger who came rejoiced our soul; and this was straightway confirmed by the relation of our colleagues, who were present at thy consecration, who bare thee such testimony as was meet to one who had been elected from elsewhere [Antioch]. For thou hadst lived before with so high estimation, that another city envied thee to thy own people . . . Evil (as far as we see) has followed on thy good beginnings; beginnings, so good, so well reported of to us, that, in our answer to the relation of the brethren, we shewed how we were partakers of the joy.'

S. Celestine lingers even fondly over the reminiscence, which was such a sad contrast to the letter which he had to answer.

'Who could readily believe,' asks Vincentius of Lerins [77], 'that he was in error, whom he saw to have been chosen by such judgement of the Empire, the object of such estimation of the Bishops? who was so loved by the holy, in such favour with the people, who daily discoursed on the words of God, and confuted the poisonous errors of Jews and Grentiles. Whom could he not persuade that he taught aright, preached aright, held aright, who in order to make way for his own heresy persecuted the blasphemies of all [other] heresies? But to pass by Nestorius who had ever more admiration than usefulness, more fame than experience, whom human favour had made for a season great in the eyes of the people rather than Divine grace----'

The outward change was sudden, Vincentius too says,

[77] What a temptation was that lately, when this unhappy Nestorius, suddenly changed from a sheep to a wolf, began to rend the flock of Christ, when they too who were torn, in great part still believed him to be a sheep, and so the more easily fell into his jaws!'

Theodoret [78], who had for so many years defended him, after he had once condemned him at Chalcedon, spoke more severely of him than any other writer. Theodoret was of an affectionate disposition. The great bane of his life was, that he would believe any evil of S. Cyril, rather than suspect his former friend Nestorius to be in the wrong. Under this prejudice, he believed S. Cyril to be an Apollinarian which he was not, rather than suspect Nestorius to be the heretic which he was. When then S. Leo espoused his cause against the worthless successor of S. Cyril, Dioscorus, and shewed at once how the two opposite heresies of Eutyches and Nestorius were equally inconsistent with Catholic truth, his eyes may have been opened, and he may have felt towards Nestorius as the occasion to him of an almost lifelong error, from which he was rescued by his own deposition and disgrace. Nestorius too had, as far as was known, died unrepentant in an heresy which denied the Incarnation. His later account of Nestorius is,

[79] From the first, Nestorius shewed what he was going to be all his life through: that he cultivated a mere popular eloquence, eliciting empty applause and attracting to himself the unstable multitude; that he went about, clad in a mourning garment, walking heavily, avoiding public throngs, seeking by the pallor of his looks to appear ascetic, at home mostly given to books and living quietly by himself. He went on to advanced age enticing the many by such habits and counterfeits, seeking to seem to be a Christian rather than to be one, and preferring his own glory to the glory of Christ.'

The course of his heresy Theodoret describes in summary.

[79] The first step of his innovation was that we must not confess the Holy Virgin who bare the Word of God having taken flesh of her, to be Theotocos, but Christotocos only, whereas the heralds of the orthodox faith long ago taught to call her Theotocos, and believe her the Mother of the Lord.'

Then he mentions the plea of Nestorius,

'that the name Christ signifies the two Natures, the Godhead and Manhood of the Only-Begotten, but that of God absolutely the simple and incorporeal essence of God the Word; and that of man the human nature alone; therefore it is necessary to confess the Virgin to be Christotocos and not Theotocos, lest unawares we say that God the Word took the beginning of His Being from the

holy Virgin, and so should be obliged consistently to confess that the Mother was older than He Who was born of her.'

Lastly he mentions the preaching of Nestorius, that in the Church of the orthodox he shouted out many such words as 'Mary, my good man, did not bear God; she bore a man the instrument of God;' 'and again among other follies,' 'The Gentile is blameless, when he gives a mother to the gods.'

Such is the outline of his teaching at Constantinople. His efforts were concentrated on the substitution of Christotocos for Theotocos; for 'God made Man,' a human Christ connected with God, corrupting by flippant sayings the minds which he could influence.

He gained favour with Theodosius who leaned on those around him. His elevation to the Patriarchate was a marked distinction, as being a call from a different Patriarchate, at the nomination of the Emperor Theodosius, and the people received him with joy. He seemed to himself called to great things. 'He had not,' Socrates says [80], 'tasted, according to the proverb, the waters of the city,' when in an inaugural oration before the Emperor and a large concourse of people, he apostrophised the Emperor, "Give me, O king, the land clear from heretics and I in turn will give thee heaven. Destroy the heretics with me, and I will destroy the Persians with thee." He must have meant, of course, that he could promise victory over the Persians in the name of God. Men noticed, we are told [80], the vanity and passionateness and vainglory of the speech. It was, at the least, a calling in of the civil sword against those, of whom he himself knew nothing, and for whose conversion his predecessors had waited patiently, and promising victory over a warlike people, not upon self-humiliation before God, but upon the extirpation of men who had not the same errors with himself. An Arian congregation, seeing their church destroyed, in desperation fired it and threw themselves into the flames. This gained to Nestorius, with all the faithful as well as heretics, the title of 'the Incendiary.' The persecution occasioned much bloodshed at Miletus and Sardis. The Emperor had to repress his violence against the Novatians. The Macedonians [81] and the Quartodecimans in Asia, Lydia, Caria, were also persecuted. He had conferred with Theodore of Mopsuestia in his way from Antioch to his See; so that it was even thought that he had imbibed his heresy then [82]. Those whom he brought with him were of the same school [83].

He began at first warily. He used ambiguous language, but all directed against the one crucial term Theotocos. Unless the blessed Virgin 'bare God,' i. e. Him Who was at once both God and Man, our Lord plainly would not have been God. And therewith would have perished the doctrine of the Atonement too, which also Nestorius did not believe. For a "brother cannot redeem a man; he cannot give to God [84] a ransom for him. Too dear is the redemption of their souls, and it ceaseth for ever."

He used what terms he could, to eke out the poverty of his conception. He could think of our Lord as a man, an instrument of Deity;' ' [85] a temple created of the Virgin for God the Word to inhabit,' and haying a close or continual or the highest connection with God; but still the 'connection' was different in degree, not in kind, from that with any Saint.

The hereditary title of the Mother of the Lord, which even Theodoret, when his strife with S. Cyril was over, recognised as ' [86] the Apostolical tradition,' excluded this humanising of our Lord. And so Nestorius (a grave historian says [87]) continuously teaching hereon in the Church, endeavoured in all ways to expel the term Theotocos, and dreaded the term as they do hobgoblins [88]. This he did, Socrates adds, 'out of great ignorance.'

'Being by nature fluent of speech, he was thought to have been educated; but in truth, he was ill-trained, and disdained to learn the books of the ancient interpreters. For being puffed up for his fluency of speech, he did not attend accurately to the ancients, but thought himself superior to all.'

Yet the term Theotocos had been in such familiar use by every school for nearly two centuries, that the aversion of Nestorius to it can hardly have been simple ignorance. It was probably the instinctive aversion of heresy to the term which condemns it. Socrates himself mentions that it was used by Origen and Eusebius: it was used alike by Alexander, the predecessor of S. Athanasius [89], whose Council first condemned Arius; by S. Athanasius himself [90]; by the Arian Eusebius [91]; and by S. Cyril of Jerusalem [92], who did not use the word Homoousion. The Apostate Emperor Julian said, in controversy with the Christians, ' [93] Did Isaiah say that a Virgin should bear God? but ye do not cease calling Mary Theotocos,' attesting that the word was in the mouths of all Christians. A little later it was used by the two S. Gregories [94]. It was used also by the great predecessor of Nestorius in the see of Constantinople, S. Chrysostom, as also by Ammon Bishop of Adrianople in Egypt, and by Antiochus Bishop of Ptolemais in Phoenicia [95]. The corresponding title, Mater Dei, was used in the Latin Church by S. Ambrose [96], Cassian [97], and Vincent of Lerins [98].

John of Antioch, at a later period, entreating Nestorius to accept the term, in order to prevent the impending schism, said to him,

'This name no one of the ecclesiastical teachers has declined. For those who have used it have been many and eminent, and those who have not used it have never imputed any error to those who used it.'

John endeavoured to smoothe to him the adoption of the word.

[99] The ten days, which Celestine allowed, are very short, but it might be made matter of a single day, perhaps only of a few hours. For to use a convenient word in the dispensation of our Sovereign Ruler Christ for us, which has been used by many of the fathers, and is true as to the saving Birth of the Virgin, is easy; which thy holiness ought not to decline, nor take that into account, that one ought not to do things contrary. For if thy mind is the same as that of the fathers and teachers of the Church (for this, my lord, I have heard from many common friends), what grief has it, to utter a pious thought in a corresponding word?'

Nestorius seems to have thought it to have been his office to convert the Church to his misbelief. He says,

[100] I see in our people much reverence and most fervent piety, but that they are blinded as to the dogma of the knowledge of God. But this is not the fault of the people, but (how shall I say it courteously?) that the teachers had not opportunity to set before you aught of the more accurate teaching.'

This was strong language, that the people of Constantinople were in error as to the faith through the fault of its former Bishops; but he also owned thereby, that his faith was different from theirs. 'Art thou then,' Cassian [101] apostrophises him, 'the amender of former Bishops, the condemner of former Priests? art thou more excellent than Gregory, more approved than Nectarius, surpassing John?'

Nestorius seems to have chosen for himself the office of arbiter between ideal parties. In his third Epistle to S. Celestine he says,

'[102] *It is known to your Blessedness, that if two sects stand over against one another, and one of them only uses the word Theotocos, and the other only Anthropotocos, and each sect draws the other to its own confession, so that, if it do not obtain this, there is peril lest it fall from the Church, it will be necessary, that one deputed to the consideration of this matter, having care for each sect, should remedy the peril of either party, by a word delivered by the Evangelist which signifies both natures. For that word, Christotocos, tempers the assertion of both, because it both removes the blasphemy of the Samosatene which is spoken of Christ, the Lord of all, as if He were a pure man, and also puts to flight the malice of Arius and Apollinarius.'*

It is strange that he did not see (if indeed he did not see what every one else saw), that Christotocos, as opposed to Theotocos, could only mean 'mother of the Messiah,' i. e. mother of Him who should be the Messiah. Vincent of Lerins uses the homely illustration,

'[103] *as we speak of the mother of a Presbyter or a Bishop, not that she bare one who was already a Presbyter or a Bishop, but a man who was afterwards made a Presbyter or Bishop.'*

S. John Damascene says,

'[104] *We do not call the holy Virgin Christotocos, because Nestorius invented it to deny the word Theotocos.'*

The name 'Anthropotocos' must have been a fiction of his own, in order to make room for his own term Christotocos, as an intermediate term. No one would give the name as a descriptive name, however they may have held our Lord to be a mere man; and Nestorius speaks of those, who called the Blessed Virgin Anthropotocos, as in the Church.

However, in his own Patriarchate, for three years Nestorius had his own way. S. Cyril names that period in his full letter of explanation to Acacius of Beroea, who must have been cognizant of the accuracy of the statement.

'[105] *But when we all waited for Nestorius, while he spent a period of three years in blaspheming, and we and your holiness and the whole Council with us tried to bring him back from them, and to those doctrines which appertain to rightness and truth.'*

Peter, the notary, rehearsed the same in the first session of the Council.'[106] Not many days having elapsed' [after his consecration]. S. Cyril in his letter to S. Celestine says,

'107 *During the past I have kept silence and have written absolutely nothing either to your Religiousness, or any of our Fellow-ministers, about him who is now at Constantinople and ruleth the Church, believing that hastiness in these things is not without blame.'*

Within Constantinople, Nestorius, twice apparently, gave occasion to a great expression of popular feeling by utterances which he sanctioned, absolutely denying the doctrine of the Incarnation. The first was by Anastasius, a priest [108] whom he had brought from Antioch, whom 'he held in great honour, and employed as a counsellor; a fiery lover of Nestorius and his Jewish dogmas.' He burst out in a sermon openly, ' [109] let no one call Mary theotocos: for Mary was human; but it is impossible that one human should bear God.' This the people could ill-endure. Nestorius supported it with vehemence.

The other statement which reached S. Cyril, and which he mentioned to some at Constantinople, who blamed him for his letter to the monks [110], was by Dorotheus Bishop of Marcianopolis, who said openly, 'Anathema, if any call the holy Mary, Theotocos.'

This went much further than the former. It pronounced Anathema (as S. Cyril saw) upon all who held what all held and expressed, upon the whole Catholic Church. Nestorius at once received him to Communion.

Nestorius supported the denial of the Theotocos. In his first Sermon he says, that he had been asked whether the Blessed Virgin was to be called 'Anthropotocos or Theotocos.' He appealed to his hearers,

'111 *Has God a mother? Then heathendom may be excused, bringing in mothers to its gods. Then Paul is a liar, who saith of the Deity of Christ, 'without father, without mother, without descent.' Mary bore not God, my good friends. For that which is born of the flesh is flesh, and that which is born of the Spirit is spirit. The creature bare not the Uncreated: the Father did not beget God the Word. For 'in the beginning was the Word,' as John saith. The creature did not bear the Creator, but she bare a Man, the instrument of Deity: the Holy Spirit did not create God the Word; for that which was born of her was of the Holy Spirit; but He framed of the Virgin for God the Word a temple wherein He should dwell.'*

Nestorius continued to preach the same, sometimes in terms, in themselves sound, but in the context of what is unsound.

From his position as Patriarch in New Rome, the residence of the Emperor, or his personal influence with Theodosius, he could overbear most opposition. What opposition there was came, it had been observed, first from the Laity, then from the Clergy, lastly from the Bishops.

Nestorius, in his first epistle to S. Celestine, told him that he had daily used both 'anger and gentleness' in repressing the Theotocos. His idea of 'anger and gentleness' may be gathered from a formal petition to the Emperors from Basil, a deacon and Archimandrite, and Thalassius a reader and monk, in their petition to the Emperors. In the words of this petition,

^{n112} *By his command and invitation, we went to the See-house, to be fully instructed whether what we had heard concerning him is true. He put us off a second and a third time, and then scarcely bade us say what we wished. But when he had heard from us, that what he had said, that 'Mary only bore a man consubstantial with herself,' and 'what is born of the flesh is flesh,' is not orthodox language, immediately he had us seized, and thence, beaten by the crowd of the officers, we were led to the prison, and there they stripped us naked as prisoners and subject to punishment, bound us to pillars, threw us down and kicked us. What in the civil courts we do not say that Clerks, Archimandrites, or monks, nay, or any secular persons do not suffer, we endured in the Church lawlessly from the lawless ones. Oppressed, famished, we remained a long time under guard, and his mania was not satisfied with this, but after all this, by some deceit we were delivered over to the most Excellent Eparch of this renowned city, and loaded with irons we were led back to the prison, and afterwards were brought up in the Praetorium in the same way with chains, and since there was no accuser, we were again led back by the guard in the prison and thus he again chastised us smiting us on the face, and having discoursed and agreed deceitfully (as appeared from what followed) about Him Who is by nature Son of Grod, that He was born of the holy Mary the Theotocos, since there is another Son; so he dismissed us.'*

Basil who relates this, says also,

^{n113} *Some of the most reverend Presbyters frequently rebuked to the face him who is now entrusted with the Episcopate (if he should be called a Bishop) and, because of his self-will that he will not call the Holy Virgin Theotocos, or Christ by nature true God, have put themselves out of his communion, and so still remain; others do so secretly; others, because they spoke in this holy Church Eirene-by-the-sea against the ill-renewal of this dogma, have been silenced. On this the people, desiring to have the wonted sound teaching, cried out, 'A King we have; a Bishop we have not.' But this essay of the people did not remain unavenged; some were seized by the attendants, and beaten in divers ways in the royal city, as is not practised even among the Barbarians. Some contradicted him publicly to the face in the Church and underwent no little trouble. A monk of the simpler sort was constrained by zeal in the midst of the Church to hinder this herald of impiety from entering in at the Celebration, being a heretic. Him having beaten, he delivered to the Magnificent Governors and being again beaten and paraded publicly, the crier proclaiming (his offence), he [Nestorius] sent him into exile. And not this only, but even in the most holy Church after his impious homily, those on his side who held down every thing, would have shed blood, had not the aid of God prevented it.'*

They conclude by asking the Emperor to convene a General Council, 'not, Grod knows, to avenge our wrongs,' but 'to unite the most holy Church, restore the priests of the true faith, before the untrue teaching spread abroad.' They speak of Nestorius as

'intimidating, threatening, driving, expelling, maltreating, acting recklessly and ill, and doing all unsparingly to establish his own mania and ungodliness, neither fearing God, nor ashamed before men, but clothed with contempt of all,

confident in his wrath and in the might of some who have been corrupted, and (to speak fearlessly) in your Majesty.'

It is strong language, but language, the more responsible, as formally addressed to one who held absolute power, who used it as no modern Sovereign could, and who was known to favour the Patriarch, against whom it was directed.

Nestorius boasted to S. Celestine of his success against those who had departed from him.

'[114] *Moreover they have dared to call the Virgin who bare Christ (Christotocos) in a certain way Theotocos. For they do not shudder at calling her Theotocos, although those holy fathers above all praise at Nice are read to have said nothing more as to the holy Virgin than that our Lord Jesus Christ was incarnate of the Holy Ghost and the Virgin Mary. I do not speak of the Holy Scriptures, which every where, both by Angels and Apostles, set forth the Virgin as the mother of Christ, not of God the Word. For which things' sake what strifes we have endured, I suppose that report has, before this, instructed your Blessedness; observing this also, that we have not striven in vain, but by the grace of the Lord, many of those who were departing from us have been amended.'*

To S. Cyril he says,

'[115] *Know that thou hast been deceived by the Clerks of thine own persuasion, who have been deprived here by the holy Synod, because they were minded as the Manichees.'*

S. Cyril in the Synodal letter [116] from Alexandria, announcing his impending excommunication, mentions those whom Nestorius had excommunicated or degraded, as he had 'indicated to Celestine the most holy Bishop of Great Rome and our fellow-bishop.' S. Celestine also requires as a condition of Communion that he should ' [117] restore to the Church all excluded for the sake of Christ its Head.' In his letter to John of Antioch he supposes that this may have been done by others also.

Within Constantinople Nestorius was opposed by those whose position secured them from his aggression: by S. Proclus, appointed Bishop of Cyzicus, whom the Cyzicans declined, wishing to appoint their own Bishop, and who remained a Bishop without a see; and by Eusebius of Dorylaeum, who

'[118] *being of great piety and skill among the laymen, having gathered within himself no mean learning, was moved with fervent and devout zeal, and said with piercing cry, that the Word Himself Who is before the ages endured a second Generation by that after the flesh and from a woman.'*

Nestorius answered him by speaking of the 'pollution' of these wretches and saying, "that if there were two births, there must be two sons," i. e. that our 'one Lord Jesus Christ' 'could not be Begotten of the Father before all worlds' and yet 'for us men and for our salvation' be born of the Virgin Mary.

Leontius [119] says that Eusebius was also said to be the author of the parallel between Paul of Samosata and Nestorius.

Different accounts are given of the way in which the minds of the people were affected. S. Cyril says that on the Anathema pronounced by Dorotheus,

'[120] There was a great cry from all the people, and a running out [of the Church.] For they would not communicate with those so minded. And now too the people of Constantinople remain out of communion, except some of the lighter sort and his flatterers. But nearly all the monasteries and their Archimandrites and many of the senate do not communicate: fearing lest they should be wronged as to his faith and that of those with him, whom he brought when he came up from Antioch, who all speak perverse things.'

Nestorius, on the other hand, boasts at the close of his answer to S. Cyril's second letter [121],

'Church matters with us advance daily, and the people through the grace of God so grow, that those who see their multitude, cry out with the prophet, that the earth is filled with the knowledge of the Lord, as much water covereth the sea, and the Emperors are in exceeding joy, being enlightened as to the doctrine; and, to speak briefly, one may see daily, as to all the heresies which fight with God and the orthodoxy of the Church, that word is daily fulfilled with us, the house of Saul waxed weaker and weaker, and the house of David waxed stronger and stronger.'

It is not much that the Emperor told S. Cyril [122], that the Churches were united and would be yet more, and that he [S. Cyril] was forgiven; (for Nestorius had persuaded him that S. Cyril was a mere disturber of the peace) or that Nestorius on one occasion speaks of the people being thronged [123]. But some were even ready to turn against those who objected to his teaching [124], and 'many Clergy and laymen from Constantinople coming to Antioch and Beroea agreed with the saying of Dorotheus, as having nothing contrary to Apostolic doctrine or the faith of Nicaea [125].'

In these three years, S. Cyril had only broken silence three times; once in his letter to the monks in Egypt; a letter to Nestorius, explaining the occasion of that letter when he heard that Nestorius was offended by it; and the second full statement of doctrine in the Epistle, which was received by the Council of Ephesus.

i. The first was his 'letter to the Monks of Egypt.' Grave perplexity had been occasioned to some of them, even as to the Divinity of our Lord, through some writings attributed to Nestorius. S. Cyril answered them, but without any mention of Nestorius. He himself gives the account of his writing,

' [126] When his [Nestorius'] homilies were brought to Egypt, I learnt that some of the lighter sort were carried away, and said doubtingly among themselves, 'does he say right?' 'Is he in error?' Fearing lest the disease should root in the minds of the simple, I wrote a general Epistle to the monasteries of Egypt, confirming them to the right faith.'

No Bishop, competent for his office, could have done otherwise than set himself to remove those perplexities in the minds of the people committed to his charge. Others circulated what he had written, in Constantinople. S. Cyril continues his account,

> 'Some took copies to Constantinople. And those who read them were much benefited, so that very many of those in office wrote, thanking me. But that too was fresh nutriment of displeasure against me, and he [Nestorius] contended against me as an enemy, having no other ground of censure than that I cannot think as he does.'

ii. iii. S. Cyril's two Epistles to Nestorius (previous to the sentence of condemnation which he was commissioned to announce, unless Nestorius should retract) were letters of explanation.

The first was to remove the offence, which Nestorius had taken at 'the letter to the monks.' It runs;

'[127] *Persons deserving of all credit have come to Alexandria and have informed me that thy Piety is exceeding angry, and setting every thing in motion to grieve me. And when I would learn the cause of the grief of thy Piety, they said that some from Alexandria were circulating the letter written to the holy Monks, and that this was the occasion of the hatred and displeasure. I wondered then, that thy Piety did not rather think with Itself, that the disturbance as to the faith did not originate with my letter, but with some, whether written by thy Piety or no, but any how papers or exegeses which were circulated. We then toiled, wishing to restore those misled. For some would hardly admit that Christ is God; but that He was rather an organ or instrument of the Deity and a God-bearing man, and things even beyond this. I had then reason to complain of the things, which thy Piety did or did not write. (For I do not much trust the papers which are carried about.) How then should I be silent, when faith is so injured and so many are perverted? Shall we not be placed before the Judgement-seat of Christ? Shall we not give account for the unseasonable silence, having been appointed by Him to say what is meet? What shall I do now? For I must consult with thy Piety. And that, when the most religious and God-beloved Bishop of the Roman Church, and the God-beloved Bishops with him, report about the papers brought thither, I know not how, whether by thy Piety or no. For they write, as exceedingly scandalized. And how shall we soothe those who come from the East from all the Churches, and murmur against the papers? Or does thy Piety think, that only a little disturbance has sprung up in the Churches from such homilies? We are all struggling and toiling, bringing back those who are somehow mispersuaded to think otherwise. When then it is thy Piety, who made all of necessity murmur, how does It justly find fault? Why does It cry out against me, and that to no purpose, and does not rather correct Its own speech, to stop this world-wide scandal? For though the speech is past, yet as being diffused among the people, let it be set straight by revision, and do thou vouchsafe to concede one word to those who are offended, by calling the holy Virgin Theotocos, that soothing those who have been grieved, and having a right repute among all, we may celebrate the Communions amid the peace and harmony of the peoples. But let not thy Piety doubt, that we are ready to endure all things for the Faith in*

Christ and to undergo imprisonments and death itself. But I say the truth, that even while Atticus of blessed memory still survived, I composed a book on the Holy and Consubstantial Trinity, in which I wrote also about the Incarnation of the Only-Begotten agreeably to what I have now written, and I read it to Bishops and Clerks and those of the laity who were fond of hearing, but I have not given it out hitherto to any one. If then it should be published, it is probable that I may again be blamed, whereas the little tract was composed even before the consecration of thy Piety.'

It was, of course, an unpleasant office to write to a Patriarch, in high favour with the Sovereign of both, who had no slight opinion of himself and of his writings, and was very angry with S. Cyril himself for writing against them, to tell him that he was in fact himself in the wrong; that he, S. Cyril, could not have done otherwise than he did, having before him the judgement-seat of Christ, and that Nestorius had to undo what he had done, which had set East and West against him. They were not smooth things to write; but I do not know how they could have been conveyed more smoothly. S. Cyril assures Nestorius, that there was nothing personal in what he had written, for he did not even know certainly, whose writings he was answering, but that they were conveying wrong doctrine among those with whom S. Cyril was put in trust; wrong doctrine, which Nestorius would not go along with; that he [S. Cyril] had had no part in the circulation of what he had written in Constantinople; that he had written the like many years before, and that this too might become a fresh subject of incrimination, if it should be published, whereas from its date it could have no bearing on Nestorius. One only request he makes him, the same, which John of Antioch the friend of Nestorius also made, by acceding to which he might have escaped his own evil memory and being the author of the miserable rent in the body of Christ, that he would vouchsafe to concede one word, Theotocos. But it would have been to give up his heresy.

The Presbyter Lampon who took S. Cyril's letter, could only obtain from Nestorius the following haughty answer, in which he avoided every topic of the letter of S. Cyril.

' 128 *[Nothing is mightier than Christian equity. We have then been constrained thereby to the present letter through the most religious presbyter Lampon, who said many things about thy Piety to us, and heard also much, and at last did not give way to us, until he wrung the letter from us, and we have been conquered by the man's importunity. For I own that I have great awe of all Christian goodness of every man, as having God residing in him. We then, although many things have been done by your Religiousness (to speak mildly) not according to brotherly love, continue in long-suffering and the friendly intercourse of letters. But experience will shew, what is the fruit of the constraint of the most religious Presbyter Lampon. I and those with me salute all the brotherhood together with thee.'*

The answer of Nestorius was in fact an apology to himself for vouchsafing to write to S. Cyril.

The second Epistle of S. Cyril is also Apologetic,

'¹²⁹ [in answer to some who are babbling to thy Piety against my reputation and that incessantly, watching, above all, the seasons of the meetings of those in power.'

The Epistle is throughout doctrinal. But there is not the slightest controversy with Nestorius, except in the appeal at the end that he would think and teach these things. It is only a careful statement of the doctrine of the Incarnation, expressly excluding what Nestorius called Apollinarian.

The answer of Nestorius [130] is in a tone of ironical condescension. He professes to pass by 'the contumelies of thy wondrous letters, as needing a medicinal long-suffering;' 'the all-wise words of thy Love;' advises him to attend to doctrine, i. e. not as he had, reading superficially the tradition of the all-holy fathers [the Nicene Creed] to shew an ignorance, which needed forgiveness; treated his letter as self-contradictory and ended in a tone of triumph. Further correspondence was of course useless. Indeed, the quotation from S. Paul seems intended by Nestorius to close the subject.

'These are the counsels from us, as from a brother to a brother. But if any one seem to be contentious, to such an one Paul will cry out through us also, We have no such custom, neither the Church of God.'

It may be that S. Cyril's letters to the Imperial family may have been occasioned by the statement which Nestorius gives of the joy of the Sovereign on being enlightened as to the dogma. But although he states the fact clearly to them, he neither mentions Nestorius, nor quotes any known saying of his.

He himself waited. He had learned probably from his fiery adhesion to his uncle and early benefactor, Theophilus, and its injustice to the memory of S. Chrysostom. He says to those who reproached him for his letter to the monks of Egypt, that he might have returned anathema for anathema,

'[131] *Since we who are yet living, and the Bishops throughout the world, and our fathers who have departed to God have been anathematised. For what hindered me too from writing the converse of his words, 'If any one say not that Mary is Theotocos, be he anathema?' But I have not done this hitherto for his sake, lest any should say, that the Bishop of Alexandria, i. e. the Egyptian Synod, has anathematised him. But if the most religious Bishops in East and West shall learn, that all have been anathematised, (for all say and confess that the holy Mary is Theotocos) how will they be disposed? How will they not be grieved, if not for themselves, yet for the holy fathers, in whose writings we find the holy Virgin Mary named Theotocos? If I did not think it would be burdensome, I would send many books of the holy Fathers, in which you may find not once but many times this word used, whereby they confess that the holy Virgin Mary is Theotocos.'*

When at last he wrote to ask the advice of S. Celestine [132], he says.

'During the time past I have been silent and have written absolutely nothing concerning him who is now at Constantinople and rules the Church, either to your Piety or to any other of our fellow-ministers, believing that precipitancy in these things is not without blame.'

Yet the confusion was already not slight. S. Cyril says to a friend of Nestorius;

' [133] *There is no one from any city or country, who does not say that these things are in every one's mouth, and, what new learning is being brought into the Churches?'*

To Nestorius himself he said, ' [134] the books of your exegeses are circulated every where.'

Vanity probably precipitated the condemnation of Nestorius. He had a low estimate of the abilities of S. Celestine.

' [135] *[The Egyptian [S.Cyril] terrified,' he says, 'by the dread of being convicted, and seeking for some trouble to stand him in stead, betakes himself to Celestine of Rome, as one too simple to penetrate the force of dogmas. Finding moreover the simplicity of that man, he childishly circumvents his ears with the illusions of letters.'*

It did not occur to Nestorius that Divine truth is seen by simple piety, not by proud intellect. He was not aware also, that S. Celestine had a deacon who, like S. Athanasius when a deacon at Nicaea, possessed that intuitive perception of truth which was afterwards to be developed on these very subjects; him, who became S. Leo the Great, who entrusted the letters of Nestorius to be translated and refuted by Cassian [136].

To this S. Celestine, of whom he thought so lightly, Nestorius wrote two letters [137], ostensibly to consult him about Julian and other Pelagians, but in reality to propound his own heresy in as plausible a manner as he could. He began by laying down,

'We owe to each other brotherly conference, as having to fight in harmony together against the devil, the enemy of peace. To what end this preface?'

Julian and others, alleging that they were Bishops of the West, complained both to the Emperor and to him, that they were persecuted being orthodox; so he, being in ignorance of the merits of the case, asked S. Celestine to inform him. 'For a new sect claims great watchfulness from true pastors.'

In the second letter, he says that he had 'often' [written about these Pelagian Bishops. He himself might have known (S. Celestine reminds him) since Atticus his predecessor had written to S. Celestine, what he had done in their matter. In both letters, he speaks of his efforts against 'something akin to Apollinarianism:' in his second, that he is at much pains to 'extirpate' it. S. Cyril, in his letter to Juvenal [138], says that Nestorius wrote this letter to the Church of the Romans, hoping to carry it away with him.

By these letters to S. Celestine, he was himself the occasion of a letter, in which S. Cyril at last consulted him about the matter of Nestorius, being shewn to S. Celestine. For S. Cyril had given instructions to his Deacon Posidonius[139],' if he should find the books of his [Nestorius] exegeses and his letters delivered to him [S. Celestine], deliver my letters also; if not, bring them here [to S.

Cyril] undelivered. He then, finding the exegeses and the letters delivered, had himself also to deliver them.'

A synod then was held at Rome, in which, after many sessions [140], the Bishops declared him to have devised a new very grievous heresy, and condemned him.

A fragment of a speech of S. Celestine is preserved [141], in which he cited the authorities of S. Ambrose in his Veni redemptor gentium, S. Hilary and S. Damasus. S. Celestine announced to Nestorius the result;

'Unless you teach as to Christ our God the same which the Church of the Romans and the Alexandrians and the holy Church in great Constantinople held excellently well till you, and, within the tenth day counted from the day of this admonition, annul by an open confession in writing that faithless novelty which undertakes to sever what holy Scripture unites, thou art cast out of all communion with the Catholic Church.'

S. Celestine wrote the same to John of Antioch [142]. This judgement he had entrusted to S. Cyril, holding his place. S. Cyril wrote what had passed and the condemnation of Nestorius by the Roman Synod to John of Antioch [143], telling him, that the Council had written the like to 'Rufus Bishop of Thessalonica, and other Bishops of Macedonia, who always agree with them,' and to Juvenal Bishop of Aelia; that he himself should follow their decision, and asking him to consider what to do to hinder this breach of communion.

John of Antioch was alarmed at this prospect of a rent, and wrote to Nestorius to prevent it by accepting the word Theotocos [144]. He wrote not in his own name only, but in that of six other Bishops who were then with him, among them Theodoret. He wrote in entire sympathy with Nestorius, in antagonism to those opposed to him. He speaks of the many, as 'unrestrained against us,' and asks, 'what will they be, now that they have gained support from these wretched letters? He takes it for granted that the faith of Nestorius was sound; he had heard that he had said that he would use the word [Theotocos] if any of those in high repute in the Church suggested it, tells him that he does not exhort him to disreputable change, or, so to say, 'boyish contradiction;' that 'though my lord Celestine had fixed a very narrow time for the answer, yet one day, perhaps a few hours would be enough; and urges him to take the counsel of those of his own mind, allowing them to speak fearlessly what was useful, not what was pleasant.' John himself held and stated the true faith, and thought the word Theotocos the convenient and true way to express it, and that to reject it would jeopardise the unspeakable mystery of the Only-Begotten Son of God.

Nestorius had however taken his line. He answers in apparent amazement;

' [145] [I thought that people could have set anything in motion against me rather than the calumny that I do not hold aright as to the piety of faith, I who hitherto have been delighted that many thousand hostilities rise against me on account of the battle which I have against all heretics. But this temptation too I must bear with joy; for it too, if we watch very carefully, may confer on us much confidence to piety.'

He says in answer, that 'the word Theotocos is assumed by many heretics as their own;' that 'some here, using the word incautiously, fall thereby into heretical and irreligious thoughts, especially those of the impious Arius and Apollinarius:' that his own solution was that 'the word Theotocos should be explained harmoniously after the deliberation of us all.' He bids John

'dismiss all anxiety, knowing that by the grace of God we have and do think the same in what relates to the piety of faith. For it is plain that if we meet, since He has given us this Synod which we hope, we shall dispose this and whatever else must be done for the correction and benefit of the whole, without scandal and in harmony; so that all things which may be ordained by a common and universal decree may receive the dignity of matters of faith, and shall give no one an occasion of contradiction even if he be very ready for it. But as to the wonted presumption of the Egyptian, your Religiousness ought not to wonder, since we have of old very many instances of this. After a little, if God shall will, our counsel herein also will be matter of praise.'

He adds in a postscript,

'We have by the grace of God attracted more both the Clergy and people and those who are in the imperial mansions, through the Epistles of your Religiousness, to that doctrine which we give publicly in the Church.'

To S. Celestine, after writing in his wonted strain about the terms Theotocos, Anthropotocos, Christotocos, he writes exultingly:

' [146] *[The most pious Emperors have been pleased, with the help of God, to appoint a Synod of the whole world, from which no one is to excuse himself [inexcusabiliter] for the enquiry into other ecclesiastical matters. For any doubt about words will not, I suppose, involve any difficult enquiry, nor be a hindrance to treating of the Divinity of the Lord Jesus.'*

S. Celestine says [147],

'He asks a field for battle; he calls for a sacerdotal examination, at which he would not be present. Who would have thought that he who asked for a synod [petitorem synodi] would be absent from the Synod?'

The relation of the Emperor to the Synod is best explained by the personal letter which he wrote to S. Cyril, commanding his attendance at it. The letter can hardly have had any other object than to intimidate S. Cyril. For he had already received the circular summons to the Council, of which the only extant copy is addressed to him. The letter was written altogether in the mind of Nestorius [148]. For he treats S. Cyril as the author of the existing confusion, and the doctrine as one hereafter to be examined and settled by the Council.

' [149] *[It is plain to every one that religion has its firmness not from any one's bidding but from intelligence. Now then let thy Piety instruct Us, why, overlooking Us (whom thou knowest to have such care of godliness) and all the priests every where, who could better have solved this dispute, thou hast, as far as in thee lies, cast confusion and severance into the Church. As if a rash impetuosity became questions as to godliness, rather than accuracy; or as if carefulness had not more weight with Ourselves than rashness; or as if intricacy in these things were more pleasing to Us than, simplicity. And yet we did not think that Our high estimation would be so received by thy Piety, or that every thing would be thrown into confusion, inasmuch as We too know how to be displeased. But now We shall take heed to the sacred calm. But know that thou hast disturbed every thing as thou oughtest not.'*

Then, having reproached him, as having tried to sow dissension in the Imperial family, by his letters to him and the Empress Eudocia, and his sister Augusta Pulcheria, and told him that it belonged to one and the same, to wish to dissever Churches and Royalties, as though there were no other way of obtaining distinction, he resumes,

'But that thou mayest know Our state, be assured that the Churches and the kingdoms are united, and will be yet more united at Our command, with the providence of our Saviour Christ, and that thy Piety is forgiven, that thou mayest have no pretext, nor be able to say that thou art blamed on account of religion For we will that all shall be laid open at the holy Synod and that what shall seem good shall prevail, whether the defeated obtain forgiveness from the fathers or no. We certainly will not endure that cities and Churches should be thrown into confusion, nor that the question should remain unsifted. Of these they must sit in judgment, who every where preside over the Priesthood; and by them We have and shall have firmer possession of the true doctrine. Nor shall any one, who has ever so little share in the polity, be allowed liberty of speech, if in his self-confidence he choose to evade such a judgement. He shall not be permitted; for Our Majesty [lit. Divinity] must praise those who shall eagerly and readily come to this enquiry, and will not endure if any choose to command rather than be counselled about these matters. So then thy Reverence must come at the time appointed in the other letters, sent to all the Metropolitans; and must not expect to recover the relation to Ourselves in any other way than that, ceasing from all grievousness and turbulence, thou come willingly to the investigation of these questions. For thus thou wilt appear to have done what has hitherto been done harshly and inconsiderately, yet still in behalf of thy opinion, not through any private pique or undue hostility to any one, and to will to do with justice what remains to be done. For if thou willest to do otherwise, We will not endure it.'

A Caesar who so wrote could not be approached. It seems that he expected S. Cyril to be condemned rather than Nestorius. S. Cyril did not attempt to remove the offence of his letters to the Imperial family, until he had been allowed to return from the Council to his own diocese.

S.Cyril explains his own mind towards Nestorius to a zealous adherent[150] of Nestorius, with a singular simplicity.

' [151] *[If I were writing to one who knew not my disposition, I might have used many words, persuading that I am a person exceeding peaceful, not given to strife, not fond of warfare, but one who longs to love all and to be loved by all. But because I write to one who knows me, I say briefly, 'If a brother's grief could be removed by loss of money or goods, I would gladly have done it, that I might not seem to hold anything of more value than love. But since it is a question of faith, and all the Churches (so to say) in the whole Roman Empire are offended,----* [152] *what shall we do, who are entrusted by God with the*

Divine mysteries?' For those who are taught the faith will accuse us in the Day of Judgement, saying that they held the faith as taught by us..... Only be the faith preserved, and I am his dear friend and yield to none as loving more than myself the most God-beloved Bishop Nestorius, who (God is my witness) I would might be of good repute in Christ and efface the blot of the past, and shew that what is commonly said by some as to his faith, are untrue accusations.'

And again to Clergy at Constantinople,

' [153] *[I must make my meaning plain to you and so I write again, that although I by nature love peace, and am very ignorant of strife, yet I wish that the Churches should have peace, and that the priests of God living in peace should remember us, since Jesus Christ the Saviour of all saith, "My peace I give unto you, My peace I leave with you." Say then in conferences, that much has passed from them to injure us; yet there will be peace, when he shall cease to think or speak such things. If he profess the right faith, there will be a full and most firm peace. If he desires this, let him write the Catholic faith and send it to Alexandria. If this be written from his inmost heart, I too am ready, as far as in me lies, to write the like and publish a book and say that none of our fellow-bishops ought to be aggrieved, because we learn that his words have a right intention and manifest purpose. But if he continue in the perverseness of vain-glory and asks for peace, nothing remains but that we resist with all our might, lest we should seem to agree with him. For to me my chiefest desire is to labour and live and die for the faith which is in Christ.'*

There could scarcely be a franker offer, putting aside every thing of his own, to 'write the Catholic faith.' Nestorius is tied down to no Theological expressions, but to the simple faith. He could not write it, because he had ceased to hold it.

The Bishops assembled in that Synod were of no ordinary character. Vincentius of Lerins, writing about three years after it was holden, speaks of its

' [154] *great humility and holiness, that they were for the more part metropolitans, of such condition and doctrine, that almost all could dispute about matters of faith, and yet they claimed nothing for themselves, but were careful to hand down nothing to those after them, which they had not themselves received from the Fathers.'*

S. Cyril in his Apology to the Emperor, calls them ' [155] men, very well known to your Mightiness, and exceeding well spoken of for excellence in all things.'

Nestorius came to the Council ' [156] immediately after the Feast of Easter' with 10 or 15 Bishops, his adherents [157]. He was also supported by a few Pelagian Bishops, whom he had admitted to Communion, and who for the time were retained in their office by the requirement of Theodosius, that everything should remain as it was, until the decision of the Council. He is said to have found many Bishops present. If so, they must have been Bishops from the Exarchate of Ephesus. For the rest are related to have arrived later. The Council was the plan of Nestorius, and he naturally came among the first, to guide, as he hoped, its decisions. S. Cyril, on his arrival, found that there had been active, though ineffectual, efforts against the faith. He wrote, ' [158] [The Evil one, the sleepless beast, is going about, plotting against the faith of Christ, but avails nothing.' The Evil one is, of course, Satan; but Satan acts through human agents. Nestorius says, that he had no intercourse with S. Cyril. He wrote to Scholasticus, an Eunuch of the Emperor and his friend; 'Cyril has both heretofore entirely avoided any converse with us, and until now avoids it, thinking that he shall thereby escape the conviction of the Chapters [the anathemas] because without contradiction they are heretical [159].' If (as has been conjectured) it was at this time that S. Cyril made the extracts from the works of Nestorius, and possibly those from older writers [160], containing the true doctrine, he had enough to do. There is no reason to think that S. Cyril preached at this time against Nestorius [161].

The pure humanitarianism of Nestorius was elicited by the attempts of Theodotus of Ancyra, and his pious friend, Acacius, Bishop of Melitene, to bring him back to the faith. To Theodotus and several others, he repeated the well-known blasphemies about our Lord's sacred Infancy and Childhood, that he would not call Him God, who was two or three months old, or who was nurtured at the breast, or who fled into Egypt [162]. This was stated upon oath to the Council. There was nothing further to investigate. It supplied what was yet wanting, the knowledge that Nestorius had not laid aside the heresy, for which he had been condemned the year before. S. Celestine had given the formal advice to S. Cyril [163], that if Nestorius came to a better mind, he should be received. He had, up to the moment of the opening of the Council, made things worse. He had taken into his own mouth the blasphemies, which before he had sanctioned in his adherent, Dorotheus. If one who nakedly denied the Incarnation was not fit to be Patriarch of Constantinople, Nestorius had decided against himself. It brought out what lay in his letter to S. Cyril which was formally condemned by the Council, that our Lord's relation to God was the same in kind, although not in degree, as that of any devout Christian.

There could be no question among any who listened to the evidence, as there was none among any of those who heard it. He was deposed on the evidence of his own letter to S. Cyril, of twenty sayings in his acknowledged works, and of contradictions to the faith in Ephesus itself.

S. Celestine had, it seems, collected a new Synod [164] at Rome, from which he wrote to the Council. The Council itself reported that

'[165] *although the whole multitude of Bishops were hindered from coming to Ephesus by the distance, yet being gathered in those parts, they, Celestine presiding, with entire consent, uttered our mind as to the faith. Those who came, explained to this our Synod by letter the mind of the whole Western Church.*'

Philip, a presbyter, and Roman legate, after reading the Acts, declared that all things had been adjudged ' [166] *according to the Canons and Ecclesiastical discipline.*'

After long canvass on the part of the deputies of John's party to obtain a rescinding of the sentence of the Synod, the Prefect at last wrote to Nestorius,

'[167] *We have delayed long what seemed to be done by the judgment of the Synod, although many greatly blamed us and were instant that it should be. But* now the letters of your Holiness have been delivered to us, shewing that the lingering at Ephesus is distasteful to you, and that your Religiousness desires to journey, we have directed those, who ought to minister to you along the whole journey, to minister to you [by sea or land], on the whole way to your monastery.....We do not suppose that you need consolation, considering the wisdom of your soul, and the many thousand goods by which you are endowed above all others.'

Nestorius in his answer accepts as a gift the command to live in his monastery.

'[168] [For nothing is more honourable to us, than a removal for piety. But I beseech your Highness, for the sake of religion, often to remind the pious Prince to set a note everywhere, by public Imperial letters, on the verbosities of Cyril which his Piety has adjudged, so that it should be read throughout the orthodox Churches, lest in the absence of letters of the pious Emperor, if the writings of Cyril should be said to be condemned by him, an occasion of scandal should arise to the simple, as if it were not said truly.'

Nestorius does not seem to mind his own deposition, so that the sentence against Cyril and Memnon be also confirmed; as Count John reported to the Emperor, that the party of John bore patiently the notice of the deposition of Nestorius, when united with that of Cyril and Memnon [169].

The public account which Nestorius gave [170], was, that 'he was allowed, at his own request, to retire to his monastery,' which was not more than two furlongs outside of Antioch.

There, Nestorius says, he 'received all sorts of honours and respectful presents.'

There, he himself says, he remained for four years. The adjuration of S. Celestine to Theodosius [171] to 'remove him from all intercourse [with others], that he might have no facility to destroy others,' remained unheeded. After four years, by the decree of Theodosius, he was banished to the Oasis. Evagrius[172] supplies the fact, that his former friend John of Antioch reported to the Emperor his continued blasphemies, and so 'Theodosius condemned him to perpetual banishment.'

He was removed from propagating his heresy personally, but could and did write in defence of it. The Oasis, to which he was finally removed, was a place not unpleasant in itself. It was however open to the incursions of a hostile tribe, the Blemmyes. With his sufferings there, in consequence of edicts of the Emperor, the Church had nothing to do. His treatment by the Emperor is unexplained. But the sufferings were God's temporal judgement inflicted through the State. The Church was guiltless of them. Yet since "whom the Lord loveth He chasteneth," they shewed that God had not abandoned him to the last.

**

S. Cyril's relation to Nestorius ended with the sentence upon him. His own troubles then began. S. Cyril himself, on his arrival, had anticipated a speedy close of the Council [173]. The Bishops had urged S. Cyril to hasten the hearing.'
[174] [Some of the Bishops were weighed down by years; some were in peril of

life through illness; some had died; some were straitened by poverty.' The Council had waited 16 days after the day of Pentecost, which the Emperor had peremptorily fixed for the opening of the Council. The whole Synod had exclaimed that he did not wish to be present. They supposed that he feared, '[175] lest the Most Reverend Nestorius, who had been taken from the Church under his jurisdiction, should be deposed, and was perhaps ashamed of the business.'

John's delay might well be puzzling in those days when tidings travelled slowly. He himself did not explain it to the Council, although he did subsequently to the Emperor. There had been a scarcity at Antioch and consequent tumults among the people, so that much time was wasted in setting out. Incessant rains made the roads bad. Of all this the Bishops at Ephesus naturally knew nothing. They knew only that he had chosen the slow land-journey instead of coming by sea, and even thus, under ordinary circumstances, he might have been punctual. Antioch was, by land, only 30 days' [176] journey from Ephesus. From the close of Easter-week to Pentecost there are 41 days, and 14 more had elapsed before there was any notice of his arrival. Why should he delay, except that he did not wish to be there? Even Eutherius [177], a Nestorian, thought that he delayed on purpose.

According to the statement of John, S. Cyril wrote to him two days before the opening of the Council, that the whole Council was awaiting his arrival. He meant then to wait for him. Moderns speak of S. Cyril as arbitrary; no one has ventured to say he was fickle. Something then must have intervened, which occasioned him to yield to the wish of the Bishops. The change would be explained, if S. Cyril had come in the meantime to know of the mind, in which the Antiochenes were coming to the Council. They made no secret of it. Their deputies may have informed S. Cyril. Theodoret, who was one of them, and who at that time used Nestorianising language which was condemned at the 5th General Council, says,

'[178] *Before we departed to Ephesus, the blessed John wrote to the most-God-beloved Bishop Eutherius of Tyana, and Firmus of Caesarea, and Theodotus of Ancyra, calling these Chapters, teaching of Apollinarius. And at Ephesus our deposing him of Alexandria and him of Ephesus had for its ground the setting forth and confirmation of the Chapters. And there were many Synodical letters written to the Victorious Emperor, and the High Magistrates, and in like way to the people at Constantinople, and the most reverend Clergy. And moreover, when summoned to Constantinople, we had five resolutions in the presence of the Emperor himself, and we sent three protests to him subsequently.'*

These charges were the pith of the different documents put forth by John's Conciliabulum. Of course, contravention of the Emperor's orders was put in the forefront; but no assembly, calling itself a Synod, could have deposed a Patriarch and a Bishop for neglecting or contravening the orders of an Emperor. The heresy alleged could be the only ground of deposition. John set forth this in the preamble which was accepted by his Conciliabulum.

'[179] *I would that no one of those set apart as priests of God should be cast out of the Church. But since the excision of incurable members is necessary for the health of the whole body, it is meet that Cyril and Memnon should be deposed, as the chiefs of the past lawlessness and of the trampling upon Ecclesiastical ordinances and the pious decrees of our most pious Emperor, and on account of the heretical meaning of the aforesaid Chapters, and that those subject to them should be excommunicated, until, recognizing their offence, they anathematize the heretical Chapters of Cyril, and agree to abide by the holy faith set forth by the holy fathers assembled at Nice, not superadding any thing other than it or foreign to godliness, and come together according to the pious letter of our most pious Emperor and examine as brothers the subjects of enquiry, and establish the pious faith.'*

This same note sounds throughout, in every document of John's Conciliabulum [180].

If S. Cyril had any intimation of this mind of the Antiochenes, it accounts for his sudden resolve not to wait for them, but to accede to the wishes of the other Bishops and open the Council without them. The mind of the Church had been expressed in the previous year. The Council itself was only a device of Nestorius to ward off his condemnation. He had already been severed from the Communion of the greater part of Christendom. The Council represented the whole West, North Africa, Egypt, Jerusalem, Macedonia, Illyricum, Pontus, Cappadocia, Armenia. The 15 or 17 [181] Bishops of John of Antioch, even if united with the 10 or 15 [182] Bishops of Nestorius, were but a fraction of the Church. No injustice was done to Nestorius. But grave confusion and scandal might have ensued upon John's arrival. If John had brought into the Council the charge of heresy, which his Conciliabulum alleged so perseveringly against S. Cyril and Memnon, it would have rested with Candidian, the friend of Nestorius, to rule in what order the charges should be taken. Candidian threw himself so entirely into John's side (even in intercepting the Relation of the Council to the Emperor), that he would, without doubt, have preferred the charge of heresy against S. Cyril. What the result would have been, He only can know, Who sees the things which have not been, as if they had been. We cannot write the things which have not been, since God Alone knows the hearts which He made, and how they would have developed under trials which He spared. But Nestorius had shewn himself practised in inflicting violence, as Dioscorus up to the eve of the Latrocinium had not. Soldiers of Theodosius had not much respect for Bishops. Those who carried the news of the deposition of Nestorius to Count Irenaeus brought back to the Council the marks of their ill-treatment [183]. Nestorius had brought his own guard of soldiers and a great number of peasants and others from the worst parts of Constantinople. Candidian had drawn troops from the garrison at Tripoli in Lydia. It has been noticed that the seamen who brought S. Cyril were ready to support him, and the peasantry of the lands of the see of Ephesus to support Memnon. The whole population of Ephesus were enthusiastic in behalf of the ancient doctrine, as they shewed by their exuberant joy [184], when the sentence, for which they had waited from morning to evening, was announced.

It would be mere matter of imagination to picture anything further. But the second Council of Ephesus, which became the Latrocinium under the guidance of Dioscorus, was called just as legitimately as the first.

However this may have been, it does not require much humility to think that S. Cyril, in the midst of the events, knew more than we, who see them only through some fragmentary records of the past. Even apart from the menace of

Candidian, one so long-sighted as S. Cyril must have known that he would incur the grave displeasure of Theodosius, by superseding his orders; that there was a strong prima-facie case of contravening them against him; and that the Emperor, who had written to him as he had, was not one to be trifled with. Yet he braved it all. It was of moment to the Church, that the heresy of Nestorius should be condemned. The sentence once passed could not be reversed; because the whole Church except the Antiochenes agreed in it.

So S. Cyril assented to the wish of the Council not to delay, and braved the Emperor's displeasure, expecting it to fall on himself alone.

His earthly future, after the Council was over, remained for some time in the balance. Candidian sent to the Emperor an adverse report [185]; John's Conciliabulum sent their complaints [186], as if they had been the Council; Nestorius sent his account [187]; S. Cyril was not heard. Theodosius first condemned the condemnation of Nestorius; annulled the proceedings of the Council; forbade any Bishop to leave Ephesus, to come to his Court or to return home [188]. The adherents of Nestorius in Constantinople hindered any tidings of his deposition coming both by sea and by land [189]: Candidian precluded access at a distance [190]. S. Cyril's deposition by John's Conciliabulum was reported at Constantinople, as if it were the act of the Council [191]; it was (S. Cyril understood) consequently deliberated at Court, whether he should not be banished [192].

His deposition was accepted, and he himself put under a guard of soldiers placed even at his bedroom door. Memnon wrote [193], that they were sometimes deprived of necessaries [194], were insulted by the rustics and the rabble which Nestorius had brought. S. Cyril was at peace. He wrote,

' [195] Since the letter of the most religious and Christ-loving Emperors has been read, in which it was said that the deposing of the three was to be accepted, we have been kept in ward, not knowing what will be the issue. But we give thanks to God, if we be thought worthy for His Name's sake not to be prisoners only, but also to endure all besides. For it is not without its reward.----As the blessed David says, "I am ready for the scourge." '

At the wish of the Council, he employed the leisure of his imprisonment in explaining his Anathematisms [196].

The Conciliabulum, in transmitting 'the Alexandrian's new exposition of the heretical chapters,' said that he 'thereby shewed his impiety more evidently[197].' They even wondered at the perseverance of the Council, notwithstanding the imprisonment of Cyril and Memnon. They write as a Synod,

' [198] Count John holds in most guarded custody Cyril and Memnon, thrusting [detrudens] each apart, and placing a multitude of soldiers around the house of each. Yet not even thus are they still, who turn every thing upside down and have filled the world with confusion and sedition, but acting as usual, make a confusion, and set in motion a rule against themselves. For, being excommunicated, they have audaciously assumed to themselves the ministry of the priesthood, &c.'

And again in their Epistle to Acacius of Berrhoea,

'199 Your Religiousness should know that they [the Bishops of the Council] have been excommunicated by us, because they co-operated with the insanity of the heretic Cyril and what he did unlawfully and iniquitously, and have presumed to exercise their office and to communicate with the condemned.---- And these things they commit, knowing that those most injurious persons Cyril and Memnon have been thrust [trusi] away and are kept by a multitude of soldiers. For thrusting [trudentes] each apart, they guard them night and day; wherefore let your Holiness pray &c.'

The Bishops of the Council seem also to have thought that it was the intention of the Nestorianisers to wear them out to undo what they had done. A brief memorial at the end of their letter to the Clergy of Constantinople says,

'200 [We are being killed with the heat through the heaviness of the air, and some one is buried almost daily; so that all the servants are sent home, and all the other Bishops are in the same state. Whence we pray your Reverences to go to the gracious Sovereign and say that the Synod is oppressed by those, who prevent any term being given, so that we are altogether perishing by exhaustion. But your Reverences should know, that although they press upon us till we all die, we will not do any thing other than our Saviour Christ has taught us to decree.'

The cordon was drawn with all safety to hinder any report from the Council reaching the Emperor's ears. It was snapped by a mendicant. The Clergy of Constantinople wrote,

'201 Since no one can do any thing against God (for what is man?), by the ordering of God there arrived an Epistle written from Ephesus to the holy Bishops and monks sent by a beggar who tied it within a reed, and thus, begging and carrying his reed, brought it. Forthwith all the monasteries with the Archimandrites arose and went to the palace. The holy Dalmatius, one of the Archimandrites, had not left his monastery for 48 years, but remained enclosed. Our most pious Emperor went to him and saw him. There being ofttimes earthquakes in Constantinople, the Emperor ofttimes requested him to come forth and say litanies; he never would. But when he was praying about this, a voice came down from heaven bidding him go forth. For He did not will that His flock should perish utterly.'

The Archimandrites, who were admitted, prevailed. Theodosius learnt with surprise [202] that while the Nestorians had free ingress and regress, the deputies of the Council had been refused access to him.

The Emperor tried in vain to reconcile the Antiochenes with S. Cyril.

The Antiochenes, in their third indignant protest [203], reproached the Emperor with their obedience, reminded him that the East was no small part of his Empire, that he needed the true faith to prevail in the war which then encircled Africa, that God would fight for him, if he would defend the holy faith, and would not allow the body of the Church to be cut of, but it would be cut off, if the meaning superinduced on the faith by Cyril and confirmed by others should stand; that persons intermixed with the Churches taught the doctrine of Apollinarius and Arius and Eunomius, and unlawfully and irregularly exercised the office of the priesthood. They conclude with the prayer that he would not allow any thing to be stealthily introduced against the faith of the holy fathers who met at Nice. If after this admonition before God the Emperor did not acquiesce, they 'with S. Paul shook off the dust from their feet against them, saying, "We are clean from the blood of all men." "We have not ceased night and day, from the time we came to the holy Synod to protest to the Emperor, Judges, soldiers, priests, and laymen, not to be the betrayers of the faith delivered by the fathers.'

It was an internecine war, continued even after the return of the Eastern Bishops to their sees; the Easterns still absolutely demanded the deposition of S. Cyril Memnon and all their adherents, and that their teaching should be proscribed.

***

S. Cyril shewed his peace-loving disposition on his return to Egypt. The Orientals had brought upon him his imprisonment, its privations and indignities, and the prospect of banishment. This they had done by aping a Council, yet without the formalities of a Council, without enquiring into anything which the real Council had done, assuming that they had done what they had not done----formally sanctioned the Anathematisms which S. Cyril had framed, not as a rule of faith but to cut off the evasions of Nestorius, and that these Anathemas were heretical. They had persuaded the Emperor, that their 40 Bishops, who represented one Patriarchate, were the Council of the whole world, which he had convoked. Until they found it useless to mention the name of Nestorius to the Emperor [204], they urged his restoration and the deposition of S. Cyril. He had escaped in despite of them. They would not be persuaded that Nestorius was the heretic which he was; and they would repeat that S. Cyril was an Arian, Eunomian, Apollinarian, although they must have known that at the least he was neither Eunomian nor Arian.

There was nothing then for S. Cyril to do in regard to them. They had fallen into the trap which Nestorius had laid for them by sending the Anathemas meant to test his own sincerity, without the Epistle which would have explained them. It became an axiom with Theodoret that they were heretical. S. Cyril then could but wait. S. Sixtus iii., a peace-loving Bishop who had succeeded S. Celestine, bears him witness that he had shewed at once how mindful he was of the faith and how regardless of contumelies, which he suffered gloriously, according to the Apostle, wishing that the Churches should be well-ordered, rather than that he should be righted himself; that one [Nestorius] having wrecked himself, he was anxious that all the rest should be saved out of the waves. 'The same mind is in us also; to act tenderly towards them, when they cease to be impious towards God. Let those then, who will to return to the right way, be received.' He addresses S. Cyril himself,

[205] *[Hold fast, most beloved brother, what has been done by the Council, and what has been defined by us. For a brother dismisses contumelies which benefit him before the Lord of all. For such contumely is victory. Whence he has borne meekly all the sharp blows, nor did those things grieve him, wherein he now rejoices; for he strove for a crown. For he knows what prizes are in store for the victors in such conflicts.'*

S. Sixtus coincided altogether with S. Cyril, but spoke strongly; 'let him [John] know that he shall be one of the Catholic body, if, undoing all undone by the Synod, he shew himself a Catholic priest.'

S. Cyril required nothing for himself. The Bishops, whom the Emperor assembled at Constantinople, propounded the terms, at which the Emperor was 'exceedingly pleased.'

[206] *[The Bishop, full of piety, John of Antioch, must anathematise the doctrine of Nestorius, and acknowledge in writing his deposition; and this being done, the Bishop of Alexandria will, out of love, forget altogether and regard as nothing the contumelies which he endured at Ephesus, very grievous as they were, and hard to endure.'*

John's party would not accept them. The first conditions of peace on John's side, which Aristolaus, the Emperor's deputy, selected as the mildest [207], were in fact, of unconditional submission.

The terms were,

[208] *[We acknowledge the Nicene Creed as sufficient, but the letter of S. Athanasius to Epictetus explains its meaning. We abide therefore therein, and cast off all doctrines recently superinduced, either by Epistles or Chapters, as disturbing the common faith:'*

i. e. he was to acknowledge that he, not Nestorius, had been the disturber of the Church. S. Cyril most gladly [209] received the Epistle to Epictetus [210], but shewed them that their own copies had been corrupted by heretics [211]. For the rest, he said that to withdraw what he had written would be to unsay all which had been said against the heresy of Nestorius. He was, in fact, to withdraw by his single act Epistles, of which one had been accepted by the Council of Ephesus, individually and as a body, the other, with the anathemas, had been placed among its Acts (no one excepting), and undo his whole work at the dictum of John and five other Bishops.

The Orientals then selected a wiser envoy, Paul of Emesa. Yet even him they burthened with complaints, 'as if some things had been said and done wrongly' in the Synod. This occasioned the only reminiscence of the past ill-treatment, ' [212] [They who ought to seek pardon for the past, how do they add fresh contumelies?' When these were withdrawn, S. Cyril says, 'we were filled with gladness of heart;' and 'contrary perhaps to his expectations,' Paul found him fully disposed for peace [213]. S. Cyril's relation shews how deeply he felt the rent as a work of Satan. He accepted at once a Confession, written (John said in his letter to S. Cyril) 'by us in harmony [214].' He gave to Paul a statement of faith, which John accepted. Paul preached in the great Church of Alexandria [215]. 'The people cried out, This is the Faith, the gift of God, orthodox Cyril. This we sought to hear.' S. Cyril wrote to John the exulting letter, beginning with the words of the Psalm, 'Let the heavens rejoice and the earth be glad. For the middle-wall of partition is dissolved; what saddened has ceased; all manner of discord is removed. For Christ, the Saviour of us all, has bestowed peace upon all His Churches.'

He says, in a sort of under-tone to Maximian [216] [who had succeeded Nestorius,

'Strife and contention reign not among us, but we have all one mark, looking to peace. And if those who from the first have differed in opinion from us and cut themselves off from us, had willed, there would have been no strife or difference among the Churches. But blessed be the Saviour, Who hath lulled the storm &c.'

It was S. Cyril's lot, then as now, to be misunderstood. He was blamed as to the peace, as, before, for the conflict. Theodoret could not but acquiesce in the acceptance of his own Synodal letter, but held it to be directly contradictory of the twelve Chapters [217]. To his lord and truly God-loving and venerable holy father Nestorius' he apologises for the peace, and assures him, that he holds Cyril in abhorrence, as being the author of all the disturbance of the whole world [218]. The Nestorianizers were of course very angry; but he had to explain himself, even to his old friend Acacius of Melitene as also to others[219]. He whom the Orientals had so unrelentingly persecuted was now their defender, shewing that they were not Nestorians, and trying patiently to win back to the Communion of the Church individuals still alienated.

He had to bear what was still harder, the reproaches of S. Isidore, to whom he had a filial affection [220]. S. Isidore [221] had told him before of 'the jeers of many at Ephesus, as if thou wert wreaking thine own enmity, and not seeking, as one orthodox, the things of Jesus Christ. For, say they, he is a nephew of Theophilus.'

He had again set forth to him the faith of the Incarnation [222] as something which 'thou thyself wouldest not deny,' and now, when S. Cyril had himself accepted the same statement as propounded by him, he wrote,

[223] *Wondrous man, thou oughtest to remain ever unchanged, not betraying the things of heaven, nor appearing contradictory to thyself. For if thou comparest what thou hast now written with thy former writings, thou wilt seem chargeable with flattery, or the minister of off-handed ness, yielding to vain-glory, instead of imitating the strivings of all those great holy combatants, who endured to be ill-treated all their life in a foreign land, rather than even hear a thought of evil doctrine.'*

S. Isidore, in his zeal for S. Cyril's perfecting, seems to have written to him according to the sayings of others. It must have been hard to be so unjustly blamed by a saint, but S. Cyril seems to have received the undeserved censure in silence.

***

One more occasion is recorded in which a public expression of opinion was asked of him, as to the writings of Theodore of Mopsuestia.

The Council, while sparing his name, had already condemned a Creed of his, which had been presented by some Nestorians to many Quartodecimans and Novatians who wished to return to the Church [224]. S. Proclus sent to John of Antioch a Tome containing Nestorian passages of Theodore (equally sparing his name), requesting him to have them condemned. Maximus, the bearer, contrary to his instructions, inserted the name. The Antiochenes, after this, would not condemn the passages, even without the name [225]. Maximus [226], an

Archimandrite, came to Alexandria, 'speaking much and strongly' against the Easterns, the 'orthodox have no room there nor freedom to speak the faith.' '[227] A noble officer of the Palace presented to S. Cyril, when at Jerusalem, a long Epistle of many Clergy and monks and laity, accusing the Eastern Bishops, that they, suppressing the name of Nestorius, professed to be averse to him, and bounded down to the books of Theodore on the Incarnation, in which lie many more grievous blasphemies than those of Nestorius. For he was the father of the ill-doctrines of Nestorius, and by speaking his words, the ungodly man is in his present condition.' The Alexandrians, having refused to sign the Tome of S. Proclus, appealed to S. Cyril [228]. S. Cyril indignantly set aside any likeness of 'the ill-reputed doctrine of Diodore and Theodore' to that of the great fathers whom John alleged [229]. To John of Antioch he wrote [230], that no one should utter in Church the ungodly doctrines of Theodore; but he dwelt on the tenderness, with which those returning should be received, and not be reproached for the past: to Proclus [231], that Theodore had died in the communion of the Church; that in rejecting his Creed the Council had purposely spared his name, lest some should separate from the Church; that in rejecting the blasphemies of Nestorius they had virtually condemned what was like them; that if it could be done without disturbance, it would be best for the sake of others; but that since John of Antioch wrote, that 'they would rather be burned with fire than do anything of that sort, why should we fan the stilled flame?' that those who wished the writings to be condemned might be persuaded to be quiet rather than give occasion of scandal to the Church. To Maximus, who would not communicate with John because of some suspected of Nestorianism, he wrote [232] urging the reception of those willing to return to communion, even though ashamed to own their fall.

Everywhere he is the peace-maker. The veteran pilot, who, under God, had guided the ship through the storm, sat, watching each cloud, as it arose. His one thought was, 'Peace has been restored; take we heed that it be not again broken.'

S. Cyril thought it indeed right to correct in writing the errors of Theodore; but this disturbed no peace, since Theodore was gone. Theodoret, as usual, wrote against him, but Theodoret had not S. Cyril's accurate Theological mind. S. Cyril, in his 9th Anathematism, called God the Holy Ghost, 'the Very own Spirit of our Lord Jesus Christ' adopting the language of S. Athanasius, that '[233] the Holy Spirit was the Very own Spirit of the Son.' Theodoret declaimed chiefly, as if S. Cyril had said this of the Humanity of our Lord, not of His Godhead; but adds, at the end, the sad words, 'If he so calls Him as One in Nature and proceeding from the Father, we will receive it; but if, as having His existence from the Son or through the Son, we will fling it away as blasphemous and ungodly.' Theodoret could not have been, at that time, acquainted with the great writers before him, S. Dionysius of Alexandria, S. Athanasius, S. Basil, S. Gregory of Nyssa, Didymus, S. Epiphanius, S. Cyril of Jerusalem [234], who used the 'from' or the 'through' which he 'flings' from him. S. Cyril's well-weighed and full language has continued to teach man until now. The impetuous language of Theodoret, if it had had any lasting weight, would have fostered the disbelief of any relation between God the Son and God the Holy Ghost, contrary to our Baptismal Creed.

Theodoret thought good to defend Theodore against S. Cyril, arguing against all the authorities which S. Cyril had adduced [235]. The one fragment which remains is written sharply [236]. S. Cyril had explained and re-explained his Anathematisms against Theodoret's attacks; for the alienated Antiochenes had to be reconciled, and a breach to be healed. This censure of his work against Theodore concerned only himself, so he went on his way in peace.

***

S. Cyril's strong natural love has been incidentally noticed [237]. One could hardly picture him, such as he has been ordinarily represented, in advancing years, enfolding and kissing the letter of his friend Acacius, Bishop of Melitene, enquiring about a type in the Old Testament, 'the scapegoat [238].' Yet since all service to God must involve self-denial, perhaps one of strong natural love was the fitter instrument of God for the hard service of that dreary warfare, as it must have aided him in the congenial office of reconciling the alienated.

Outward events give but little insight into the inward mind. S. Cyril is now chiefly known (as far as he is known at all) as the zealous defender of the Faith. But it was the Faith in Him, his God and his All. Many must have been his peaceful years before he was called out by the needs of his own people, to defend the truth of God against a living assailant. His work against the Emperor Julian (which even his opponent Theodoret admired [239], in the midst of his hottest hostility) was written, he says, on the exhortation of many, because the heathen perplexed Christians, alleging that he was not refuted, because he could not [240]. This then too was written out of a love for souls. He himself explained to Nestorius that, in his book on the Holy Trinity, he had written some things akin to what he then wrote, but with no reference to him, since it was written before Nestorius himself wrote.

Controversy was not his natural element. Cassiodorus counts him among those who were said [241] at least to have commented on the whole of Holy Scripture. His Commentaries are the largest portion of His extant works, yet these are but a part of a larger whole [242]. From these peaceful meditations on God's word he was roused by the disturbance of his monks through writings of Nestorius.

It has been noticed already [243] that types of our Lord were the chief object of interest to him in his first book on the Pentateuch, 'on the adoration in spirit and in truth:' his faith in the Incarnation and our union to God through It, are naturally prominent, as indeed it gleams through everywhere [244]. His was the exact contrary of the mind of Theodore of Mopsuestia of the Antiochene school: as has been said of our Bishop Horne and another, 'the one sees Christ every where, the other no where.' A mind which so meditates on God's word, not on particular expressions, but on the whole, is not that of the fierce controversialist which some of late have pictured him.

***

It remains only to collect what has been said as to the contents of this volume.

i. The Five books against Nestorius. 'These,' it has been said [245], 'may be well called, a Defence of S. Proclus. For S. Cyril in it mainly answers the sermons preached by Nestorius against S. Proclus. For the first two books are on the Virgin being Theotokos, and the term 'birth' ascribed to God; the third is of His being our Priest, Who is God; the fourth and fifth are for the most part on God suffering and dying.'

S. Cyril himself says that he undertook the work with reluctance, but that the homilies were written in a popular and attractive style and were full of heavy accusations against the doctrines of the truth, and left him no choice[246]. Nestorius is not named in it. Hence it has been inferred that the work was written before the Council of Ephesus [247]. Photius notices that 'in the first book, he refutes six heads of the blasphemies of Nestorius; in the second, 14; in the third, 6; in the fourth and fifth, 7 each.' He adds [248] that 'his mode of interpretation is framed according to his wonted way of expression, yet brought down to a lower style.'

ii. The Scholia are said by Photius to 'contain much which is useful.' S. Cyril, with his wonted simplicity, speaks of them as ' [249] brief expositions of the dispensation of Christ, very good and useful.' A modern writer says, ' [250] The value of the work may be inferred from this, that scarce any subsequent writer, who employed the authority of Cyril in explaining the mystery of the Incarnation, failed to take a passage or more from the Scholia.' This work also was quoted, with two other passages of S. Cyril, among the testimonies from the books of Catholic fathers, appended to the Epistle of S. Leo to the Emperor Leo [251]. It closed the collection laid before the Council of Chalcedon [252] and then ensued the acclamations, 'Eternal be the memory of Cyril.----Leo and Cyril taught alike.' It is quoted even by Theodoret [253] with sayings of 19 other fathers, in proof that 'Saints distinguished the Natures after the Union.' He alleges three places from it [254], two from his Commentary on the Epistle to the Hebrews [255], one from the Epistle to Nestorius [256], one from the defence against the Easterns [257], and two more not identified. The Scholia are quoted also by Facundus [258], Leontius of Byzantium [259], and S. Ephrem of Antioch repeatedly [260]. They not only quote it as S. Cyril's, but confirm the faith by testimonies from it.

It was translated into Latin by S. Cyril's contemporary, Marius Mercator. It is extant also in a Syriac translation, from which my son, here and there, corrected or explained the Latin text of Mercator.

Garnier remarks upon the careful arrangement which S. Cyril employed in its construction. 'He first explains single words; what is Christ; what, Emmanuel; what, Jesus; what, One; what, Union. Then, he turns to the propositions, commonly used herein, and discusses in what way Christ is One; Emmanuel, One; Jesus, One; i.e. One Lord, &c. Further, how the Word is said to have been 'emptied,' united with the flesh, made Man, and yet not therefore changed, or ceasing to be God. Thence, how Christ is not a man Theophoros, [bearing God,] or inspired by God, but is really man-God [better, God-Man]; then, in what way the Word is said to dwell in us, to be sent to us, to have His own proper Body, and how the Holy Virgin is said to be Theotocos. Lastly, that the Only-Begotten, appearing in visible flesh is called God and Man; how He suffered: in which last he refutes those who suppose, that things belonging to man can be spoken of God, relatively only. I have already said, that almost every chapter is full of distinctions useful in turning aside the objections of heretics.' Photius divides it into ten heads; ' [261] These things,' he said, 'are clearly explained in it; What is Christ; in what way the word 'Emmanuel' is to be understood, and what is 'Jesus the Christ;' and in what respect the Word of God is called Man; then, in what respect the Word of God is said to have been emptied; and how Christ is One, and how Emmanuel is One; and what we say is the Union, and about the coal which Elias saw, and other things like these.'

iii. That Christ is One. The treatise must have been written after the condemnation of Nestorius, since he is refuted by name in it. It must, however, have been written not later than A. D. 441, since it is quoted by Andrew of Samosata. It is quoted with praise by S. Eulogius [262] and Leontius of Byzantium [263] ... The Père Garnier says of it; ' [264] Eo nihil exactius elucubratiusque ad historiam dogmatis Cyrillus scripsit, ut videatur opus artificis praecedentibus laboribus absolute eruditi.'

iv. S. Cyril wrote the three books against Diodore and Theodore of Mopsuestia and that against the Synousiastae or Apollinarians at a later period, when, the writings of Nestorius being proscribed, Nestorianisers betook themselves to those of Diodore and Theodore, the real originators of Nestorianism. The fragments have been collected with great pains from every source, hitherto known. Some were ready at hand, having been collected for the 5th General Council, and embodied in its Acts; others were collected by John, Bishop of Caesarea, in his defence of the Council of Chalcedon, which is still extant in MS., in Syriac and in Greek at Venice and at Cairo (where my son saw it); others by Severus of Antioch [265]. The sources, whence the extracts are derived, are mentioned in the notes. The originals, as extant in Greek and Syriac, are among the collection of Fragments appended to my son's third volume of S. Cyril's Commentary on S. John [266]. It is the completest collection extant.

***

S. Cyril was my own early teacher on the connection of the doctrine of the Incarnation and the Holy Eucharist, which Hooker all but reached. It was at my wish that, in his uniform filial love, my son took as the central work of his life, to make the text of his works as exact as it could be made. For this he visited libraries in France, Spain, Italy, Germany, Russia, Mt. Athos, Cairo, Mt. Sinai, and applied to this the knowledge of Syriac, which he had perfected in view of another object which I had suggested to him, the re-editing of that now much undervalued Critical authority, the Peshito. Almighty God was pleased to break off the work "in the midst of the years." If in this completion of his Preface to his volume I have cleared any thing as to the self-forgetful, God-devoted character of my early Benefactor, S. Cyril, thanks be for this also to Him Who gave and Who took away.

E. B. P.
CHRISTMAS EVE, 1881.

Footnotes:

1. S. Cyrille d' Alex. Art. i. init.
2. Ep. 370.
3. Ep. 25.
4. Synodicon c. 56.
5. So the three Paschal homilies of the Archbishop Theophilus preserved by S. Jerome, are addressed, To the Bishops of the whole of Egypt, t. i. 555, 577, 605 Vall.

6. hom. 7. p. 87 init.
7. hom. 1. 3 c. 4 a.
8. pp. 174 d e 175, 176.
9. "With chapter 7 compare S. Greg. Nazianzen's very similar Anathema directed against Appollinarius' teaching, in his Letter to Cledonius.
10. p. 263.
11. [Had he sent the Epistle, John must have known them to have been S. Cyril's.]
12. Synod. c. 4.
13. [Passages from Theodoret's reply to the first, second, fourth and tenth anathematism and from his letter to the monks were read in the 5th General Council before the condemnation of his writings against S. Cyril. Also from allocutions in behalf of Nestorius from Chalcedon after his condemnation at Ephesus; from a letter to Andrew of Samosata, in which he speaks of Egypt [i.e. S. Cyril and the Egyptian bishops] being 'again mad against God,' but owns that those of Egypt, Palestine, Pontus, Asia, and with them the West are against him, and that the greatest part of the world has taken the disease; a letter of sympathy with Nestorius after the reunion of the Easterns with S. Cyril, declaring that, if his two hands were cut off, he would never agree to what had been done against Nestorius, (which however he did when required by the Bishops at Chalcedon); a letter to John of Antioch still condemning the Anathematisms, although accepting the subsequent explanation. Apart from the 'atrocious letter' full of conceits which it is inconceivable how any one could have written, Mercator, a contemporary, says it was one of the charges against Archbishop Domnus, that he had been present when Theodoret preached a sermon, exulting in the peace which would ensue from S. Cyril's death. 'No one now compels to blaspheme. Where are they who say, that He Who was crucified is God?' Mercator from, Gesta quae contra Domnum Antioch. Ep. conscripta sunt p. 276. ed. Garn.]
14. There is extant a very careful letter of Theodoret on the Incarnation, written to Eusebius scholasticus, in which Theodoret says, "Nevertheless we do not deny the properties of the Matures, but as we deem those ungodly who divide into Two sons the One Lord Jesus Christ, so do we call them enemies of the Truth who attempt to confuse the natures: for we believe that an union without confusion has taken place and we know what are the properties of the human nature, what of the Godhead." Then after mentioning the two natures of a man which do not part him into two, "thus do we know that our Lord and God, I mean the Son of God the Lord Christ, is One Son after His Incarnation too; for the Union is inseverable even as without confusion." Ep. 21. p. 1085.
15. Ep. 151.
16. See bel. p. 20 n. k; p. 24 n. 9; p. 243 n. i.
17. Ep. 147.
18. Hom. Pasch. vii. 102 d.
19. Thes. Dial. i. p. 398 c. quoted p. 192 n. i.
20. Hab. iii. 2, 550 d.
21. Ep. 1 ad Nest. Epp. 20 b.
22. Ep. 1 ad Monach. Epp. 3. a b.
23. See S. Cyril's first letter to Nestorius, Epp. pp. 19 e 20 a.
24. Nestorius alludes to this, in the sermon which he preached on the Saturday after he had received

S. Celestine's final Letter. Mercat. Opp. p. 76 Bal.

25.b see his sermon just quoted, p. 78 Bal.

26. Conc. Eph. P. i. c. 16.

27. Ib. c. 17.

28. Ib. i. 9.

29. Epist. v. in Garn. Diss. v. ap. Theodoret Opp. T. v. p. 625 ed. Schulz.

30. The passage occurs, just as Nestorius accused S. Cyril of garbling it, in Book ii. § 4 p. 54. "We do not possess the complete sermon from which this extract is taken: we do possess in Mercator's translation four sermons on the subject of the Incarnation, from the second of which S. Cyril has several extracts. In the case of this sermon the context leaves no doubt that Nestorius spoke of our Lord's manhood as a separate man, whom our Lord had indefinitely connected with Himself. This long extract of Nestorius has been given in full as matter of candour. The thing itself we have not the means of explaining. Although he makes S. Cyril's extracts from his writings the cause of S. Celestine's belief that his teaching was heretical. S. Celestine, in his letter to himself, says expressly, that his conviction came from his own letters.

"In your letters you have given sentence not so much in respect of our Faith as of your own self, choosing to speak of God the Word differently from what is the Faith of all." Ep. Celestin. ad Nestorium, Conc. Eph. 1. n. 18.

Again to the Clergy and people of Constantinople S. Celestine says,

"he preaches things not to be uttered, persuades things which ought to be shunned, as both his writings sent us by himself with his own signature, and also the memorial of my holy brother and co-Bishop Cyril" &c. Ib. n. 19.

and again writing to John Archbishop of Antioch S. Celestine says,

"he pours into the people most devoted to Christ certain perverse things against the reverence of the Virgin-birth and the hope of our salvation. These things have come to us from the sorrow of the faithful; these things have been published in the books himself sent, and stronger proof yet, these things have been so conveyed to us in letters fortified with the very signature of their author, that one may not any longer doubt." Ib. n. 20.

Helladius bishop of Tarsus and Eutherius Bishop of Tyana in their memorial to S. Sixtus, against S. Cyril, the Council of Ephesus, and the reconciliation thereto of John Archbishop of Antioch, mention this "garbled extract," Synodicon c. 117.

31. See pp. 185-236.

32. § 27, pp. 214, 215.

33. § 36 and 37.

34. pp. 228, 229 and 232, 233.

35. See it in S. Cyril's 3 Epistles pp. 55. sqq Oxford, 1872.

36. p. 1C.

37. see p. 321.

38. p. 16 b.

39. p. 690 a.

40. p. 18 d.

41. p. 692 b.

42. Opp. v. P. ii. 2. 131 a.

43. Hist. Conc. § 129 near the end.

44. See S. Cyril's books against Nestorius, pp. 20, 51, 141, 164.
45. see Ib. p. 51.
46. see p. 141.
47. sec p. 164. g.
48. Synod. c. 3.
49. Ep. Conciliab. Eph. (post Conc. Eph. Act.i.) ad Imp.
50. S. Cyrilli Apol. ad Imp. p. 252 c.
51. Conc. Eph. Act. v. n. 2.
52. l. c. p. 251 b c.
53. Synod, c. 7.
54. It forms Vol. 7 of his collected works, also published by Stephen Baluz, is incorporated into subsequent editions of the Concilia, and again with some additions and corrections, after a fresh inspection of the manuscript by Mansi.
55. Epp. Opp. v. 2. p. 152 c.
56. See the Compiler's words at the end of cap. 94, "are put in order by Irenaeus in what is called his Tragedy."
57. Published by Assemani, Bibl. Or. t. 3. 1. pp. 4 sqq.
58. c. 25.
59. Ib. pp. .38, 39.
60. c. 20.
61. p. 341.
62. See on this Formula Card. Newman's exhaustive treatise, 'On S. Cyril's formula of the mia phusis.' Tracts Theological and Ecclesiastical, 1874; who however says 'whether S. Athanasius himself used it, is a contested point.' p. 335.
63. Leontius Scholast. Byzant. de sectis, Actio 8. §§ 4, 5 in Gall. Bibl. Vett. Patr. xii. 651, 652.
64. Apol. adv. Orient, cap. 8 p. 178 b c d e.
65. See below p. 320. n. a.
66. Ep. 1 ad Succens. p. 135. d e: see below p. 321 note. Photius saw it in various writings of his, "These were contained therein [in the codex] various essays of Diodore of Tarsus on the Holy Spirit, in which he too is convicted of having been sick beforehand with the disease of Nestorius." cod. 102 p. 86. Bekk.
67. Contr. Nest. et Eutych. L. iii. de Nestorianorum impietate secrcto tradita principio. Bibl. Patr. T. ix. p. 696.
68. Assem. B. O. iii. 1. p. (233 arab.) 236.
69. Assem. B. 0. i. 347, 348. quoted in Card. Newman's Arians of the 4th. Cent. p. 24. ed. 4.
70. Contestatio publice proposita &c. Conc. Eph. P. i. n. 13.
71. c. Apollin. L. iii. in Synod. v. Coll. iv. n. 1.
72. 'Uniens eum sibi affectu voluntatis, majorem quandam praestabat ei gratiam.' de Incarn. L. 14. Ib. n. 54.
73. "He too, meriting adoption by grace, calls God His God, because in like way with other men he received his being." on S. John L. 6, Ib. n. 13.
74. aischrogenes. S. Cyr. Hom. div. p. 383.
75. Apol. ad Theodos. Conc. Eph. P. 3. c. 13.
76. Ep. S. Celestin. ad Nest. Conc. Eph. P. i. c. 18.
77. Commonit. l. c. 16.
78. Haeret. Fab. iv. 12. Leontius (A. D. 610.) quotes this work in proof how Theodoret held Nestorius in abhorrence, (against a spurious correspondence between Theodoret and Nestorius in which they were made to acknowledge each other) de sectis. iv. 5. Photius (cod. 56.) says of this work of Theodoret, which he had read, 'he goes down to Nestorius and his heresy, pouring upon him unmingled censure. He goes on

also to the Eutychian heresy,' (the two last chapters of the ivth. book.) No one attends now to Garnier's paradox that the account of Nestorius was substituted from a younger Theodoret for the original statement of Theodoret, while the account of Eutyches connected with it is to be from Theodoret himself.

79. Haeret. Fab. iv. 12.
80. Socr. vii. 29.
81. Ib. 31.
82. Evagrius says this on the authority of Theodulus [a presbyter of Coelesyria about A.D. 480.] i. 2.
83. S. Cyril Ep. 9 ad S. Celestin. p. 37.
84. Ps. xlix. 7, 8.
85. Expressions of Nestorius, while denying the Theotocos. Serm. 1. ap. Mercator.
86. Theod. Haeret. Tab. iv. 12.
87. Socr. H. E. vii. 32.
88. ta mormolukia.
89. Ep. ad Alex. in Theod. H. E. i. 3.
90. Against Arians Orat. iii. n. 14, 29, 30. Orat. iv. 32. Incarn. c. Ar. 8, 22. quoted in Newman's S. Athanasius ag. the Arians. Disc. iii. 25. 8. p. 420. n. 1. Oxf. Tr.
91. Vit. Const, iii. 43. in Ps. 109, 4 p. 703. Montf. Nov. Coll.
92. Catech. x. 19.
93. in S. Cyril c. Jul. L. 8. p. 262.
94. S. Greg. Nyss. Ep. ad Eustath. p. 1093. S. Greg. Naz. Orat. 29, 4. Ep. 101. p. 85. Ben.
95. both quoted by S. Cyril de recta fide 49, 50.
96. de Virg. ii. 7.
97. de Incarn. ii. 5. vii. 25.
98. Common. ii. 21. The above are all quoted in Newman's notes on S. Athanasius against the Arians Disc. iii. 26. nn. u and x. Dr. Bright adds Tertullian, de patientia n. 3, 'Nasci se Deus in utero patitur Matris,' and S. Irenaeus, 'ut portaret Deum,' v. 19. See further Dr. Bright's History of the Church p. 312. ed. 3.

99. Joh. Ant. ad Nest. Conc. Eph. P. 1. c. 25.
100. Serm. 2 in Marius Mercator ii. 9. ed. Garn.
101. de Incarn. vii. 30.
102. in Mercat. pp. 80, 81.
103. quoted by Pet. de Incarn. v. 15.
104. Damasc. de fide Chr. vii. 12.
105. Synod, n. 56.
106. Conc. Eph. Act. i. init.
107. Ep. 9. ad Celestin. p. 36.
108. Socr. vii. 32.
109. Evagr. i. 2.
110. Ep. 6. p. 30.
111. Nest. Serm, i. in Merc. p. 5.
112. Conc. Eph. P. i. n. 30.
113. Ib.
114. Ep. 1. ad Celestin. Conc. Eph. p. i. c. 16.
115. ad S.Cyril. Ep. 5. p. 29.
116. Conc. Eph. P. i. n. 26.
117. Ep. ad Nest. fin.
118. See below ad Nest. i. 6. pp. 25, 26.
119. Cont. Nest. et Eutych. L. iii. He says 'ut aiunt.'
120. Ep. ad Celest. Conc. Eph. P . 1. n. 16.
121. Conc. Eph. P. 1. n. 9.
122. Sacr. Theod. ad Cyril. Conc. Eph. P . i. n. 31.
123. constipatione laboratis. Nest. Serm. 13. p. 93. Garn.
124. Merc. Nest. Blasph. Capit. xii. p. 117. Garn.
125. Ep. Acac. Ber. Cyrillo Conc. Eph. P. i. n. 23.
126. Ep. ad Celest.
127. S. Cyr. Ep. 2. Sec an abstract of it, ab. p. xxv.
128. ap. S. Cyr. Ep. 3.
129. Ep. 4.
130. Ib. Ep. 5.

131. Ep. 6. p. 30.

132. ad Celestin. Ep. 9. p. 30.

133. ad quend. Nestorii studiosum Ep. 7. p. 31.

134. Ep. 3 ad Nest.

135. Synod, c. 6.

136. de Christi Tncarnatione adv. Nestorium. Libb. 7.

137. Ep. ad Celestin. Conc. Eph. P. 1. nn. 16, 17.

138. Conc. Eph. P. i. n. 24.

139. Conc. Eph. Act. i. init.

140. S. Cyril Ep. ad Joh. Ant. Ib. P. i. c. 21.

141. Arnob. jun. c. Serapion. Bibl. Patr. T. 8. p. 222.

142. Conc. Eph. P. i. n. 20.

143. Ib. n. 21.

144. Ib. n. 25.

145. Synod. Ep. 3.

146. Ep. Nest. ad Celestin. in Mercator. P. 2. p. 81. Evagrius quotes from a book, which he wrote in answer to those who blamed him for having wrongly requested that the Synod at Ephesus should be convoked, i. 7.

147. Conc. Eph. P. 3, c. 23.

148. Liberatus (c. 4.) says that Nestorius obtained it from him.

149. Conc. Eph. P. 1. c. 31.

150. zeloten.

151. Ep. 7. p. 31. Neither the date of the Epistle nor the person to whom it was written is known. It must have been written before the heresy of Nestorius had become so plain.

152. as ab. p. lxiv.

153. As translated by Mercator. Opp. T. 2. pp. 53, 54. § xix-xxi. ed. Garn.

154. Common. i. 42.

155. Apol. ad Imp. Conc. Eph. P. 3. n. 13.

156. Socr. vii. 34.

157. Ten Bishops signed with him "the relation of Nestorius and the Bishops with him to the Emperor concerning the things done in the holy Synod &c." Conc. Eph. Act. i. n. 6. In Baluzii Conc. nova coll. p. 699. six names are added, one omitted.

158. Ep. ad Alex. Conc. Eph. P. 1. c. 34.

159. Synodicon c. 15.

160. S. Cyril has been criticised, because words of Apollinarius were quoted among the authorities as from S. Julius. The words themselves, in their simple meaning, express the truth, and contradict Apollinarianism. Leontius (A.D. 590), who first detected the forgery by use of MSS. says, it contains nothing 'quod nobis adversetur,' i.e. to the Catholic Faith. (de sectis Act. 8.) The words are, 'perfectus Deus in carne et perfectus homo in Spiritu.' Vitalis confessed that 'Christ was a perfect man,' but explained it to mean, 'We say so far that Christ was a perfect man, that we ascribe Divinity to Him instead of a mind.' S. Epiph. Haer. 77. n. 23. See Coustant. Epp. Rom. Pont. App. p. 71. sqq.

161. The language which Mr. Neale censures [Hist. of the Holy-Eastern Church B. ii. s. 2. p. 237.] occurs in a Homily utterly unlike S. Cyril's style, which Aubert admitted among his homilies, [T. v. 2. p. 279] but not the Editors of the Councils. [See further Dr. Bright's Hist. of the Church, p. 330. n. o.] Of the homilies delivered at Ephesus, the hoi tois hierois [Aub. p. 350] is said in the collection of Baluzius [pp. 546-551] to have been delivered after the deposition of Nestorius. So is the 2nd tes men ton hagion Aub. p. 352. These have no allusion to him, nor has the ho makarios prophetes p. 354. The phaidron horo to sustema [Aub. p. 354 also in the Acta Conc. Eph. Act. 1. n.

13. upon which the homily quoted by Mr. Neale seems to be founded] speaks of the condemnation of Nestorius as past, seauton exeleiphas, p. 357. ho Theos katheile se kai exetile. p. 358. The homily, edei men arkeisthai placed by both after the deposition [Aub. p. 358. Bal. p. 548.] scarcely alludes to Nestorius.

162. Conc. Eph. Act. 1. A Bishop, among his associates, justified the Jews, as having only slain a man.

163. Ep. ad Cyrill. in Conc. Eph. Act. 2. n. 3.

164. See Baronius H. E. A. 431. n. 7. sqq. and Pagi. Ib.

165. Relat. Conc. Eph. ad Imper. Act. iii. n. 1.

166. Conc. Eph. Act. iii. init.

167. Synodicon c. 24. The report mentioned by the delegates of John's party that Nestorius 'was sent from Ephesus, to go where he liked' [Epist. Schismat. ad suos. in Eph. Conciliab. n. 12] was accordingly inaccurate.

168. Synod. c. 25.

169. Synodicon c. 26.

170. In a writing, which Evagrius had seen. Evagr. i. 7.

171. S. Celest. Ep. ad Theodos. Conc. Eph. P. iii. n. 21.

172. l. c.

173. Conc. Eph. P. 1. n. 34.

174. Relatio Synodi ad Imp. Conc. Eph. Act. l. n. 7.

175. S. Cyrill. Epist. ad Com. et Potam. Ib. n. 5.

176. Evagr. H. E. i. 3.

177. Synodicon Ep. 201.

178. Ep. 112. ad Domnum.

179. Acta Conciliab. post Conc. Eph. Act. 1.

180. The Synod speaks of 'the Chapters sent lately to Constantinople by Cyril, as agreeing mostly with the impiety of Arius, Apollinarius, and Eunomius;' 'the Sentence' states that the Synod was 'hurried by Cyril, in order that the Chapters which agree with the evil and ungodly doctrine of Apollinarius and Arms and Eunomius might not be enquired into.' The letter to the other Bishops of the Council whom they had excommunicated, says that they had 'abetted the lawless things done by Cyril of Alexandria and Memnon the Ephesian, and maintained intercourse with men of an heretical mind.' They tell the Emperor, that they had so done, 'until they cast out and anathematize the Chapters sent out by Cyril, full of the evil doctrine of Apollinarius and Eunomius and Arius.' John, in his own letter to the Clergy of Constantinople, says that the sentence was passed 'until they anathematize the heretical Chapters of Cyril the Alexandrian, and receive without guile the faith of the holy fathers gathered at Nice.' To the Senate in Constantinople, they speak of their 'ceasing from their heretical and evil doctrine and recovering the faith of the holy fathers of Nice,' as the condition of their being restored. To the people of Constantinople they say, that they 'do not refuse repentance to the deposed and excommunicate, but would open the doors of loving-kindness, if they will very speedily anathematize the Chapters sent out by Cyril, which are alien from the Apostolic and Evangelic teaching.' They still repeat in their Relation to the Queens, that they 'had deposed Cyril and Memnon, and removed them from the Episcopate, until they become conscious of their wounds and truly repent and anathematize the heretical Chapters of Cyril, agreeing with this impiety of

Apollinarius etc.' (Acta Conciliabuli post Act. 1, Conc. Eph.) The like was repeated in the later Acta of the Conciliabulum and in Theodoret.

181. See Tillemont, S. Cyrille, Note 43.
182. See ab. p. lxxiii.
183. Epist. Memnon. ad Cler. Const. Conc. Eph. Act. vi. n. 14.
184. S. Cyr. Ep. ad Cler. Const. Conc. Eph. Act. 1. n. 9.
185. Acta Conciliab. init. (post Conc. Eph. Act. i.)
186. Lit. Conciliab. ad Imperat. l. c.
187. Nest. &c. Relat. ad Imp., Conc. Eph. Act. i. n. 6.
188. Sacra, ap. Acta Conciliab. post Conc. Eph. Act. vi. n. 3.
189. Rescript. Epp. Const., Conc. Eph. Act. vi. n. 9
190. Relat. Conc. Ib. n. 8.
191. Relat. Synod. ad Imp. l. c. Act. v. n. 1. and more fully Relat. 2. Act. vi. n. 12.
192. Epist. S. Cyr. ad cler. et pop. Const. Act. vi. n. 13.
193. Ep. Memnon. ib. n. 14.
194. panton homou ton epitedeion.
195. Ep. ad Theopempt. Ib. Act. vi. n. 18.
196. Conc. Eph. P. iii. n. 1.
197. Orient. Ep. ad suos in Const., Acta Conciliab. post Act. vi. Conc. Eph. n. 20.
198. Svnodicon c. 18.
199. Ib. c. 19.
200. Common. ad Cler. Const. Conc. Eph. Act. vi. n. 16.
201. Rescript. Epist. Const., Conc. Eph. Act. vi. n. 9.
202. Emperor. 'If it be so, let the Bishops who have arrived come.' Dalm. 'No one allows them to come.' Emp. 'No one hinders.' Dalm. ' They have been controlled and hindered from coming.'
203. Synodicon c. 35.
204. Ep. Theodoret. ad Alex. Hierap. Acta 2. Conciliab. n. 13.
205. Xysti Ep. ad Cyr. in Coteler. Eccl. Gr. Mon. T. i. pp. 46, 47.
206. S. Cyr. Ep. ad Acac. Melit. Conc. Eph. P. 3. c. 35.
207. Ep. Alex, ad Andr. Samos. Synod, c. 58.
208. Propositiones directae ab Acacio Berrh. Cyrillo Alex, in Concilio &c. Synodicon c. 53. The Bishops in whose names Acacius sent it, were John of Antioch, Alexander Hierop., Macarius of Laodicea, Andr. Samos., and Theodoret.
209. Gratissime.
210. Epist. Joh. Antioch. per Paul. Emis. Cyrillo, Synod. c. 80.
211. S. Cyr. Ep. 31. ad Joann. fin. p. 109. Ep. 38. ad Success. v. fin. p. 140.
212. S. Cyr. Ep. ad Donat. Conc. Eph. P. 3. n. 38.
213. S. Cyr. Ep. ad Joh. Ant. Conc. Eph. P. 3. c. 34.
214. Conc. Eph. P. iii. n. 30. It is translated by Dr. Bright, Hist. of the Church, pp. 350, 351.
215. Homil. Paul. Ib. n. 31.
216. Conc. Eph. P. iii. n. 39.
217. Ep. 171 ad Joh. Ant.
218. Ep. 172. A very bitter letter against S. Cyril is ascribed to Theodoret in the Synodicon c. 121.
219. See Tillemont S. Cyrille d'Alex. Art. 126. and the extracts in Liberatus Breviarium c. ix. 'De Cyrilli Epistolis pro Orientalibus scriptis.'
220. see above p. viii.
221. S. Isid. Epp. i. 310.
222. 'That the Very and supreme God became Very Man, not changed from what He was, and taking what He was not, being from two natures One Son, without beginning and without end, recent and Eternal, thou thyself wouldest

not deny, having very many evidences thereof from our holy father Athanasius, a man, who, above nature, soared aloft to the things of God.' Ep. i. 323.

223. Ib. 324.

224. Conc. Eph. Act. vi. S. Cyril says that it was the Creed of Theodore, in his Epistle to S. Proclus Ep. 54. p. 199.

225. Fac. pro def. 3 Capp. viii. 2.

226. S. Cyr. Ep. 59, ad Cler. et Lampon. p. 194.

227. Ib.

228. Johan. Ant. et Syn. S. Cyrillo, in S. Cyril. Ep. 50. pp. 192, 193. This in itself refutes the calumny of his old enemy, Count Irenaeus, that S. Cyril, for private reasons, suggested this censure of writings of Theodore.

229. S. Cyr. ad Joann. Ep. 51. p. 195. ad Acac. Ep. 52. p. 197.

230. Ep. 51. p. 196.

231. Ep. 54. p. 199, 200.

232. Ep. 49. p. 192.

233. Ep. i. ad Serapion. n. 32. p. 681

234. See at length in 'On the Clause "And the Son," in regard, to the Eastern Church &c.' pp. 113-123. or Preface to S. Cyril's Commentary on S. John T. i. pp. xxi sqq. 1874. Oxf.

235. Leont. de sect. Act. 8. B. P. x. 672.

236. Conc. v. Coll. v.

237. by my son above, p. xxix.

238. Ep. 36 ad Acac. p.121.

239. mentioned Ep. 83.

240. Praef. ad libb. c. Julian. Opp. T. vi. P. ii. p. 6. Aub.

241. 'Ferunt.' Cassiod. Praef. ad Institt. init.

242. His Commentaries on select passages of the Pentateuch, on Isaiah, the Minor Prophets, S. John, are known to all, as forming four out of the seven volumes of his works. Besides these, much of the Commentary on the Gospel of S. Luke has been preserved in the Syriac [published with a translation by Dr. Payne Smith]. Fragments of the Commentary of the Epistles to the Romans, the Corinthians, and the Hebrews were recovered from Catenae by Cardinal Mai and Dr. Cramer. The Collection, weeded of some passages wrongly ascribed to S. Cyril (as is the wont of Catenae), was edited by my son: some things were added from a MS. of Mount Athos, and the Syriac MSS. in the British Museum [S. Cyril. in D. Joan. Evang. Vol. iii. Oxon.]. Various old authorities say that he also wrote a Commentary on S.Matthew, (Tillemont, S. Cyr. d'Alexandrie Art. 158. v. fin). [The fragments on the Acts and Catholic Epistles, published by the Abbe Migne, did not appear to my son to furnish evidence of having formed a part of a regular Commentary l. c. p. 441. 445]. Of the O.T. large fragments of the Commentary on the Psalms and fragments of a Comm. on Jeremiah have been recovered by Card. Mai. It is certain that he wrote a Commentary on Ezekiel. There are not a few fragments of his Comment. on the Canticles. He also wrote on the book of Wisdom. (See Card. Mai Bibl. Nov. Patr. T. iii. Praef.)

243. see ab. p. x.

244. see ab. p. xix.

245. Garnier, Pref. to 'the fifth Sermon of Nestorius de Deo nato et Virgine Qeoto&kw|, the second against S. Proclus,' in his edition of Marius Mercator P. 2. p. 29.

246. p. 4.

247. Tillemont Art S. Cyrille d'Alex. c. 156.

248. cod. 169.

249. Common. ad Eulogium. Conc. Eph. P. 3. n. 37.

250. Garnier Praef. in Scholia in M. Mercator. p. 218.

251. Ep. 165 ed.Ball.

252. Conc. Chalc. Act. ii. fin. The passages quoted are from c. 4. init., below p. 189. and c. 13. p. 201.

253. Dial. ii. fin.

254. § 4 init. bel. p. 189. § 13. bel. pp. 200, 201. § 27. bel. p. 215.

255. See my son's S. Cyrilli Comm. in D. Joann. T. iii. App. pp. 420, 421.

256. S. Cyr. Opp. T. v. P. ii. p. 23. Aub.

257. Ib. T. vi. p. 157 sq.

258. pro defens. 3 Capp. L. vi. 3. xi. 7.

259. c. Nest. et Eutych. L i. quoting c. 35 bel. p. 224.

260. in Photius cod. 229.

261. Cod. 169.

262. in Photius Cod. 230. p. 272 Bekk.

263. Act, 10. p. 329. d. e.

264. Diss. 1 [ma de haeresi et libris Nestorii, in his edition of Marius Mercator p. 319.

265. See below, p. 321 note.

266. S. Cyrilli in B. Joannis Evang. Vol. iii. è Typogr. Clar. 1872.

Cyril of Alexandria, Five Tomes Against Nestorius - Book 1

Cyril the most Holy Archbishop of Alexandria a Five-Book Contradiction of the Blasphemies of Nestorius of the Five Tomes of S. Cyril
[Translated by P.E. Pusey]

Truth of human writings must be tested by Scripture. Arian errors and against Holy Ghost. Errors of heretics on their heads. Nestorius' book of Homilies. S. John i. 1,3,14,18. True Union of Person. Mother of God. "Made Flesh;" Manichees have no plea; without it, the curse and decay would still have been our lot. "Mother of God" except it express a Truth, may no ways be allowed. 'Passed through,' objected to. To be Incarnate, belongs to one who was, before He was Man. " Mixture " of old used in right sense. One of Nestorius' sermons quoted as owning God and Man in one. sunapheia. A mother, mother of a man, though the body only is taken of her. Elizabeth mother of S. John the Baptist. Eusebius of Dorylaeum opposes Nestorius in church. GOD the SON had two Births. The Creed of Nicea on the Incarnation. The Creed recited. Nestorius cites from that of Constantinople. "Incarnate" begotten after the flesh. If it did but mean indwelt it would be common to all. S. John's most careful accurate language. That the Virgin Mary bare God, does not exclude the Eternal Generation, nor render her an object of worship.

THOSE who wish to explore the holy Scripture and who drive away negligence in doing so, and thirst rather for the attainment thereof, and apply themselves vigorously and apart from all sloth----the being in every good shall be their's, for they fill their mind with the Divine Light: and then applying it to the doctrines of the Church, they admit every thing that is right and unadulterate, and that most readily, and lay it up in the hidden treasures of their soul, and rejoice as much in what they in their desire of knowledge have collected, as others who are worldly, in insatiably collecting Indian gems or gold, yea rather, yet more: for wisdom is better than costly stones, and every precious thing is not worthy of her, as it is written. For I say that they who are wise and prudent and skilled in the Divine doctrines, ought to remember what has been profitably written by one of the holy Disciples, Brethren try the spirits whether they he of God. And the Divine Paul says that to the saints has been given discerning of spirits.

For the one who say Lord Jesus, will say it none otherwise than through the Holy Ghost: and they who out of unlearning let loose a contradicting tongue against them, and wherein those think rightly, these all but say Jesus Anathema, from Beelzebub will they do so. We must then studying to prove all things subtilly and in a finished manner and with mind awake, light on the writings of certain, and test skillfully what words they use of Christ the Saviour of us all, and imitate, and that aright, the most approved and experienced of money dealers, who admit proved coin, and diligently reject the counterfeit and amiss. And to this the blessed Paul invites us saying, Be ye skilful [1] bankers, prove all things, hold fast that which is good, abstain from every form of evil. And it is in other ways also all-disgraceful and unseemly, that in the affairs of this life we should be seen no whit sparing of what conduceth to profit, but rather make it of moment to aim and strive after those things whereby we may live splendidly, and neglect things so sacred and count for nothing the salvation of the soul, but let it sink down in pits and swamps, sometimes exposing unto the mere pleasure of those who choose to say what they ought not, our mind, not vigilant for the truth, nor choosing to search diligently what is the true and profitable meaning of what has been read, what the perverted one and that outsteps accuracy in doctrine and works loss in the soul that looks to it. Yet to the soul is there nought equal in value in their sight who are perfect in understanding.

We must try therefore and that most straitly, writings on the Divine doctrines, and if any should go along with the sacred Scriptures and speed its clear and most unerring way therein, let it be acclaimed by us too with testimonies to its orthodoxy: but if it form its language cold and astray and amiss, yea rather giver of destruction to the readers, let it hear from every mouth, But ye are uttering and telling us another error.

Therefore either let them make the tree good and his fruit good, or let them make the tree corrupt and his fruit corrupt; for the good man out of the good treasure of his heart bringeth forth good things, and the evil man out of the evil treasure of his heart bring eth forth evil things, according to the unlying word of the Saviour. For the god of this world blinded the understandings of the unbelieving heretics, lest the light of the gospel of the glory of Christ should shine: and they have been deceived manifoldly. For some (miserable!) say that the Word sprung of God the Father is lesser than He that begot Him, and have not shuddered at apportioning to Him an alien and slave-befitting measure; others, whetting against the Holy Ghost their unholy and intemperate mouth, do rightly hear the Prophet say, But draw YE near hither, ungodly sons, seed of the adulterers and the whore, against Whom did ye sport yourselves? and against Whom opened ye your mouth and on Whom let loose your tongue? are YE not children of destruction, a lawless seed? But these shall walk in their own light and find the flames that themselves kindled: for us whose care is orthodoxy, it is meet that we should give a wise and accurate account of each of the Divine doctrines and should shun the charges [put forth by] their unbridled mouth, lest in ought stumbling and sinning against the brethren and wounding their weak conscience, we sin against Christ, Let us therefore hearken unto Him Who saith, If the enemy had reproached Me, I could have borne it, and if he that hated Me had spoken proudly against Me, I would have hid Myself from him, but THOU, a man Mine intimate, My guide and My friend, who sweetenedst food together with Me, in the house of God we went in harmony. But let these things go upon the heads of the enemy, who war against the glory of our Saviour, and esteem blasphemy against Him, their delicate meat: for us it is meet and necessary (as I said) that we, zealous to savour those things that please Him, should not follow [doctrine] which is alien from truth or which diverges in any other direction, and tends to decay, [but follow] that which is for the good of our flock and is crowned by the Truth itself with testimonies to its rightness. [2]

And this I say having met with a certain book compiled by some one, having a large collection of homilies, orderly and systematically arranged and in no wise lacking in due appliances for the reader. And if ought had been said by its author, which by passing into forgetfulness should come to nought, I would have deemed it a duty both myself to hold my peace and to counsel others to do the same; lest things so unmeetly and unheedfully said should become known to many others, and to those after us. But since a multitude of blasphemies has been heaped into this book and some great accusation has been made, baying against the doctrines of the truth, how was it not necessary that we in turn should (so to say) strip for combat and should fight in behalf of its readers, that they may not take harm thence, but may rather know how to repulse bravely the damage from what is unrightly said? For the Divine John was called by Christ the Saviour of us all the Son of thunder, and with reason, for that he well-nigh sounded forth o'er all beneath the heaven and thundered over the earth, uttering something vast and immense . For he makes known full well the truly dread and mighty Mystery of the Incarnation of the Only-Begotten: for he said, In the, beginning was the Word, and the Word was with God, and the Word was God: all things were made through Him, and without Him was not any thing made. But when he had made accurate and complete initiation, and declared that the Only-Begotten being God and ineffably begotten of God by Nature, is Maker and Creator of all things; then, then, in fit season, does he at length begin the allwise economy that for our sakes and in our behalf was wrought, and says, And the Word was made flesh and tabernacled in us (and we saw His glory, the glory as of the Only-Begotten of the Father) full of grace and truth. For he said that the Word was flesh, shewing the force of the true union, i.e., understood as one "of Person:" and by saying that He tabernacled in us, he does not allow us to conceive that the Word which is out of God by Nature passed into flesh which is of the earth. For one not thoroughly exact as to what the Divine Nature Which surpasses every thing generate is, might (I suppose) have deemed that It was haply recipient of change and could become regardless of Its own Essentially-accruing goods, and change (so to say) into something other than what It is, and be brought down to the measures of the creation, subjected in unlooked-for way to changes and alterations. But that this is utterly impossible (for the Nature of God is stablished and hath unshaken abidance in that wherein it is), he hath testified saying, that the Word tabernacled in us, albeit made flesh: both skilfully explaining the wisdom of the Economy and guarding full well that the Nature of the Word be not accused by any as though It had become flesh by change and turning aside.

  We ourselves too then say, tracking the aim of the inspired, and in no way outstepping the definition of the Faith, that He Who is out of [3] God by Nature, the Only-Begotten, He Which is in the Bosom of the Father, He through Whom are all things and in Whom all things, albeit having before every age and time His Own Existence, and ever co-existing with Him Who begot Him, descended unto voluntary emptiness in the last times of the world, and took the servant's form, i.e., became in our condition and Man economically, and was made like in all things unto His brethren, by partaking similarly of blood and flesh, and that He thus underwent birth with us and like us, and took into Himself the passing into being of His own Flesh, not as needing a second beginning unto being (for the Word was in the beginning and was God) but, that He might gather together the human race, a second first-fruits of all things after that first one, born after the flesh of a woman, according to the Scriptures. For so being Rich, became He poor, bringing us again unto His own wealth and having all in Himself through the flesh which was united to Him. For thus have we been buried with Christ through Holy Baptism, have been raised and made to sit with Him in heavenly places. For so hath written the steward of His mysteries, the herald and Apostle, and minister of the Gospel oracles, the most wise Paul. Necessary therefore, alike to the faith of the Mystery and to the exact demonstration thereof, is the fact of true Union, I mean of Person, that the mode of generation according to the flesh of the Only-Begotten may be without blame, Who was (as I said) called to no second existence (for Himself is the Maker of the worlds), but lowered Himself economically to manhood for our sakes, and despised not the laws of human nature but chose rather to have as His own together with the flesh the fleshly generation too. Therefore do we say that He was born after the flesh Who is ever Co-existent with the Father. For thus condemned He sin in the flesh and He hath brought to nought the might of death in us, made as we, Who knew no sin, in Whom we live and move and are.

But some (I know not how) wrong the most sacred beauty of the dogmas of the Church and wrinkle the holy and all-pure Virgin, bringing her down to the unseemly rottenness of their own ideas and arming against us a multitude of new-fangled inventions. For they accuse, as something bastard and uncomely, yea rather as going beyond all fit language, the word Mother of God, which the holy fathers before us have constructed for the holy Virgin; and sunder, dividing into two several sons, the One Lord Jesus Christ, and take away from God the Word the sufferings of the Flesh, though not even we have said that He suffered in His own Nature, as God, but we attribute rather to Him along with the Flesh the Sufferings also that befel the Flesh, that He too may be confessed to be Saviour (for with His stripes were WE healed, as it is written, and He has been wounded for our transgressions, albeit not recipient of suffering any wound): and WE have been saved by His undergoing death for us through His own Body.

But I will essay to demonstrate clearly what I said, for I will now read the words of him who has compiled this book, and first of all those which he made, inveighing in no slight terms against the word Mother of God. But since he repeatedly goes through the same words, and it is necessary that we should repeatedly go through the same ideas, pardon (I pray) pardon us who do not wilfully repeat ourselves but have resolved that in whatever direction the aim of his words goes off, thither we too ought to oppose. He then spake thus, debasing the title of the Holy Virgin, I mean Mother of God:

Nestorius. *"I often (he says) asked them"* (i. e., those who contradict him) *"do you say that the Godhead has been begotten of the holy Virgin? They straightway recoil at the saying: who (says one) is sick of such exceeding blasphemy, as to say that in her who bare the temple by the Spirit, in her was God formed? then when I reply to this, What then that is incongruous do WE say in advising to flee the word, and come to the common phrase significant of the two natures? then seems it to them that what is said is blasphemy. Either clearly acknowledge that the Godhead has been born of the blessed Mary, or if you flee this expression as blasphemy, why saying the same as I, dost thou feign thou sayest it not?"*

§1. They therefore who think contrary to what yourself said and think good (I know not how) to hold, these have been clearly testified to by your own mouth as having a right and most unerring opinion in regard to Christ the Saviour of us all, and as holding with their mind the faith which they had delivered to the churches which from the beginning were eye-witnesses and ministers of the word and priests of our Mysteries and faithful stewards. For they shake off (and that most rightly) as a patent proof of unlearning alike and extremest impiety, the mere imagining that the Word from forth God the Father has been called unto a second beginning of being or took flesh of the holy Virgin as a root of His own existence: still they call her Mother of God, as having borne Immanuel Who is by Nature God: for the Word has been made with us, being God by Nature and above us. Do they therefore say contrary to what they think? For some one of those who think with thee will (I suppose) say, "If thou say that the Nature of the Word is not Offspring of the flesh, and free thyself from this charge, how dost thou affirm that the holy Virgin bare God?" But thou in turn wilt hear from us, The God-inspired Scripture says that the Word out of God the Father was made Flesh, i. e., was without confusion and Personally united to flesh: for not alien to Him is the Body which was united to Him and born of a woman, but as with each of us his body is his own, in this same way is the Body of the Only Begotten His own and none other's: for thus was He also born according to the flesh. Then how (tell me) would He have been made Flesh, except He had received birth of a woman, the laws of human nature calling Him thereto, and bodily existence being able no otherwise to have its beginning? For not (I suppose) giving heed to the juggleries of the Greeks, shall we too romance that the bodies of men are born of oak or rock: but our laws nature set us, yea rather nature's Creator, for as of each of existing things is the kin to it born, so of ourselves too, and no otherwise (how could it be?) For nought at all of what It willeth to accomplish is impracticable to the Divine and Ineffable Power, yet doth It proceed through what befits the nature of things that are, not dishonouring the laws set by Itself. And it were not impracticable to the Word That can do all things, having determined indeed for our sakes to become as we, yet to refuse the birth of a woman, and from without to fashion to Himself a body by His own Power, just as we say was done in the case of our forefather, Adam: for God took (it says) dust of the ground and formed man. But since this were occasion to the unbelievers who desire to accuse the Mystery of the Incarnation, and (before all) to the unholy Manichees, whom thou sayest over and over that thou fearest lest they should spring upon those who call the holy Virgin Mother of God, as though they were affirming that the Incarnation of the Word existed in mere phantasy; needs did He progress through the laws of human nature, and since His aim was to assure all that He hath become truly Man, He took hold of the seed of Abraham, and the blessed Virgin being the mean to this same end, He took part like us in blood and flesh; for so and no otherwise could He become God with us. Most needful in another way too unto those on the earth was the Incarnation or Inhumanation of the Word. For if He had not been born as we according to the flesh, if He had not taken part like us of the same, He would not have freed the nature of man from the blame [contracted] in Adam, nor would He have driven away from our bodies the decay, nor would the might of the curse have ceased which we say came on the first woman; for it was said to her, In sorrows shalt thou bring forth children.

But the nature of man hath fallen into the disease of disobedience in Adam, it has become now approved in Christ through the utter obedience: for it is written, As by one mail's disobedience many were made sinners, so too by the obedience of one shall many be made righteous. For in Adam hath it suffered, Dust thou art and unto dust shalt thou return, in Christ hath it gained the riches of being able to be superior to the toils of death, and (so to say) to exult over decay, saying those words of the Prophet, O death, where thy victory? o grave, where thy sting? it became accursed, as I said, but in Christ was this too brought to nought. And verily it has been said somewhere to the holy Virgin, Elizabeth prophesying in spirit, Blessed art thou among women and blessed is the fruit of thy womb. Sin hath reigned over us and the inventor and father of sins behaved himself proudly over all beneath the skies, objecting [to them] the transgression of the Divine Laws: but in Christ we see the nature of man, as in a second firstfruits of our race, having confidence with God. For He said clearly, The prince of this world cometh, and in Me shall find nothing.

But, good sir (would I with reason say) except the Only-Begotten had become as we, had become as we no otherwise than by means of birth in the flesh from forth a woman, WE had not been enriched with what is His. For as the most wise Paul writeth to us, Emmanuel the second Adam hath appeared to us, not from the earth like the first, but from Heaven. For the Word That is from above and from forth the Father hath come down not into the flesh of any one nor into alien flesh (as I already said), nor again hath He descended upon any one of those like us to dwell in him, as He was in the Prophets; but having made His own the body which was from forth a woman and born from her after the Flesh, He gathered up man's birth through Himself, made as we after the flesh, Who is before all ages from the Father. This confession of faith the Divine Scriptures delivered to us. But THOU feignest to fear lest any of us should suppose that the Word Begotten of God had the beginning of His Being from earthly flesh: thou takest away utterly the Mystery of the Economy with flesh, saying that the holy Virgin ought not to be called by us Mother of God: thou turnest round those who call her Mother of God unto a confession inevitable and as of necessity, of supposing that the Word out of God became fruit of flesh. But it is not so, far from it. For He That hath His Being of God the Father before all time (for He is the Framer of the ages), in the last times of the age, since He became Flesh, is said to have been begotten after the flesh. For if the Body is conceived of as His own, how will He not wholly and entirely appropriate the birth of His own Body? Yea yourself too would have approved the right and undefiled faith of these who thus hold, if you would have persuaded yourself to reason and to confess that Christ is truly God, the One and Only of God the Father, not severed into man separately and likewise into God, but the Same, both Word out of God the Father and Man out of woman as we, while He abideth God.

But that thou dost accuse the Birth after the flesh of the Word, every way declaring two sons and dividing the One Lord Jesus Christ, shall be shewn not by my words but by thine own.

"Look what follows, heretic. I grudge not the word to the Virgin mother-of-Christ, but I know that she is august who received God, through whom the Lord of all passed, and through whom the Sun of righteousness beamed. Again I suspect your applause: how did ye understand passed through? I have not said

passed through, in the sense of born, for not so quickly do I forget my own words: that God passed through from out the Virgin mother of Christ was I taught by the Divine Scripture, that God was born from her, was I nowhere taught." And after more; "Never therefore does the Divine Scripture say that God was born of the mother of Christ, but that Jesus, Christ, Son, Lord, [was so born]."

And hereto he subjoins that Christ was not truly God, but rather a God-bearing man, as he supposes, putting forward the Angel's voice saying to blessed Joseph, Arise take the young child, and says that the Angels too, though wiser than we, knew that He was a child.

§2. Herein therefore he stiles heretic him who holds the right and admirable faith about Christ, and who since He is truly God, calls her mother of God who bare Him. But there will be no doubt to any of those who think aright, that it is himself who, fastening the blame of heresies on them who choose to deem aright, is establishing the unbeauty of his own words, and has all but confessed openly that he is being borne outside of the straight way, and is making crooked paths. Next how (tell me) do you not grudge this title to the holy Virgin, albeit you take away the dignity of the Divine Birth, and say that she is not Mother of God? but debasing the expression and affirming that it is full of blasphemy, how do you bid those who so will, to apply it to the holy Virgin (though I hear you call her august)? and then deem the so blasphemous word (as you alone think it) meet to adorn the most august one, and you feign to crown her, putting about her as some choice honour, a calumny against God the Word? For if it be wholly abhorrent to the Word Who is sprung of God to endure fleshly birth and you permit her who did not bear God to be called Mother of God, is it not true to say that you have openly depised the Lord's will? will you not be caught insulting rather the august one, than (as you suppose and say) electing to honour her, by allotting to her a name hated of God? For not to those whom we determine to honour [do] we give names whereby the glory of the Supreme Nature is dishonoured, first of all we shall unawares be involving our own selves in the charge of such impiety, next we shall do them no slight wrong, decking as if in honour those we praise with what is no praise, and weaving for them a laudation hated of God.

One may moreover marvel at this too: that striking right and left at the words of the unholy heretics and in no wise allowing them to prevail, because they take away the truth of the Divine doctrines, next allotting no slight blame to the word Mother of God and accusing it amongst other things as untrue and impious, you said that you pardon it and will not grudge it to the Virgin even if one should choose to call her Mother of God. Will you permit it therefore to those too who are diseased with the madness of Arius, to say that the Son is inferior to the Father? or again to the rest who bring down the Nature of the Holy Ghost from its God-befitting excellency? But you would not choose to do this; and if any one desire to learn why, you will (I suppose) surely say, I do not endure a blasphemous word. Hence if she be not Mother of God, and you permit this to be said, know that you are deserting the truth, and reck little about any longer appearing wise. For do you not say that Elisabeth too or any other of the holy women is worthy of all reverence? will you then not grudge it, if any one choose to call them too mothers of God? But I suppose that you will surely and utterly withstand them and say, This is not so; for they bare sanctified men and none among them was God by Nature. Hence either drive away this from every woman; or if you allow the holy Virgin alone among all to have it, what words will you use for your defence? For if it be true of her and she has truly borne God, in that the Word of God has been made flesh, confess this with us, and you will free yourself from the charge of impiety: but if she hath not borne God, to permit any to call her Mother of God is to partake of their impiety. But she is Mother of God, because the Only-Begotten has been made man as we, united of a truth to flesh, and enduring fleshly birth and not dishonouring the laws of our nature, as I said before.

But since he says that he knows that she, i.e. the holy Virgin, is august, come I pray come let us consider the reason too of the reverence that was done her: "for I know (he says) that she is august [4], through whom the Lord of all passed, through whom the Sun of righteousness beamed." How then do you say that she received God? or in what way did the Lord of all pass through her? or how beamed the Sun of righteousness? For if she hath not borne God, after the flesh I mean, how received she God? how passed He through her? But haply you will say this wise word of yours as you think and dare to speak it " The Word was God both connected with man and indwelling him." But the tradition of the faith makes itself ready against your words as to this, No God-bearing man, but God Incarnate have we been taught to worship: but not so speakest THOU: how then do you not see that you are babbling and falsely marking the truth that is in the Divine dogmas? For the Word has been made flesh. How did you now say that she received God except you have believed that she hath borne Emmanuel Who is God by Nature? how passed the Lord of all through her and how beamed the Sun of righteousness? And who is he that you think fit to embellish by such names? is he a common man, like one of us, yet hallowed, as having the Word of God indwelling? Then how will such an one be Lord of all, and Sun of righteousness? For the power of lordship and dominion over all and of illumining things possessing intelligence, will pertain not to our measures, but will be attributed to the Supreme and Most High Nature alone.

But since taking (I know not whence) the word passed through, you have applied it to God, explain the word; the meaning of the passage through here spoken of, will belong to your wisdom to tell us who know it not. For if the Word of God so passed through her, as to pass from one place to another, you cast Him down forthwith; for you will hear Him saying by the voice of the saints, Do not I fill Heaven and earth saith the Lord? For not in place is the Godhead nor knoweth It bodily changes of place, for it filleth all things. But if while awaiting the fit period of birth, He made an incidental indwelling in man, and so you say that God made passage through the holy Virgin, or passed through her (for I will use in all thy holy words): we see nought in the holy Virgin more than in other women. For Elisabeth bare the blessed Baptist who had been hallowed through the Spirit through Whom the Son Himself also makes His abode in us. And the wise John will witness saying, Hereby know we that He is in us, because He gave us of His Spirit. The Word of God therefore passed through Elisabeth herself too, indwelling in the babe through the Spirit even before its birth.

But you feel suspicious of the applause as though it came to you from the people for having chosen to speak right things? for having called Him Who was born of the holy Virgin Sun of righteousness and Lord of all; you then again feign to speak with precision, and find fault with the applause, and accuse again those who are rejoicing over you of not having understood. O great strength which is in your words! you have made no delay in the needed vexing of them, you turned straightway their joy into mourning, you rent off their rejoicing and girt them with sackcloth, straightway adding, "Again I suspect your applause, how did ye understand passed through? I have not said passed through in the sense of was born, for not so quickly do I forget my own words. That God passed through from out the Virgin Mother of Christ, was I taught by the Divine Scriptures, that God was born of her, was I nowhere taught."

Those therefore are thy perverted sayings; the applause was of love, in that your mind had some guise of orthodoxy. But I will press on now too no less and say, What is passed through, if it mean not birth? will you say that the Word out of God Himself by Himself and apart from flesh hastened through the Virgin? yet how would not this be replete with all folly? For it would be necessary to suppose that the Godhead were recipient of quantity, and of movement [which bears from one place to another; or if the Godhead be unembodied, at large and everywhere, and not in place and [circumscript, how will it pass through a single body? But whatever it be that you are saying, how do you not need to clear it up and say it more openly, if confident in your own opinions about it, you are able to testify to their incorruption? where (I pray) have you heard the God-inspired Scripture say that the Word of God passed through the holy Virgin? For that brief and contracted is the life of those upon earth, the blessed David taught saying, Man, I his days as grass, as a flower of the field so he flourisheth; for the wind passeth through him and he shall not be, but of the holy Virgin what thing of this sort can you say has been written? That God has been born of her, after the flesh I mean, God-inspired Scripture has clearly shewn.

But I will go again to your own words, O all-excellent, for you have yourself too confessed and this most often that the Word has been made Flesh, and you reject it not. And this too you say besides: for you say that the Godhead of the Only-Begotten was clearly and openly Incarnate. You have written in this wise,

> "Thus it says elsewhere too, He spoke to us in His Son Whom He appointed Heir of all things through Whom also He made the worlds, Who being the Brightness of His Glory: [5] having put Son, it calls Him fearlessly both Brightness of His Glory, and appointed Heir; Heir, appointed after the Flesh, Brightness of the Father's Glory after the Godhead: for He departed not, made flesh, from likeness to the Father. And in addition it again says thus, for the times of ignorance God winked at, but now commandeth all men to repent, because He fixed a Day in which He will judge the world by the Man Whom He appointed, having given assurance unto all men in that He raised Him from the dead. Having first said, By the Man, he then adds, In that He raised Him from the dead, that no one might suppose that the Godhead Incarnate had died."

§3. Who then is He Who was Incarnate, or in what way was He incarnate, what Godhead was incarnate, tell (O most excellent sir) to us who would learn it. Shall we grant that the Word, God out of God, was Incarnate, and say that He was made Man, as having been made as we and born in flesh? or shall we allow this in no wise, but suppose that a man came hereto, connected with God, according to thee? But you will (I suppose) say, that it is better and wise to think that the Word out of God was Incarnate and made flesh, according to the Scriptures: for one is not I suppose seen assuming that wherein one is, but if one come somehow to be in that wherein one was not at first, reason will forthwith admit that something new has been wrought regarding him. Hence it is unlearned to say that any of us having stepped forth of the definitions of human nature have been incarnate and been made flesh; but the Incarnation, or being made flesh, will beseem (and that with much reason) the Nature That is beyond humanity. But if He was truly Incarnate and has been made flesh, He is accredited as Man, and not connected with a man, by mere indwelling or external relation or connection, as you say. Yet even though He became Man, He possesseth the being God in all security, nor do we say that any change took place of the flesh into the Nature of Godhead, and we hold that neither did the reverse take place, for the nature of the Word hath remained what it is even when united to flesh. What no one therefore even in bare idea thinks of holding, why do you putting this in your book, as though actually uttered, pretend to be contending for the doctrines of piety? For the name mixture, some of the holy fathers too have put: but since you say that you are afraid lest any confusion be deemed to take place, as in the case of liquids mingled with one another, I rid you from your fears, for not so did they deem (how could they?) but they used the word improperly, anxious to declare the extreme union [of the things that had come together; and we say that the Word of God came together with His proper Flesh, in union indissoluble and unalterable. And we find that the God-inspired Scripture itself too, does not look minutely into the word, but uses it rather improperly and simply. And verily the Divine Paul hath written of some, But the Word preached did not profit them, who wore not mixed [in faith with its hearers. Were they of whom he spoke going to be mixed one with another, after this fashion, as wine with water, and to undergo a confusion of persons, or were they rather to be united in soul, as it is written in the Acts of the holy Apostles, And of the multitude of them that believed was the heart and the soul one? But this I suppose is the truth, not the other. Be free then from all fear on this score, for firmly established is the mind of the saints.

But since to say that the Nature of the Word was Incarnate is (I deem) nought else than to hold that It has been made Man and not without birth of woman (for this only way does the nature of human bodies know of), how were you not taught by the God-inspired Scripture the Birth after the flesh of the Only-Begotten? albeit yourself too, when the prophetic lessons were before you, Unto us a Child was horn, unto us a Son was given, say thus of the Child that was born, " Great the mystery of the gift, for this is the Babe That is seen, this the new-born That appears, this that needed bodily swaddling bands, this the just-born after the Essence that is seen, in the hidden part [Everlasting Son, Son Creator of all, Son Who by the swaddling-bands of His own aid binds the instability of the creation. " And elsewhere again, " And the Babe is God All-free, so far removed is God the Word, O Arius, from being subject to God." In which words he styled even the body connected with Him God. And again, We recognise therefore the human nature of the Babe and His Godhead, we preserve the oneness of the Sonship in the nature of manhood and Godhead. " Lo here with all clearness you say that the Babe, the just-born, the visible, the new-born, the swaddled, is Son and Creator of all; and the Babe the holy Virgin hath borne to us. You know therefore that God has been born after the flesh, and this you have learnt out of the God-inspired Scripture. For who will be conceived to be Creator of all, save He alone through Whom the Father hath made all?

But I said (you will haply say) " in the secret part Son and Creator of all." Well, I agree, but I will ask you: You say that the hidden is the Word of God and that this is the Creator of all: how then did you but now point out as with your finger the Babe just-born and new-born and in swaddling clothes, and called this same both Son of God and Creator of all? or do you haply suppose that the Word out of God has been transformed into the nature of the flesh, and accuse yourself, not others, of daring to say this? Surely if the Babe be the hidden Son and Creator of all, and have been born of the holy Virgin, you have acknowledged with us even against your will that she is Mother of God in some unlooked-for way, since how is a babe God all-free? For if you use the word, all-free , in the sense in which each one of us too may be so conceived, as entrusted by God with the reins of his own free-will, what is there special in Him beyond the rest? or why do you put about Him the freedom, as some God-befitting and truly choice Dignity? albeit it is in the power of all upon the earth to possess it and indeed they already have it. But if the freedom here signify the being not subject to the laws of another, and He be free in such sort as the Divine Nature itself too is conceived of, how do you say that the new-born Babe is in case so august and befitting only the Supreme Nature and glory? albeit that all which is called into being is subject unto God and runs under the yoke of bondage. But you will perchance deem that that empty word [6] of yours suffices unto all this, that I mean in respect of the natures being connected one with another, and that, not Personally, but rather in honour unvarying [in each] and equality of rank: for this is what you are always unlearnedly saying to us. But that in saying such things, you will be caught to be staying yourself upon rotten and fragile conceptions, will be shewn and not at length, when opportunity offers to us to speak upon this too.

But to these he subjoins some others by which he deems that he can shew and that skillfully that the mode of a generation like ours is unmeet and impossible. And our words he arrays against himself, and deems that he can over-master them easily and shew that they are nothing although they set forth the truth. He says thus:

"'If Christ (says he [7]) be God, and Christ be born of the blessed Mary, how is not the Virgin mother of God?' I hide none of their objections: for the lover of the truth takes and objects to himself all that comes of the falsehood;" and then he endeavours to apply the solution, using some such conceptions as these. "For the babe (he says) is formed in the womb, but so long as it have not yet been formed, it hath no soul, but being formed at length, it has a soul made it of God. As then the woman bears the body, God ensouls it, and the woman is not called mother of soul, because she bare a man endowed with soul, but rather mother of man, so (he says) the blessed Virgin too, even though she have borne a man, the Word of God passing forth along with him" (for this word did he use) "not therefore is she mother of God."

§4. Is therefore (tell me) that blamed by you which is said by us? does it seem right to you without understanding to find fault with what is so rightly and purely said, and do you not rather attach the blame of not being able to think aright to your own understanding? For they to whom the truth is repugnant, to them will belong (and too readily) the receptivity of what is not so, and the rebuke of those who are wont to speak most excellently, will not be without its harm, yea rather will be even a manifest demonstration of the having declined unto falsehood and of choosing to honour what it would be more right to hate, in that one has missed of right reason. But no man, having conceived of things so base. . . [8], he said that himself was the lover of the truth, and that we had contrived the lie; albeit one may see on the contrary that ours is right and true. For the advocate of the lie and fraud endeavours to fasten the blame of his falsehood on the champions of the truth, haply driven to forgetfulness of the Prophet who says, Woe unto them that call evil good and good evil, that put darkness for light and light for darkness.

But I will endeavour to shew by the example adduced by him that he does not even clearly know what he is saying. For flesh confessedly is born of flesh, and the Artificer of all performs the ensouling in the mode and way that He knows. Yet is the woman who bears, albeit she is the source of the flesh only, believed to bear the whole man, made up (I mean) of soul and body, although she contribute nothing of her own to the being of the soul. Yet when one says man, one signifies surely the soul united to the body. As therefore the woman, albeit she bear the body alone, is said to bear him that is made up of soul and body, and this no wise damages the account of the soul, as though it found in flesh the origin of its being; so will you conceive as to the blessed Virgin too: for even though she be mother of the holy Flesh, she hath nevertheless borne God the Word out of God truly united thereto [9], and though any call her Mother of God, he will not be defining a more recent beginning of God the Word nor that the flesh hath been made the commencement of His Being: but will understand rather the mode of the economy and wondering at it will say, O Lord, I have heard Thy hearing and was afraid, I considered Thy works and was astonished.

Bat our all-wise and prudent expounder, having pondered the force of the example says, "Thus the holy Virgin, too, even though she hath borne man, God the Word passing along with him, yet not therefore is she Mother of God: for not from the blessed Virgin was the Dignity of the Word, but He was God by Nature."

What therefore is the meaning of, that the Word passed forth along with the flesh, he alone knows, but I marvel much at his subtil refinement. For the word of truth sets forth that the Word of God has been Personally united to the Flesh; and he keeps affirming the passing forth along with, meaning I know not what. Next, when our [10] discussion was all about nature and Personal Union, and aimed at enquiring not what the Word out of God is in respect to Dignity, but whether He has been made Man economically, making His own the flesh born of a woman: he removing the question to quite other matters says, "Not from the holy Virgin was the Dignity of the Word, but He was God by Nature:" albeit how are not Dignity and Nature two entirely different things? But our discourse hereupon does not need overmuch skill [4]: we must therefore see what comes next. For he fortifies yet another outpost against what has been said by us, as he thinks invincible and competent to shew with all force that the Birth out of woman of Emmanuel is empty talk of ours: he says again thus,

"The blessed John Baptist is fore-heralded by the holy Angels, that the babe shall be filled with the Holy Ghost even from his mother's womb, and having the Holy Ghost, was this blessed Baptist born. What then? call you Elizabeth mother of the Spirit? apply your mind here, although there be some among you who are startled at what is said, pardon their inexperience."

§5. And who on hearing such words will not straightway say in Prophet's voice, For the fool will utter folly and his heart will conceive vanity, to accomplish iniquity and to utter error against the Lord? For error confessedly is it and nought else, to trust in such frigid and childish thoughts as though they were true. One may then marvel at him for his gentleness, for he said that they ought to be esteemed worthy of pardon and clemency who had no acquaintance with those words of his: yet were it a thing thrice-longed for by us ourselves (if so be), yea rather by all too who are Christians; for how should not all long to be rid from words so burdensome and perverse? But we say this: Elizabeth hath confessedly borne the blessed Baptist anointed in the womb with the Holy Ghost: and if it had been any where said by the God-inspired Scriptures, that the Spirit too was made flesh, rightly would you have said that she ought to be called by us mother of the Spirit; but if the bairn is said to have been honoured with bare anointing only, why deem you it right to put the fact of incarnation on an equal footing with the grace of participation? for it is not the same thing, to say that the Word was made flesh and that one has been anointed through the Spirit with prophetic spirit. For of the holy Virgin it is written, Behold a Virgin shall conceive and bear a Son, and He who is born is called the fruit and moreover Emmanuel, which being interpreted is, God with us; but of Elizabeth, she shall bear a son who shall go before Him in the spirit and power of Elias, and shall go before the face of the Lord to prepare His ways. By no means therefore is Elizabeth mother of the Spirit, for she bare a prophet of the Highest: but the holy Virgin is truly mother of God [11], for she hath borne carnally, i. e., according to the flesh, God united to flesh. For since she is human who bare, therefore and rightly do we say that the mode of generation has been wrought in human wise; for thus and no otherwise was it possible that He Who is over all nature could become as we, not slighting the being what He is (how could He?) but rather abiding what He was and is and will be: for superior to change is the Divine and Most High Nature.

That we therefore think aright in affirming that God has been born according to the flesh for the salvation of all,... God-inspired Scripture hath testified: but since to his most novel dogmas he opposes the truth and the very symbol of the Church's Faith, which the fathers once gathered together at Nicea through the illumination of the Spirit defined; he, fearing lest any should keep whole the Faith, instructed unto the Truth by their words, endeavours to calumniate it and alters the significance of the words, and dares to coin with false stamp the very force of its ideas. For while himself in the midst of the Church was using profane babblings, a certain man [12] of those who were of great piety and yet among the laity, but who had gathered within himself no mean learning, was moved with fervent and devout zeal and with piercing cry[13] said that the Word Himself Who is before the ages endured a second Generation also, viz., that after the flesh and forth of a woman; the people being disturbed hereat, and the more part and wiser having honoured him with no mean praises, as pious and most full of wisdom and not imparticipate in uprightness of doctrine, the rest being mad against him, he [Nestorius] interrupting, straightway approves those whom by teaching his own he had destroyed, and whets his tongue against him who could not endure his words, yea and against the holy fathers who have decreed for us the pious definition of the Faith which we have as an anchor of the soul both sure and steadfast, as it is written.

> *"For (said he) I rejoice at beholding your zeal; but from the thing itself is a clear confutation of what has been said by the pollution of this wretched man*[14]*; for whereof the births are two, two sons are they, but the Church knoweth one Son Christ the Lord."*

§6. Most foolishly therefore put he forth the definition of his ideas on this matter saying, "for whereof the births are two two sons are they." But letting alone for a while his subtil accuracy herein, come, come let us gather what pertains to accurate investigation for the consideration of the matter. He therefore made it inadmissible [to speak of two generations [15]] but says that one ought to be confessed by us, that we conceive not of two sons (as though it were necessary if the births be two, that two sons also should be introduced): let him come forward and tell us which of the generations he will admit, that before the ages from out the Father, wherein the Word was God not yet Incarnate, or this one, recent and out of a woman.

If then he say that alone, I mean the one before the ages from out the Father, that one alone will be Son Who is out of Him by Nature and not yet participate of flesh and blood: and vainly (as it seems) is the Mystery of the Incarnation uttered, and in no wise hath He emptied Himself nor been made in servant's form, but hath remained thus, rejecting the true concurrence with flesh even until now. But he who is in the last times out of woman, shall be styled by himself son, and we will admit this one generation, I mean out of woman; needs has the Word out of God the Father fallen away from being by Nature Son.

But the pious man sees full surely the absurdity of such ideas and its exceeding swerving unto impiety. In order then that we may proceed along the royal road, we say. that two were the Births, one the Son through both, the Word out of God not yet made in flesh, the Same afterwards Incarnate and enduring for us the birth of a woman after the flesh. For if one said in regard of men that two sons must surely be conceived of, if we speak of two births, he would say rightly and it would be true; but since the Mystery of Christ and the mode of the Incarnation hath another path, and is not beheld in like wise with what is ours, why is he, looking at our habits, and then fastening his mind on what is marvellous and above speech, caught fall ing into feeblest and unlearned pettiness of belief? What surprises me is this: he confessing herein that the Church knows one Son, and adding, The Lord Christ, hath no longer kept One, for he sunders one from another things united, and putteth each apart, not enquiring what the Word is by Nature, what the flesh also; but gathering rather into one, man and God in equality of glory only, as he deemeth, which is a thing utterly implausible, yea rather impossible, he casts down the scheme of the mystery unto uncomeliness. Thus he saith:

"But we must (for it has now come into my mind) learn that the Synod of Nicea too nowhere durst say that God was born of Mary; for it said, We believe in One God the Father Almighty and in One Lord Jesus Christ. Observe that having first put the word Christ, which is the indication of the two natures, they did not say, in one God the Word, but took the name that signifies both, in order that when lower down you hear of death, you think it not strange; in order that the words crucified and buried may not strike the ear as though the Godhead suffered these things." Then it goes on, "We believe in One Lord Jesus Christ, the Only Begotten Son, the Begotten out of the Father, the Consubstantial with the Father, Who came down from the heavens for our sakes, and was Incarnate of the Holy Ghost. They said not, and begotten of the Holy Ghost." And he says that the holy fathers interpreting what is the meaning of Incarnate say, Made Man. And what being made Man means he himself making clear, said again, "His own Nature not undergoing change into flesh, but inhabitation in man."

§7. Will any one of those who rank as Christians endure either the infatuation that there is in these words or the impiety of his ideas? To those of really sound mind are not these things a manifest ribaldry, and no mean kind of openmouthedness against Christ? for he slanders the truth, he says that He is not truly Son, allotting this to another (for " observe, he says, that having first put the word Christ which is the indication of the two natures, they did not say, We believe in One God the Word)." And as regards the Name, I mean Christ,[16] I will presently enquire whether it be significative of the two Natures or not, but what is before us we will exercise ourselves in, as we can. For in no wise to be borne may those things be that are so absurdly and heedlessly babbled forth by him, but one might (I deem) say, speaking in behalf of the holy fathers, What art thou doing, noble sir, putting forth rude tongue against holy men, to whom will beseem that which was said by Christ Himself the Saviour of us all, It is not YE that speak, but the Spirit of your Father Which speaketh in you? for what has there not been conceived of by them of things exceeding well polished unto an admirable subtilty? what of needful doctrines has been overlooked, or what method of safeguard neglected by them? " They have not dared (he says) insert in their words concerning the Faith that God the Word was born of Mary." If therefore thou for this reason accuse those who have been before us, and sayest thou art aggrieved because they are not found to use thy exact words, it is time (I suppose) to accuse along with them the holy Apostles and Evangelists too, for they have compiled the books of instruction [concerning Christ, yet one will not find them using word for word your expressions. But (if it please you) pass this over as [17] ....but consider rather that they have well wrought out their explanation of this matter, for faith in the Holy and Consubstantial Trinity is exacted of us. But since they say that they believe in One God the Father Almighty, Maker of all things both visible and invisible, and in One Lord Jesus Christ His Son, and none other (according to us) is Jesus Christ the Lord than the One and by Nature and truly Son, Who beaming from out of God and being God the Word has been made Man, by birth (that is) out of woman, how will they who proclaim the mode of the economy not be found to speak also of His Birth of a woman after the flesh? for then in truth has the Word which is God and Wisdom and Life and Light, the Son, been named Christ Jesus. It is manifest therefore that the time of such naming has concurrent with it the Birth, that I mean through the holy-Virgin. That believing on Christ Jesus, we believe in the One and by Nature and truly Son, our faith mounting up unto the Father through Him, will be clear, in that He Himself hath cried aloud to the whole world, He that believeth on Me believeth not on Me but on Him that sent Me, and he that seeth Me seeth Him that sent Me, and again, Believe on God, and believe on Me. And we do not (I suppose) say that He asks of us two faiths, but rather He teaches that if any admit the faith to Himward, he hath believed on the Father Himself.

But since (as is probable) he will be making use of the community of the names, saying that Christ and Lord, yea and Son, are common titles, and will be affirming that they suit the Word That sprung of the Father even though He be conceived of as alone and not yet participate of flesh, and likewise the Temple that sprang of a virgin, this matter needs (I think) considerable investigation: putting it off for the present to a season (as I said) fitly belonging to it, let us go to another utterance of the holy Synod which this man perverting unto his own liking, does violence to the force of truth. For he says that the fathers have written, We believe in One Lord Jesus Christ, the Only-Begotten Son, the Begotten from forth the Father, the Consubstantial with the Father, Who came down for our sakes, and was Incarnate of the Holy Ghost. He adds hereto and says of che holy fathers, " lower down they interpret that He who was made man, He it is who is said to be Incarnate, the Divine Nature not enduring change into flesh but inhabitation in man." In his explanation he again keeps hold of the same mind and moreover says thus;

"They followed the Evangelist, for the Evangelist too when he comes to the being made man, shunned saying Birth in respect of God the Word, and hath put Incarnation. Where? Hear, And the Word was made flesh; he said not, Was born through the flesh. For where the Apostles or the Evangelists make mention of the Son, they put that He was born of a woman. Give heed to what is said, I beseech you; for where they utter the name of the Son, and that He was borne from forth a woman, they put the word, Born; where they mention the Word, no one of them durst speak of birth through the human nature. For the blessed John the Evangelist, when he came to the Word and to His Incarnation, hear what he says, The Word was made flesh."

§8. Come therefore putting beside what he said, the definition of our Creed, let us see if ought has been innovated by this man regarding it too.

WE BELIEVE IN ONE GOD THE FATHER ALMIGHTY, MAKER OF ALL THINGS VISIBLE AND INVISIBLE, AND IN ONE LORD JESUS CHRIST, THE SON OF GOD, BEGOTTEN OUT OF THE FATHER, ONLY-BEGOTTEN THAT IS OUT OF HIS ESSENCE, GOD OUT OF GOD LIGHT OUT OF LIGHT VERY GOD OUT OF VERY GOD, BEGOTTEN NOT MADE, CONSUBSTANTIAL WITH THE FATHER, THROUGH WHOM ALL THINGS WERE MADE, BOTH THOSE IN HEAVEN AND THOSE ON EARTH: WHO FOR US MEN AND FOR OUR SALVATION CAME DOWN AND WAS INCARNATE AND MADE MAN, SUFFERED AND ROSE THE THIRD DAY, ASCENDED INTO THE HEAVENS, COMETH TO JUDGE QUICK AND DEAD, AND IN THE HOLY GHOST.

Come now therefore, noble sir, where (tell me) have they put of the Son, Incarnate of the Holy Ghost and the Virgin Mary [18]? but this he can by no means shew. But consider this. They say that the Word out of God, the Only-Begotten, He That is from forth the Essence of the Father, He through Whom are all things, the Very Light, was both incarnate and made man, suffered and rose, and too, that He will in season come again the Judge.

But in order that submitting to accurate scrutiny his words also, we may see what is the amount of the unlearning that is in them, he affirms in plain terms that they say that the Word out of God was both incarnate and made man, and he crowns them with his vote unto their truth as saying what was convenient. Do they therefore (tell me) in saying that He was both Incarnate and made Man mean ought else than that He was begotten after the flesh? for this would be (and alone) the mode of incarnation to one who has his existence both external to flesh and in his proper nature; for no one would say (I suppose) that flesh has been made flesh nor will any one be made what he was [already]. But if one should conceive a certain economic change to have been made regarding him unto somewhat else which he was not, the expression will then have great fitness. Hence if they say that the Only-Begotten has been Incarnate, and this would be wrought (I suppose) through fleshly generation and in no other way, how have they not plainly said that the Word being God has been begotten after the flesh?

But (he says) the Birth is not named in plain terms. Yes, but the nature of the thing knows (as I already said) no other way of being incarnate. So that, although it be not in plain terms said in matters of this kind, we will not for this, forsaking the only way recognized by nature, go off to another. For it is written in the Book of Genesis, And to Seth there was made a son, and he called his name Enos. Shall we then, because the Scripture has put, was made, not admit the mode of birth? how would not this be unlearned? for the very nature of the thing will all but compel us even against our will to confess the idea of birth. How then on hearing of the Incarnation does he not forthwith admit the idea of Birth? and when the being made man has been plainly mentioned, how did he not straightway understand, that being made man would befit not a man, lest he should seem to be made that he already was, but the Word originating from God? But where being made man is believed to truly take place, there is full surely the birth whereby he may be seen to be made man.

But not thus does it seem to you is the saying to be conceived of, that the Word of God was both Incarnate and was made Man; for you said again, endeavouring to oppose the idea of every one else, that the being made man, means, not the change into flesh of the Divine Nature [19], but its indwelling in man. He says then that the conversion into flesh of the Divine Nature is both impossible and that it in no wise befalls it (and very rightly, for we will approve him who herein has chosen to speak aright; for I say that It is stable and that It will not be transformed into ought else than what It is believed to be): but that his discourse hath missed of the fitting and true, in that he maintained that the being made Man is the indwelling in man, I shall essay to shew. For if he says that this matter is true of Emmanuel singly and alone, let him teach the reason why (for I cannot learn it), or no one will tolerate him as a definer and layer down of the law in respect of those things as to which he is pleased to speak inconsiderately. But perchance the force of the things defined does not extend unto one [alone], there will then be no blame, even though it extend unto all. Hence not once for all but many times over shall we find that God has been made man, and not only the Word out of God the Father, but I will add both the

Father Himself and besides, the Holy Ghost. For He said through one of the holy Prophets of them that have been justified in faith, I will dwell in them and walk in them and I will be their God and they shall be My people. And Christ Himself also said, And if any man hear Me, we will come I and My Father and make Our abode with him and lodge in him [20]. The most wise Paul too hath somewhere written, And Moses was faithful in all his house as a servant, for a testimony of the things which were to be spoken of, but Christ as a Son over Bis own house whose house are WE; and moreover of the Holy Ghost too, Know ye not that ye are the temple of God and that the Spirit of God dwelleth in you? Hence if when the God of all is said to dwell in any, if this be the being made man or the incarnation, let it be said in respect of each one also of those who were made partakers of the Divine Nature and have moreover had Him indwelling them, that he has both been made man and besides was incarnate. This now being so and admitted as true, the Word out of God the Father might even be said to have been most often made flesh, yea and He indwelleth even now in many of those who fear Him.

Yea (he says) for it is written of God the Word, that He tabernacled in us; the Divine-uttering Paul too said of Christ the Saviour of us all, that in Him hath dwelt all the fulness of the Godhead bodily.

He tabernacled in us confessedly, for so it is written; and moreover that He hath dwelt: I will not oppose you saying it, but rather will I search into the words of the Divines. For the blessed Evangelist, having aforesaid, And the Word was made flesh, profitably added too the, tabernacled in us, that by means of both he might work in us unmutilated the knowledge of the mystery Christward. For that the Word out of God the Father was united Personally to flesh, he hath openly declared [21] by saying that He was made flesh: that made flesh, He hath not passed into the nature of flesh, undergoing change into what He was not, but together with becoming as we, hath abode what He was, he again clearly states, adding to the former, the tabernacled in us. And the Divine-uttering Paul saith that in Christ dwelt all the fullness of the Godhead bodily, that no one might suppose that the Indwelling was simple or accidental but (as I said just now) Very and Personal. For that the Word of God is Incorporeal and not subject to touch, the Spirit-clad was not ignorant; but since it was needful that the declaration of the mystery should be seen to be in no wise a matter of blame, but should be made so accurate and exact unto what is right and true as to be beyond all marvel:----he is doing violence (it seems) and all but overlooking what befits the Unembodied and Supreme Nature, for he hath added, Bodily, being able in no other way to speak than may be attained by our mind and tongue.

Do not therefore, when he tells us of simple indwelling, think that he is saying ought that needs not the strongest reprobation. For overthrowing as he thinks and that with vigour the birth according to the flesh of the Son, he compounds an argument befitting old wives and foolish and having no foundation of truth. For he writes again after this manner; his discourse was made touching the Arians:

"Yet [22] though they prate that God the Word is junior to the greater Godhead, these make Him second to the blessed Mary, and over the Godhead, Creator of times, they set a mother born in time, yea rather they do not even allow that she who bare Christ is mother of Christ. For if not the nature of man

but God the Word was, as these say, that which is of her, she that bare was no mother of that which was born. For how will any one be mother of him who is alien from her nature? But if she be called mother by them, that which is born is manhood not Godhead, for it is the property of every mother to bear what is consubstantial [with her]. Either then she will not be mother, not bearing what is consubstantial with herself, or being called mother by them, she bare that which was in essence like to herself."

§9. How deep the matter of his cogitations! dread and hard to escape is clearly the compulsion resulting from the reasonings of him who hath compiled such things! Whence comes he having gathered into the midst unto us such fables? or who ever sank down to this extent of unlearning in his conceptions, as to think or say that the Godhead of the Only-Begotten has not its existence before the ages from the Father but rather makes flesh and blood the beginning of its passing into being? who is so distraught and slight of understanding and wholly without car for the holy Scriptures? who remembereth not Isaiah who hath cried aloud of Him, Who shall declare His generation? John too who hath written clearly, In the beginning was the Word and the Word was with God and the Word was God; all things were made through Him and without Him was not any thing made? And if all things through Him, how will He Who is before every age and time be later in birth than the things that were made through Him? why then do you bring in what is repudiated by all, as though it had been said? cease accusing those who rightly blame what you say, and who laugh at the vastness of the unlearning that is therein. Since therefore there is no one who says that the Virgin hath borne from forth her own flesh the nature of the Godhead, do not contend to no purpose, twining for us reasonings not made out of premises that are true and acknowledged by all.

But what was it that persuaded you to let loose a tongue so sheer and unguarded against those who are zealous to think aright, and to pour down accusal dire and all-cruel upon every worshipper of God? For you said again in Church,

"But I have already full often said that if any simpler one either among us or any other, rejoice in the word Mother of God, I have no grudge against the word; only let him not make the Virgin a goddess."

§10. Again dost thou rail upon us, and put on a mouth so bitter? and reproachest the congregation of the Lord, as it is written? But WE, my friend, who call her mother of God, have never at all deified any one of those that are numbered among creatures, but are accustomed to know as God the One and by Nature and truly so: and we know that the blessed Virgin was woman as we. But thyself wilt be caught, and that at no long interval, representing to us Emmanuel as a God-bearing man, and putting upon another the condemnation due to your own essays.

Footnotes:

1. trophimoi, reared up, unless it be an error of the single Manuscript which has preserved to us this work for the usual dokimoi, approved. For the citation itself see Translation of S. Cyril's homilies on S. Luke by the Very Rev. R. P. Smith, p. 149 note y.

2. The Greek as it stands is hardly translateable.

3. ek. See "on the clause And the Son, in regard to the Eastern Church and the Bonn Conference," Oxford 1870. pp.128 sqq.

4. The words, who received God, alluded to immediately after, appear to have dropped out of the single existent Manuscript. The passage is one of those cited before the council of Ephesus (Act. i. t. iii. 1064 ed. Col.), and translated by Marius Mercator, p. 202 ed. Bal. Mercator seems to translate less correctly, conceived.

5. Serm. 2. p. 59 Bal.

6. This word sunapto and its noun sunapheia, S. Cyril had used long before to express the kind of Union which Christ gives us with Himself. S. Cyril says, "For as elsewhere He says that He is a Vine, we the branches, shewing that not alien nor of other kind are the branches from the Vine but of it by nature, so here He says that He is our foundation (1 Cor. iii. 11) in order to shew the natural kindship to Him when He was made man, of them which are built upon Him. For then are we connected (...) with Him by nature too, and suspended as it were from our relation to Him as the branches from the vine, we bear the fruit of piety to God-ward," Thes. cap. 15. p. 171 c d. "If on receiving Christ's Spirit we are through It brought near to God the Father, as made partakers of His Divine Nature, how is It a thing made, through which we are connected (...) with God as being now His offspring?" Thes. cap. 34 p. 360 D. And in his treatise de Trinitate written more than five years before this date, S. Cyril says, "Nor could human nature any otherwise have been partaker of the Divine Nature, had it not gained this through the Son as Mediator, receiving it as a natural (...) mode of connection (...)," Dial. i. p. 406 a: "we are temples of the Spirit Who existeth and is, we are called therefore gods as being participant with the Divine and Ineffable Nature, by connection (...) with It," Dial. 7 p. 639 fin. Of God the SON's union with His human nature, S. Cyril says, "But that the SON was Lord, before His concurrence with flesh and His connection therewith through union (...) we shall see without any trouble," Dial. 6. p. 605 d. S. Cyril then used the word to denote our union with Christ in which our own personality is preserved to us entire. When he speaks of the Incarnation in which God the Son's human nature was so made His own, by Union with Him, as to have no distinct or separate personality, S. Cyril uses connection by way of union, a connection that makes the Two natures but One.

Nestorius on the other hand following his own earlier teaching speaks of a connection between God the Son and His human nature no closer than that of any holy person with Christ.

The empty word is found in the creed against which Charisius priest and steward of the Church in Philadelphia brought a complaint before the Council of Ephesus (t. iii. 1205 sqq. ed. Col.), and of which Marius Mercator gives a Latin Translation (see On the Clause And the Son, pp. 76, 77 and note): he gives it at pp. 41 sqq. ed. Baluz. with the heading, Now the setting forth of the corrupt faith of the above mentioned Theodore, and further on, pp. 186 sqq. when giving the session that was holden about Charisius, he gives it over again in a slightly different translation with the heading Nestorian Creed. This Theodore to whom it is attributed was a contemporary of S. Chry-sostom about half a century before and was Bishop of Mopsuestia in Cilicia.

To this empty word S. Cyril opposed his Personal Union (...) . Fleury (Eccl. Hist. Bk. 25 § 8 fin.) speaks of, as the first place in which he has met the expression S. Cyril's 2nd Letter (the first (Ecumenical Letter) to Nestorius in which he says, "The Word having united to Himself Personally flesh ensouled with a rational soul" (see 3 Epistles Parker 1872 p. 56). In the final Letter which S. Cyril and his Council of Alexandria wrote A. D. 430 to Nestorius were appended 12 Anathemas which Nestorius was required to sign (3 Epistles p. 68). These Anathemas or Chapters were much misunderstood by John Archbishop of Antioch, and his suffragans in Cilicia, Palestine, Euphratesia &c, who thought that they contained Apollinarian error; Liberatus who wrote about 125 years after tells us in his Breviarium (cap. 4 Gallandi Bibl. Patr. Vet. xii. 127) that John of Antioch "sent to Andrew and Theodoret, Bishops of his Council to reply in writing to the 12 chapters as renewing the dogma of Apollinaris." Theodoret too in sending his replies back to John sends him aletter beginning," I was greatly grieved on reading the Anathemas which you sent me, bidding me answer them in writing and lay bare to all their heretical meaning." S. Cyril defended his Anathemas or Chapters against the exceptions made by Andrew and Theodoret separately: in the close of his Letter to his Priest Eulogius, his Proctor at Constantinople, he says that he sends the Provost (inter alia) copies of his answers to each of these Bishops. The second chapter begins, "If any confess not that the Word out of God the Father has been united to flesh Personally, ..." No possible misunderstanding of this term, Personal Union, united Personally, seems to have occurred to S.Cyril, for in his Explanation of his Chapters made at the request of the Synod in order that they should he clearer (as the title tells us), during the days while the Council was awaiting its dismissal, as Alexander of Hierapolis writes to Constantinople to John of Antioch, S.Cyril does not allude to this. There is no trace of Andrew Bishop of Samosata having written against this 2nd chapter nor against the fifth and sixth: so prohably no objection occurred to him either. Nor does Eutherius bishop of Tyana in his Letter to John of Antioch, running briefly through the chapters, except against the Personal Union. Theodoret objects to the term, Personal Union, from its novelty and from its appearing to imply mixture. Again in his letter to the monks of Euphratesia, Osroene, Syria, Phoenicia and Cilicia, giving briefly his objections to some of the chapters, he repeats that the expressions

Personal Union and concurrence (...) by Natural Union, teach some mixture and confusion of the Form of God and the form of the servant (Ep. 151 p. 1292 fin.) In answer to Theodore t's objection to the second chapter(written perhaps but a few weeks after this present treatise,) S. Cyril explains the term and says, Seeing that Nestorius is always undoing the birth after the flesh of God the Word and insinuating merely an union of dignities and saying that man is connected (...) with God, honoured with the co-name of Sonship; needs do WE opposing his words say that a Personal Union took place, Personal (...) having no other meaning than only that the nature or Person of the Word, i.e. the Word Himself, united in truth to human nature, apart from any turning and confusion (as we have full often said) is conceived of and is, One Christ, the Same God and Man.

S. Cyril uses the word habitually e.g. it occurs five times in his Treatise to the Princesses Arcadia and Marina on the right faith: he uses also other like expressions, true union, true and Natural Union, inseverable, indissoluble. S. Eulogius, one of S. Cyril's successors in his see (A. D. 581) and a contemporary of Pope S. Gregory, in his famous explanation that the Council of Ephesus forbad oppositions to, not definitions of, the Faith, alludes to this expression and says, For it [the Council of Ephesus] does define what none before it defined. Nay its he kath' hupostasin henosis is a definition not made by the elder Synods. (S. Eulogius in Phot. Bibl. cod. 230 translated in the above-cited On the clause, And the Son in regard &c. p. 80.)

7. i. e. Nestorius is citing S. Cyril himself in his letter to the monks ; see Epp. p. 3 d, and S. Cyril's reply just below, is that blamed by you which has been said by us ?

8. The Roman Editors of the Concilia, who first published this treatise in 1608, conjectured that oudeis, no one, might be a slip for ouden , nothing, translating, But with no thought of how base these things are. Perhaps some words have slipped out.

9. See S. Ath. against Arians, iii. § 29 p. 410. O.T. note e. where this passage is translated. S.Cyril in his 16th Paschal homily, about this same time (A.D. 430) says, "Yet He was (as I said) God in the manhood too, allowing to the nature that is ours to advance through its own laws, yet along therewith preserving the genuineness of the Godhead: for thus and no otherwise will both the bairn (to techthen) be conceived of as by Nature God, and the Virgin which bare will be said to be mother, not of flesh and blood simply, like the mothers with us, but of the Lord and of God Who hath hidden Himself under our likeness." . . . "For as the Precious and all-holy Flesh which was forth of the holy Virgin hath become the own of the Word who is forth of God the Father, so too all things beseeming the flesh save only sin: but chiefly and before all else will birth of a woman beseem the flesh. Hence the Godhead by Itself if it be conceived of apart from flesh will be 'without mother' and that full rightly: but when the mystery Christ-ward is brought forward, the truth as to this will be other and subtil exceedingly. For we shall deem, if we choose to think aright and go the most unerring way, that

the Virgin bare not bare (gumnon) Godhead but rather the Word from forth of God the Father, Incarnate and United to flesh, she who was taken to aid in bearing after the flesh Him who was united to flesh. Emmanuel therefore is God: and mother of God will she too be called who bare after the flesh God who for our sakes appeared in flesh." t. v. ii. pp. 227. 228.

10. i. e. S. Cyril's Letter to the Monks, above-cited, which Nestorius was in part contradicting in the sermon to which the extract belongs.

11. S. Cyril uses exactly the same expression in his Letter to the Monks (Epp. 8 c) and in the first of the chapters that he appended to his great Letter to Nestorius (see note k), "If any confess not that Emmanuel is God in truth and consequently the holy Virgin Mother of God: for she hath borne after the flesh the Word from forth of God made flesh, be he anathema." But the word carnally or after the flesh was not understood by many: e. g. Andrew Bishop of Samosata thought that it contradicted the miraculous Birth from a virgin. S. Cyril explains his meaning in his reply to Andrew; " we said that the Virgin bare the Word of God made flesh according to the Scriptures, i. e, Man: bare Him carnally, i.e. according to the flesh. . . . Saying according to the flesh is not taking away the miraculousness of the Birth .... but teaches that as God begets Divinely or in God-befitting manner according to His own Nature, so too man humanly or flesh carnally." Def. xii capp. adv. Episc. orient, cap. 1. p. 100 d e. See also below Schol. §31.& above p. 22. note o. Theodoret's objection to S. Cyril's first chapter is of a different kind and is identical with that of Nestorius (above p. 7, below p. 33 and note b): the notion that gegenneke , she hath borne, necessitates the conversion of the Godhead into flesh. In Andrew's case, the meaning of the word carnally was misunderstood, in Theodoret's, the word was apparently unnoticed.

12. Eusebius an Advocate at Constantinople; he afterwards put out a protest addressed to the Clergy and Laity of that City (Conc. Eph. part. i. cap. 13 t. iii. 888 ed. Col.) that Nestorius was reviving the false teaching of Paul of Samosata, condemned nearly two centuries before (Marius Mercator, whose translation into Latin of S. Cyril's Defences of his 12 chapters or Anathemas against Nestorius' errors and of his Scholia on the Incarnation, has come down to us, likewise put out a paper of like kind, Opera pp. 50 sqq. ed. Baluz 1684). Many years on we read of Eusebius, as Bishop of Dorylaeum in Phrygia, as a friend of Eutyches, but after fruitless efforts to reclaim him, also his accuser before S. Flavian, Archbishop of Constantinople. In November 448, a Synod was called of Bishops who chanced from one cause or another to be there: these amounted to thirty. The circumstance of Constantinople being the capital of the Eastern Empire occasioned Bishops to be often there. (The Archbishop of Alexandria though apparently he had habitually one of nis Deacons there, as a sort of deputy, or Proctor, in the Imperial City, seems on more especial occasions to have had a Bishop there: e.g. S.Cyril sent his great Synodal Letter to Nestorius by four Bishops, Theopemptus, Daniel, Potamon

and Comarius: of these Theopemptus Bishop of Cabasa and Daniel Bishop of Darnis, went to Ephesus and voted in the Council: Potamon and Comarius remained at Constantinople, for one of S. Cyril's earliest Letters after the Council (Epp. p. 81) was directed to them conjointly with the great Archimandrite Dalmatius, the Priest Eulogius, S. Cyril's Proctor, and another. A brief letter of S. Cyril's written a few days later (pp. 91 sq.) when he was in ward at Ephesus, is directed to Theopemptus, Potamon and Daniel. Fleury (bk. 26 § 3) suggests that Theopemptus and Daniel went back to Constantinople with Letters from the Council.) Before this Synod the Bishop Eusebius accused Eutyches, who was condemned. The August of the next year, 449, the Robber-Council of Ephesus deposed S.Flavian (whose Martyrdom followed immediately for he was driven into exile to Epipa in Lydia and died there) and Eusebius. Eusebius was likewise ejected from his See and stayed at Rome as Pope S. Leo tells the Empress Pulcheria in a letter (S. Leo ad Pulch. 59 [79] col. 1037 ed. Ball.] cited by Fleury 27, 49 english translation): Eusebius was at the Council of Chalcedon, he was vindicated at the close of the 1st Session (t. iv. 1189 Col). In the third Session he presents to the Council a petition against Dioscorus (ib. 1249,1251). In the fifth Session he was one of those engaged in the handling concerning the holy faith, traktai?santon peri tes hagias pisteo (ib. 1452): he signs in the sixteenth session (ib. 1737). A rescript of the Emperor Marcian annuls all that had been done against him. This Rescript addressed to Palladius, Praetorian Prefect, Valentinian, Praefect of Illyria, Tatian Praefect of the City, Vincomalus Master of the offices (see Theod. Ep. 140 tit.) and Consul-designate, is given as a sequel to the Acts of the Council of Chalcedon (part. 3 cap. xi. t. iv. 1809 ed. Col.). See Fleury Eccl. Hist. Books xxv. xxvii.and xxviii. in the English translation edited by Dr. Newman, Oxford, 1844.

Eusebius' brave and loyal conduct on this present occasion while yet a layman, is mentioned in the Council of Chalcedon itself; for when that Council had heard the Letter of S. Cyril to John Archbishop of Antioch to which they gave the Ecumenical sanction of the Church, some of the Bishops called out, ..., Eusebius deposed Nestorius. It is likewise mentioned by Evagrius (Eccl. Hist. i. 9) who says, ... , exercising the Bishop's office at Dorylaeum, who while yet an advocate first convicted the blasphemy of Nestorius. Leontius (in the 7th century) writing against Nestorius and Eutyches (contra Nest. et Eutych. lib. 3 in Galland. Bibl. Vet. Patrum xii. 697) speaks of it too.

13. The people's applause during the sermons of S. Augustine and S. Chrysostom are often mentioned: Nestorius alludes to the applause of his own sermons a little above, p. 11. Two or three years later when the troubles which followed on the council through the Eastern Bishops misunderstanding S. Cyril and his language, were beginning to be allayed, and one of them, the pious and aged Paul Bishop of Emesa, was preaching at Alexandria before the Archbishop, the very words that the people uttered in their delight are preserved to us

(concilia t. iii. 1617, 1621 ed. Col.). Here Eusebius' cry was one of zeal for the Faith, contradicting the denial of Truth which he heard.

14. i.e. Eusebius afterwards bishop of Dorylaeum.

15. See the same objection brought forward in the treatise Quod Unus Christus, given below.

16. see Book 2, beginning of Book 5 and §§ 4.5. Def. xii capp. contr.Theod. cap. 7 init. de recta fide to the Emperor, pp. 32, 37, 38, to the Princesses, 47 b 70 e 85 c 115 c d 120 d, to the Empresses Pulcheria and Eudoxia 131 b & § 18 p. 148 b Quod Unus Christus see below. See also Theodoret in his letter to Bishop Timothy (Ep.130).

17. Here the MS. leaves a blank of about 12 letters: these blanks sometimes indicate that the scribe could not decipher the word in the ms. which he was copying.

18. The Creed that S. Cyril (here as elsewhere) recites above is the Nicene Creed, as actually put forth by that Council: Nestorius, being Archbishop of Constantinople, had (not unnaturally) been quoting from that of Constantinople, which is the Nicene Creed in the form in which it was afterwards put forth by the Council of Constantinople (A. D. 381), and in which it is familiar to us. See the two in Rev. Dr. Heurtley's De Fide et symbolo, pp. 5 and 17 ed. 18G9. and translated in parallel columns with the variations marked in my Father's, The Councils of the Church to the close of the second general Council of Constantinople, A. D. 381, 1857 pp. 312 sqq. For the very slow steps by which the Creed of Constantinople became well-known beyond the more immediate neighbourhood of Constantinople itself see "On the clause, And the Son, in regard &c." pp. 37 sqq; for the beginnings of its Liturgical use, in Spain, pp. 49, 65; in France p. 66; Germany, Rome p. 66; the East, note 2 pp. 184, 185. Even John Archbishop of Antioch in his Letter to S. Proclus written a few years after this treatise of S. Cyril, inserts the Creed of Nicea, Synodicon cap. 196. Conc. iv. 452 Col. Diogenes bishop of Cyzicus, in the Council of Chalcedon, said, "The holy fathers who were afterwards, explained the, was Incarnate, which the holy fathers in Nicea said, by 'From forth the Holy Ghost and Mary the Virgin.'" The Egyptians and the most pious Bishops with them called out, No one admits addition (Conc. Chalc. Act 1.1. iv. 913 ed. Col. quoted On the &c. p. 40.): probably with a keen recollection of what their great Archbishop had here said, objecting to Nestorius as adding them: for the Council was holden in 451, only 7 years after he had departed to his rest.

On the antiquity of these words though not in the actual Nicene Creed, see my Father's note P to Tertullian in the Library of the Fathers, pp. 503, 504.

19. Theodoret, having lived amid the same school of thought as Nestorius, shares with him the dread of the Divine Nature being imagined to be changed into flesh. In his objection to S. Cyril's first chapter (see above p. 24 note q) Theodoret says, "It is plain then from what has been said that the form of God was not turned into servant's form but remaining what it was, took servant's form.....having moulded Himself a Temple in the Virgin's womb, He was co-with that which was moulded and conceived and

formed and borne: wherefore we style that holy Virgin too, Mother of God, not as having borne God by Nature but man united to God Who moulded him(p. 204 c d e)." In his Letter to the Monks of the province he says, "For in his first chapter he casts out the economy that was wrought for our sakes, teaching that God the Word hath not taken human nature but was Himself changed into flesh," Ep. 151 p. 1292; Migne, t. 83. col. 1417. In his letter to the Monks of Constantinople written in his later years (Tillemont Art. xi. fin. thinks about 451) he says that SS.Basil, Gregory, Amphilochius, Pope Damasus, Ambrose, Cyprian, Athanasius, Alexander his teacher, Meletius, Flavian, lights of the East, Ephraim the lyre of the Spirit; John [Chrysostom], Atticus, Ignatius, Polycarp, Irenaeus, Justin, Hippolytus, and (he then Bishop of Rome, the most holy Leo, all taught that "One Son is the Only-Begotten Son of God and God before the ages Begotten ineffably from out the Father, and that after the Incarnation He is called both Son of man and man, not turned hereinto but assuming what is ours." Ep. 145 p. 1253. Further on in the same Epistle Theodoret speaks also of the Manhood remaining: he says that whereas our Lord raised other bodies free from all blemish, "in His own He left the tokens of sufferings that He might through the sufferings convict of erring those who deny the assumption of His Body, and through the print of the nails might teach them who imagined that the Body had been changed into another nature, that it had remained in its proper form." ib p. 1254.

20. This addition occurs in the same words on S. John i. 13 p. 107 O.T. (cf. an allusion on S.John xiv. 24) and in Scholia, § 18.

21. diamemenuken . This emendation of the Roman editors for diamemeneken is confirmed to us by citations of Niketas in his catena on S. John. (This Niketas was Archbishop of Heraklea in Thrace in the xith century, he compiled ample Commentaries on Holy Scripture made up of copious extracts from the Fathers: those on the Psalms, SS. Matthew, Luke, John, the Epistle to the Hebrews, perhaps a fragment of that to the Romans have reached us either published or in MSS.: for the psalms and S. John at least Niketas made use of the labours of those who before him had constructed catenae of Fathers and he had besides access to works of the Fathers now lost, of which he has thus preserved something.)

22. This passage is given rather fuller, and at greater length by Mercator, with the title, Also in the nineteenth quire, when he is speaking as it were against Arius. (p. 112, Bal.)

Cyril of Alexandria, Five Tomes Against Nestorius – Book 2

TOME II
[Translated by P.E. Pusey]

The Word after the Union One Incarnate Person. Similitudes of unlike things united. 'Connection' does not unite. The Name Christ means God the Son Incarnate. Jacob's pillar a type. To His human nature belong the anointing and HIs subjection to the Law: yet He is God. Cyrus how christ, the Babylonians how holy. Personal Union. Christ's glory no imparted glory but His own inherent glory. If community of names unite, Emmanuel has nought more than we. The human cannot be allotted to a distinct person. God the Son incarnate to be worshipped just as before His Incarnation. Speak not of 'hidden' and 'manifest' as though Two, they are One. Worship of Him taught by God the Father.

The tongue is a fire and an unruly evil, as it is written; thrusting from him the mischief therefrom, the Divine-uttering David says, Set a watch, O Lord, before my mouth, a door of fencing around my lips, incline not mine heart to words of wickedness. For to be able to speak aright, and to have an exact control over the tongue, as to what it should speak, what not, is of a truth God-given, and is no slight matter with those who practise a conversation not void of admiration. But recklessness in speech and unbridled licence unto trickery, are replete with danger and bear down to the pit-fall of hell those who use it. And it is written, Death and life are in the hand of the tongue, they that master it shall eat the fruits thereof. A certain other too of the wise men hath said to us, If thou hast a word of understanding, answer, if not, lay thine hand upon thy mouth; for how is not silence better than unlearned speech? But accursed is it in another way too to belch forth bitter words, and to heap down sinful sayings upon the ineffable Glory, albeit it ought to be honoured by us with unceasing praises. And when we sin against the brethren and wound their weak conscience, we sin against Christ, for so hath written the Divine-uttering Paul.

And this I say having read Nestorius' words and observing that he not only says that we ought not to say that the holy Virgin is Mother of God and that she hath borne Emmanuel Who is God, but yet in addition to this and in many ways is he minded to make war upon the glory of Christ. For he endeavours to shew us that He is God-bearing and not truly God, but man associated with God; as in equality of rank. For thus seems good to him alone apart from every one else, to think and to speak, albeit the Catholic Church, which Christ Himself presented to Himself, has not the wrinkles of him who has compiled such things, but rather as unblemished, she keeps wholly without rebuke her knowledge of Him, and hath made full well her tradition of the Faith. For we believe in One God, the Father Almighty, of all things both visible and invisible the Maker, and in One Lord Jesus the Christ, and in the Holy Ghost: and following the confessions annexed hereto of the holy Fathers, we say that the Very Word Essentially sprung from forth God the Father, was made as we and was Incarnate and made Man, that is, took to Himself a Body from forth the holy Virgin, and made it His Own: for thus will He be truly One Lord Jesus Christ, thus let us worship Him as One, not putting apart Man and God, but believing that He is One and the Same, in Godhead and in Manhood, that is, God alike and Man.

But the inventor of the most recent impiety, albeit making feint of saying One Christ, ever divides the Natures and sets Each by itself, saying that they did not truly come together; but making excuses in sins, as it is written, devises some mode of connection, of merely (as I said) equality of rank, as shall be shewn from his own words: and he makes the Word out of God indwell by participation, as in a common man, and distributes the sayings in the Gospels, so as one while to attribute certain to the Word alone [1] and by Himself, other while to him that is born from forth a woman separately. Yet how is it not obvious to all that the Only-Begotten being God by Nature has been made man, not by connection simply (as he says) considered as external or accidental, but by true union, ineffable and passing understanding. And thus He is conceived of as One and Only, and every thing said [befits Him and all will be said of One Person. For the Incarnate Nature [2] of the Word Himself is after the Union now conceived of as One, just as will reasonably be conceived in regard to ourselves too, for man is really One, compounded of unlike things, soul I mean and body. But it is necessary now too to notify that we say that the Body united to God the Word is ensouled with a reasonable Soul. And I will for profit's sake add this too: other than the Word out of God is the flesh, in regard to its proper nature, other again Essentially the Nature of the Word Itself. But even though the things named be conceived of as diverse and sundered in diverseness of nature, yet is Christ conceived of as One out of both, the Godhead and manhood having come together one to another in true union.

And the God-inspired Scripture confirms us hereto by ten thousand words and acts: using similitudes whereby one may (and that without labour) clearly advance so as we may behold the Mystery of Christ. The blessed Prophet Isaiah said therefore, And there was sent to me one of the Seraphim and in his hand a live coal which he had taken with the tongs from off the altar and he touched my mouth and said, Lo this hath touched thy lips and shall take away thine iniquities and purge thy sins. And searching according to our power into the depth of the vision, we say that none other save our Lord Jesus Christ is the spiritual coal laid on the altar whereon by us it gives forth the sweet savour of incense to God the Father: for through Him have we had access and are acceptable, offering the spiritual worship. This Divine Coal therefore, when it touches the lips of him who approaches thereto, will straightway exhibit 'him pure and wholly imparticipate in any sin. And in what way it touches our lips, the blessed Paul will teach saying, Nigh thee is the word, in thy mouth and in thy heart, that if thou say with thy mouth Lord Jesus and believe in thy heart that God hath raised, Him from the dead, thou shalt be saved, for with the heart man believeth unto righteousness, and with the mouth confession is made unto salvation. And He is compared to a Coal, because conceived of as from two unlike things, yet by a true concurrence they are all but knit together unto union. For the fire entering into the wood, will transelement it somehow into its own glory and might albeit it hath retained what it was.

Our Lord Jesus Christ again likens Himself to a Pearl, saying, The kingdom of heaven is like unto a merchant man seeking goodly pearls, who when he had found one Pearl of great price hath gone and sold all that he had and bought it. I hear Him in another way manifesting Himself to us and saying, I am the flower of the plain, the lily of the valleys. For He has in His Proper Nature the God-befitting Brightness of God the Father, and gives forth again His Savour, in respect I mean of spiritual fragrance. As therefore in the pearl and also the lily, the thing itself is conceived of as body, the brilliancy or fragrance therein considered in its proper definition as other than they in whom they are, yet are the things inseparably innate again the own properties and not alien from those which possess them:---- in this way (I deem) shall we both reason and think of Emmanuel too. For of diverse kind by nature are Godhead and flesh [3], yet was the Body of the Word His own, and not severed from His Body is the Word which is united thereto; for thus and not otherwise will Emmanuel, i.e., God with us, be conceived of. Hence one while as Man, and making Himself manifest to us from the measures of the emptiness too, He said, No man takes My life from Me, another while again conceived of as God the Word and out of Heaven and One with His proper flesh, He says, No man hath ascended up to Heaven but He That came down from Heaven, the Son of Man.

The Holy Scripture therefore from every side knitting together unto inseverable and true union the Son and bearing us back in faith unto One Person, this extraordinary man manifoldly severs, and hath babbled idly, calling the Word out of God the Father God of Christ Himself too, as our discourse as it advances will clearly demonstrate in its own time and place. For he feigns that he is afraid lest any overcome by reverence for the holy Virgin, and calling her Mother of God, should, supposing that there is a mixture and immingling of the Persons one with another pour forth uncomeliness upon the doctrines of the Church, albeit no one thus thinks: and rectifying (as he deems) a thing so dire, he utterly confuses all things, regardless of ideas which pertain to rightness and truth: for he said thus;

> "If in simple faith you had been putting forward the word Mother of God, I would not have grudged it you, on examining the sense of the word. But since I see that you, on plea of honouring the blessed Mary, are maintaining the blasphemy of the heretics, I therefore ward off the putting forth of the word, suspecting the danger that is concealed therein. But to speak clearly and more intelligibly to all, it is the aim of the party of Arius and Eunomius and Apolinarius and of all who are of like brotherhood, [4] to bring in Theotokus, as though, a mingling having taken place and the two natures not divided, nought of the meaner things were taken of the human nature, and they had place at length against the Divinity, [5] as though all things were spoken of One, not in regard to the rank from connection, but to Nature. For One is Christ, and One Lord: but in respect of Christ, I mean of the Only-Begotten Son, both Christ and Son are said, one while, of the Godhead, another while of the Manhood and Godhead."

§1. Seest thou how with manifold inventions of ideas he impiously embellishes the generation after the flesh also of the Only-Begotten, how he essays to shew that it will take place no otherwise than by some infusion or commingling of the substances having place: albeit the Teachers of the Church do not initiate us this fashion; for we say that a true concurrence had place, the Word uniting to Himself the Body, yet abiding what He was. But this man taking nought of these things to mind, hath blasphemed in no mean degree, parting Him into two persons and hypostases wholly severed one from the other, and attributing to either separately the words to it belonging: and again he says One Lord Jesus Christ, as though man were connected with God by rank only, not by true Union i. e., by Nature. How then is He One [6] Christ and Son and Lord, if to both severally will belong, as thou sayest, the being thus called and so being in truth, by reason of the hypostases coming together in no wise by union one with another, but being united in respect of rank only or sway or authority? And yet if we examine into the nature of things, we shall observe that things which are in equality of dignity, have not for this reason parted with their individual existence: nor yet will the having equal degree in point of glory, suffice to union, as for example, Peter and John were both of them Apostles and holy and adorned with equal honours and might through the Spirit by Christ the Saviour of us all. For they along with the rest heard, Ye are the light of the world, and again, Heal the sick, raise the dead, cleanse the lepers, cast out devils. Shall we therefore say that from their equality of rank or sway accrues to them that they too should be counted as one man, and this is sufficient for unity, I mean unity of their persons? And how will not such an opinion be with reason conceived of as foolish exceedingly? Why then dost thou feign that thou art right in the Faith, saying that One is Christ Jesus the Lord, and then, severing into two persona and hypostases the One, dishonourest the mode of the True Union through which the Christ is One and Alone, and unlearnedly callest equality of honour connection? What is this mode of connection? knowest thou not that dear it always is to those in this life who are rich in honours from the rulers to be in worldly renown? yet they being in. equal dignity sometimes, are yet separate one from another in individual being and moreover in their desire of thinking and doing the same things. But if the kind of rank were any necessary bond gathering them into unity just like a physical coming together;----they would not, being in equality of honours or rank, have been parted one from another in persons and mind so as to be one and another. Where then shall we put thy connection, what shall we count that it wrought? did it persuade them to be of one league, did it cause that they should come together unto a mystic [union? But you cannot say this, for reason has shewn that the connection is utterly weak to both these.

Tell me this too (for I will ask it as well, as matter of necessity), what good did the rank do for the man born from out a woman who was (as you said) connected with God the Word? for did it make him equal in glory and excellency, and render him as great as He too is believed to be? And how then will He not speak falsely saying, My Glory will I not give to another, and vainly hath the Divine-uttering Psalmist too prated, saying on this wise, Who among the clouds shall be made equal to the Lord? who shall be made like to the Lord among the sons of God? Is not he other than the Word, One and by Nature and forth of God the Father, who in his proper person has been verily parted from union with Him? and how is this not clear to all? Now rank has not made equal to God the Word that which was connected, but it is seen to be and is in lower place: how then dost thou say One Christ and Son and Lord, although one excels, at least according to the force of reasoning, the other settles down below equality with Him and glory? Besides (for I will add this too to what I said) the Word That is forth of God the Father has given (according to him) His proper rank to him that is born of a woman: but how he says that this very thing has been wrought, it is meet to examine. Has he too been made Very Light? is he by Nature God and Life and Creator and Wisdom and Might, Image and Brightness of the Person of the Father? and the Endowments of the Supreme Glory, have they passed Naturally into some one of things made? what then is the Excellence in God by Nature? what great and above us, if it is possible for the creature to be rich and that essentially [7], in the good things wherein Itself is? But perchance it has been clad in rank, as participant of the Divine Preeminence? there are again two undoubted sons, if it is true that something other and inferior by nature to Him Who wrought in him the participation is that which is honoured with relationship to Him: you are therefore caught now as not even knowing what you are saying. For why do you blame those who attribute the words in the Gospels to One Person? is it not because you are inventing two sons? for how is there any longer One Lord and Christ and Son, if each have his proper person and mode of being and moreover hypostasis withdrawing unto diverse-ness, repudiating the reality of true union and having utter irreconcilability with the other? And what is strange and shews the loathsomeness of his blasphemies, he says that the names are common. I mean Son and Christ and Lord. And if he say that they are common, i. e., to One Christ and to others besides Him, his statement would have probability: but if he ignorantly sever and supposes that these terms befit the Word by Himself and moreover him that is forth of a woman, there are again surely and unmistakably two christs and sons and lords. For he said, "The name Christ must one while be put for the Godhead Itself, other while for the Manhood too, or also for both." But the community of name will help him not a whit to conceive of one Christ and Son and Lord while he severs (even though the hypostases themselves part not one from another), and the Persons are disjoined in their own proper diverseness.

For making manifest to us the force of his innate unlearning he subjoins and says,

> "When therefore the Divine Scripture is about to speak of either the birth of Christ which was forth of the blessed Virgin, or His Death, it is never seen to put God, but either Christ or Son or Lord, seeing that these three are significant of the two natures, one while of this, other while of that, other while of this and that. As for example when the Scripture declares to us the Generation out of man, what says it? God sent forth His Son; it did not say, God sent forth God the Word [8], but it takes the name which indicates the two natures. For since the Son is Man and God, it says, Sent forth His Son made from out a woman, that when you hear the word made out of a woman, then you may see the name put forth which indicates the two natures, that you may call the Birth from forth the blessed Virgin, the Son's Birth, for the Virgin mother of Christ too bare the Son of God. But since the Son of God is two-fold in His Natures, she bare indeed the Son of God, but bare the manhood which is son by reason of the connected Son."

§2. But WE my friend, who know how to think better than thine empty whistlings and who track out the order of the God-inspired Scripture which says that One is God the Father out of whom are all things and One Lord Jesus Christ through Whom all things were brought into being: when we hear that Christ has been born of the holy Virgin, then, then in all wisdom and zealous to go the straight way of the Truth, do wo say that the Word Which sprang forth of God the Father was both Incarnate and united Personally to flesh and born after the flesh: and we will not endure thy trickery, but to One and Only, the Son That is by Nature, will we allot the name Christ, with reason, when the Birth through the holy Virgin is spoken of. For common (as I said) to Him with others also will such names confessedly "be, for many are sons by grace and gods and lords both in heaven and in earth, as the Divine-uttering Paul too writes to us: yet [they are so] as participating with Him Who is so by Nature and in imitation [of Him]. Still the name Christ and its reality will pertain in no wise to the bare Word from forth the Father, conceived of by us as bare [Word] by Himself and apart from flesh: but if now He be said to have emptied Himself and to have come down [to be] in servant's form and been made as we by reason of the flesh, He too will be called by reason of the anointing, Christ; for not in His own Nature has the Word being God been Anointed, but the anointing hath happened to Him in regard to His Humanity. Thus therefore when that has first entered in, in regard to which the anointing takes place (for His is the Incarnation whereto belongs the anointing), when Christ is named by us we will not (according to thy unbridled speech) suppose that just a man, severed from the Word and put apart, has been born of the holy Virgin but the very Word (as I said) out of God the Father united to flesh and anointed humanly with the oil of gladness by God the Father.

But that the anointing hath happened to God the Word in respect of the manhood, when He became as we, holy Scripture will prove to us; for the Divine-uttering Jacob departing from his father's hearth was hastening on his way unto Mesopotamia and going to Laban the son of Bethuel, and having lighted on a certain place on the way thither he was lodging there and, laying his head on a stone, he sleeps: and having seen a ladder, stretching on high from earth to heaven and angels both ascending and descending by means of it and the Lord resting thereupon, he marvelled much at the vision and taking the stone he set it up as a pillar and poured oil upon the top of it. Regard now herein our Lord Jesus Christ, the One and only and truly Son, as a pillared stone. For indeed He is a choice stone, a head corner-stone, precious, set for the head of the corner and for the foundation of Zion by God the Father. Regard (I pray) moreover how it was anointed, for not the whole stone throughout did the Divine-uttering Jacob bedew with oil, but rather poured it upon the top of it. Therefore not wholly (so to speak) nor in that the Only-Begotten is Word, has He been anointed in respect of His proper Nature (for how could He be conceived of as participate of His own Spirit?) but rather is anointed (as I said) on the surface, i. e., externally and as in part and on the surface on the Body that was His own by true union: and as He is said to suffer in the flesh humanly, albeit by Nature Impassible as God; so is He conceived of as anointed in regard to the human nature, albeit Himself anointing with His own Spirit those whom it befits to partake of His holiness.

Thus are WE minded to think and are accustomed to walk aright, going on the royal and unperverted road: but he saying that such names are indicative of the two natures, allots to either with authority what seems good to him and is ashamed of the lowliness of speech belonging to the economy with flesh, and though you hear the blessed Paul say, God sent forth His Son made from out a woman, made under the law, Away, says this man, think not that the Word Which sprang forth of God has been sent, for He has not been made from out a woman, He has not been made under the law.

And that our words are no empty guile, but we have used rather his own speech, I will again bring forward the very things he said,

"For God (he says) sent forth His Son made of a woman, if made under the law. Here he points out the two natures, he says what took place as to the human nature, for demand of the wrangler [9], Who was made under the law? was it God the Word?"

§3. And how will not he be verily distraught, who essays to overturn, as far as in him lies, things so clear and known of all and undoubted? Whom hath the Father sent to us out of heaven, Saviour and Redeemer? was it not the Word Which sprang forth of His Essence? Who is He That descended and ascended far above the Heavens that He might fill all things? Dost thou say that the being able to fill all things is the work of our nature and will you affix it to the measures of humanity? of whom hath the blessed John written, He that cometh from above is above all? Or will haply Himself too lie in rebuking the people of the Jews and saying, Ye are from beneath, I am from above, and again, I am not of this world? For if He were man out of woman like one of the rest, and not rather the Word That is from above and out of God the Father, Incarnate and appearing in human form, how will He be conceived of as both above and out of heaven? how above all and not of this world? albeit a part of the world by reason of the flesh and (so to speak), according to the measure that befits the human nature, made along with all under God. Therefore He called the Father His God, though He too is God by Nature and beamed forth out of His Essence Only-Begotten Son. Of whom says the blessed David, He sent forth His Word and healed them? for no elder, no angel but the Lord Himself hath saved us, according to the Scriptures.

"But yea, he saith, God the Word able to fill all things has been sent. How? for where do we say that He is not? or whither will He be sent?"

Will you accuse therefore the all-wise Moses too, as having wronged in no slight degree the Ineffable glory of God? for he said that God descended in the form of fire upon the Mount Sinai. And if you hear the blessed David say unto God mighty over all, Thou shalt send forth Thy Spirit and they shall be created and Thou shalt renew the face of the earth, wilt thou then perchance put aside the Spirit-clad and suppose that he speaks falsely? for no motion involving change of place does the Godhead make, nor will It pass from place to place, as though the being in all and filling all things were not inherent in It. These things (I suppose)........thyself too [10] ; but you will be reasoning again, and rising up against the true doctrines, choosing to follow yourself alone. But you would surely have better thoughts if you reasoned thus, that our whole speech as to God has been framed in human wise, but is understood as befits Him Alone.

Cyril of Alexandria

But it has troubled him not a little that the Word out of God the Father is said to have been made under the Law. But the fear herein is nought, for He hath remained what He was, Lawgiver (that is) and God. And if He have not been made man, He hath not been made under the Law; but since it is true that He hath humbled Himself Who in His own Nature is above and high, hath been made as we Who is above the whole creation, and being Rich became poor through being made as we, how will He not be said with us to have been made under the Law too? Shall we not, if we think aright, conclude that the measure of man's nature is defined to lie in his having to be subject to the Law? for the exempt and above the Law and by Nature and in truth free will be none other than the Godhead. Hence when He was made flesh then was He made under the Law too, for He paid to the collectors the didrachm [11], albeit in His own Nature Free as God and Son oven when He was made flesh. But if to thee it seems good to sever into two the One and to declare to us that he which was forth of a woman is man apart by himself, how will he be said to have been made under the Law too, who is of the nature which is under the Law? for not that which hath to be subject to the Law, will be made under the Law, but that which, hath a Nature above Law and external to Law. For the Divine and Most High Nature alone (as I said) is both beyond law and also free, and hath no master whatever, but Itself rather ruleth all and subjecteth all to His own yoke.

But this man having missed right reasoning, slid down to this extent of impiety in his ideas and arrived at such height of awkwardness, from dividing into two the One Lord Jesus Christ, as unshrinkingly to say that Emmanuel is neither truly God nor yet by Nature Son, but is so called Christ and holy, as certain other too of men like us or of those who have worshipped impure devils: for thus again hath he said:

"But as we say that the Creator of all is God and Moses god; for it says, I have made thee a god unto Pharaoh: and Israel God's son, for it says, Israel is My firstborn son; and as we say that Saul was christ, for it says, I will not stretch forth my hand upon him, because he is the Lord's christ, and Cyrus likewise, Thus saith the Lord to Cyrus My christ, and the Babylonian holy, for I (it says) marshal them [12]: so do we say that the Lord is christ and god and son and holy. But the community of names is similar, the rank not the same."

§4. What are you saying? what word are you belching forth out of your own heart and not out of the mouth of the Lord, as it is written? No one calleth Jesus Anathema save in Beelzebub. As Moses for instance may be conceived of or called by us God, so will Christ too? after the likeness of Israel, will He too be Son, tell me? O impiety! O words that reck not of lifting up themselves against the glory of our Saviour! O sheer stupidity! and that overcomes all hesitancy in respect I mean of unholy daring against the doctrines of the Church. Let the blessed David now too sing, The enemies of the Lord lied unto Him: for the Divine-uttering Moses was by nature a man as we and nought else: but when on God saying, Come I am sending thee to Pharaoh king of Egypt and thou shalt bring the children of Israel forth of the land of Egypt, he was putting forward as reason for begging off, his slowness of speech [and want of utterance, since yesterday and the third day, he heard God say, See I have made thee a god to Pharaoh and Aaron thy brother shall be thy interpreter. For feeble was the law to rid any from bondage unto the devil, but on Christ becoming our

Mediator, this too has been achieved, just as here when Aaron was along with the Divine-uttering Moses, Israel was delivered from the bondage in Egypt. But since Christ was about in due course of time to be made under the Law too, in that He was as we and was man, Aaron was put in second place to Moses [13]. And the plan of the mystery is thus,----but if one should choose to say this too, that by the calling of God has that mighty Moses too been honoured, according to this which has been said to us in common and as by God's favour and munificence, I said, Ye are gods and all of you sons of the Most High:----is Christ in this way God? yet how is not this madness and the empty froth of an unlearned mind? for the one (as I said) being man by nature has been honoured with the mere title only, the Other is truly God (for the Word was God) in human form, having the preeminence over all of His own Nature unmutilated (for not in change for the worse will be the Divine Nature by reason of Its descending to communicate in blood and flesh), and verily He is recognized as God when appearing as Man also. And a clear demonstration of this are the things that have been written in the Gospels concerning Him. For the Divine-uttering John said, Now when He was in Jerusalem in the feast, many believed in His Name when they saw the miracles which He was doing, but Jesus Himself did not trust Himself to them, because He knew all things and needed not that any one should testify of man, for He knew what was in man: albeit the being able to see the heart of man and to know its secrets, will not belong to any one (whence should it?) of men like us, nor yet to ought other of things made, but rather to Him Alone Who is said to fashion our hearts by Himself. Then how has Emmanuel, being called God, been honoured like Moses with the mere title alone, and is not rather in truth that which He is also said to be? Thus again does John write of Him, for He whom God sent speaketh the words of God and giveth not the Spirit by measure. Understandest thou then how, albeit beheld a man as we, He speaketh the words of God? For to God Alone Who is by Nature and truly will pertain as something choice and above the creature, the being able by a word to achieve what He will and to render partakers of the Holy Ghost them who have been justified in faith:----and one may see that Christ is in this case. For He said to the leper, I will, be clean. to the widow's son, Young man, to thee say I, Arise: and His own Disciples He manifested partakers of the Holy Ghost, for He breathed on them, saying, Receive ye the Holy Ghost. Then how will He Who has advanced to this point and been crowned with God-befitting renown be god after such sort as was Moses? whose heart knew he? who hath believed on his name? whom hath he justified through faith in himself? where hath he as son spoken the words of God? albeit he hath openly cried unto them of Israel, Thus saith the Lord, [14] and hath a servant's measure, for he was made faithful as a servant in the house of God.

And if Emmanuel was son in the same way too as was Israel who was made so after the flesh, thou hast brought down among bondservants Him Who is in His own Nature Free, even though He became in the form of a bondman by reason of the flesh and the things thereto pertaining: thou hast set in equal measure with the sons by grace Him on account of whom they have been enriched with the grace of sonship: for He has been called first-born of us by reason of the manhood, yet even so hath remained Only-begotten as God. [15] Therefore (as saith the most wise Paul) the powers above are bidden to worship the First-begotten when introduced by the Father into the world, and on learning the mystery regarding Him, with ceaseless praises do they extol the One and by Nature and truly Son. For if He gives authority to them that received Him to become children of God, as John saith, and if it is true that His Spirit effects that we too should become sons (for God sent forth the Spirit of His Son into our hearts crying Abba, Father), none who are accustomed to think aright will endure this man saying that He too is son in such manner as was Israel.

And how was He in such wise too christ and holy, as may be called christ both Cyrus the King of the Persians and yet again the Persians and Medes themselves? for it were time to say that neither has Christ been sanctified humanly albeit the Holy Ghost soared down upon Him in form of a dove. For Cyrus son of Cambyses led an expedition against the land of the Babylonians in his time, but he was in error, and used to offer worship to foul devils: but when, on God stirring him up and rousing him into wrath, he took the land of the Babylonians, by a name common, albeit not anointed with the Holy Ghost, he was called christ. And in this way were the Persians and Medes holy who were his fellows (for they too served the creature more than God the Creator and worshipped the works of their own hands); but since the offering that was once, according to the words of the Mosaic Law, separated unto God, whether calf or sheep, was called holy; therefore have they too been called holy through the Prophet's voice, by reason they were set apart by the Divine assent to take captive the land of the Babylonians. If then Emmanuel is in such sort christ as was Cyrus too, and in such wise holy as were the Medes and Persians, one might with reason say as of their absurdity of notion that neither hath He been anointed with the Holy Ghost nor is He holy at all. The Divine David will therefore lie saying unto Him, Thou lovedst righteousness and hatedst wrong, therefore God, Thy God, anointed Thee with the oil of gladness above Thy fellows.

And he chattering after this sort against the Preeminence and glory of our Saviour, thinks that he thrusts away the charge of impiety, by saying something childish and without understanding, "for the community (he says) of names is like, not the rank the same." How, tell me, for I do not understand? For if He is in such wise God as was Moses too, and in such wise son as was Israel, and in such wise christ as was Cyrus and moreover in such wise holy as were the Medes, how will He escape having to be in equality of rank with them?

Now therefore you will be caught in having blasphemed against the very Nature of the Word too, for thou saidst again,

"Say of Him Who assumed that He is God, add of that which is assumed that it is the servant's form, bring in next the dignity of connection, that of the two the sway is common, that of the two the dignity is the same; while the natures remain, acknowledge the union of rank."

§5. He divides therefore again into two, in exceeding lack of understanding he lavishes on rank the force of union, haply not understanding what union is, and what the rank really is. But this we say; he said that of the two natures one is the sway, one the Dignity. Since then he who is in equality of glory with God the Word will not surpass Moses in respect of being god, it is I suppose clear that the very Word which is forth of God, will have equal status in nature and glory with Moses, for if the mean be like and in every respect have exact resemblance with the first and third, the plan of their nature will not be diverse.

But haply he will say that the mode of rank is not nature: how therefore do you deem it fit to gather into one (as yourself say) sway and to crown with equal rank things essentially so far severed from participation one with another and also from equality? for where a nature is wholly in inferior place, the other overtopping it, how will there accrue to it both equality of honours and even dignity and the mode of glory be not diverse?

But that on mentioning connection, haply conceived of as that of mere proximity and juxtaposition, or as an accidental one, himself rises up against his own words, building what he undid and setting up what has been overthrown, will be clear by this again also: for he said thus;

"Therefore [16] I would have you hold fast with all assurance: there is no severance of the connection of the dignity of the sonship, there is no severance of his being Christ, of the Godhead and Manhood there is a severance; Christ is indivisible, in that He is Christ, for we have not two christs nor two sons, for there is not with us a first and a second, nor yet other and other, nor again another son and another again; but the One is Himself twofold, not in rank but in nature."

§6. Tell me again what it is you term inseverable connection: is it the union, I mean in respect of Person, which WE set forth, striving together for the doctrines of the Truth? or is it this which is conceived of as one of juxtaposition and proximity of any to anything? for thus does the God-inspired Scripture take the word. And verily He spake to the most holy Moses, when He was discoursing with him respecting that olden tabernacle, And thou shalt make fifty taches of gold and connect the curtains one to other with the taches. For being five and each having individually the being other than the rest, they were connected by the taches. But not thus do WE say that the union has been wrought as to Christ, for neither as one may be connected with another, either in respect to like mindedness or bodily nearness, was He too like this, but (as I have repeatedly said) He made His own the Body which was taken from forth the holy Virgin; and we say that the Word out of God has been truly united to flesh not without a soul.

Hence if the force of the connection which has been spoken of by him, signify the union which we mean, i. e. of Person, reasonably will he have said that there is no severance of Christ, in that He is Christ; for He is "not one and another, nor yet son and son, other and other, first and second," but One both before flesh and with flesh: [for thus will He be in respect of rank (as THOU sayest) and also of sway, inseverable, yea rather the Same. Then how dost thou say that the One and Inseverable is twofold, and that not in regard of rank but of nature? for not because the Word out of God the Father having taken flesh, proceeded forth man as we, will He for this reason be called also twofold, for One and that not without flesh is He Who is in His proper Nature external to flesh and body. [17] [For as, were one to kill a man such as we are, he would not with reason be accused of having wronged two men but one alone, even though the man be conceived of as being of soul and body, and the nature of the things that have been brought together be not the same, but diverse: so again must we conceive of Christ, for He is not twofold, but One and Only Lord and Son is the

Word from forth God the Father, not without flesh. For that of Manhood and Godhead most vast is the difference or interval I myself too would allow, for other in respect of the mode of their being and nothing like one to another are plainly the things which have been named. But when the mystery Christ-ward is brought before us, the plan of the union ignores not indeed the difference, but puts aside the severance, not confounding the natures or immingling them but, because the Word of God when He partook of flesh and blood, even thus is conceived of and called One Son. But you in saying that they ought not to be called two christs, nor should one confess two sons, and hereby filching the semblance of rightness in dogma, are caught in the act of saying two christs, and dividing into his own diverseness man and God, and you endeavour to shew that the one is operated, the other operates: for your words are thus,

"The [18] good glory of the Only-Begotten one while is ascribed to the Father, for it is, He says, My Father which glorifieth Me, other while to the Spirit, for the Spirit of Truth, He says, shall glorify Me, other while to the power of Christ, for they, it says, went forth and preached the word everywhere, the Lord co-working and confirming the word through the signs that followed."

§7. If he says that the Only-Begotten Word of God, as though lacking glory in that He is and is conceived of as Word and not yet Incarnate, is glorified by the Father and the Holy Ghost:----that he both blunders and has missed the truth, I will leave saying for the present (for occasion leads us to something else); but he seems to me to have forgotten what he had just now thought out and said, for he said, "Not one and another is Christ, not other and other son, for we have not two Christs and two sons." But, O most understanding, would I say, if thou affirm that the good glory of the Only-Begotten is ascribed to the power of Christ, how will He be not one and another, or how not wholly and surely two? for if not the same be giver and receiver, or he ascribe to another than himself the things which accrue to him by nature, Christ hath wrought being possessed, as being other than the Only-Begotten: for if the good glory of the Only-Begotten have been (as you say) ascribed to him; and the Divine-uttering disciples using the power that came from him, preached and wrought miracles, how is that not true that I said? for he hath wrought using other's power, that he which wrought and not himself rather may be glorified by those in the world. What then (tell me) appears there more in Him than in the holy Apostles? for they have wrought wonders not by their own power, and this themselves clearly confessed, for they were worthy of admiration in knowing this too and glorifying Him Who worketh in them. Then how ought not Christ Who according to thee was possessed by another and had from without the good glory of the Only-Begotten, to have proclaimed to those who approach Him as God, and supplicate succour from Him, In the name of the Only-Begotten, or in His Might, be to thee this good thing: for so used to do the all-wise disciples, every where naming Jesus of Nazareth. But to no one whatever hath He declared this, but rather to His own power used He to attribute what was accomplished, one time saying to the blind man, Believe ye that I am able to do this? and requiring [their assent, at another ordering with authority saying, I will, be clean. Why dost thou not, letting go the fables fit for old women which have been invented by thyself alone, occupy thyself with wise mind about the depth of the mystery? [19][

But one may see that he little recks of things needful unto profit, but is afraid lest he let drop ought true and be caught thinking anything praiseworthy: and thinks every thing that is most discordant and makes a condemnation utterly inconsiderate of the doctrines of the church, albeit he should have remembered God saying by the mouth of Ezekiel to those who are over the spiritual flocks, Ye ate the good pasture and drank the pure water and troubled the residue with your feet, and My flock fed on the treadings down of your feet and drank the water troubled by your feet. For when WE apply our minds to the God-inspired Scriptures, we eat the good pasture, as it is written, and we drink the untroubled water, i. e. the unmixed with falsehood, translucent and most pure word of the Spirit: but if we thicken it and immingle therewith like mud the cheerlessness of our own devices, we plot against the flocks of the Saviour.

And that this too is true, the things which he has thought out and heedlessly said of Christ, will shew; for it is thus:

"For God the Word even before the Incarnation was Son and God and of one mind with the Father, but in the last times He took the form of a servant. Yet being before this Son, and being [so] called, after the assumption He cannot be called Son separately, lest we teach the doctrine of two sons. But since he has been connected with Him which is in the beginning Son, Him who was connected with him, he may not admit of severance in respect of the dignity of sonship, in respect I say of the dignity of sonship, not in respect of the natures. Wherefore God the Word is called Christ also, since He has His connection with Christ perpetual. And it is not possible that God the Word should do ought without the manhood, for it has been with all exactitude brought unto exact connection, not unto deification, as the wise ones of the neo-dogmatists say."

§8. He that durst say that the good glory of the Only-Begotten has been ascribed to the power of Christ, and that plucked asunder the bond of Oneness, gathers again into union and again dissolves it and parts the natures one from other. And most plentifully does he vainly talk and rhodomontade to us respecting these things, so that even though he should say ought that tendeth unto orthodoxy, he may be clearly convicted of not knowing what he saith. For he says here that the Word of God "is both Son and God even before the Incarnation, moreover that in the last times He took the form of a servant." Tell me therefore, if I do not seem to thee to say what is meet, Who is it now that is said to be made man? and what dost thou say that being made man is? who is he that took the servant's form? and how was it taken by him? That in saying therefore that a man was made man, you will display as worthy of ridicule your own understanding, how can one doubt? for he that is man by nature, [20] [how will he be made what he was, and pass as though to somewhat else, in respect I mean of nature? that which in its own nature is not free, how will it be said to have become bond, as though it were not so at the beginning? Hence to have been made man, will not pertain unto a man, far from it, and to take the form of a servant, belongs not to him who even at the beginning has the measure of bondservice, but to Him rather Who being not man by Nature, is believed to have been made so, and Who being Lord of all as God, abased Himself in our condition, uniting to Himself Personally the human nature, and taking the form of the servant. For thus will that too be true which thou saidst, that "after the assumption, He cannot be called Son separately lest we teach the doctrine of two sons."

And the right and unperverted and straight-going path of doctrines, is this and no other. But he again who mentioned to us the being-made-man of the Word Which is forth of the Father, borne almost straightway unto forgetfulness of what he said, severs again into two the One, both in vile sort floating in feeblest ideas and using ever words untested, for he said, "But since he has been connected with Him, Who is in the beginning Son, Who was connected with him, he may not admit of severance, as regards the dignity of sonship, as regards dignity I say of sonship, not as regards the natures." Rightly, my friend, dost thou reject as unprofitable that which seems to be insecure, studiously has it been set before thee to use ever vigilant mode of speech. For lo, lo, severing the natures, thou gatherest them into union as regards the dignity of sonship. Sufficeth therefore unto true union in things by nature severed one from another, the sameness or identity of names and the dignity in respect of this? for thus too does it seem good to thee to say. Therefore since the name Christ, and moreover son and lord, have been given to others too as names common [to several] (for very many have been made christs and have been called sonsand lords); they too will be as regards the dignity of sonship, both disseverable one from another and all of them one in respect of the union which you think was wrought in respect of Christ too. But a man such as we will be wholly distinct from the Word out of God: how therefore they have not been severed, how too there is one son, I cannot conceive, unless we say that the human nature and the Word have come together by a true union.

But since one must, on account of these words of his, carry round the argument even unto absurdity, that on all sides he may be convicted of having thought not aright, come now, come, let us say this too. For if the dignity of sonship suffices unto union, since the Word Which is from forth Him is called and is Son of God the Father, and the name is common to many more, where is the harm (tell me) of saying that the rest too all of them have themselves been united with Him, in order that Emmanuel may have nought more than they? for the claim [7] of the same names will (it seems) be contending with Him and be striving for equality, and the mode of connection will lie in bare and mere appellation or community of name. What then is being made man understood to be? what too the descent in the servant's form? for if the mode of the being made man is (according to him) a mere connection, and consist in the dignity only of sonship what is to hinder our saying that it has been effected in regard to all the rest too? But the friend of learning sees assuredly the uncomeliness of what is said. Whither therefore is he now borne off, distraught, unto things not lawful? by us shall be said to him what is uttered by Jeremiah's voice, Thou waxedst weary in much journeying, for he is tossed to and fro borne about with every wind, as saith the most wise Paul. Therefore receive the anchor of the soul sure and stedfast, set thy feet upon a rock. If thou sayest that the Word of God was made man, this will suffice to shew that He Who is above all the creation was made as we. He took the servant's form although He possessed freedom as God; for He was in equality with the Father, Who possesseth dominion over all. Cease to sever the natures after the union: for that one thing and another is the Divine Nature and the nature of man it will be fit to know, and needful I deem to those who are sound in mind (for they are parted one from another by incomparable differences), but in regard to Christ the Saviour of us all, do thou having brought them togetherinto union true andof Person, reject severance, for thus wilt thou confess one Christ and Son and Lord.

But I know not how the inventor of feeble doctrines has made exceeding petty account of the fact of union, and thrusting away both it (as seems) and the might of the truth, hath gone again unto what liketh himself and saith, "Therefore is God the Word called Christ also, seeing that He hath His connection with Christ perpetual. And it is not possible for God the Word to work ought without the manhood; for it hath been accurately adjusted unto exact connection, not deification, as the wise ones of the neo-dogmatists say." When therefore he says that the Word from forth God the Father has been separately called Christ, as having connection with Christ, i. e., with another, how has he not idly prated in saying that after the assumption He cannot be so styled separately? since not as One is that conceived of by us which is said to have been accidentally connected with ought else, for two of a surety will be rightly conceived to be the things which come together, and not one, itself connected with itself. False speech therefore are his words, and in another sense are they idle talk: but WE after the union, though one name God the Word, conceive not of Him apart from His own flesh; though one say Christ, we recognize the Word Incarnate. [21] [What then is the mode of the connection which you speak of conceived to be? for if you say that the human nature has been united Personally with the Word That sprang forth from God, why (tell me) do you insult the Divine Flesh? albeit you refuse not to worship it, while the duty of being worshipped belongs only to the Divine and Ineffable Nature: but if you do not think that a true union took place, but call rather by the name of connection, the rank which consists in identity of name and in mere and only equality of style, why do you prate in solemn language , saying that he that is born of the woman has "been accurately adjusted unto exact connection," i. e., with the Word? for they are synonymous [one with another, son with son, and lord with lord, nor are the names a whit inferior one to another, and to inquire into any superiority in them is (I suppose) idle, for son than son qua son, hath neither greater nor less. You are therefore talking superfluously (clearly so) in saying that he has been "accurately adjusted unto exact connection." But to say that they have been accurately adjusted one to another will belong (as appears to me) not to things possessing an identity of name, but to those rather, which obtain the equality and likeness in every thing of things that are believed to be one. As for example we say that there hath been accurately adjusted unto exact correspondence to the form of such an one, either the son that is begotten from out him, or one might say his image: but as regards connection, how can things be conceived of and said to have been accurately adjusted?

But himself interpreted to us the force of connection: for "it is not possible (he says) that God the Word should do ought without the human nature." Likeminded therefore with one another and harmonious according to thee, and from common counsel advancing unto each action shall we believe the pair of sons spoken of by thee. How then are there not two christs and sons and lords? But you affirm (it is like) that the Word used His Body as an instrument. Yet if you say One Son and One Person, the Incarnate Person of the Word, He will not be an instrument of Deity, but rather will use as an instrument His own Body, just as a man's soul too does. Therefore confess One, not dividing the natures, at the same time knowing and holding, that of the flesh the count is one; of the Godhead again, that which beseems It alone: for we say that the flesh of the Word by no means became Godhead, but rather Divine, as being His own. For if the flesh of a man is called human, what hinders that that of God the Word should be called Divine? why then dost them mock at the beauty of the Truth, telling us of the deification of the holy flesh, and all but casting in the teeth of those who have chosen to think aright, a god-making, albeit thyself sayest,

> "In order therefore that it might be pointed out to the Magi too, Who this is That is worshipped by them, and to Whom the grace of the Holy Ghost led them----that it was not to a mere babe viewed by itself, but to a body connected ineffably with God."

§9. Since therefore he says that the body has been ineffably united to God, and that which is truly ineffable is beyond understanding and speech, true of a surety is the union or the (according to him) connection. For such things are ineffable, and of things that thus come together with one another one would not (I deem) know the mode. But if thou art able to say it, and deemest that thou canst declare the force of the connection, how is it any longer ineffable?

But I marvel that albeit he says that the Body has been connected with God and that ineffably, he does not say that it is His very own, in order that it might be conceived of as one with Him, but parts again into man and God, separately and apart, the One Christ and Lord Jesus, and feigns that he thinks aright, when he says,

> "Yet [22] not mere man is Christ (o accuser) but Man alike and God: had He been God alone, it had been right, of Apolinarius, to say, Why seek ye to kill Me, God, Who have told you the truth? This is He Who was encircled with the Thorny Crown, this He Who said, My God, My God, why forsookest Thou Me? this He Who endured the three days death, this do I worship with the Godhead as co-partner in the Divine sway."

§10. View now I pray again how he snatches at and puts around his own words the form of the truth (for "not mere man, says he, is Christ, but Man alike and God,") yet severs again and says that He is not One, and stupidly takes hold of something without foundation and constructs what pleases himself. For as though some one were saying that the Word had appeared to us upon earth bare and without flesh, and had conversed with us, and wrought His Divine signs, or that He was common man and that not the Word Himself has been made Man:----he says, "Not mere man is Christ, but God also." But WE, most excellent sir (will I say), even though we say that He is Man alike and God, do not speak thus as putting them apart, but rather knowing that the Same even before the Incarnation was Son and God and Word of the Father, and after it hath become man as we and been made flesh. But he asserting that He ought not to be conceived of as mere man but God and Man, allots the Thorny Crown and the rest of the Sufferings to man severally and apart, while he confesses that he worships this man with the Godhead, and yet greater impiety, as not being (it is like) truly God and Son, but co-partner in the sway of the Word. For that he clearly severs, his confession that he ought to be worshipped along with the Godhead will clearly shew. For that which is co-worshipped with other is altogether other than that with which it is co-worshipped. But WE are accustomed to worship Emmanuel with one worship, not severing from the Word the Body That was Personally united to Him.

But it is meet to investigate what the being "advocate of the Divine Sway" means. For did our Lord Jesus Christ Himself too like one of the holy Apostles and Evangelists preach to the world another christ or son and lord, as having the Divine Sway or Authority over all, and Himself too speak for the glory of another? albeit the choir of God's heralds proclaim to the world Jesus Christ who is forth of the seed of David according to the flesh, and the plan of our faith advances through our confession to Himward, and we are justified, believing not on a mere man like us, but on Him Who is by Nature and truly God. And the Gentiles indeed were living in the world without God, when they knew not Christ, as blessed Paul saith, but since they knew Him they have not remained in ignorance of Him Who is by Nature God. Let him therefore teach us Whose glory and sway it was that Christ spoke for, albeit of them that came to Him He demanded faith in Himself, and this faith in Him He attributed to the Father: and verily He said, Believe in Me and in God believe, and again, He that believeth on Me believeth not on Me but on Him That sent Me, and he that seeth Me seeth Him That sent Me.

But haply to speak for according to him may mean the same as to speak as: I concede, albeit the word has other meaning. Then how may man speak as God (according to thee) when enduring the contumelies of the Jews? For come let us view the speech befitting each. It will be meet for Him Who is in truth God by Nature to say, I am invisible, impalpable and superior to suffering, moreover Incorporeal, Life and Life-giving and above all as God: the other expounding to us his own nature how it is, will reasonably say, I am visible and palpable, passible, subject to decay and subject to God. Will then he who says such things speak as He That excels and is superior, as regards the count of His own Nature? how were this not an unlearned thing to say? for one surely will speak falsely, either that one or this. But in saying advocacy or speaking for, that it is nought else than to speak for another, you confess even against your will who tell us of connection and of One Christ and Lord: and severing them into two you worship them, yea rather you co-worship, and think that you are freeing the Church from the charge of god-making, yourself engoddening a man, and not saying One Son even though He be not conceived of apart from His own flesh: for then would you worship Him unblamed, and will know where you were, as it is written , going astray from the doctrines of the truth.

"But yea (saith he) he hath said to the leper, I will, be thou cleansed, and to the ruler of the synagogue's daughter, Maid, arise, and to the sea, Peace, be still, and herein was he a co-partner, for he uttered the Divine words whereby it was possible to achieve all things easily." Two then are they that command, and let us grant that the words on all matters belong to both. When then it says, Why seek ye to kill me, a man which have told you the truth, whose words (tell me) do you say that these be? or dost thou allot those to the Word, these to a man born of a woman as other than He? Where then wilt thou put the most holy Paul who says clearly, But to us One God the Father out of Whom all things and we unto Him, and One Lord Jesus Christ through Whom all things and we through Him. But he, over and over saying, "One Son and not one and other, nor yet

Christ and a second christ," contends against his own words, and to two persons and distinct hypostases allots the expressions of the Divines and His own.

Yet not regardless of his own notions, he puts forth again,

"I [23] [venerate him as image of Almighty Godhead; for He highly exalted Him and gave Him a Name which is above every name, that at the name of Jesus Christ every knee should bow, of heavenly and earthly and beneath the earth and every tongue should confess Lord Jesus Christ."

§11. And who again will be conceived of as he whom (as he supposes) he confesses he venerates and pretends to honour with likeness to God, save surely him whom he but now mentioned to us, calling him an advocate or co-worker of the Divine sway? whom he foolishly said ought to be co-worshipped with the Godhead, as son other and severally than the Word of God: he says that he has also been exalted by God the Father, that he moreover received the Name which is above every name, that to him should both every knee how, of heavenly and earthly and neath the earth and every tongue confess Lord Jesus Christ.

If therefore the Father hath placed Him, being God by Nature, on high even before the here-mentioned exaltation: on investigating the mode of the intervening abasement, we shall find some wise Economy in regard to which dishonoured meanwhile, He had become again in the exaltation wherein He ever was, exaltation essentially inexisting and verily Proper to Him. If this be not so (as he deems and says) but He made some other than the Word of God, the man connected with Him, an object of worship by heaven and earth and those lower yet:----He hath engodded a man like us: no longer will He meetly blame us as though we desired to engod him that is not God, whereas one must fasten on God the Father Himself the charge of the transgression hereto pertaining. He that is studious for learning sees therefore in what direction his words burst forth, and the inventions of his untempered miscounsel at what a word they terminate. For WE say that the Son being by Nature God, i. e., the Word out of God the Father, descended unto voluntary emptying, ascended again with the flesh too unto the God-befitting Dignity of His inherent Excellence: for He is worshipped with flesh too, as being an object of worship even before it, for He was even yet by Nature God, both before the emptying and when He is said to endure the emptiness, made as we. But this man disdaining so august and spotless doctrines connecteth a man with God by mere outward accident, and is not ashamed to co-worship him as in equality of dignity and as one with another, and maintains (he says) that he received as somewhat unwonted and strange and as a matter of favour that to him every knee should bow, and besides that every tongue should confess Lord Jesus Christ. And shouldst thou say that he was made God by Nature, he hath blasphemed openly saying that the Nature of the Godhead is generate; and if not by Nature but he receive the dignity of gift and from outside and by mere title, how is he not openly saying that we worship him who is not by Nature God? And together with us (it is like) the gravity of the spirits above too is in error. And the Father Himself is the beginning and plea to us of these things. How then will He yet find fault with them who have chosen to worship the creature rather than Himself? and why does He indict and punish those that have erred, if the error have been by the will of Himself, in exhibiting to us as an object of worship him who is not by Nature God?

But since citing here this word, I mean the one before us, that to Him shall bow every knee and every tongue shall confess Lord Jesus Christ, he (I know not how minded) pretermitted what remains and was of necessity added in order by the blessed Paul, come let us adding it say this, for every tongue confesses Lord Jesus Christ to the glory of God the Father. Hence if He be not by Nature God, but he says that on account of accidental connection, I mean with the Word out of God, he is worshipped both by ourselves and by the holy angels:----some mode of honour has been invented by the Father, so that the creature should be engodded along with Himself, and to no purpose has He displeasure against any for having done this: and if this thing were to His honour, how should He not deem worthy of recompense, praise and glory them who have chosen to do this?

But haply they will say this, How is it any honour to the Father that every knee should bow to Emmanuel?

Because the Word being by Nature God and out of Him, that is, out of His Essence, has been made flesh, and is worshipped (as I said) as One and Alone and Truly Son with His proper Flesh. And the Father is glorified as God, having Very Son Him who was begotten from forth His Essence, whom made flesh also He hath given for us, in order that He having suffered in the flesh might save all under Heaven, that every one who believeth on Him should not perish but have everlasting life, that every one that seeth Him might see the Father. Now that this too is to us verily a life-giving thing, the Son Himself hath shewn: for He said, This is Life Eternal that they might know Thee, the Only Very God and Jesus Christ whom Thou sentest.

And this and none other is the way to the right and most unerring line of thought, but he utterly confounding every thing says,

"Because of the wearer I reverence the worn, because of the hidden I worship him that is seen. [24]"

§12. View again (I pray) how he every where shuns the union and fears the truth and refuses the rightness of the Divine doctrines. Not other than the worn was He who weareth, but rather the same conceived of in concurrence [of Godhead and manhood, and One and Alone in truth Son of God the Father. Worship therefore the Word out of God as One with His own Flesh. For tell me, if I do not seem to thee to think aright, thrusting aside as feeble thy slow speech herein. For suppose one should choose to say of any man such as we are or of any one of the kings of the earth, Because of the king's soul I reverence his body, because of the hidden I worship him that is seen, would not one straightway chide him and say, O sir what are you doing? one man surely is the Ruler, even though he be evidently compounded of two, soul I mean and body. Why then are you idly blabbing to us, speaking of a wearer and a worn, a hidden and an apparent, and confessing that you co-worship as one with another and dishonouring the mode of union, whereas the God-inspired Scriptures reveals to us One Christ and Lord, the Word out of God the Father with His own Body? Knowest thou not that He healed in Jerusalem the blind from his birth, afterward finding him in the temple, He engrafted into him a firm and stablished faith in Himself? for He came to him and asked, Dost

THOU believe on the Son of God? and when to this he cried out, Who is He, Lord, that I might believe on Him? He again said, Thou hast both seen Him and it is He that talketh with thee. [[25] Thou seest how He hath shewn him not the wearer, not the hidden within, but rather Himself as One with the flesh? And verily the wise John says, That Which was from the beginning, which we have heard, which we have seen with our eyes, which we viewed and our hands handled, of the Word of Life. Albeit the Godhead is impalpable, yet the Word has been made palpable through His own flesh; invisible by Nature, He was yet manifest through the Body; but Thou again completely severest and dealest subtilly with the truth, parting the natures, uniting (as you say) the worship. But if you part the natures, along with them will diverge the natural properties too of either, the count of their difference will speed apart: hence two are they confessedly.

But tell me who ask, what is it that severs the natures one from another and what will be the mode of their difference. You will (I suppose) surely answer that one thing by nature is man or the manhood, another God or the Godhead: and the one exalted incomparably above the other, and it as much inferior as is man less than God. How then (tell me) dost thou deem right to honour with one worship things of so unlike nature and parted, as regards their mode of being, by incomparable differences? For would you, if you put about a horse a man's glory, be doing anything praiseworthy? would you not rather be insulting the superior, dragging down the better nature into dishonour?

But he has invented something clever in his defence, for he subjoins:

"Not [26] [by itself God is that which was formed in the womb, not by itself God that which was formed forth of the Spirit, not by itself God that which was buried in the tomb; for so should we have been man-worshippers and very worshippers of the dead. But since God is in that which is assumed, from that which assumeth is the assumed co-named God, as connected with the assumer."

§13. Lo again is he who every where telleth us of connection, and feareth the charge of man-worship, caught in the act of being a man-worshipper, and is holden in the meshes of his own mis-counsel and is detected falling into a reprobate mind. 'For (says he) that which is born from the womb is not by itself God.' How I marvel at thy shrewdness and thy so subtle mind: for who ever is there who hath dared to say this? or who that knows not that that which is born of the flesh is flesh? yet was it the own flesh of the Word and He is conceived of as one with it, just as we said but now that the soul of man too is one with his own body. If therefore one should choose say of us too, The body by itself is not man, would not such an one reasonably be called superfluous in his words and a random talker? for none will deny that the body by itself is not man, but it will be rather called the body of a man: natheless one will not severing them asunder and putting soul and body apart say that the body is co-named with the soul in order to signify a single man, for such a speech would not have been made orderly but would rather be replete with unlearning; but on bringing both together by physical union
[27] unto the condition of one man, he will then style him a man, and will not in this way seem to say what is paltry and uncomely. One must therefore if one would be in all wise and sensible say, A body which is from forth a woman, and confess that conjoined by personal union to the Word, it has rendered the

Same, God and Man, One Christ and Son and Lord. But now pretermitting this, falling quite away from the straight road he thinks...... [b the perverted way, and proclaims unto us two gods: one, as if by Nature and in truth, the Word forth of God the Father, and other than He, him who is co-named with Him. For just as no one of us would be said to live (for example) with himself alone, but rather he would live with another, and if any one were to say that any of the kings of the earth co-reigned with himself, such an one would reasonably incur ridicule, and would be blabbing [8], putting and saying what belonged to one only, as though [he were speaking] of two: just so is it exceeding lack of understanding to suppose that to be co-named can have place in respect of one only. For they will surely be two; and the one is God by Nature, the other having (it seems) the mere being co-named [as something] from without and accruing to him, is exhibited to us as a new god. Does therefore He That is by Nature and truly God of all lie in saying to us, If thou wilt hearken unto Me, there shall be no new god be in thee, neither shalt thou worship an alien god? Then how have we worshipped Christ and how to Him shall every knee bow? how dost thou confess that thou veneratest Him? albeit thou fearest (as thou saidst) to be called a [man-worshipper.

But he has as he thinks some clever answer to this, "he is co-named god as connected with the assumer:" how was he assumed (tell) or what the mode of the connection? If therefore by true union, I mean of Person, cease dividing what has been united; for seasonably (I deem) by us too shall be said to thee who art severing the inseverable, What, therefore God joined together let not man put asunder. But if thou say that the assumption or the connection is extraneous and of accident, how knowest thou not that in us too is God and WE are connected to Him relatively and have been made partakers of His Divine Nature? yea the Divine-uttering David singeth, My soul is fast joined after Thee. Shall WE too therefore be co-named with God by Nature gods according to him, to us too shall every knee bow? What God the Father hath enjoined to the spirits above let the Divine-uttering Paul come forward and teach; For when (saith he) He bringeth the First-begotten into the world He saith, And let all the Angels of God worship Him. Since therefore herein thy wise word has not been added, but He has enjoined rather that He should be worshipped as of a surety One and not one along with another: who is He who is worshipped by the Angels, albeit the Divine Scripture calls Him First-born? We say that the Word out of God the Father has been called First-born albeit He is God by Nature and Only-Begotten Son and not reckoned with the creature, as far as regards Godhead, because He was made Man and First-born among many brethren.

One therefore is He Who is worshipped by the spirits above, the Word forth of God the Father with His own flesh: for then did He bear Him and, as having the preeminence in all things, is He conceived of as First-born. And the God-inspired Scriptures wholly proclaim One Christ and Son and Lord: but this too-curious man says Two and he is not ashamed to add a worshipped man to the Holy and Consubstantial Trinity: for he says again,

> "But this kinsman after the flesh of Israel, man according to what is manifest, begotten according to Paul's voice of the seed of David, is by connection Almighty God" and then adds, [28] "Hear Paul proclaiming both, he confesses the man first and then deifies what is manifest by connection with God, that none may suspect the Christian of being a man-worshipper. Keep we

therefore unconfused the connection of the natures, confess we One God, reverence we the man who is co-worshipped by a Divine connection along with the Almighty God."

§14. If therefore on naming Man thou knowest that He is with this God by Nature, it is well and I will stop: but if severing the natures, not merely in respect of knowing which is the human, which again the Divine, but rather parting them from their concurrence unto unity, confessedly thou art a man-worshipper, and it shall be said to thee by us, Thou shalt eat the fruit of thy labours: and being hard and spurning admonition, go alone on the perverted way. But WE, tracking the pious and blameless path of the holy fathers, instructed full well in the writings of the Apostles and Evangelists, will honour together with God the Father and the Holy Ghost, with one worship, the One Lord Jesus Christ, through Whom and with Whom to God the Father be glory with the Holy Ghost unto ages of ages.

Footnotes:

1. See S. Cyril's fourth chapter, " If any one allot to two Persons or Hypostases the words in the Gospel and Apostolic writings, said either of Christ by the saints or by Him of Himself, and ascribe some to a man conceived of by himself apart from the Word That is of God, others as God-befitting to the Word alone That is of God the Father, be he anathema." Neither Andrew nor Theodoret understood this chapter; Andrew allows that the words must not be allotted to two persons, and uses the term akra of the Union of God and Man both here and on chapter 11 end, just as S. Cyril Hom. Pasch. 7, p. 102 d had said to eis akron henoun and in the Hom. 16 (A.D. 429) so often quoted by Andrew, p. 230 b (as well as at p. 17 above and elsewhere) had used the expression ten eis akron henosin [Nestorius § 8, below p. 64 had called it akra sunapheia]; but appears to think that S. Cyril had denied any distinction of the words at all. Theodoret after an allotment to the Human nature of our Lord of words said by Him of His Human nature, shews his misunderstanding of S. Cyril's chapter by adding what is quite true, but is equally admitted by S. Cyril, "Hence, the things spoken and wrought in God-befitting sort, we will allot to God the Word, those spoken and wrought in lowly wise to the servant's form, lest we fall into the sickness of Arius' and Eunomius' blasphemy."

What S. Cyril is objecting to is the notion that He who is One with the Father is God the Son absolutely distinct from His own Manhood, that He who said. My God My God why forsookest Thou Me is, not God the Son, speaking of and through the Manhood which He had for ever united to Himself but, a man distinct and apart. But even in his quite early writings S. Cyril had never overlooked what the Eastern Bishops were (a year or two after this treatise was written) so anxious to have brought prominently forward, viz. that "as to the Gospel and Apostolic words concerning the Lord, we know that Divines make some common, as to One Person, apportion others, as to two Natures, and give to Christ the God-befitting according to His

Godhead, the lowly ones according to His Manhood " (Confession of Eastern Bishops, approved by S. Cyril and incorporated by him in his Ecumenical letter to John of Antioch, Three Epistles p. 72). In his Thesaurus cap. x init., S. Cyril says, "But we must know and believe that the Word being God and Consubstantial in all things with the Father, put on man's nature and hath been made Man, in order that He may both sometimes speak as man by reason of the Economy with flesh, and may also as God utter the things above man as so being by Nature and when opportunity introduces the need of this. But if any one should wish to refer the things which are more humanly and economically spoken (as I said) to His Godhead and again to refer the things which are Divinely spoken to the time wherein He has been made man, such an one will wrong the nature of things and will destroy the Economy: for one while He saith as God, Verily I say to you, before Abraham was, I am, and again, I have come down from out of heaven. If one wishes to preserve to Him only the God-befitting Dignity, he will utterly take away His being made man in the last times (for He was not in human nature before Abraham was nor yet has He as man come down from Heaven): and again if one should choose to attribute to bare God the Word before the Incarnation the words and acts of the human nature, such an one will do impiously: for what will he do when Christ says Now has My Soul been troubled and is very sorrowful? will he admit that sorrow and dismay befel the Nature of God and that fear of death gat hold thereof? what when he sees Him crucified, will he admit that the Godhead of the Son suffered this just as man? or will he repudiate the blasphemy? Therefore let what is suitable thereto be kept to each time and fact and let Theology practise herself not surely in those things whence it is clear that He is speaking as man, but those whence He is from forth the Father as Son and God; and let it allow to the Economy with flesh that He should sometimes say what does not belong to the Godhead bare and by Itself." pp. 72,73. See also de Trinitate ad Herm. dial. 1. p. 398, dial. 6. p. 600 a b, 602 fin. Hom. Pasch. 7 (A.D. 420) "For as to create in God-befitting manner is not conceived of as pertaining to a man, so is to die alien from God." p. 104 b and through the Homily. These belong to the earlier years of S. Cyril's Episcopate: they do not differ from what S. Cyril wrote about this time, in explanation of his fourth chapter, and in reply to Andrew's criticisms, p. 171 a b, nor from what, in A.D. 432 when the Egyptian and Eastern Churches had explained to one another what each meant, S. Cyril wrote to Acacius Bishop of Melitene as being what the Eastern Bishops said and as being one of the essential points in which they differed from Nestorius (Epp. pp. 117, 118 a).

2. .... S. Cyril in his second Letter to Successus bishop of Diocaesarea in Isauria, written probably about 3 years after this, explains the Term One Nature Incarnate thus, " For even if the Only-Begotten Son of God Incarnate and Made man be said by us to be One, He has not therefore been mixed up (as some please to think) nor has the Nature of the

Word passed into the nature of the flesh nor yet that of the flesh into His Nature, but, while each abides and is conceived of in its natural property, He united unspeakably and unutterably shewed us One Nature of the Son, yet (as I said) Incarnate. For not merely of things which are simple by nature is the One rightly used, but also of those which are brought together as compounded; such as is man, of soul and body: for such things are diverse in form and not consubstantial one to another; yet united, they made up one nature of man, albeit in the plan of the compounding, the difference of nature in the things brought together into Union exists." Epp. p. 143 a b c. The great estimation in which this letter was held is indicated by its frequent citations in controversies on the Incarnation. See also the Letter to Acacius Bishop Melitene, Epp. pp. 115, 116.

3. See S. Cyril's first Letter to Successus, Epp. p. 137 d.

4. The following extract from Tillemont (Hist. Eccles. Les Apollinaristes, Art 2. t. vii pp. 001, 605 ed. 2. Paris 1700), will illustrate that dread of Apollinarianism, which not only Nestorius but John of Antioch (see a letter of his to S.Cyril, Synodicon cap. 80. Baluz. Nova Collectio Conciliorum t. i. 783; iv. 346 Col.) Theodoret and the Bishops of that Archiepiscopate felt. Apollinarianism had been their last great heretical onslaught, only about 60 years previous, and Antioch its head-quarters. Tillemont says, "Car ne voulant pas reconnoistre qu'il y eust deux substances et deux natures en J. C, l'une divine et l'autre humaine, ou bien l'une de Dieu et l'autre de la chair, non seulement ils [les Apollinaristes] soutenoient, après les Ariens, qu'il avoit une seule nature mixte et composée de la divine et de l'humaine : mais ils se reduisoient à dire que sa chair estoit consubstantielle à sa divinité, qu'une partie du Verbe avoit esté changée en chair, en os, en cheveux, en un mot en un corps et en une nature toute différente de la sienne, que ce n'avoit pas esté un corps comme le nostre, qu'il en avoit seulement la forme et l'apparence extérieure, mais qu'il estoit coeternel à la nature divine, formé de la substance mesme de la sagesse éternelle et de celle du Verbe changée en un corps passible: Qu'ainsi c'estoit la substance mesme de la sagesse qui avoit creé le monde, et la divinité du Fils consubstantielle au Père, qui avoit esté circoncise et attachée a la croix ; et non un corps terrestre comme le nostre.

Ils ajoutaient, par une consequence bien naturelle de ce faux principe, que la substance de son corps n'estait pas prise de Marie, mais avoit seulement passé par elle comme par un canal [this was the ancient blasphemy of a portion of the Gnostics, see S. Iren. 3. 11. 3. p. 231 O.T.] : d'où vient qu'ils luy refusoient le titre de Mere de Dieu, et qu'ils pretendoient qu'on ne pouvoit dire que le corps de J. C. fust tiré d'elle, sans mettre une quaternité en Dieu au lieu de la Trinité ; de sorte qu'il est visible que selon eux, le corps de J. C. estoit compris dans la Trinité. Ils disaient aussi que ce corps avait esté avant Marie et que J. C. l'avoit toujours eu, ayant toujours esté fils de l'homme, qu'il l'avoit pris du ciel [S. Cyril in his Ecumenic Letter to John Archbishop of Antioch (see 3

Epistles p. 72) says that some had reported that he himself had held this very thing], qu'il n'avoit eu qu'à descendre en terre avec son corps qui luy estoit uni substantiellement, qu'ainsi ce corps estoit non seulement consubstantiel à la divinité, mais aussi céleste et increé."

When therefore S. Cyril insists on the Word having been made flesh, the Eastern Bishops thought that while using S. John the Evangelist's words, he was pressing the gegone to mean hath become, been actually turned into: and the "One Incarnate Hypostasis of the Word" seemed to them to mean not Union but the mixture and confusion of the Apollinarians. Theodoret, in his objections to the 12 chapters which S. Cyril and his Council had drawn up for Nestorius to sign, does not in general use language that differs very much from S. Cyril's own mind; but sets out with the conviction that S. Cyril was an Apollinarian and so reads and interprets the chapters as really intended to bring in Apollinarian error secretly by use of veiled language. Thus in reply to S. Cyril's "for she [the blessed Virgin] hath borne after the flesh the Word from out of God made flesh" (chapter 1), Theodoret remarks, "we say that He has not been made flesh by nature nor was God the Word changed into flesh," "it is plain therefore that the Form of God was not turned into form of servant:" in objection to Chapter 2, "Superfluous therefore is Personal union, which as I think he is putting forward instead of mixture:" the objection to chapter 3 ends with the words, "he who is teaching us mixture by means of other names:" in objection to chapter 5, "but that the Word has been made flesh by any turning, we not only do not say, but we accuse of impiety them that say so:" the objection to chapter 6 closes, "for not by being turned did God the Word become flesh, but assumed flesh possessed of an intellectual soul;" in the objection to chapter 8 occur similarly the words, "For neither did God the Word receive transformation [tropen see S. James i. 17] nor again did man lose what he was, and become changed into the nature of God:" the objection to chapter 10 begins, "Not into nature of flesh was the Unchangeable Nature turned:" in the objection to chapter 11 occur the words, "for first of all, he nowhere mentioned flesh endowed with mind nor confessed that he which was assumed is perfect man, but everywhere he says flesh, following the doctrine of Apollinarius; next he intersperses in his words the notion of mixture, infusing it by means of other words." Hence it is clear that Theodoret's objection was not to the chapters themselves but to the chapters in that he approached them possessed with the notion that S. Cyril was an Apollinarian and was endeavouring to disseminate their error by dishonest use of apparently orthodox language.

5. Nestorius means that whereas it was the object of the Arians and Eunomians to assert that God the Son was inferior to God the Father, supposing all the lowly actions that are recorded of God our Saviour and His purely Human actions, His hunger and thirst and weariness and sorrow and pain, could be referred to His Godhead, it would go to make out their case. Whereas the actions are not referred to the Godhead

considered by Itself, but all the actions recorded of our Lord after His Birth in the flesh, whether Divine or Human, are referred to One Person, God and Man in One, of God the Son. Just as (to use our little comparisons to help our frail understanding) no distinction is made in human actions; we say, he ate, he slept, he read, he wrote, he thought: we do not distinguish and say, his body ate, his body slept, his soul read, or wrote, or thought. Part of this passage is quoted by S. Cyril in his defence of his fourth chapter against Andrew. For the last portion of the extract compare serm 2, p. 68, Bal.

6. One is added on the authority of a Syriac citation in a MS. in the British Museum, Cod add. 14533 fol. 9and again fol. 30. The Roman editors had given it in their margin as a conjectural emendation.

7. i.e. as one of the things not imparted to it, but so part of its own being, that it may not lose it without ceasing to be what it is.

8. Nestorius in the fourth of the sermons which Mercator has published (preached after he had received from S. Cyril the Great Letter of the Alexandrine Synod with the 12 Chapters appended, accompanied by Pope S. Celestine's Letter), preached against opponents of his and re-affirms what he had said before, repeating a few words here and there from the older sermon from which these extracts were taken: a sermon not perhaps belonging to the volume which was first published (see above p. 4) but preached (as was certainly the next piece, p. 51) to oppose S. Cyril's letter to monks, p. 13 b. In this sermon 4, p. 82 Nestorius says, " God sent His Son, a name common to the natures, i. e., of man and God. He did not say, God sending God the Word." See too further on where other similarities or re-capitulations are referred to in margin. The passage which stands at the head of § 13 (see below p. 77) is from serm. 2. p. 65 Bal. and some of it also in serm. 1. p. 55.

The whole passage as cited here and in the Council of Ephesus (see next note) is given by Mercator with the title, From the book of Nestorius himself, out of the 16th quire, on dogma. In the volume from which the extracts were taken for the Council of Ephesus, the sermon on dogma seems to have nearly followed that which Mercator gives us complete pp. 56-70, and which is there called sermon 2: for the extracts from this sermon 2 are extracted from the 15th and 10th quires, see Mercatoris opera pp. 205, 207, 210 Bal.: while the two extracts given from the sermon on Dogma are from the 16th and 17th quires, viz. this one from the 16th (Merc. p. 201, or 17th as Greek edd.) and the extract at the head of § 8 below from the 17th quire (Merc. p. 205). The Greek editions of the council however agree with Mercator in styling this extract eis dogma, but omit the words in the title to the other extract, appending it instead to two citations from the 15th quire; one of which is, in part, at the head of § 14, the other is given by S. Cyril both there and in his letter to Acacius of Melitene written after the reconcilation with the Eastern Bishops, Epp. p. 115. 1.5-9.

9. i. e. S. Cyril himself: for Nestorius looked not kindly on S. Cyril's Letter to the monks, to which (p. 13 b) he is here referring, see note on book 4 § 6 below.

10. The present text as it now stands is tauta pou kai sauton, the Roman Editors conjecture kata for kai, but it is just as likely that the difficulty is occasioned by omission from homoeoteleuton, from which even a good MS. (as is the one in which the Greek text of these books is preserved) is rarely exempt.

11. i. e., the tribute money of half a shekel which was the acknowledgement of God's sovereignty appointed in the first instance by God, Exod. xxx. 12-16. (It does not appear to have been a regular tax, though there seems an allusion to it in 2 Kings xii. 4, the money of every one that passeth the account. This tax our Lord paid, S. Matt, xvii. 24-27, yet told S. Peter that He was free, as a Son.) Every male who had attained the age of 20 was to pay: it amounted to a hundred talents, 1775 shekels of silver: with the hundred talents were cast a hundred silver sockets for the sanctuary and the vail, the 1775 silver shekels were used in making hooks for the pillars and in overlaying the chapiters (Exod. xxxviii, 25-28).

Dr. Edersheim, learned in Jewish customs and deeply versed in their books, tells us, " It had only been about a century before [our Lord's payment for Himself and S. Peter], during the reign of Salome-Alexandra (about 78 B. C), that the Pharisaical party, being then in power, had carried an enactment by which the Temple-tribute was to be enforced at law.....It is a matter of doubt whether the half-shekel had ever been intended as an annual payment. Its first enactment was under exceptional circumstances, and the mode in which, as we are informed a similar collection was made during the reign of Joash(2 Chron.xxiv.6-11) suggests the question whether the original institution by Moses was not treated rather as affording a precedent than as laying down a binding rule. At the time of Nehemiah we read only of a self-imposed ordinance and at the rate of a third, not a half shekel (Neh. x. 32-34). But long before the coming of Christ very different views prevailed." The Temple, its ministry and Services pp. 49, 50 (Religious Tract Society). Dr. Edersheim tells us that the money was paid in the month previous to the Passover, pp. 47, 48.

12. In this passage as cited before the Council of Ephesus are given the words which S. Cyril also (see de Trin.dial. 6. p. 589 e and elsewhere,) with the Alexandrine MS. of the LXX. reads, hegiasmenoi eisin, they have been sanctified (corresponding to My sanctified ones in our version) and I lead them. These words are required to explain Nestorius' assertion that the Babylonian was called holy.

13. See this at greater length in S. Cyril's Glaphyra on Exodus, lib. i. cap. 4. pp. 305 sq. and especially 306 c; also lib. iii. 3. pp. 327 sq.

14. This contrast between our Master and our fellow-servants to whom He had delegated His authority before His own Advent, is argued on by S. Cyril below, Schol. § 26, also Thes. cap. 12 p. 108 c d and often.

15. S. Cyril in his Thesaurus, cap. 25 p. 238 d says, " He is therefore Only-Begotten by Nature, as Only out of the Father, God out of God, and Light beaming forth of Light: First-Begotten for our sakes, in order

that all the creation engrafted as it were in a certain immortal root and springing up out of Him Who ever is (for all things have been made through Him and consist) might itself too be preserved for aye." (... is Aubert's text slightly emended from the beautiful Munich Codex 331, written in the tenth century). See also De Trin. ad Herm. dial. l.p. 405 c: and 7th Paschal homily (A.D. 420) p. 103; 10th Paschal homily (A.D. 423) p. 159 e.

16. This is given differently in Marius Mercator's collection of extracts made by S.Cyril from Nestorius'writings. The 17th extract is as follows, " Also from another tractate quire 25. Wherefore I would have you secure in your assent or acclamation [..., no doubt rightly]. There is no severance of the connection and of Godhead [deitatis, perhaps, dignitatis, dignity] nor of the sway. In that the Son is Christ, there is no severance in these, but in regard to Godhead and manhood there is severance. In that He is Christ, the Son is undivided, in that He is Son, He is undivided. For we have not two christs and two sons, nor is there with us a first christ and a second, nor one and another, nor again one son and again another son, but Himself the Same, Himself a twofold Son, not in respect of dignity but of nature." p. 117 ed. Baluz.

17. flesh and body. Thus I heave translated, following the translation given of this piece of S. Cyril hy the Syriac MS. in the British Museum (Add. 17154 fol. 21 v) written in the seventh century. The MS. contains a correspondence betweeh Severus Archbishop of Antioch and Sergius the Grammarian on the controversy about the two Natures in the Incarnation. Severus quotes S. Cyril throughout his writings, and this passage is cited in Severus' reply to Sergius' second letter. The Greek has the more usual phrase, flesh and blood.

18. S. Cyril had looked on these words of Nestorius as replete with gravest untruth, for S. Cyril's seventh chapter is, "If any says that Jesus has been in-wrought-in as man by God the Word and that the good glory of the Only-Begotten has been put around Him as though He were other than He, be he anathema." They may belong to one of Nestorius' earlier sermons. Mercator (p. 110 ed. Bal.) cites them as being out of the second volume, first quire (i. e. of one of the volumes of published sermons, see above p. 48 note n). Mercator tells us that this volume began, "I have yet much to say to you." (Mercator has apparently only three extracts out of the first volume, i.e. two on the Creed, and the one given above p. 51.) In the extracts made for the Council of Ephesus, part of the passage is also cited and there too as taken out of the first quire: see Merc. p. 207, top of page, and the corresponding place in the different editions of the Council of Ephesus.

19. S. Cyril in his sixth Dialogue to Hermias explains that "Hence He is glorified by the Father not as though He needed glory while conceived of as apart from flesh, and believed God forth of God : but since He was man, which does not possess as fruit of his proper nature, the power of working God-befitting acts, He receives the power by the Union and Concurrence (...) Unspeakable such as is conceived to be that of the Word with His human nature."

De Trin. ad Herm. dial. 6. p. 601 a b.

20. See this also in the Quod Unus Christus, below.

21. i.e. S. Cyril says here and elsewhere (de recta fide ad Imperatorem 32 e, ad Arcadiam Marinamque 47 b 70 e 85 e 115 d 120 d, ad Pulcheriam et Eudociam 131 b 148 b, in his Explanation of XIth chapter, and three or four times in the treatise Quod Unus Christus) that the name Jesus Christ does not belong to God the Son before the Incarnation, except as looking on to the Incarnation (de recta fide ad Arcadiam Marinamque 120 d) but is the name of God the Son Incarnate God and Man : not as though there were a connection with Christ but because "God and Man are One Christ."

22. This passage again is from sermon 2 in Mercator's selection: it occurs at p. 64 Bal. In the sermon itself, after who have told you the truth, is added, but now He says, why seek ye to kill Me that Man who was crowned &c. Words here and there are quoted by the same Mercator, as translations of S. Cyril's citations of Nestorius (p. 114 Bal.) and some other words among the passages cited before Council of Ephesus where they are said to be taken from the sixteenth quire, (ib. p. 207 & Conc. t. iii. 1068 Col.)

23. These words are also a portion of serm. 2 (see p. 65 Baluz.). The closing words, and that every tongue should confess Lord Jesus Christ, are there omitted but seem to have formed part of the sermon, since S. Cyril a little below says that Nestorius for some reason or other had omitted to add, to the glory of God the Father. We do not know where Nestorius used the words cited a little before, But yea He said to the leper, I will, &c.

24. These words are extant in Nestorius' first sermon p. 55 Baluz, but some phrases are repeated in serm. 2 p. 65 just following S. Cyril's last citation. The words, Because of the wearer I reverence the worn, are not in this part of the second sermon, yet are quoted (pp. 114, 115) in a long piece extracted (all but these words) from serm. 2, and again in page 207 in an extract from the 16th quire in which this sermon was. The words here cited are likewise cited by S. Cyril in his Great Letter to Nestorius. Three Epistles, p. 64.

25. S. Cyril loves to quote this loyal adoration of our Master on the part of the born-blind and our Master's acceptance of it; see it mentioned again below Schol. § 36 and de recta fide to the Emperor Theodosius, 31 a.

26. This belongs to serm. 2. and follows the last quotation, a few words only intervening. A few words are also quoted in the Great Letter to Nest. see note v.

27. See this expression physical union or unity of Nature of the Union of the Nature of God and the Nature of man in Christ in S. Cyril's third chapter. S, Cyril says in his Explanation of his third chapter that he used physical in the sense of true. The word physical or natural, perplexed Andrew of Samosata, who in his objection to that chapter supposes natural to have been used in contrast with supernatural.

Theodoret, in his objection, replies that even man himself, though really one, is allowed to be spoken of as twofold. S. Cyril does not object to this : he speaks in regard to our Lord, of dividing the

Natures in one's conception of them. " Hence in regard of thought and of only seeing with the eyes of the soul how the Only-Begotten became man, we say that the natures united are two, but that the Word of God Incarnate and made man, is One Christ and Son and Lord." Ep. 1 to Successus, p. 137 e. Again, " But they [i. e. they who thought one ought to speak of two natures as actually existent] did not know that things which are severed otherwise than in mere conception of them, these will full surely part off one from the other wholly and separately into diverseness. Take for example a man: we conceive of two natures in him, one, of the soul, the other, of the body. But severing them in mere idea, and in subtil conception or fantasy of the mind, admitting the difference, we do not put the natures apart nor give them their force throughout by severing, but we conceive of One ; so that the two are no longer two, but through both is One living creature made up. Hence though one speak of the nature of manhood and Godhead in Emmanuel, yet has the manhood become the Word's own, and He is conceived of as One Son with it." Ep. 2. to Successus, p. 145 b c.

28. something seems to have dropped out here. The Roman Editors conjectured ietai hastens along for oietai thinks: "he hastens along the perverted way, falling from the straight path."

29. These two pieces are both quoted before the Council of Ephesus, see pp. 204, 206 Bal. where they are called from the fifteenth quire; the Greek editions add on dogma. S. Cyril cites also the last portion in his letter to Acacius of Melitene Epp. p. 115 a, see above p. 49 note n.

Cyril of Alexandria, Five Tomes Against Nestorius – Book 3

TOME III
[Translated by P.E. Pusey]

Ps. xviii. 11 hints at the depth of Christ's mystery. Gifts through Incarnation. Is, xlv. 14, 15 the Incarnate Son. S. John i. 14. 2 Sam. vii. 12-14 explained by S. Paul. 1 Sam. ii. 35. The WORD Incarnate worshipped by Angels worships with us and is our High Priest. GOD the WORD sent and how: so our High Priest. Sent and High Priest when Incarnate., Possessor of Godhead, a misnomer. Heb. v. 1. He makes us His brothers. 'Yesterday to-day and for ever.' S. John i. 30: iii. 13: Micah v. 2, Is. liii. 8. Gen. xxxii. 24 sqq. High Priesthood belongs to Incarnation. 'Sent' of God is a human word and to be understood worthily of God. The Son Incarnate gives the Holy Ghost as God, receives as man. High priesthood. Growth "in wisdom and stature and favour." Union alone permits to attribute to One the properties of either manhood or Godhead. The Paschal Lamb and the sacrifice for sin of a young bullock types of the sinlessness of our Sacrifice.

Great confessedly is the mystery of godliness, and marvelled at by the holy Angels themselves also, and hereto the most wise Paul confirms us saying, To the intent that now unto the principalities and powers in heavenly places might be known through the Church the manifold wisdom of God according to the eternal purpose which He purposed in our Lord Jesus Christ, in Whom we have boldness and access with confidence through faith. For wisdom verily, and that not human (how could it?) but Divine rather and deposited in certain ineffable depths and incomprehensibilities, is the Mystery of Christ. And the blessed David singeth, And He made darkness His secret place, around Him His pavilion dark water in clouds of the skies, palling darkness (I suppose) nought else save altogether the dim conception of ideas, falling like mist upon the eyes of the understanding.

We say therefore that the mystery of Christ hath by no means needed subtil investigations and search beyond the reach of mind, but faith rather that holds the tradition simple and guileless. Thus we ourselves also have been taught and believed that God the Father sent His own Son who is by Nature God, made Man and born of a woman after the flesh, that He might justify them that believe on Him and having freed from stumblings through ignorance, by His Good and most gentle authority, might present them clean and undefiled through Him to God the Father, and might make partakers of His own Divine Nature them who are under death and decay, yea and might preach recovery of sight to the blind, and might bring over the flocks which had strayed into the light of the true knowledge of God, and might teach at length who it is Who is by Nature and truly God and the Creator of all. For He became the savour of the knowledge of God the Father, and in Him we have beheld Him out of Whom He was begotten by Nature and know clearly the way that leadeth us unto everlasting life. That thus the Son should beam upon the crowd of the Gentiles too, hath the blessed Prophet Isaiah cried beforehand saying, Thus saith the Lord, Egypt toiled and the merchandise of the Ethiopians, and the Sabeans, men of stature, shall pass over unto Thee and they shall be Thy servants, and they shall come after Thee bound in fetters: and they shall worship Thee, and in Thee shall they pray; for in Thee is God, and there is no God save Thee, for THOU art God and we knew it not, the God of Israel the Saviour. And it is said somewhere to the Son, as from the Person again of God the Father, Lo, I have set Thee for a covenant of the race, for a light of the nations, that Thou mayest be for salvation unto the end of the earth. For He hath instituted to them of the blood and race of Israel, the new covenant, the first having waxen old, and He beamed as far as the boundaries of that beneath the sky also, to the nations and people in every place and city. For they have worshipped Him yea and they follow Him spiritually, holden by the indissoluble chains of love, as in fetters and well-nigh say what is in the Prophet Jeremiah, Behold WE will be Thine for THOU art the Lord our God. See (I pray) the vigilance of the Prophet's thoughts, They shall worship Thee (he says) and in Thee shall they pray, for in Thee is God, and there is no God beside Thee. He knew then confessedly as being Spirit-clad the Word Out of God the Father, Who should tabernacle in us, as saith the blessed Evangelist John: therefore he saith that God is in Thee; yet hath he not suffered Emmanuel to be Severed into two gods, but even though the Only-Begotten was made man, he acknowledged Him even so as One and straightway added, There is no God save Thee. For Consider accurately the Prophet's utterance. For having first declared (as I said) that God is in Thee, he hath not added, And there is no God save He that is in Thee, but gathering it into the Unity of the Economy, says There is no God beside Thee.

But that the Only-Begotten Word of God made man, is declared to us by the (so to speak) whole God-inspired Scripture, is easy to shew without toil by very many proofs: but I think it is enough for the present to say this. God said somewhere to blessed David, And I will set up out of thy seed after thee Him who shall proceed out of thy bowels and I will prepare His Kingdom: He shall build an house for My Name and I will stablish His Throne for ever, and\ will be to Him a Father and He shall be to Me a Son. But some one (I suppose) will say that these things were said not of Emmanuel, but of Solomon rather: yet the most wise Paul will strenuously oppose those who would thus understand it, for he takes the words of Christ and says that it is He to Whom it has been said by God the Father, I will be to Him a Father and He shall be to Me a Son. But that when made like unto us, i. e., Man, He should offer to God the Father, all beneath the sky saved through faith in Him, He made known saying elsewhere, And I will raise Me up a faithful Priest who shall do all which is in Mine heart and in My soul, and I will build Him a sure house and He shall walk before Me for ever. Observe (I pray) that having elsewhere said, He shall build an house for My Name, the Father here promises to rear the house for the Son. And the Divine Paul understanding this, said that Moses was faithful in all My house having the measure pertaining to a servant, but Christ as a Son over His own house, Whose House are WE; and the mode of the ministry, things pertaining to us, not the blood of bulls and of calves, but the confession of the faith of us all.

And blessed Paul will again certify it, writing thus, Wherefore holy brethren partakers of the heavenly calling, consider the Apostle and High Priest of our confession, Jesus, who was faithful to Him That appointed Him. We say therefore that the Word out of God the Father, when receiving servant's form He is said to have been emptied for our sake, then too did abase Himself in the measure of the human nature, whereto will pertain (and very reasonably) both the seeming to be sent and the accounting the ministry the token of the very highest honour. For if when He became as we, He have worshipped with us as Man, albeit the Host above and the holy spirits worship Him, and Moses says of Him, Rejoice O ye heavens with Him and let all the sons of God worship Him; what is there strange or what inconvenient to the nature of the Economy if He have been called High Priest as offering for us for an odour of a sweet smell Himself and us through Himself and in Himself to God the Father? for we are a sweet savour of Christ, as it is written. But this noble person again affirms that these things have been wrought in no fit order, and all but smiles at those who conceive that these things were so, and impiously finding fault with the Divine purposes, says thus:

> *"For they hearing the name of Apostle, deem that God the Word was Apostle; reading the name High Priest, they fancy that the Godhead was High Priest, by a species of paradoxical craziness: for who learning of the ministry of an Apostle, would not forthwith know that a man is indicated? who on hearing the appellation of High Priest, would suppose that the Essence of Godhead were High Priest? for if the Godhead be High Priest, who is he who is served by the ministry of the High Priesthood? if God be the Offerer, there is none to whom offering is made: for what is there worthy of Godhead that as less It should offer to the greater?"* And hereto he adds, *"Whence then is God supposed by them to have been now called High Priest Who needeth not sacrifices for His own advancement like the high priests? Is the possessor of Godhead, taken from among men, ordained for men in things God-ward?"*

§1. Therefore dost thou say that the Word of God has not been even sent into the world? The most wise Paul hath cozened (it appears) those who were called through him, for he said, God sent forth His Son made of a woman, made under the law: the blessed David too will be found according to thee idly romancing and seeking impossible things, for he said somewhere to God the Father in Heaven, O send out Thy Light and Thy Truth. And what (tell me) will not the Son Himself too speak falsely in saying, For God sent not His Son into the world to judge the world, but that the world through Him might be saved, and again, I came forth from the Father and am come. The wise John too writes somewhere of Him, He that receiveth His testimony set to his seal that God is true, for He Whom God sent speaketh God's words. But we say that the Word of God hath been sent, having with the measures of the emptying the name and fact of being sent: but YOU why do you unlearnedly fear and blush to allot to Him the name and fact both of the apostolate and the High-priesthood? would it befit (do you suppose) as other than He, the man born of a woman having (according to you) a mere connection and that in equality of dignity only? how then is the Word being God seen to profit any longer our condition, if we have been even presented to God the Father through another? for no longer have we had the access through Him, but a man like us has become our mediator having the name of Godhead put on.

Yea (says he) the priest's office is petty to the Word begotten out of God the Father. Petty confessedly, I agree with you enunciating the truth, but not in bare [Godhead did He dawn on those upon the earth, but rather made man as we, to whom the priesthood is some great and choice thing. But if He refused the priest's office as belonging to man, or indeed ought that appertains to the measure of bond-service, how were it not better far, before this to refuse too the Incarnation?

Yet He rejected not for our sakes the Birth. But this man (as I said) is ashamed of the truth, shewing himself unwise and unskilled, albeit the blessed Paul saith, For I am not ashamed of the Gospel, for it is the power of God unto salvation to every one that believeth. And one may well marvel that the Word of God for the salvation and life of all endured to suffer so great abasement, which the inventor for us of idle teachings is (I know not how) ashamed merely to acknowledge, albeit he ought to wonder hereat and to cry with the blessed Prophet, O Lord, I have heard Thy report and was afraid, I considered Thy works and was amazed. But since the whole God-inspired Scripture in a manner rises up against him, and arrays against him the truth, shewing that his discourse in favour of his own inventions, cold and without any real being and destitute of support from any quarter, lacks in no small degree the conceptions and ideas that tend unto Tightness and truth; hence what no one of those well reported of for rightness of doctrine, ever either thought or said, this he makes the occasion of his discourse, and fights with shadows and strains himself to no purpose, no one opposing him or wishing to contend about these matters. And this (I deem) is to beat the air. For he said "Who on learning of the ministry of an apostle would not forthwith know that a man is indicated? who on hearing the appellation of High Priest would suppose that the Essence of Godhead were High-Priest?" Since therefore there is no one who says this, with whom (tell me) are you striving, and as though yourself alone were overthrowing what is condemned by the voice of all, are haply thinking that your opposition is worthy even of honours? albeit how is it not true that since no one saith this, it is you who are bringing forward what it were better to be silent on and not to instil into the souls of the more simple? For who is so crazed as to, suppose that the Essence 'of Godhead were High Priest?' Aaron was a man, albeit he obtained preeminence of the rest in Divine Priesthood. How then will any one suppose that the Essence of Godhead is High Priest, or how will he not wholly and surely confess that mention is made of a man when the brother of Moses is named to us as High Priest? Yet he putting forth some language that commonly belongs to and befits every High Priest of those among us, essays to undo the marvel of the Economy understood in Christ, and dares to shake from the very foundations our Divine Mystery, not considering that Christ hath founded the Church upon a rock, and the gates of Hell shall not prevail against her. For he no wise condescends to follow the common doctrine and that of all who are wont to think aright, but he alone innovates without examination what he pleases. For WE (as I said before) say that the Word out of God the Father, made Man, offered to Himself and to the Father the confession of our faith and wrought an Economy befitting and by no means out of harmony with the measures of the emptying. [1] But not so does it seem to him, but he taking separately and apart him that is from forth the holy Virgin as though another

Christ than the Word That is out of God the Father, says that he became the Apostle and high priest of our confession and supposes that he is thinking what conduce unto piety when he says, "If God be the offerer, there is none to whom offering is made, for what is there worthy of Godhead that as though less It should make offering to the greater?" Now if there were any who were contending and saying that He That is truly Word out of God the Father had been appointed to office of priesthood even before the Incarnation and were in the measure of ministry and were for this reason to be called High Priest and Apostle, he would have given a wise rebuke, and one would say that his argument hereon had been made in season. For not in lack of priests is the Nature That rules all, that Himself should minister therein. But since the Only-Begotten, being God by Nature and receiving from the hands of those who execute the Priest's office their ministrations, hath descended unto the measure of those appointed unto the priesthood, having become Man (as I said), nought strange will it be if He be called by us High Priest too. Hath He not come down in servant's form, having taken that is the form of a servant, albeit Impress and Brightness of the Father's Glory? None will doubt it. When therefore He Who is in His own Nature Free as God, He Who is in the Form and Equality of the Father, has been called bond, economically not thrusting from Him the measure of those who are under the yoke of bondage, why dost thou fear to call Him High Priest too by reason of the Manhood? for He dedicates us for an odour of a sweet smell through faith, and Himself hath He offered for us as a most sweet-smelling offering to the Father.

But he (saying I know not what) straightway subjoins to these things; "Whence then were God supposed by them to have been now called High Priest Who needeth not sacrifices for His own advancement? is the possessor of Godhead taken from among men appointed for men in things God-ward?" Whence then Christ, i. e., the Word out of God made man, was, or why He was called, Apostle and High Priest, our discourse has already clearly shewn, but I think it right not to leave unexamined his unwonted and strange utterance. For doth he say that the Word out of God is Possessor of Godhead, even though any should wish to conceive of Him apart and without flesh? doth he define His Godhead as other than He? whereof I don't know how (as he saith) He hath become possessor, as though it accrued to Him and came to Him from without, although once not God by Nature, like what was said by that ancient woman, I mean Eve, when she bare Seth, I gat a man through God. But this I deem is wholly to be spurned by him and by all. Why then doth he speak with inexactness, and fling about words without understanding, in matters so cogent? would not one earn laughter and accusal of insanity, if one chose to say that any among us were the possessor of human nature, or a horse of horse-nature? who then is the possessor of Godhead, who taken from men is ordained in things to Godward? Haply he will say severing into two the One Christ, Him that is forth of the Holy Virgin: for to this I suppose now too is his aim directed.

Hath the Godhead then (tell me) become the acquisition [of a man, and hath it befallen any one of us, to become God by Nature and in truth and to be rich in the excellence of the Essence that is above all and Supreme? Away with the ill-counsel, o man, for none of those accounted among things generate may acquire and have as his own the Nature of Godhead: His own was the Body of the Word and as one therewith God and Christ and Son and Lord hath the creation worshipped, and the Heavens do praise and we with them. For as the Prophet saith, His Goodness covered the Heavens and of His Praise was the earth full, not as though a man gat Godhead (for how or whence could he?) but that the Word out of God the Father had come into possession of flesh of man. But be it that he who was taken out of men was owner of Godhead (as seems good to yourself), how is he ordained in things to Godward, i. e., as High Priest? will he therefore bare of the Godhead which he gat, minister in the Priest's office to God, or already having it as his own? for this and nought else will the saying that he gat it signify. But if bare of it, he gat it not; if having it as his own, Godhead will surely minister in the Priest's office to God. Why then do you wander distractedly and jumble all together and blush not, stamping with false mark the tradition of the Faith?

The Word out of God the Father hath cogent reason even though He be said to execute the Priest's Office before the Father; for He has been styled Priest not apart from flesh, but made (as I said) as we, to whom the glory of the priesthood is accounted an honour.

In another way too it is not hard to see that it is the absurdest possible thing and replete with much folly to say that he who was taken out of men and ordained unto God-ward, is possessor of Godhead; for if he were taken by God, how possessed he the Nature Which took him? for that which is taken will rather belong to him who took it, as a possession, not that which is taken be the possessor. As for example, A man has become the possessor of wealth, or again of skill unto anything: is it not plain to all that he will not himself be the possession of wealth or again of the skill that accrued to him, but rather the possessor of what he has gotten? but this is I think in no way doubtful.

Hence if on enquiring into the mode of the Incarnation of the Only-Begotten, we find that man became God as coming into possession of Godhead, let him be called (after your phrase) possessor of Godhead, for his hath the Godhead become. But if the Word being God came into possession of the seed of Abraham, and being in the form of the Father, hath become Man, receiving the servant's form, how would one not be distraught, if he chose to say that that which was taken possessed the Nature That acquired it and hath not rather become the very own of Him Who took it?

But that he carries round the force of his own words and inventions and moreover the very name of high Priesthood in unlearned wise unto a mere man born from forth a woman, bearing it away from the Only-Begotten and Word That is out of the Father, he will make manifest by what follows too: for he has written again on this wise:

"Not [2] Angels doth He take hold of, but Abraham's seed He taketh hold of. Is the Godhead Abraham's seed? Hear the following utterance too: Wherefore it behoved Him, he saith, in all things to be made like unto His brethren. Had God the Word any brothers like unto His Godhead? Mark what is straightway joined on to these, That He might be made a merciful and faithful High Priest in things to God-ward, for in that He Himself hath suffered being tempted, He is able to succour them that are tempted. Therefore He Who suffered is a merciful High Priest: passible is the Temple, not the quickening God of him that has suffered: the seed of Abraham is he which is yesterday and to-day, as Paul saith, not He That saith, Before Abraham was I am. Like to his brethren in

all things is he which assumed brother-hood of human soul and flesh and not He which saith, He that hath seen Me hath seen the Father."

§2. The Word therefore being God took (as he too hath just now confessed) Abraham's seed; how then is he that is forth of the seed of Abraham any longer possessor of Godhead, if he were taken by God, did not himself take Godhead? The seed of Abraham then will by no means be the Nature of Godhead, but rather hath become the Body of God the Word, according to the Scriptures, and His Own, and He Who in His own proper Nature is uncounted among the creation as God, when He became Man who is part of the creation, then, then and with reason deigns He to call us brothers saying, I will declare Thy Name unto My brethren. But that by reason of the measure of emptiness, the Word out of God the Father hath descended even to having to call those upon the earth His brothers, the most wise Paul will clearly shew, writing of Him and us, For both He That sanctifieth and they who are being sanctified are all out of one, for which cause He is not ashamed to call them brethren saying, I will declare Thy Name unto My brethren. For before the Incarnation, exceeding petty to the Word Which sprang of God was the name of brotherhood with us: but when He had descended unto voluntary emptiness, petty was it thus too, yet hath it come fitly in, for He hath partaken of blood and flesh and of those in flesh and blood has been styled Brother. For if He is sanctified in that He have become Man albeit God by Nature and Himself the Giver of the Spirit, how if He be called Brother too, will it not be so said in due order? for for this cause He hath become as we that He might render us brothers and free, for as many (it says) as received Him, to them gave He authority to become children of God, to them that believe on His Name, which were begotten not out of blood nor out of the will of the flesh nor out of the will of man but out of God. For the Word out of God the Father has been with us born after the flesh that we too might be enriched with the birth out of God through the Spirit, no longer termed children of flesh but transelemented rather into what was above nature and termed sons of God by grace: for He has been made as one of us who is by Nature and truly Only-Begotten Son.

And unerring is the word; the Divine-uttering Paul will give us assurance thereto, saying on this wise, And because ye are sons, God sent forth the Spirit of His Son into your hearts, crying Abba Father. Why then do you offer violence to the wisdom of the economy as though it appeared to have been wrought in no fitting order, in that you say, "Is the Godhead Abraham's seed? had He any brothers like to the Godhead?" Is not this clear madness? for the absurdly enquiring into and bearing away unto blasphemy, things so right and unblameable in respect of the Economy in Christ, what else is it than proof of the most utter distraction? for confessedly in respect of the nature of the body or of human nature perfect as far as itself is concerned, has the Word out of God the Father been made like unto us and in every thing like save sin alone. But I will ask him who says "Had God the Word any brothers like to the Godhead?" what idea (I pray) had the most holy Paul in his mind when he wrote to certain, Little children of whom I travail in birth again until Christ be formed in you, and elsewhere too to those who through faith are perfected in spirit, But WE all with unveiled face reflecting the glory of the Lord are changed into His image from glory to glory as by the Lord the Spirit; now the Lord is the Spirit, and where the Spirit of the Lord, there liberty? Doth he therefore say this to the Galatians as not having the impress in regard to bodily freedom, of that which is of the seed of David after the flesh, but is he travailing again with them that Christ after the flesh may somehow be engraven on them and formed in them? albeit how will not every body (I suppose) unhesitatingly say, that all who are on the earth are conformed one to another and to Christ Himself, in so far as He is conceived of as man, Who is both Man and with us? what formation then unto Christ was it that was sought for in them? or how are WE transformed from glory to glory, what form leaving, unto what are we transelemented? Let therefore the Divine initiator come forward and teach us, the Priest of the Divine Mysteries, the teacher of the Gentiles in faith and verity; for whom (says he) He knew, and predestinated to be conformed to the image of His Son, them, He also called. Therefore (as I said just now) in that He was made man and was of the seed of Abraham, we all are conformed to Him: all therefore who are on earth, the Father both fore-knew and fore-ordained; and these having called He sanctified and glorified. But verily not all were fore-ordained, not all were sanctified or glorified:----the fact therefore of conformation unto the Son will not be conceived of as existing in the nature alone of the flesh or of manhood, but in another way also, and this the blessed Paul sets before ua saying, And as we bare the image of the earthy we shall bear the image too of the heavenly; calling the image of the earthy, that of our forefather Adam, of the heavenly, that of Christ. What then first is the image of our forefather? proneness to sin, becoming under death and decay. What again that of the heavenly? being in no wise overcome of passions, not knowing to transgress, not being subject to death and decay, holiness, righteousness, and whatever are akin to and like these. But these (I suppose) will befit the Divine and Untaint Nature to possess: for superior to both sin and decay is Holiness and Righteousness. Herein does the Word out of God the Father restore us too, rendering us partakers of His own Divine Nature through the Spirit.

He has therefore brothers like to Himself and bearing the image of His Divine Nature, in regard of holiness; for thus is Christ formed in us, the Holy Ghost as it were transelementing us from things human unto those that are His own. Therefore to us too said the blessed Paul, But YE are not in the flesh, but in the spirit. Therefore the Son transfers not ought at all of things that have been made into the Nature of His own Godhead (for that were impossible): but there is impressed on those who have been made partakers of His Divine Nature through their partaking of the Holy Ghost the spiritual Likeness with Him, and the Beauty of the Ineffable Godhead flashes upon the souls of the saints. Why then dost thou assigning the mere and alone likeness of the flesh, not blush, disregarding the Divine and Spiritual forming, yea rather taking it utterly away? Yet the Lord of all and Only-Begotten God lowered Himself unto emptiness for our sakes, that He might bestow on us the Dignity of brotherhood with Him and the Beauty worthy of all love, of His Innate Nobility: and this man, bereaving us of all that is most lovely, says that a mere man hath become our brother and shews that sure (as he supposes) is his account hereof, adding "Mark too what is straightway joined on to these, That He might be a merciful and faithful High Priest in things God-ward, for in that He Himself hath suffered being tempted, He is able to succour them that are tempted. Therefore a merciful High Priest is He That suffered: passible is the Temple, not the quickening God of him which hath suffered." Therefore that by choosing thus to think and moreover daring to say it too, he severs again into distinct hypostases and into two Persons, the Word from forth God the Father and him whom himself has just introduced to us as a God-bearing man, if so be that one and apart by himself is he that suffered, and another he that quickeneth, I suppose that no one whatever will doubt.

But in another way also is he beside himself, having quaffed wine from forth the vine of Sodom, and drunk with error and haply not even knowing what he saith: for where hath the Word out of God the Father been called (I shudder at saying it) the God of Christ? for there is One Lord Jesus Christ, and one faith in Him, not as though in two distinct persons, but as through one Baptism into One Son and God and Lord, the Word out of God the Father even when He became Man. For not because He became as we, will He lose the being God (how should He?) nor yet because He is God by Nature, doth He hold the likeness to us inadmissible nor will He reject the being man; but as He hath remained in human nature God, so being both in the Nature and Pre-eminence of the Godhead, none the less is He Man. Both therefore in the Same, and One God and Man is Emmanuel.

But this good man rejecting the mode of the Economy as uncomely, removeth from God the Word the human, that He may at last be clearly seen to have in no way aided our condition. For he says that not He became an High Priest both Merciful and Faithful, but allots this rather to him that suffered as being other than He. Yet how should he not, if he had desired to be a wise initiator, have made an exact muster of the expressions and ideas that are in the God-inspired Scripture and considered that this is a thing which is both truly God-befitting and not apart from what befits and beseems the emptying: and how we will say as briefly as we can.

The God of all uttered the Law to them of old, Moses being mediator. But there was not in the Law the power of achieving good without any blame, to those who wished it (for it hath perfected nothing). But neither was the first covenant found faultless, but the all-wise Paul called it the ministry of condemnation. I hear him say, We know that what things soever the law saith, it saith to them who are under the law, that every mouth may be stopped and all the world may become under sentence before God, because by the deeds of the law there shall no flesh be justified in His sight, (for the Law worketh unto wrath, and the Letter killeth), and as himself somewhere saith, He that despised Moses' law dieth without mercy under two or three witnesses. Seeing therefore that the Law condemneth them that sin and decreeth sometimes the uttermost punishment to them that disregard it, and in no wise pitieth, how was not the manifestation to them on the earth of a Compassionate and truly Merciful High Priest necessary? of One Who should make the curse to cease, should stop the condemnation and free sinners with forgiving grace and with the bending [of clemency? for I (He says) am He that blotteth out thy transgressions and will not remember. For we have been justified by faith and not out of the works of the Law, as it is written. On Whom then believing are we justified? is it not on Him who suffered death for us after the flesh? is it not on One Lord Jesus Christ? have we not on declaring His Death and confessing His Resurrection been redeemed? If therefore we have believed on a man like us and not rather on God, the thing is man-worship, and confessedly nothing else: but if we believe that He That suffered in the flesh is God, Who hath been made also our High Priest, we have no ways erred, but acknowledge the Word out of God made Man: and thus is required of us faith God-ward, Who putteth out of condemnation and freeth from sin those that are taken thereby. For the Son of man hath authority on the earth also to forgive sins, as Himself too saith. Contrasting therefore with the salvation and grace that is through Christ the harshness (so to speak) of the law's severity, we say that Christ was made a Merciful High Priest. For He was and is God Good by Nature and Compassionate and Merciful always, and hath not become this in time but was so manifested to us. And He has been named Faithful, [3] as abiding what He is always, according to what is said of the Father Himself too, But God is faithful Who will not suffer you to be tempted above that ye are able.

A merciful and faithful High-Priest therefore has Emmanuel been made unto us; for (as Paul saith) the one were many priests because they were by death hindered from remaining, He, because He continneth for ever, hath a priest-hood that passeth not, wherefore He is able to save also unto the uttermost them that come unto God through Him, ever living to intercede for them. That the Word out of the Father hath remained God, albeit made priest, as it is written, on account of the fashion and mode that befitteth the Economy with flesh, the word of the blessed Paul hath been sufficient unto our full assurance, for he said again, Now of the things which have been said this is the sum, We have such an High Priest, Who sat at the Right Hand of the Throne of the Majesty in the heavens, a Minister of the sanctuary and of the Very Tabernacle which the Lord pitched and not man. Yiew therefore view the Word Which sprang of God illustrious as God in supremest excellencies and in the Seat of Godhead, and the Same executing the Priest's Office as man and offering to the Father no sacrifice of earth but Divine rather and spiritual and how He has Heaven as His Holy Tabernacle. For not after the law of a carnal commandment has He been made High Priest, but after the power of an indissoluble life, as it is written. Faithful therefore is He in this too, and sure to them who come to Him, that He is able full easily to save them quite, for with His own Blood and with One Offering hath He perfected for ever them that are sanctified. For this I deem doth the holy Paul shew us saying, for in that He Himself hath suffered, being tempted, He is able to succour them that are tempted. Why then unrecking of thoughts which pertain unto piety and straying from words of rightness and truth, does he say, "He That suffered is a Merciful High Priest, Passible the Temple, not the Life-giving God of Him Who suffered?"

That the Word of God then hath of His own Will suffered in the flesh for our sakes, shall be shewn in its own time: but that he is severing the Inseverable and setting forth two christs by the effect of his ideas, even though he clearly say One Christ, he shall be no less convicted through what has been forthwith subjoined, for he said again,

> "Abraham's seed is He Who was yesterday and to-day, according to the voice of Paul, not He Who saith, Before Abraham was, I am. Like to His brethren in all things, He Who assumed brotherhood of human soul and body, not He Who saith, He that hath seen Me hath seen the Father, He was sent Who is consubstantial with us and has been anointed to preach remission to the captives and recovery of sight to the blind, for the Spirit of the Lord is upon Me, wherefore He anointed Me."

§3. Thou severest therefore into two again and that patently, then how art thou not convicted of being sensual and having not the Spirit, as saith the disciple of the Saviour? but the might of the Truth will array itself (o man) against thy words. For we affirm that the Word Himself out of God the Father took hold of Abraham's seed, and made His own body having a reasonable soul the body which was assumed of the holy Virgin. And verily by true union do we say that One and the Same is He Who was yesterday and to-day and for ever, and Who before Abraham Divinely, was made man after and underwent birth of a woman. Hence He will not lie in saying, Verily I say unto you, Before Abraham was I am.

But he does not the least understand what yesterday and to-day and for ever is. For that he may shew that the Word of God is Eternal and that by Nature and superior to change and turn, even though He have been made Man, he parted the whole of time into three periods, and puts yesterday of past time, to-day of the present, and for ever of the future. But this boorish man against reason [says] that yesterday and to-day are spoken by him of a common man, not considering that it will full surely shew Him to have been older and pre-existent to His own Birth, if He were at all of yesterday, which is indicative of time past. That not one is He that is yesterday and to-day, Jesus Christ, another He Who saith, before Abraham was I am, but One and the Same by a true Union, the Word having been made Man as we and having preserved to His own Nature, even when He was made man, the being without beginning in time, one may see and that without trouble, in the God-inspired Scripture. For as the blessed Evangelist John saith of Christ the Saviour of us all, John beareth witness of Him and hath cried saying, He That cometh after me has been made before me, for He was before me, and again, The next day he looketh at Jesus coming unto him and saith, Behold the Lamb of God Which taketh away the sin of the world, This is He of Whom I said, After me cometh a Man Which has been made before me, for He was before me. Thou seest then and that very clearly the Divine-uttering Baptist calling Jesus a Man and coming after, as being late-born and after him, yet preceding him and pre-existing, for this, I deem, the words, for He was before me and has been made before me, mean. How then if He is a Man, is He conceived of as pre-existing and is said to be before: him who had the start of Him in time and had his birth in the flesh older than His? For if this were said of a man like us, every body would (I suppose) be at a loss to defend it, but in regard to Christ the Saviour of us all, there is no difficulty. For He Who is out of God makes His own the birth of His own flesh, yet is He not ignorant that He is Maker of the worlds and hath pre-existence as God, and is Co-eternal with His own Father. For we do not say that He hath His Being contemporaneous with the birth of His own body, but was (as I said) ineffably begotten of the Essence of God the Father. Therefore having His Being before Abraham as God even though He was made Man, He will not speak falsely in saying, as One in truth both Son and Lord, Before Abraham was I am.

And marvel not if He hath apportioned to His own Nature the being before Abraham, but consider rather that albeit He had taken a body of the holy Virgin, He said to Nicodemus, If I have told you earthly things and ye believe not, how shall ye believe if I tell you heavenly things? and no man hath ascended up into heaven but He That came down from Heaven, the Son of Man, albeit He was called son of man too, born of a woman after the flesh. Will

He then be false in saying that there hath come down from Heaven the son of man, i. e., Himself? Not so, for He is Himself the Truth. How then will the son of man be rightly conceived of as from above? because the Word being God and out of the Essence That is above all, is said to have come down and to have taken the servant's form. Therefore He converseth with us, not as any longer bare Word, but man as we, and as already conceived of as One with the Flesh united to Him. And as by reason of what beseemeth the emptiness, He maketh His own all that belongs to His own Flesh, albeit by Nature unembodied; so Himself being from above and out of Heaven, He allotteth again the coming from above to Himself even when He hath been made Man, even though He hath been born according to the flesh with us of a woman. The properties therefore of the human nature have become the very own of the Word, those again of the Word Himself, the very own of the human nature: for thus is conceived of One Christ and Son and Lord.

But since this innovator has added that " like to His brethren in all things is He Who assumed brotherhood of human soul and flesh, not He Who saith, He that hath seen Me hath seen the Father," come now let us again consider as we can what it is which he here saith. For that the Son is the Image and Impress of God the Father, he too hath confessed: who again "He is Who of human soul and body assumed brotherhood," i. e., with us, let him come forward and teach; for no one would say that a man like us, such as (for example) Barnabas or Paul or any other of those who are reckoned among men, would be said to take brotherhood of human soul and body, as though he were ought else than this, and so took it, but he is so rather in being what he is. Not one therefore who is man could be conceived as taking the being what he is, as though it were other than he: but it will beseem rather the Word which sprang forth of God, having no rank among us in regard to the count of His own Nature, to take "brotherhood of human soul and body" with us. And the word of the truth contends on our side and the tradition of the undefiled Faith. It holds then that God the Word in the Form of God the Father has been made our Brother in all things, taking "brotherhood of human soul and body," and will not speak falsely in saying, He that hath seen Me hath seen the Father. For if any among us had fallen into such unlearning in his ideas as to suppose that God the Father Himself Which is in Heaven must needs come down, even to the having likeness with us (I mean bodily); he might well have feared lest that when Christ says, He that hath seen Me hath seen the Father, he might be imagining that He too out of Whom He is, was in form as we, and in fashion of body. But since when He was made man, He preserved the being God, and holdeth the Beauty of His own Nature untarnished, I would no wise shrink from saying that He possesseth likeness with us, in respect of His being man as we, Who is of soul and body, albeit God by Nature and Impress of the Person of Him Who hath begotten Him. One therefore and the Same is He, like to His brethren after the flesh, yet shewing in His own Nature Him too Who begat Him, in regard I say to His being God.

But this man doth not understand this (whence should he?) but adulterating (so to speak) the plan of the mystery which is right and unalloyed, he introduces to us one and another christ, and caught in Jewish accusals, perceives not where he is nor in what reach of ills he hath come. For they of the blood of Israel heard God crying aloud through one of the holy Prophets respecting Emmanuel, And THOU Bethlehem house of Ephratha, little art thou to be among the thousands of Judah; out of thee shall He come to Me to be ruler in Israel, and His goings forth from the beginning from the days of eternity: and again, His generation who shall tell? because His life is raised from the earth. And they, no wise understanding the mystery nor yet knowing that albeit God by Nature and having the origin of His Being Invisible and Incomprehensible, He was called Bethlehemite as being there born after the flesh out of the root of Jesse and David, said one to another, Is not this He Whom they seek to kill? lo, He speaketh boldly and they say nothing unto Him; do the rulers know that This Man is the Christ? Yet we know this Man whence He is, but Christ when He cometh, no man knoweth whence He is. For they heard (as I said) the Prophet saying plainly, His generation who shall tell? and that He hath His goings forth or His Being before every age. View again (I pray) the vastness of Jewish stupor: for on saying The Christ when He cometh, no one knoweth whence He is, they said again one to another, Of a truth this is the Prophet: others (it says) said, Shall Christ come out of Galilee? said not the Scripture that out of the seed of David and from Bethlehem the village where was David, the Christ cometh? Seest thou how they stagger, confessing both His being apart from beginning, Divinely, and His fleshly Generation in time? But they would not have been carried away into mis-counsel thus extravagant, if they had known truly that the Word being God, proceeded Man out of the root of Jesse and David and of the holy Virgin, and that the Lord of earth and Heaven and of all was called a Bethlehemite too, for He shared poverty with us being Rich, as it is written.

    Why therefore plunging thee in the sleights of the Jews dost thou both deem and say what it is neither lawful to say nor yet harmless to conceive of? confess with us One Christ, and do not severing into two again say this, "He was sent that is consubstantial with us and has been anointed to preach remission to the captives and recovery of sight to the blind." Whither then will go the word of the divines, who have been initiators of all under Heaven? for they have cried aloud that the very Word out of God the Father, was made Saviour and Redeemer of all, not as though a man other than He were mediating, like as Moses, but rather as come down to us in bodily likeness and form, for thus has He been anointed as High Priest and Apostle. And indeed He rebuked the Jews saying, Is it not written in your Law, I said, Ye are gods? if he called them gods to whom the word of God came and the scripture cannot be broken: Him Whom the Father sanctified and sent into the world, do YE say [to Him], thou blasphemest, because I said, I am the Son of God? why (I pray) shall we put Him Who abased Himself unto emptiness that He might save all under Heaven, forth of the most God-befitting and truly admirable achievements that have been wrought unto us-ward, by saying that there has been sent some other than He consubstantial with ourselves? albeit how were it not better to say and thus to chuse to think, that He has been both sent and hath been made consubstantial with us, i. e., man: yet abiding Consubstantial with God the Father Himself too, as He is both conceived of and was and is God? for He is, He is what He was, even when He assumed the humanity, and having sameness of Essence with God the Father Which is in Heaven, He grasped in wisdom the likeness with us too; as Mediator too has He been set forth, combining through Himself unto an union of relation things completely dissevered one from another as to the plan of their nature. For He being God by Nature has been made man in truth, that we too might be called offspring, no more of the first, that is, of the earthy, to whom it was said by God, Earth thou art and unto earth shalt thou return, who conducteth even unto death, but of the second, from above and out of Heaven, Christ I mean Who bringeth us again unto purest life, and rendereth incorrupt that which is holden of death and freeth from sins that which was enfolden by the toils of sin. Thus saith somewhere the Father Himself to the Son, Behold I have given Thee for a Covenant of the race for a Light of the [Gentiles, to open the eyes of the blind, to bring forth of chains the bound and of the prison-house them that sat in darkness; and again by the voice of Isaiah, The beasts of the field shall honour Me, the Sirens and the daughters of the ostriches, because I gave water in the wilderness and rivers in the thirsty land to give drink to Mine offspring, chosen, My people whom I won for Myself, to declare My Virtues. The which understanding very well of those of the Gentiles called through faith unto true knowledge of God, the Divine-uttering Peter writeth and saith, But YE are a chosen race, a royal priesthood, an holy nation, a peculiar people, that ye should tell out the Virtues of Him Who calleth you out of darkness into His wondrous light, of old not a people, but now a people.

But if as seems good to thee to think and say, "he was sent who is consubstantial with us," no longer with the Father, in no wise have WE been made partakers of the Divine Nature, but have abode as I said, and are yet offspring of the first, of him who conducteth unto curse and death and under penalty of sin. We have therefore been deceived [4] and are no less now too in that case wherein we were of old and before the Advent. How then did old things pass away and lo they have become new? and where is, If any be in Christ, he is a new creature?

But are you ashamed to confess the Word of God God made man as we? do you therefore chide Him and say that He hath planned no wise matter when He emptied Himself for our sakes? Therefore thou shalt hear Him say, Get thee behind Me Satan, thou art an offence unto Me, for thou savourest not the things that be of God but those of men. Search with us the God-inspired Scripture; He appeared of old to the Patriarch Jacob too when he was departing from Laban's hearth, and was at the very fords of Jabok, as it is written: for Jacob was left alone and there was wrestling a man with him until morning, and he knows that he prevaileth not against him and he touched the flat of his thigh and the flat of Jacob's thigh stiffened in his wrestling with him; and he said to him, Dismiss me for the dawn hath gone up, and he said, I will not dismiss Thee except Thou bless me. And after other again, And Jacob called the name of that place, The Form of God, for I saw God Face to face and my life was preserved; and the sun rose upon him when he passed by the Form of God. Understand therefore how not as incorporeal and impalpable Word did He deign to shew Himself then to the Patriarch, foreshewing to him the type of the mystery, but He Who wrestled and consumed the whole night thereupon was a man. But when the day was dawning and it was morning, He says, Dismiss Me, which was clearly the word of one who was bringing to an end the wrestling.

And what is the plan of the mystery, it is necessary to say. With them who abide as it were in night and darkness, and have a spiritual mist o'er mind and heart and I cannot yet understand the mystery Him-ward, He useth to wrestle and fight and overcome; but with them who are []now in light and so to speak in spiritual morning and have good understanding of the Mystery, He thinketh not good any longer to wrestle, but dispenseth to them instead spiritual blessings. Hence if even at length and hardly you should enter in yourself too into the light and so to speak into the morning, He Who conquereth all would cease fighting with you. And see how whereas it was a man who wrestled, the Divine-uttering Jacob says that he had seen God Face to face: and the sacred Scripture added that the sun arose upon him when he passed by the Form of God. Why therefore (I pray) are you ashamed at the measures of the emptiness, albeit every one (I suppose) who both holds the right faith and examines accurately the aim of the God-inspired Scripture says that the Word out of God the Father was both Incarnate and made Man? He therefore Who is consubstantial with us, in that He has been made Man, and to the Father Himself, in that He hath remained God even in human nature, was sent preaching remission to the captives and recovery of sight to the blind, and to heal the broken in heart, and to call the acceptable year of the Lord: for His Alone and of none other are the deeds which have been wrought us, and one of the holy Prophets shall be our pledge, thus saying, No ambassador, no angel, but the Lord Himself saved us, who also most clearly saith to us, Therefore My people shall know My Name in that day, I Who speak am present. Albeit if he who has been sent were some mere man, how would Himself be conceived of as having spoken the Law which was long ago given to them of old? for not at all proceeding as man, would He be said to have been made man, lest He should be seen to have an existence elder to His coming into being: but preexisting as God, He hath spoken indeed the Law, but says that He is present in some strange and unwonted way when He has been made Man.

"But yes (says he) the Word being God fulfils all things: how then was He also sent, for where was He not Who fulfils all things?" what (tell me) shall we admit that the Divine and Consubstantial Trinity has been contracted rather than that it is spread over all and fulfils all things? Then how hath the great Moses, when some of them of old were building the Heaven-reaching tower, introduced God saying, Come let us go down and there confound their tongues? what descent needed the Nature That fills both Heaven and earth? it is written of the Holy Ghost too, The Spirit of the Lord hath filled the earth; the blessed David sings and says of them that lie in the earth to God Who is mighty to quicken, Thou shalt send forth Thy Spirit and they shall be created and Thou shalt renew the face of the earth. How is That sent forth which filleth all things? Do not therefore (putting forward as something clever and hard to be overturned, that He Who is mighty to fulfil all things, the Word out of God the Father, has His mission an impossibility) hasten to undo the truth and to overturn the power of the Mystery; but consider rather that He speaketh in human wise of the things that belong to God and they are conceived of by us in such sort as both Himself Alone may know, and as He is wont to act.

But since as little and human and in boundless degree below the dignity of the Only Begotten He receives the unction, come let us say what is reasonable upon this point too, undoing occasions of offence. If therefore He have not been made Man, let Him shake off things human, let Him repudiate the Economy as putting Him in inferior position and setting Him behind the Supreme Glory and God-befitting Excellence; for petty to the Word is what is ours. But since the Mystery is of a truth wise and the fact of the emptying not to be rejected by Him, why dost thou foolhardily find fault with things that are right? and turn away as uncomely what is crowned with His Approval? didst thou see Him anointed humanly? behold the same also anointing Divinely [5] [: for it is written that John too bare record saying, I saw the Spirit descending like a dove and abiding upon Him and I knew Him not, but He That sent me to baptize with water, He said unto me, Upon Whom thou shalt see the Spirit descending and remaining on Him, This is He which baptizeth with the Holy Ghost, and I have seen and borne record that This is the Son of God, For dost thou say that it is the work of the human nature to have power to baptize with the Holy Ghost them that believe? albeit how were it not folly to think that this were so? for how would the less bestow the participation of that which is immeasurably superior? And observe that this very person upon Whom the Spirit is said to soar down and to remain upon Him, baptizeth with the Holy Ghost, anointing (it is plain) as God with His own Spirit them that believe. And verily He rose from the dead, and breathed on His disciples, saying, Receive ye the Holy Ghost. And they receiving, say, WE received not the spirit of the world but the Spirit Which is out of God, that we might know the things that were freely given to us of God. The most wise Paul too writes, They that are in the flesh cannot please God, but YE are not in the flesh but in the spirit if so be that the Spirit of God dwell in you: if any man have not the Spirit of Christ, this man is not His. And elsewhere too, For as many as are led by the Spirit of God, these are the sons of God. Therefore when thou seest Him anointed with His own Spirit, remember the economy with flesh and take count of the human nature: when thou seest Him give the Spirit, with this marvel at God in human nature too.

But taking no account of these things this contentious man says again thus:

"This [6] is he who was made a faithful High Priest to God, for he was made so, he was not so from eternity, this, heretic, is he who by little and little advanced unto the dignity of the high priesthood. Hear a clearer voice calling out to thee, Who in the days (it says) of His Flesh, when He offered up prayers and supplications with mighty cry and tears unto Him That was able to save Him from death and was heard for His Piety, though He were Son, He learned obedience by the things He suffered and, made perfect, became unto them that obey Him the Author of indissoluble salvation. That is perfected which advances by little and little, heretic. Respecting which John too cries out in the Gospels, Jesus was advancing in stature and wisdom and grace, conformably to which things Paul too speaking says, Made perfect He became unto all them that obey Him the Author of eternal salvation, called of God an High Priest after the order of Melchisedelc, this is he who is compared with Moses in regard to generalship, that is called seed of Abraham, that is like in all things to his brethren, that was made High Priest in time, that was perfected through sufferings, that in that he suffered beting tempted is able to succour them that are tempted, that is called an High Priest after the order of Melchisedek. Why then interpret contrary to Paul, commingling the Impassible God the Word with earthly body and making Him a passible High Priest?"

§4. Most vigorous onslaught, my friend, and truly spirited hast thou made upon the doctrines of piety. And the Divine-uttering Baruch, pointing out the Word of God already Incarnate and seen in likeness to us, says, This is our God, there shall none other be accounted of in comparison of Him, He found out all the way of knowledge and gave it to Jacob His servant and to Israel His beloved: afterward did He shew Himself upon earth and conversed with men.

But THOU calling out and that full often, This, yea all but putting forth thine hand;----who is it that you manifest to believers and cause to be seen of them, yea, and say that he advanced by little and little unto High Priesthood? I suppose it is surely he of whom but now specifying thou saidst, "Therefore a Merciful High Priest is he that suffered, not the quickening God of him that suffered: the seed of Abraham he who is yesterday and to-day, as Paul saith, not he who saith, Before Abraham was I am; like to his brethren in all things he that assumed brotherhood of human soul and flesh, not He Who saith, He that hath seen Me, hath seen the Father." And that in affirming that the Life-giving Word of God is God of him who suffered, involving yourself in the charge of inevitable blasphemy, you have done no slight wrong, sufficient reasoning made clear to us. But I marvel that thyself oblivious of thine own words, thou deemest right to say alike and think that He by little and little advanced unto the dignity of the High Priest, Whom thou sayest is even God Almighty. For the Epistle written to the Hebrews being before thee, thou art caught saying, "Yet is This man Who after the flesh is akin to Israel, Who in that which is visible is Man, Who according to Paul's speech was made out of the seed of David, by connection God Almighty." How did He yet advance, according to that idle talk, to the dignity of High Priest albeit testified by thy voice too as Almighty God?

And though you utter the ill-famed connection and invented I know not whence by yourself alone, I will pass it over for the present: but I will ask, bidding the argument advance straight on its own befitting and proper course, Does not that which advances unto Priesthood and glory make its advance or progress unto the better and more excellent? and how will not every one whatever give his vote for the truth of this? Greater therefore than the being Almighty God, is the High Priesthood. Then how does he whose lot is the Priesthood minister too and stand as a worshipper by God, and as a servant by his master, offering what is customable and bringing sacrifices, and He Who is crowned with the Supreme glory receives the sacrifices and is honoured by the service?

But thou sayest (I suppose) this, Being God Almighty the Same hath become High-Priest. He hath been emptied [7] therefore and hath abased Himself by descent into the inferior. How therefore did He yet advance unto dignity when made an High Priest? Remember again thine own words, for thus thou saidst a little above, "If the Godhead be High Priest, who is He who is served by the ministry of the High Priesthood? if He Who offereth be God, there is none to whom the offering is made, for what is there worthy of Godhead that as inferior It should make offering to a greater?" Stand now at least to your own words; but this you cannot do, for you will be borne about (so to say) by every wind, and perceive not that you are being driven about, one while springing off from those into these, other while again from these into those, and in no wise are you afraid of what Paul saith, For if what I destroyed this I build again, I make myself a transgressor.

But you will perhaps say, Affirming that the Word out of God the Father is everywhere One Christ and Son and Lord, with His own Flesh, how sayest thou now that He has been set forth as an High Priest and Apostle? dost thou not in so saying insult the Supreme Dignity of His Divine Glory?

Because, good Sir, (shall I say) the Only Begotten Word of God has been made man and in the measures of the human nature, the fact of Priesthood will not unbefit Him, and moreover the saying that He has been sent, for He despised the shame, as the Divine-uttering Paul writes, and endured yet lower and worser things for our sakes: for He gave His bach to the scourges, His Face He turned not away from the shame of spittings, and endurant He bore the contumelies of the Jews. But thou deemest not meet to call Him Priest, as being God? admit the words pertaining to the Economy, consider the emptying, the descent unto the servant's form. For we say not that the Word of God advanced and hastened unto dignity, if He have been styled our High Priest, but rather that He descended herein too unto emptiness. Since how has He been emptied and is He said to have been abased, albeit He possesseth unchangeableness and is in Form and Equality in everything with His Father? how too advanced He by little and little and this (as thyself sayest) unto the dignity of the High Priesthood? what sort of growth received He hereunto? If then it were a bodily one, I will ask again, Doth bodily growth lead up to the glory of the Priesthood: be then this common [to all] and let this method of reasoning of yours belong to every one who advanceth bodily, But of a truth the Priesthood beseemeth not all those who customably advance unto bodily growth; how therefore blushest thou not in putting forth unto us for demonstration of those things which thou saidst, what was spoken by the Divine-uttering Luke, But Jesus was advancing in stature and wisdom and grace?

But thou sayest that the growth was unto wisdom, albeit how is not this without learning? for we believe that out of the very belly and womb of the Virgin, Emmanuel being God proceeded forth Man, full surely of the wisdom and grace that are inherent of Nature. What sort of growth then will He admit of, in Whom are all the treasures of wisdom, Who is with God the Father Co-giver of the grace from above? how then is He said to advance? it is, I deem, by God the Word co-measuring with the increase and stature of His own Body, the manifestation of the most God-befitting goods that are in Him. For let us consider that although He has been made Man as we, He was zealous to lie hid at the first, and administered by little and little as it were noiselessly and in silence the might of the Mystery; and of this God the Father Himself will be our assurance saying, Jacob My Servant, I will defend Him, Israel My chosen, My Soul received Him, I gave My Spirit upon Him, He shall bring forth judgement to the Gentiles: He shall not cry nor lift up, nor shall His voice be heard without: a bruised reed. He shall not break and smoking flax He shall not quench. And He was somewhere rebuking the holy Apostles themselves that they should not make Him, known. Hence a thing unwonted and strange and worthy of looking into, would have been shewn, if being yet a babe, He had made a God-befitting demonstration of wisdom: but He little and little and proportionably to bodily stature, extending it and making it manifest to all, will be said to advance and that with reason. [8] How therefore did He advance by little and little unto the Priesthood, tell me, by being perfected in virtue? Then how or whence may one doubt that that which faileth of perfection in virtue, will be under blame, and not wholly an object of admiration, yea rather haply under charge of sin? But it is indeed true that He hath done no sin neither was guile found in His Mouth, as it is written. Full-perfect therefore is He being such unto every thing, and in no wise will He have the lack of being complete unto the achievement of virtue. And when was He That was God in the womb too not Perfect unto good, of Whom the Prophet Isaiah too saith, Butter and honey shall He eat, before He have knowledge to prefer evil, He shall choose the good, because before the Child shall know good or ill, He shall disobey vice to choose the good? where then will you be able to demonstrate Christ's yet imperfectness unto good? or what advance will He need who is so Perfect as to disobey vice and to prefer to it, yea only choose, good?

Yet I know not how he who affirmeth and saith "This is he who by little and little advanced to the dignity of the high priesthood," and who brought forward in proof of his words, Jesus advanced in stature and wisdom and grace, all but marking out the uncomeliness of his own words and gliding into forgetfulness of the things of which he assumed were right, affirms to us that the mode of perfection was wrought in another way, saying, "This is he who in time has been made High Priest, who was perfected through sufferings." Is not this manifest distraction? yea rather a proof of utter recklessness? for our Lord Jesus Christ has been made perfect through sufferings, but this man albeit he was not ignorant of the mode of being made perfect, carries away the minds of the simpler unto certain strange perversions of ideas and says that He advanced unto being High Priest and has been perfected unto this, "Who is said to have been emptied because this took place. And as though he had full clearly shewn that neither was the Word of God made flesh, nor yet proceeded Man out of woman, he chides those who have chosen thus to hold and says, "Why therefore doth thou mis-interpret Paul, commingling with earthly body the Impassive God the Word and making Him a passible High Priest?" Hear therefore from us too, to whom rather the truth is dear, Why dost thou mis-interpret Paul, yea rather slanderest the whole God-inspired Scripture, withdrawing the Word of God from the economy with flesh, and settest over us as priest a man honoured with mere connection? albeit thou hearest that the Same is at once High Priest and Co-Throned with God the Father, as we have already said. For Paul said, We have such an High Priest, Who sat on the Right Hand of the Throne of the Majesty in the heavens. For that the Word out of God the Father is Impassible, is I suppose clear to every one: that He hath suffered for us in the flesh, the voice of inspired men will seal up for a truth. But if thyself bear away the Word out of God from earthly body, the whole will come to nothing. For if He have not been made Man, neither did He die for us, and if He have not given unto death His own Body, how is He said to be the first begotten from the dead? Hence Christ neither died nor revived. Let the Divine-uttering Paul therefore come forward, let him cry aloud saying, If the dead are not raised, neither has been Christ raised, if Christ have not been raised, vain is your faith, ye are yet in your sins: they also which fell asleep in Christ perished. But Christ has been raised from the dead, for the Only-Begotten Word of God has been made Man and, taking an earthly body and uniting it Personally to Him, by the grace of God, as it is written, tasted death for every man. He has been named first-fruits of them that slept, having been raised from the dead. Sure therefore and not vain is now our faith, which we have as an anchor of the soul both sure and stedfast, as it is written.

And he, as though he had in no wise wronged the plan of the economy with flesh, through saying such things and pouring forth untempered and foulest vomit upon the doctrines of the truth, proceeds to another mis-counsel, yea rather manifest blasphemy and says,

Cyril of Alexandria

"This man alone [9] therefore being our High Priest, feeling and kin and sure, turn ye not away from the faith Him-ward; for He was sent, the blessing which was proraised us out of the seed of Abraham, as offering the sacrifice of His Body for Himself alike and His race."

§5. Thou sayest that a High Priest both kin to us and feeling and sure and moreover only, is he whom thy discourse but now clearly taught us of. For thou saidst, "The seed of Abraham is he who is yesterday and to-day, as Paul saith, not He Who saith, Before Abraham was I am; Like to His brethren in all things, he who assumed brother-hood of human soul and flesh, not He Who said, He that hath seen Me hath seen the Father; sent was he who is consubstantial with us and has been anointed to preach remission unto the captives and recovery of sight to the blind." This man therefore will be conceived of as of kin too to those on the earth, and not as THOU sayest, He That saith, He that hath seen Me hath seen the Father. For if gathering both into one according to true union thou with us confessest One Son, thou hast laboured in vain, in bearing away each separately and apart from other, severing into hypostases and persons, completely, not in the mere knowledge that the nature of flesh is other than the Divine Nature yet by concurrence unto true union hath become Its own: if on the other hand desiring to shew thyself irreconcileable in opinion with us and utterly repudiating the union, thou sayest that He is one and another, and that the One has been begotten out of God the Father, the other of kin and consubstantial with us; how (tell me) dost thou say that we ought not now to turn aside from faith to Him-ward? and we shall believe him to be our kin, letting go Him Who saith, Before Abraham was I am: we shall take as our god him who assumed brotherhood with us of human soul and flesh, letting go Him Who saith, He that hath seen Me hath seen the Father, albeit Himself saith, For so God loved the world that He gave His Only-Begotten Son that whosoever believeth in Him should not perish but have everlasting life, and again, He that believeth on Him is not condemned, but he that believeth not is condemned already, because he hath not believed in the Name of the Only-Begotten Son of God. Is he therefore who is forth of the seed of Abraham conceived of as Only-Begotten apart and by himself, albeit John hath clearly written, The Only-Begotten Son which is in the Bosom of the Father, He declared Him, and moreover another Holy Scripture, But when He bringeth in the First-begotten into the world, He saith, And let all Angels of God worship Him? But First-born wholly and surely will He be Who is among many brethren, not He Who is begotten Alone of the Alone God the Father: for thus far will we follow, sir, thy distinctions, keenly awaiting for the economy's sake, whither the words burst through upon us. Hence (for I will call back the argument to its commencement) "he that assumed brotherhood with us of human soul and flesh," yet was made out of the seed of Abraham, will be the Firstborn among many brethren, but He that is in the Bosom of God the Father, the Only-Begotten God the Word. Then when the God-inspired Scripture says that our faith must be had in the Only-Begotten Son of God, why dost thou, putting forward one kin and consubstantial with us, say that we ought not to turn away from faith in him-ward? It is therefore necessary to link together [3] in One Lord and Christ, by personal coalescence [that is, in order that the Same may be conceived of as Only-Begotten and First-Begotten in the Same, in that the

Word out of God the Father being God by Nature has been made Man as we and out of the seed of Abraham.

But now something clever has been found out as he thinks by him and thus again says he:

"Remember by all means what I have full often said to you, refusing two-fold natures in our Lord Christ, two-fold in nature, single in dignity: for the sway of the natures is for the connection's sake, one, the natures abiding ever in their own order, but the dignity connected as I said before unto a single sway."

§6. Yea apt at learning wert thou, who hast chosen to follow the God-inspired Scripture, which says One Lord Jesus Christ and does not put apart Him Who is out of the seed of Abraham and the Word out of God the Father. And besides one must consider this too: for one thing indeed is Godhead, another, manhood like ours, according to the inherent nature of things; but by coalescence unto true union, One Christ out of both, as we have full often said. But when the hypostases, as YOU say, have been severed into two and are conceived of as existing separately and apart, how will there be a coalescence in one Person, except one be conceived of as the property of the other: just as of a man's soul his body will be conceived of as the property, albeit of other nature than it, for not the same things are soul and body?

But (one may perchance say) how is the Holy and Adorable Trinity distinguished into Three Hypostases, yet issues in One Nature of Godhead? Because (I would say) the identity of Essence following of necessity upon the difference of ....[10], carries up the mind of believers unto One Nature of Godhead: but in respect to Emmanuel, since Godhead is something other than manhood, unless we say that the Body of the Word became His own by true Union, how will One Person be effected, when either hypostasis, apart by itself, brings before us the property of both? And except the assumed have been made the own of the assumer, connection by concurrence simply in dignity alone and sway will not suffice to effect One Only Christ, the Same God Alike and Man. For then, then, in very sooth, [it will behove not [11]] to turn aside from the faith unto Himward, even though He be conceived of as out of the seed of Abraham after the flesh. But if you say that He is one and other and then affirm that our faith must be put in him that is out of the seed of Abraham, be well assured that you are pouring down upon your own head the charge of man-worship, albeit you repudiate and rightly the repute of being a man-worshipper.

Yea and thinking it too little to deem aright, he slanders in another way too the great Mystery of godliness. For he subjoins forthwith,

"For he was sent to us, the blessing being promised out of the seed of Abraham, offering the sacrifice of his body for himself alike and his race."

Was Christ then Himself too made under sin? He through whom sin's mouth against us is stopped, according to the Psalmist's voice? did the darkness of accursed crime touch the Very Light Himself? needed then with us He through Whom is all redemption and hope of salvation a redeemer and Saviour? it will befit him (it seems) with us to offer thanksgiving, when God in His Clemency says, I am He That blotteth out thy sins and I will not remember them; him too even as we will the father of sin accuse. And then how will he not speak falsely saying, The prince of this world cometh, and in Me he shall find nothing? The presidents of the synagogue of the Jews once blasphemed against Him, for when they were worn out by the darts of envy, at seeing the blind from his birth in unwonted manner healed, they impiously said, Give glory to God, WE know that this man is a sinner, but our Lord Jesus Christ, convicting them of unbridled utterance said plainly, Which of you convicteth Me of sin? and if I say the truth, why do YE not believe Me? Hence, if He have offered sacrifice, both for us and moreover for Himself too, He surely hath needed it, even as we too who are under the yoke of sin: convict Him therefore of sin; if He hath offered sacrifice with us, shew Him co-sinner with us. Being the Good Shepherd, for whom hath He laid down His Life, for Himself rather or for the sheep? I hear Him saying of us, For their sakes do I sanctify Myself, and as the Divine-speaking Paul saith, By the grace of God for every man tasted He death, and again, He was delivered up because of our transgressions and was raised because of our justification, and as the Prophet Esaias saith, The chastisement of our peace was upon Him, with His stripes were WE healed, not Himself has been healed by the suffering of His own Flesh. He was delivered up because of our transgressions (not because of His own, far from it, for confessedly has the nature of man been borne down by the transgression in Adam unto curse and death, it is moreover sick of proneness to sin in the flesh), in order that the righteousness of the Law might be fulfilled in us who walk not after the flesh but after the spirit. For therefore was He also named the last Adam, not enduring to be sick of the things of the first one, but rather ridding in Himself first the nature of man from the blame of that ancient transgression. For it was condemned in Adam, but in Christ was seen most approved and worthy of wonder. Earthy therefore is he, but Christ heavenly. And it was put to shame in the first, borne down to disobedience which is sin, but in Christ hath it preserved untransgression, and as in a second firstfruits of the race, was seen both unwounded by sins, and superior to curse and doom and death and decay. And the most wise Paul confirms us herein, thus writing, For as through one man's disobedience the many were made sinners, so too by its obedience of one shall the many be made righteous. Every one who has become guilty of sin needs therefore sacrifice for his own transgressions: and Christ hath offered Himself for His kin according to the flesh, i. e., for us; but for Himself not a whit, being superior to sin, as God. For if He have been sacrificed for Himself, not WE alone have been bought by His Blood according to the Scriptures but Himself too will have been co-bought with us, no longer according to Isaiah's voice did the Lord give Him up for our sins, but He has been given rather for His own. For where is at all sacrifice and offering, there surely is also remission of sins. The Divine-uttering Paul therefore hath beguiled those throughout all under heaven by writing regarding Him, For such an High Priest became us, holy harmless undefiled, separated from sinners and made higher than the heavens, Who needeth not daily as the high priests to offer up sacrifice, first for his own sins then for the people's, for this He did once when He offered up Himself: for the Law maketh men high priests which have infirmity, but the word of the oath which was since the Law, the Son Who hath been perfected for evermore. How therefore is Christ an holy High Priest? or in what way harmless and undefiled? And if He need with us sacrifice, having made His offering for remission of transgressions and for justification of them that have sinned, how has He been separated from sinners, if He be justified along with them, the sacrifice having been offered for none else than these very persons? But I marvel that whereas Paul hath cried aloud and that full clearly that He is not like those who have been bidden to offer for their own transgressions, and then for the people's, thou wert not afraid to put forth the contrary to what he said, and durst say that after the likeness of them who were made priests according to the Law, He too offered up sacrifice for Himself. And if it be true that the Law maketh men High Priests which have infirmity, but the word of the oath which was since the Law, the Son Who hath been perfected for evermore, why makest thou connumerate with those who are used to infirmity Him Who has been removed from their multitude; and possesses the perfection which is above the Law, of His own and by Nature, if so be He be Son of a truth and therefore God?

But let us see from the legal and more ancient scripture too in what manner and for whom, Emmanuel hath offered Himself for an odour of a sweet smell unto God the Father. For a shadow confessedly was the Law, yet hath it the outline of the mystery Christ-ward and travails with the form of the Truth. And indeed Christ said somewhere when conversing with the Jews, Had ye believed Moses ye would have believed Me, for of Me he wrote. How therefore did they of the blood of Israel when about to depart out of the Land of the Egyptians sacrifice the Lamb? for their own selves alone or for the Lamb's sake too? whom did it redeem by its blood? was it them who were under the yoke of bondage, and were enduring the oppression hard to bear of the Egyptians, or itself too? whose destroyer did it scare away? to whom said the God of all, And I will see the blood and will shelter you? was it to those who needed His shelter or to the Lamb itself too?

For God the Father was representing the sacrifices that were to be made for sins, in the Law as on a tablet, outlining yet the mystery of Christ, and thus He said to the hierophant Moses, If the whole congregation of the children of Israel sin unwillingly and the thing be hid from the eyes of the assembly and they have done one of all the commandments of the Lord which should not be done, and have transgressed and the sin be known to them which they have sinned therein, the congregation shall offer a young bullock without blemish from among the herd for the sin. And having fully gone through how the details of the sacrifice should be done, He adds and says, And the priest shall make an atonement for them and the sin shall be forgiven them. Observe then that the bullock was offered as a type of Christ the All-Pure and That hath no spot, and they who offer and not surely the bullock were set free from their guilt. For He has been sacrificed not rather for Himself, as THOU sayest, but for the infirm, for whom the high priest according to the Law used to make supplication, that you may again understand Him That was made an Advocate for us, a High Priest undefiled and holy, separated from sinners.

Since therefore our opponent is on all sides sick of uncomeliness of speech, we say that the Word out of God the Father was made the High Priest and Apostle of our confession when He was made Man, abasing Himself unto emptiness and in our condition: in order that having offered Himself to the Father for an odour of sweet smell in behalf of all, He might win all under Heaven, might remove the ancient guilt, might justify by grace through faith, might render superior to death and decay, holy and hallowed and full well versed in every kind of virtue, confessing Him their Saviour and Redeemer, through Whom and with Whom to God the Father be glory with the Holy Ghost for evermore. Amen.

Footnotes:

1. S. Cyril in his Thesaurus, written chiefly against, the error of those who tried to make it seem that the SON was less than the FATHER, had said (cap. 21. pp. 213 d e 214 a b), "Not setting forth the Nature of the Word, but the Economy with flesh, does the Apostle say this. For when has He been made the High Priest of our confession? when Apostle? when faithful to Him who made Him? was it not when for our sakes and in our behalf He was made man and, as John says, the Word was made flesh? then became He faithful to Him who made Him, as man fulfilling His work, as Himself said : then was He made Apostle, sent in our behalf and for our sakes: then was He made High Priest of our confession, offering the Confession of our faith to the Father and presenting His own Body as a spotless sacrifice in order that He might cleanse all us through Him. If therefore it be said of the Son that He hath been made faithful, hath been made an Apostle, hath been made an High Priest, let not the expression be referred to His Being but to the quality of affairs. For Paul too being a man and existing already has been made an Apostle (not then beginning to be when he was called to the apostolate for existing previously, he was made an Apostle [these few words are supplied from the Munich MS. cited above p. 57 note y]): and Moses likewise has been made faithful in all his house, Aaron too has been made High Priest, outlining in himself too the Saviour. For as Aaron was not born High Priest but became so many years after, when he put on the long garment and the ephod and the rest of the priestly raiment, which was women's work: just so as to Christ also. For He was the Word in the beginning, but long time after He became High Priest for us, taking on Him as some long robe the man out of woman, or the Temple, in order that by His own Blood He might cleanse the people, offering Himself to God as a spotless Lamb: for He did not sin nor was guile found in His mouth."

2. This passage is given in full by Mercator p. 111 Bal. immediately after the foregoing, which had been from the eighth quire: a few words are also given before the council of Ephesus, from the sixth quire, p. 206 Bal.

3. "The sacred writers . . . acknowledged two senses of the word faithful in Scripture, first believing, then trustworthy, of which the former belongs to man, the latter to God. Thus Abraham was faithful because he believed God's word; and God faithful, for, as David says in the psalm, The Lord is faithful in all His words, or is trustworthy and cannot lie. Again, If any faithful woman have widows, she is so called from her right faith; but, It is a faithful saying, because what He hath spoken has a claim on our faith, for it is true and is not otherwise. Accordingly the words, who is faithful to Him That made Him, implies no parallel with others, nor means that by having faith He became well-pleasing: but that,

being Son of the True God, He too is faithful and ought to be believed in all He says and does, Himself remaining unalterable and not changed by His human economy and fleshly presence." S. Athanasius against the Arians ii. C. p. 289 O.T. " Faithful because Onely (...) and lasting and trusty unto the faith of His Promises." S. Cyril de recta fide to the Empresses Pulcheria and Eudocia, § 5, p. 135 d. "He is called faithful because He is able to save always them who approach through Him to God, and the Father too has been called faithful." Ib. §18, p. 148 fin.

4. or, reduced to emptiness, ... cf. Jer. ii. 5. ..., have become vain, have walked after empty gods and become themselves emptied out: so we too if our Mediator were but man, should have been reduced to utter emptiness.

5. See S.Ath. agst. Ar.i. §47.p.248 O.T. and note b.

6. Most of this is cited before the Council of Ephesus, from the sixth quire, p. 208 Bal. and in the concilia. A few words are added at the beginning, " Since he was saying of Christ that He had been sent to proclaim remission to the captives, as an Apostle he adds this too and says, This is he &c," as Mercator, or, from the sixth quire, speaking of Christ. "That He was sent to preach remission to the captives. As the Apostle adds and says, This is he &c," as the Greek Edd.

7. So too against the Arians who affirmed that the Son was exalted because man, S. Cyril, following S. Athanasius, says, "And what accession of honour has there been to Him Who is in the form of God, yet has put on the servant's form? how will H e not rather with reason seem to have been minished Who left the greater and took up the less? Being God He hath been made man in order to find----what reward? or how was He glorified Who hath descended from glory to dishonour? how hath He been made high Who disregarding the Dignity of Godhead came down even unto manhood? how hath He Who came down, been made above ? what advance hath abasement? what betterment He Who from what is better hath come into the inferior? If, God Most High, and dwelling in high places, He is said to he exalted, whither (I pray) after the Nature of God will that yet mount up which is exalted? how was He low which is in the Bosom of the Most High Father? what accession did God need? if He have therefore come down in order to be exalted, what was the need of the coming down? if He therefore abased Himself in order to be exalted, what was the need of the abasement? how is not he unwise who seeks with toil what he could have without toil ? how received He the Name which is above every name, Who was ever worshipped in it?" Thes. cap. 20 init. pp. 194,195, see S. Ath. against Ar. i. § 40. p. 237 O.T.

8. In S. Cyril's very famous 16th Paschal homily written at the beginning of previous year, A.D. 430, and cited by Andrew of Samosata in his objection to S. Cyril's fourth chapter and more fully by S. Cyril in his reply to that objection p. 172 e, he says, " And though thou hear that Jesus was progressing in stature and wisdom and grace, deem not that the Word of God became wise by accession but rather remember the Divine Paul writing on this wise, Christ God's Power and God's Wisdom :

nor dare idly to say that we shall allot to the man the progress in stature and wisdom and grace (for this I ween is nought else than to sever into two the One Christ), but (as I said before) the Son being Eternal, is in the last times of the world said to have been declared Son of God (Rom. i. 4), Economically making His own the birth of His proper flesh : so too being the Wisdom of Him Who begat Him, He is said to progress in wisdom albeit All-Perfect as God, reasonably receiving into Himself the properties of the human nature on account of the completeness of the union (dia ten eis akron henosin)." Pasch. Hom. p. 230 a b. Before this date S. Cyril had said, " And as for our sakes He abased Himself, so too for our sakes He admits progress, in order that WE again in Him might advance in wisdom who of old were made beasts by reason of sin, might advance in favour too, who of old have been hated because of the transgression in Adam. For all of ours for our sakes did Christ take into Himself that He might transform all things unto the better and might become the beginning of every good to the race of man." Thes. cap. 28 p. 251 a. In a treatise written at about the same date as the Books against Nestorius, S. Cyril says, "For the mode and plan of the economy with flesh knows that He is both as we and above us; surpassing the measure of the creation as God, and (so to speak) inferior to Himself in that He is man. For where is the abasement which He voluntarily underwent, if He refuse what is human? Yet not in these is the nature of the Word conceived to lie, but He rather makes them His own together with His own flesh, just as He does hunger and thirst and the being said to be wearied with the journey. When then thou hearest, The little one waxed and was strengthened, filled with wisdom, admit in reply the mystery of the economy with flesh. For that He was God in flesh, the blessed Evangelist will himself assure, saying, the grace of God was on it. For not as though He had grace from another God is He said to have the grace of God, but because the little one had grace which beseems God. For the Word was and is God even when He is seen in flesh, i.e. man like us. And if He be said to have grace or to advance in favour (grace) with both. God and men, it is not a whit incongruous, if even the Father Himself accepted the economy and the Son making His own what pertains to flesh because of what alike befits the mystery and is serviceable." de recta fide to the Empresses § 10 p. 139 b c d.

9. cited before council of Ephesus, from seventh quire, p. 209, Bal. &c.

10. The text here gives phuseon natures, in the MS. another hand has written over, hupostaseon. The Roman Editors conjecture, prosopon e hupostaseon, Persons or Hypostases: but see Dr. Newman's S. Athanasius against Arians p. 155 O.T. note f.

11. I have supplied these words from the expression used by S. Cyril at the beginning of this section. There seems to be an ellipse in the MS.

Cyril of Alexandria, Five Tomes Against Nestorius – Book 4

TOME IV
[Translated by P.E. Pusey]

Brazen serpent a type: how to be cured of the stings. In HOLY TRINITY Each Person exists yet each work is the work of the Whole TRINITY. Meaning of "Made flesh." Christ gives the SPIRIT as His own, and works as God through His own SPIRIT. Nicene Fathers spake through the HOLY GHOST. "Commended." The HOLY GHOST Spirit of the Truth, i. e., of CHRIST. All Divine Work work of Whole TRINITY. HOLY GHOST out of the FATHER and the Own of the SON. S. John xvii. 1. Flesh of CHRIST quickens in the Eucharist, because it is the flesh of the WORD. Its type the Lamb, its mode a mystery. Nestorius confessed that Godhead and manhood belong to the Same, and contradicts himself: yet the Eucharist does quicken us: and He is Man having remained GOD. No one taught confusion of Person in Christ.

The Divine-uttering Paul, shewing that not ineffective for the profit of those who have elected to live piously, is the shadow in the Law and besides full well setting before the minds of all, as a picture and representation of the truer, the things which long ago befell them of old, says, But these things happened unto them typically, but were written for our admonition unto whom the ends of the world are come. Come now therefore selecting out of the writings of the Law let us say, that they of Israel were camping in the desert of old time when they departed out of the land of the Egyptians and were speeding unto the Land of Promise: but when (wretched ones!) unmindful of the wonders in Egypt and of their love to Godward, they began unholily to murmur, they were destroyed of serpents, as it is written. Yet they escaped the bites of the venomous creatures, Moses having reared up for them the brazen Serpent, God the Saviour of all having commanded, Make thee a serpent and set it for a sign and it shall be, if a serpent have bitten a man, that every one that is bitten, seeing it shall live. The figure then was the mystery Christ-ward, for the Only-Begotten Word of God being God, and Good by Nature out of a Good Father, partook of flesh and blood, i. e., was made man, and like unto us wicked ones, in regard I mean that He is man as we. And He has been set up on high too, that is, He endured the cross on the wood and death after the flesh, even though He rose again the third day having trampled on the might of death.

When therefore of exceeding great lack of understanding murmuring against the economy with flesh and charging it with uncomeliness, we are ashamed to think or say that the Word of God became Man as we and was united to flesh in verity, then will the dragon, the prince of evil, slay us, infusing into our minds error, as it were the venom of his own perverseness: yet shall we escape and repel the damage of his crookedness, if with the eyes of our heart we look on the serpent, that is, if we consider with accurate mind the mystery of Christ. For then, then, deeming right shall we confess unhesitatingly that the Word of God has been made flesh, and proceeded forth of a woman along with remaining God, and is the Same God alike and Man, neither shaming of the measures of the human nature by reason of the Dignity of the Excellence, nor yet reft of His God-befitting Authority and Supreme Glory on account of the human nature. And they who are used full well to discern such things, clearly and by accurate scrutiny understanding through both the one, and the Mystery regarding Him, say, O the depth of the riches and wisdom and knowledge of God, how unsearchable His judgements and His ways not to be tracked; for who knew the mind of the Lord?

Yet doth somehow this man thrusting away these things as impossible and uncomely, dare to make no small accusal against the glory and excellence of our Saviour, and allotting to Him our measure and nought else, says that He has been glorified by the Holy Ghost, not using as His own Power, that through Him to work signs, but gaining from without and introduced, the power of achieving ought miraculous, that He may appear as we the recipient of a gift haply of healing, and be bound to say with blessed Paul, By the Grace of God I am what I am. For to whom being and being able to achieve ought is imported and from without, these will with reason utter such word as this.

For he desiring (as he thinks) to prove the Holy Trinity equal in operation unto all things, says again thus;

"God the Word was made Flesh and tabernacled in us. The Father co-seated with Himself the manhood which was assumed: for (it saith) The Lord said unto my Lord, Sit Thou on My Right Hand; the Spirit descending consummated the glory of that which was assumed, for when (He saith) the Spirit of Truth is come, He shall glorify Me. Desirest thou also another operation of the Trinity in respect of these very things? The Son indwelt in the body, the Father commended Him when baptized, the Spirit fashioned him in the Virgin." Then again he says of the holy Apostles, "The Son chose them out, for I (He says) chose you forth; the Father sanctified, for (He says) Father, sanctify them in Thy Truth, the Spirit rendered them orators."

§1. That his whole discourse has been framed both unwisely and unhappily, is full easy to shew. And in this too he wanders, and how, I will say. For One indeed is the Nature of the Godhead, but the Father exists in His Proper mode ¹and the Son too and likewise the Spirit: yet are all things wrought by the Father and through the Son in the Spirit, and when the Father is (so to say) moved to ought, yet does the Son surely work in the Spirit; and though the Son or the Spirit be said to fulfil ought, this is full surely of the Father: and through the whole Holy and Consubstantial Trinity runs the Operation alike and Will unto everything.

On this subject we say thus. But view again how clearly and evidently, although he says that the Word out of God has been made Flesh, he mis-coins the force of the ideas, and bears it far away from rightness, representing the Incarnation as an operation of His: for he adds forthwith, "wilt thou another operation of the Trinity besides these?" as though he had already shewn the first operation of God the Word, His being made Flesh according to the Scriptures. And what is the other after the first operation, he shews as he supposes. He says, "The Son indwelt in the body:" a God-clad man therefore is Christ. Next the Word of God the Father is shewn operating this alone for man: so that even though the blessed Evangelist say, The Word was made Flesh and tabernacled in us, [2] it indicates nothing else to us but just this alone, that the Word being God dwelt in a man just as in ourselves too. For we are temples of the living God, and herein know we that He is in us because He gave us of His Spirit. But thou wilt not (I suppose) say this, shuddering at the blasphemy, but wilt confess with us, that the Word of God has been made Man (and this is the Incarnation): and wilt agree that He hath remained God, and kept the Beauty of His proper Nature, even though He have the name, Son of Man, and have been made so of a truth. What then didst thou learn, and say that the Father co-seated with Himself the manhood that was assumed, and not rather that there sitteth on the Throne of His proper Godhead, in the Good-Pleasure of God the Father, the Word That sprang from Him, when made Man too: in order that His Human Nature be not conceived and spoken of by us as something other than He, albeit the union that is of truth [shews us that He is One and that His Flesh is not alien from Him?

In this too thou wilt therefore be caught speaking falsely and in no slight degree erring from fit reasoning. And if to say that the Word has been made Flesh is nought else than that He being in the Excellence of Godhead and abiding what He was, hath become Man, what glory from without will He be in need of, Himself the Lord of Glory? For confessedly was He being glorified, the Spirit working Divine signs; yet not as a God-clad man, gaining this thing from an alien and superior Nature, even as do WE, but rather as using of His own Spirit: for He was God by Nature and not alien to Him is His Spirit. Hence we say that not from without nor by adoption has the operation of the Spirit been given to Him, even as unto us, or to the holy Apostles: for to them hath Christ given authority over unclean spirits to cast them out, and commanded them to heal both every sickness and every ailment in the people.

From within therefore and from Himself is His Spirit, And an evident demonstration of this will be His being able to supply It to others too and not of measure, as the blessed Evangelist saith. For the God of all measured to []the saints the grace through the Spirit, and to one He gave the word of wisdom, to another the word of knowledge, to another, gifts of healing: and this I think is that those who have the operation have power of measure: but our Lord Jesus Christ, putting forth the Spirit out of His own fulness, even as doth the Father Himself, gives It not as of measure to those who are worthy to receive It. Why then, most excellent sir, dost thou make Him Who giveth the Spirit not of measure, connumerate with those who have It in measure, saying that His glory has been cemented [by the Spirit and that He has been operated on, like one of us, receiving as a grace support from Him, rather than working Divine signs through His own Spirit.

For the all-daring Jews, whetting against Him a bitter tongue, unholily said, This man casteth not out devils save in Beelzebub the prince of the devils; but our Lord Jesus Christ convicting them of no small folly yea rather of impiety, says, If I in Beelzebub, prince of devils, cast out devils, by whom do your sons cast them out? for the glorious and mighty choir of the holy Apostles, performing miracles in the Name of Jesus Christ of Nazareth, is marvelled at: and of a truth they returned rejoicing and saying, Lord even the devils are subject to. us in Thy Name. But if it be possible that in the name of any one of those operated on, others too should avail to accomplish the like, let him come, let him tell us why no one is marvelled at for rebuking unclean spirits or having accomplished ought else that passes reason, in the name of any saint.

But they are operated upon by the Spirit and have a measured grace, He, as God in-worketh, and through His own Spirit achieveth without toil the things whereby He is marvelled at. And verily the woman who was sick of the issue of blood came one time secretly behind Him (thus is it written) and touched the border of His garment and immediately her issue of blood stanched, which Christ now understanding, says Who touched Me? and when at this the Divine-speaking disciples said, Master, the multitude are thronging Thee and pressing Thee, He said again, Somebody touched Me, for I know that might went forth of Me. Understandest thou then that not as introduced from without, but from within and out of Himself hath He the power to inwork and to free from weaknesses?

And the blessed Evangelist Matthew too somewhere writeth, And the whole multitude were seeking to touch Him, for there went might out of Him and healed all. His might then is His Spirit, and the Divine-uttering David will give us proof, saying, By the Word of the Lord were the Heavens stablished and by the Spirit of His Mouth all their might. The Mouth of God the Father he says is the Word That is out of Him, by Whose Spirit the things made through Him, are stablished in being. I have now therefore said that he brings down to nothing the Mystery of Godliness, which has been marvelled at by the holy Angels themselves too, and recking nought of the dogmas that pertain unto truth, he makes light of them saying, "Wilt thou another operation of the Trinity besides these? the Son dwelt in the body, the Father commended him when baptized, the Spirit fashioned him in the Virgin." And that the truth will follow surely upon the things which we have said, and that we have made no mere condemnation of his words, but rather a clear and true conviction of them, himself will shew saying elsewhere on this wise,

"And the proof of co-work is evident, The Son became man, the Father enthroned Him, the Spirit honoured Him by signs."

§2. Will any one doubt even after this that the aim of his ideas looks to unlearning alike and unholiness, and is bold against the doctrines of piety? for like as he unwisely casts forth the Word of God from being made Flesh and says that He wrought an indwelling in man, so too again does he take the being made man, albeit the holy Churches in every region under Heaven, and the venerable Fathers themselves who put forth unto us the definition of the right and undefiled Faith, viz. (the Holy Ghost speaking in them) that the Word of God was made flesh and became Man, conceiving that this is nought else save only the being made man as we, and being born after the flesh of a woman, because He hath also been made with us under the Law, Who as God is above the Law.

But since (as I have already full often said) his aim is to undo the Truth, therefore he alone (and that strenuously) lifts himself up, and opposes the opinions of all, and brandishes arms against the Ineffable glory, and what he alone thinks, endeavours to bring in secretly as a kind of rubbish upon the churches of God: for he maintains that the Incarnation is indwelling, and not rather that the Word out of God partook like us of blood and flesh, albeit the

Word hath indwelt and indwells yet in all the saints, but has once been made as we, and has partaken Personally in a single flesh, wherein He is believed both to have died and to have risen for us: for of His own will He suffered in the flesh.

But that to no purpose is he flinging about words, and recking little of the absurdity of his language, says that Christ was ennobled by signs through the Spirit, the words which have been just cited, sufficiently (as I think) shewed: but let us examine, if you please, his other words. 'The Father (he says) commended;' what then commended here is, I cannot understand: for the word is confessedly a word of the market and the mob, and replete with commonplace trickery; but I suppose that he wanted to indicate, set forth, for example, or, hath witnessed to. How then (tell me) did the Father commend? did He exhibit one counted worthy of Divine Indwelling? or was it not this at all, but rather His own Son made man, yet abiding even in Flesh, what He was and is and shall be, i. e. God? For Jesus Christ Who was yesterday and to-day is the Same even for ever.

Come then, let us examine what is spoken of Him. What says the Evangelist? And John bare record, saying, I have seen the Spirit descending from, Heaven like a dove, ... [3] and abiding upon Him, This is He That baptizeth with the Holy Ghost: and I have seen and testified that This is the Son of God. For our Lord Jesus Christ was about to sanctify economically the Jordan, and deigned with us to be baptized, ordering the Mystery of the Economy with flesh through the ways that beseem it: for it was necessary that the Word out of God the Father should be known to have been made Man. Yet was He baptized as Man, He baptized Divinely in the Holy Ghost. And we do not say that He ministered the participation of the Holy Ghost to the baptized either as a servant or by means of any other, but hallowed them, Himself infusing into them out of His own Fulness as God by Nature. How then dost thou, disregarding words alike and thoughts that belong to rightness, say that indwelling in man was wrought by God the Word; albeit whereas very many saints have had the God of all indwelling in them, none of them baptized with his own spirit or has been said to indwell Divinely in any and has so indwelt? and Christ Himself dwells in us through the Holy Ghost, Which is His own too, even as God the Father's. And this Himself ratifies to us saying, But when the Comforter is come, Whom I will send unto you from the Father, the Spirit of the Truth, Which proceedeth from the Father, He shall testify of Me.

See then how He says that the Spirit Which proceedeth from God the Father is the own Spirit of the Truth also: and He Himself is of a surety the Truth. How then, if He be of a truth not rather God made man, but man having the Divine Indwelling as His Energy, doth He promise to send down, as His own, the Spirit of God the Father upon them who believe on Him? Yea, as I said, he shakes to nothing the glory of the Mystery, distributing the operation of the Holy Trinity in respect of the things done, and allotting to each of the Persons by Himself what the other hath not wrought.

Again he says on this wise, "The Son chose forth, for I, He says, chose you: the Father sanctified, the Spirit made orators." O distraction without measure! if all things have been done by the Father through the Son in the Spirit and nothing be done by God the Father, save in this very way;----how is he not surely distraught, who distributes to the Persons severally the Operations unto ought of the Untaint and One Godhead, and doth not rather maintain that each thing that is done has been wrought by the Father through the Son in the Spirit? For if the Son is both the Counsel and Wisdom and Might of the Father, full surely will the Father work all things through the Son, as through His Counsel and Wisdom and Might. Thus chose He for their excellence His disciples, thus do we say that those who were chosen out were sanctified, thus that they were made orators, from out One Godhead; that is, by the Father through the Son in the Spirit. For He says, Holy Father, sanctify them in Thy Truth. The Truth therefore sanctifies, i. e. the Son; He infuses ..... [4] too and renders them wise and through the operation of the Holy Ghost; devoutly eloquent. And verily He said in the book of Matthew to His own Disciples, When they deliver you up take no thought how or what ye shall speak, for it shall be given yon in that hour what ye shall speak, for not YE are the speakers, but the Spirit of your Father which speaketh in you; and through that of Luke, Settle it therefore in your hearts not to meditate before what ye shall answer, for I will give you a mouth and wisdom which all your adversaries shall not be able to gainsay or resist. Hearest thou how when the Holy Ghost speaketh in them, Himself gives the mouth? For He is as Word Giver of word and Bestower of the Spirit, as having It as His own Naturally; even as the Father Himself too. The Holy Trinity has therefore the same Operation, and whatsoever things the Father doth and willeth to accomplish, these things doth the Son too in equal manner, likewise the Spirit also. But the giving of the Operations severally to Each of the Persons individually is nought else than to set forth three gods severally and wholly distinct from one another. For the count of Natural Unity in regard to the Holy Trinity, shews I suppose one motion [unto every thing that is done. But if now we say that while One Person is moved, e. g., to work, the Two remain ineffective, how is not a gross severance privily introduced, allotting as a certain position to each Person, the being conceived of external to and isolated from the rest, not in respect of His Individual Being (for that were true), but in respect of utter diversity which does not endure language that gathers them into Natural Union? For One Nature of Godhead is conceived of in the Holy and Consubstantial Trinity [5].

But this good man dares to abridge God the Word Consubstantial with God the Father as though he knows not that He has been made Man, not casting away what He was, but assuming rather what He was not: for he is an advocate for (as has been said) the Holy Ghost and insults the Son, thus saying to some who have elected to think with Arius,

"They [6] (he says) contriving greater insult against Him, and severing from the Divine Nature the Spirit Which having formed His Human Nature (for that, it says, which is conceived in Mary is of the Holy Ghost), reformed unto righteousness that which was formed (for He was manifested, it says, in flesh, was made righteous in Spirit), Which made Him terrible to devils (for I, He says, in the Spirit of God, cast out devils); Which made His Flesh a Temple (for I saw, it says, the Spirit descending from Heaven like a dove and it abode upon Him); Which granted Him to be taken up (for, it says, having given commandment to the holy Apostles whom He chose forth, He was taken up through the Holy Ghost): This I say which bestowed on Christ so great glory they make Christ's bondman."

§3. The daring then to sever the Spirit from the Divine and Untaint Nature, is (I assent) the part of a bad and sinful mind and one far removed from what is fit (for He is Consubstantial with God the Father, and moreover with the Son Himself and is believed to be God and out of God): but I think that we should, letting this be for the present, examine the words before us and with all attention see whither they look. For says he "Doing a greater insult against Him (i. e., the Word out of God the Father) and severing from the Divine Nature the Spirit Which formed His Human Nature." Whose Human Nature, most excellent sir, sayest thou has been formed through the Spirit? albeit thou hadst but now made discourse to us about the Only-Begotten Himself Who was begotten Ineffably out of God the Father; for thou wert calling Him "Divine Nature," and His I suppose and none else's you say the Human Nature is. Therefore call to mind thine own words, for thou saidst it was the own Flesh of the Word, i. e., with a reasonable soul therein, for thus will the manhood be His. Then how, if the Word out of God the Father be One with His own Flesh, dost thou suppose that he lacks God-befitting Might and that the Holy Ghost made him terrible to devils, as though he could not do this of his own nature? and again the being able to crush Satan, as by the gift of another and hardly borrowed?

If then thou knowest that to sever the Spirit from His Divine Nature is (and justly) the most disgraceful of charges, His (it is manifest) is the Spirit, as proceeding [through His Ineffable Nature Itself and Consubstantial with Him, and He will not need the might that is from It as something external and adventitious, but will use Him rather as His own Spirit, and will render Himself terrible to the devils through Him. But if it seem good to thee to shew that they who sever are unimplicated in charges of impiety, how didst thou just now call them to us insolent? and how dost thou not perceive that thou art numbering thyself with them, if thou sayest that the Word out of God the Father united to flesh, needed just like any of ours and a mere man, the aid of the Spirit that He might be terrible to the unclean spirits? For even though He say that He casts out devils in the Spirit of God, how must one not see that the economy of the expression is worthy of marvel? For the chiefs of the Jews, envious of the renown of our Saviour and opening against Him an unbarred mouth, used to babble (miserable ones!) saying that He cast out devils in Beelzebub prince of the devils: but He with His innate clemency toward all, drawing unto what was better and true those who have erred or who were choosing to let loose their tongues upon Him, was attributing rather to God Who is by Nature, the glory of being able to crush Satan, saying that in the Spirit of God He chased away the wicked spirits: and not as putting Himself outside of being God by Nature and of having the Holy Ghost as His own: but since it was meet and worthy of God-befitting skill to intercept the wrath of those who were desiring His death and to cut off occasions from those who were offended at Him, for they were attacking Him saying, For a good work we stone Thee not but for blasphemy, because THOU, being a man, makest Thyself God: therefore skilfully does He condescending to them who were yet weak say, the Spirit of God,: for He knows, as I said, that He is God by Nature together with Him Who begot Him, and has all things of His, save only the being Father. Wherefore did He also say to Him, All Mine are Thine and Thine Mine and I have been glorified in them, and to ourselves making discourse concerning the Holy Ghost, He says, All things that the Father hath are Mine, therefore I said unto you that of Mine shall

He take and, declare it unto you. For as the Holy Ghost proceedeth out of the Father being His by Nature, in equal wise is He through the Son Himself too, His Naturally and Consubstantial with Him. Hence even though He be glorified through the Spirit, yet is He conceived of as glorifying Himself through His own Spirit, and not as though it came to Him from without even though He be seen as made Man like us.

It is besides unsafe to say this also concerning the Spirit, "Which hath made His Flesh a Temple." For it was the own Flesh of the Word, and this thyself has just now acknowledged to us, for thou saidst that His is the human nature, and the Holy Body taken out of the holy Virgin is called His Temple: His own again is His Spirit, and never will the Word out of God the Father be conceived of without His own Spirit. Better therefore were it and wiser, to say that the Body is the Temple of the Word and the flesh His own, and to believe that with the Word is ever His Spirit, just as also with the Father Himself too.

Not without blame moreover would I say that is his saying that Assumption into Heaven has been given Him by the Spirit as to a mere man. For He chose His Disciples through the Holy Ghost, He was taken up as God, not receiving this as a gift from Another; but Himself rather as a first-fruit of the human nature renewed unto immortality presenting Himself to God the Father and consecrating for us a new and living way and that entereth into the inner part of the veil, whither the forerunner is said to have entered in our behalf, after the order of Melchiscdech made an High Priest for ever. But that when Christ ascended above, the Holy Ghost was in Him as His own, none will doubt. How then didst thou not fear (tell me) to say that "This Which gave this so great glory to Christ, they make Christ's bondman?" For they who make Him Christ's bondman are confessedly impious and dishonour the Very Word Who is Consubstantial with God Himself, arraying in slave-befitting measures the Spirit Which is of Him and in Him by Nature and His own: but the saying that the glory was given Him by the Spirit, is a manifest proof of the uttermost infatuation.

But you will be caught idly babbling herein, and not understanding the Mystery to Him-ward, yea rather both thinking and saying clean contrary to yourself. For if thou hast believed that the Word being God has been made Flesh (for thou saidst that His was the human nature) why dost thou say that the Lord of glory, as though He had not glory of His own, needed it from the Spirit, and reckonest Him in the measures of the creature to which all things are from without and given? for what hast thou that thou receivedst not, will it befit the creature to hear.

Yea but (he says) I find Emmanuel saying. Father, glorify Thy Son: add therefore what remains; this is, That Thy Son too may glorify Thee. If thou assert that the Son, as lacking glory, desires that of the Father, what dost thou say, when the Father too is glorified of the Son? is it as not having glory or needing it of another? away with the mis-counsel! for verily is it trickery and unholy thought and nought else. For the Divine Nature and that passeth all natures dwelleth in the light unapproachable and hath authority over all things and to Him is ascribed the glory which most befits it alone: but when the Only-Begotten Word of God was made man and was about by the grace of God through His own flesh to taste death for every man, and undo its might hard-to-withstand, quickening as God His own Temple, He devises the prayer as Man, and wills the Father to consent with Him Who was transforming the nature of man to what it was at the beginning and renewing it unto incorruption, and displaying it superior to the meshes of death: that ancient curse and the sentence upon the First-formed being undone.

Hence since visible in flesh, He is preached Son of God by Nature and in truth, He says, Father glorify Thy Son, rendering Him as Man, superior to both death and decay, that He may be believed to be Thine, being as God Life by Nature, according to the count of His own Nature: for then will the Son too glorify Thee. Glory truly is it to God the Father that it be believed by us, that He, Very God and Life and Life-giving, begat equal and like to Himself in everything, ineffably and beyond understanding, the Son, Who was in no lesser state, even though He have been made in flesh, but preserved wholly unimpaired the Supernatural and Choice Beauty of His inherent Natural Nobility, being Himself too Life as out of Life, and all-availing and achieving without toil and bestowing in-corruption on those subject to death and decay.

Hence even though the Son be said to be glorified by the Father, consider the measure of the human nature, sever not into two [after the Union] the One Christ and Son and Lord, but confess One and the Same, God made Man [7], and the Same in like manner Lord of glory as God, and recipient of glory in His Human Nature. For consider that, albeit by Nature and in verity God and King of all and Lord, He is said to have been set King, when, made man as we, He hath humbled Himself and been made obedient to God the Father and with us under the Law. In no wise therefore will the things that pertain to the measures of the emptiness trouble the wise and understanding and settled in the faith; but from them alike and from the things that befit the Divine Nature, do they acknowledge the Son, the Same God and Man.

But he comes not forward with sound words, but having swerved exceedingly to what is unruly, he busies himself [without understanding, and deems fit to hold what please himself alone and what he thinks well to deem are understood aright. And he destroys others too, in addition to to what he has said severing into two the One Lord Jesus Christ, calumniating also our Divine Mystery itself from not enduring to confess with us, that not like one of the holy Prophets, or again Apostles and Evangelists, was Christ a God-clad man, but God rather made Man, and hath partaken in verity of blood and flesh. He said in this wise again, putting forth his words as of the Person of Christ,

"He [8] [that eateth My flesh and drinketh My Blood abideth in Me and I in him. Remember that what is said is about the flesh. As the Living Father sent Me, Me, the visible: but sometimes I misinterpret. Let us hear from what follows: As the living Father sent Me, he says the Godhead, I the Manhood: let us see who it is who is mis-interpreting. The heretic says* [he says [9]] here the Godhead, Sent Me God the Word. As the living Father sent Me, according to him, and I live, God the Word, because of the Father. After this, And he that eateth Me he too shall live. Whether do we eat, the Godhead or the flesh?"

§4. Thou sayest therefore that the flesh alone has been sent, and affirmest that it it is which is seen: it therefore suffices also alone by itself to quicken that which is tyrannized by death. Why then do the God-inspired Scriptures tell a tale to no purpose and over and over assert that the Word out of God the Father was made Flesh? for what need at all would there be of the Word, if the human nature sufficeth for us, even though conceived of alone and by itself, so as to be able to bring to nought death and to undo the might of decay? and if it is as you suppose and choose to think, not God the Word Who has been sent through being made as we, but the flesh alone which is seen has been sent by the Father, how is it not clear to all, that we have been made participant of a human body and one in no wise whatever differing from our own? [10] how therefore do you elsewhere laugh at those who so think? for thou saidst again,

> "I will speak the words too of offence. Of His own Flesh was the Lord Christ discoursing to them; Except ye eat, He says, the Flesh of the Son of Man and drink His Blood, ye have no Life in you: the hearers endured not the loftiness of what was said, they imagined of their unlearning that He was bringing in cannibalism."

§5. And how is the thing not plain cannibalism, and in what way is the Mystery yet lofty, unless we say that the Word out of God the Father has been sent, and confess that the mode of that sending was the Incarnation? For then, then we shall see clearly, that the Flesh which was united to Him and not another's flesh, avails to give Life, yet 'because it has been made the very own of Him who is mighty to quicken all things,' For if this visible fire infuses the force of its natural inherent power into those substances with which it comes in contact, and changes water itself though cold by nature into that which is contrary to its nature and makes it hot; what wonder or how can one disbelieve that the Word out of God the Father being the Life by Nature rendered the Flesh which is united to Him, Life-giving? for it is His very own and not that of another conceived of as apart from Him and of one of us. But if thou remove the Life-giving Word of God from the Mystical and true Union with His Body and sever them utterly, how canst thou shew that it is still Life-giving? And Who was it who said, He that eateth My Flesh and drinketh My Blood, abideth in Me and I in him? If then it be a man by himself and the Word of God have not rather been made as we, the deed were cannibalism and wholly unprofitable the participation (for I hear Christ Himself say, The flesh profiteth nothing, it is the Spirit that quickeneth, for as far as pertains to its own nature, the flesh is corruptible [11], and will in no wise quicken others, sick itself of the decay that is its own): but if thou say that it is the Own Body of the Word Himself, why dost thou speak portentously and utter vain things, contending that not the very Word out of God the Father has been sent, but some other than of Him, "the visible," or His Flesh, albeit the God-inspired Scripture every where proclaimeth One Christ, full well affirming that the Word was made Man as we and defining herein the tradition of the right Faith.

But out of overmuch reverence, he blushes (it appears) at the measures of emptiness and endures not to see the Son Co-Eternal with God the Father, Him who is in the Form and Equality in everything with Him Who begat Him, come down unto lowliness: he finds fault with the economy and haply leaves not unblamed the Divine Counsel and Plan. For he pretends to investigate the force of the things said by Christ, and as it were taking in the depth of the ideas; then bringing round (as he thinks) my [12] words to a seeming absurdity and ignorance; "Let us see, he says, who it is that mis-interprets. As the Living Father sent Me, for I live (according to him) God the "Word, because of the Father, and he that eateth Me he too shall live: which do we eat, the Godhead or the flesh?" Perceivest thou not therefore at length how thy mind is gone? for the

Word of God saying that He is sent, says, he also that eateth Me, he too shall live. But WE eat, not consuming the Godhead (away with the folly) but the Very Flesh of the Word Which has been made Lifergiving, because it has been made His Who liveth because of the Father. And we do not say that by a participation from without and adventitious is the Word quickened by the Father, but rather we maintain that He is Life by Nature, for He has been begotten out of the Father who is Life. For as the sun's brightness which is sent forth, though it be said (for example) to be bright because of the sender, or of that out of which it comes, yet not of participation hath it the being bright, but as of natural nobility it weareth the Excellence of him who sent it or flashed it forth: in the same way and manner, I deem, even though the Son say that He lives because of the Father, will He bear witness to Himself His own Noble Birth from forth the Father, and not with the rest of the creation promiscuously, confess that He has Life imparted and from without.

And as the Body of the Word Himself is Life-giving, He having made it His own by a true union passing understanding and language; so WE too who partake of His holy Flesh and Blood, are quickened in all respects and wholly, the Word dwelling in us Divinely through the Holy Ghost, humanly again through His Holy Flesh and Precious Blood. The most holy Paul will confirm the truth of what I said, writing thus to those in Corinth who believed in our Lord Jesus Christ, I speak as to wise men, judge YE what I say, the Cup of Blessing which we bless is it not the communion of the Blood of Christ? the Bread which we break is it not the communion of the Body of Christ? for one bread one body are we who are many, for we all are partakers of One Bread. For having partaken of the Holy Ghost, we are made one both with Christ Himself the Saviour of all and with one another: we are of the same body in this way, that we being many are one bread one body, for we all are partakers of the One Bread. For the Body of Christ which is in us binds us together into unity and is in no way divided. But that through the Body of Christ we have been brought together into unity with Him and with one another, the blessed Paul will confirm, writing, For this cause I Paul the Prisoner of Jesus Christ in behalf of you Gentiles, if ye heard of the economy of the grace of God which was given me to you-ward, how that by revelation He made known unto me the mystery, as I wrote afore in few words, whereby when ye read, ye may understand my knowledge in the mystery of Christ which in other ages was not made known to the sons of men as now it is revealed unto His holy Apostles and prophets in the Spirit, that the Gentiles should be fellow-heirs and of the same body and co-participant in the promise in Christ.

But since some of those who at first believed, ignorant of the tradition and force of the Mystery were pleased to be borne aside from what was right, celebrating in the churches banquetings and public feastings, the blessed Paul found fault with those who used so to do, writing, For have ye not houses to eat and to drink in? or despise ye the Church of God and shame them that have not? what shall I say to you? shall I praise you in this? I praise you not; for I received of the Lord what I also delivered to you, that the Lord Jesus Christ in the night in which He was delivered up, took bread and gave thanks and brake and said, This is My Body given for you, this do in remembrance of Me. Likewise the Cup too after supper saying, This Cup is the New Testament in My Blood, do this as oft as ye drink it in remembrance of Me: for as oft as ye eat this bread and drink this cup, ye are declaring the Lord's death, till He come.

And that the Mystery is Divine and the participation Life-giving and the might of this unbloody Sacrifice far better than the worship under the Law, is easy to see even from his saying that the things ordained through Moses to them of old time were a shadow, but Christ and what is His the truth. The most wise Paul too will help us herein, thus writing, One that despised Moses' Law died without mercy under two or three witnesses, of how much sorer punishment, suppose ye, shall he be thought worthy who trod under foot the Son of God and accounted common the Blood of the covenant wherein he was sanctified, and did despite unto the Spirit of grace? For they that of old did sacrifice the lamb ate thereof, but the force of the eating amounted not simply to the satisfying of the belly, nor was it for this that the sacrifices were performed under the Law: but that when death fell on the rest, they might be superior to its suffering and might escape the destroyer. And verily in one night were the first-born of the Egyptians destroyed, but these fenced by the bare type, alone were saved by it, and having the shadow for their shield, prevailed gloriously over death itself too. The types then saved those before us; in what condition are our matters, on whom at length beamed the Truth itself, that is, Christ, Who setteth before us His own Life-giving Flesh to partake of? is it not clear to all? For very exceedingly better and in vast superiority are they. And the might of the Mystery our Lord Jesus Christ making manifest saith, Verily I say to you, he that helieveth on Me hath everlasting life, I am the Bread of Life: your fathers ate the manna in the wilderness and died, this is the Bread which cometh down from Heaven that a man may eat thereof and not die, I am the Living Bread Which came down from Heaven, if any man eat of this Bread he shall live for ever and the Bread Which I will give is My Flesh Which is for the Life of the world. For since they of the blood of Israel had marvelled at Moses for the largess of manna sent down to those of that time in the desert, which fills up a type of the Mystic Eucharist (for the Law is a shadow), therefore with exceeding skill doth our Lord Jesus Christ minish the type, driving them [from it] unto the truth. For not that (He says) was the Bread of Life, but rather, I Who am out of Heaven and Who quicken all things and infuse Myself into them that eat Me, through My Flesh too that is united to Me. Which indeed He made clearer saying, Verily I say unto you, Except ye eat the flesh of the Son of Man and drink His Blood, ye have not Life in you: he that eateth My Flesh and drinketh My Blood hath eternal Life and I will raise him up at the last day, for My Flesh is true meat and My Blood is true drink; he that eateth My Flesh and drinketh My Blood abideth in Me and I in him. As the Living Father sent Me and I live because of the Father, he also that eateth Me, he too shall live. Consider then how He abideth in us and maketh us superior to corruption, infusing Himself into our bodies, as I said, through His own Flesh too, which is true meat, whereas the shadow in the Law and the worship under it possess not the truth.

And the plan of the Mystery is simple and true, not overwrought with varied devices of imaginations unto unholiness but simple as I said. For we believe that to the body born through the holy Virgin, having a reasonable soul, the Word out of God the Father having united Himself (unspeakable is the union, and wholly a Mystery!) rendered it Life-giving, being as God Life by Nature, that making us partakers of Himself spiritually alike and bodily, He might both make us superior to decay and might through Himself bring to nought the law of sin which is in the members of the flesh, might condemn sin in the flesh, as it is written. But this no wise (I deem) pleases this dogmatist of new inventions, who like some straying calf runs after only what pleases himself: and minishes the force of the mystery saying,

> "Hear the word Lord too, sometimes put of the human nature of Christ, sometimes of His Godhead, sometimes of both. As oft as ye eat this Bread and drink this Cup, ye declare the Lord's Death. Hear from the foregoing the unlearning of the gainsayers, how they read the mighty profit of the mystery, and whose memorial it imparts to men, and hear not me saying these things, but the blessed Paul, As oft as ye eat this bread, he said not, As oft as ye eat this Godhead. As oft as ye eat this bread. See what is before us concerning the Lord's Body. As oft as ye eat this Bread, whereof the Body is the antitype. Let us see therefore whose is the Death. As oft as ye eat this bread and drink this Cup, ye declare the Lord's Death. Hear yet plainer in what follows, Till He come, who is it Who is coming? They shall see the Son of Man coming in the clouds of heaven with great glory. And greater still, the Prophet before the Apostles did more clearly shew Him Who is coming and hath cried aloud proclaiming of the Jews, They shall look on Him Whom they pierced. Who then is he that was pierced? the Side: belongs the Side to the body, or the Godhead?"

§6. Again must we speak for the doctrines of the Truth, and oppose, sir, thy words, and before all else must say this to those who will hear: Thy aim is and with all diligence to represent two christs, to whom severally may belong the title of lordship, but it shall be shewn by us, without any great toil, that you go to this in most unlearned wise. For come tell me who ask thee, what Christ you are defining, whose you say is both the manhood and likewise the Godhead: if the Word out of God the Father, you have clearly confessed that the Same is man also, for you said that His is the human nature: but if him that is born of the Virgin according to thee, you will be caught no less pronouncing that He is God too: for you said that His is the Godhead also. On all sides therefore driven even against thy will to the Truth, confess with us One Christ and Lord: for thus will you cease from saying, "Hear the word Lord too, one while put of the human nature of Christ, one while of His Godhead, other while, of both:" for where there is One Son, what room is there to speak of both? and why dost thou smile at those who honour our Divine Mystery, saying most unholily, " As oft as ye eat this bread and drink the cup, ye declare the Lord's death? Hear from the foregoing the unlearning of the gainsayers, how they read the mighty profit of the mystery and Whoso memorial is set before men."

There is therefore nothing excellent in the unbloody sacrifice, but it profits exceeding little, and he will put the force of the gain thereof in just merely declaring a man's death and making a memorial of one like us. Therefore He lies in saying that He is Life-giving Who knows not how to lie, Christ: "WE too have been cozened having a vain opinion of Him: and now late and with difficulty are we being guided unto the finding of the truth, by reading these thy words. But to you who choose to think thus, shall be said what is spoken through the Prophet's voice, Lo thine eyes are not, nor thine heart comely. For he by no means understandeth, that we setting forth the Death of Christ, confessing too His Resurrection, and gaining thereby perfection in the faith, then becoming partakers of His Divine Nature and that through participating of unity with Him, are sanctified spiritually alike and bodily and are quickened. For this corruptible must put on incorruption and this mortal put on immortality: and the robe that is out of Heaven and undecaying and productive of immortality hath Christ become to us. And our proof is the most holy Paul writing, one while, Put ye on our Lord Jesus Christ, at another again, For as many of you as were baptized into Christ put on Christ, Who saith in God-befitting way and truly, I am the Resurrection and the Life.

To those things does he fearing nought put forth yet fouler impiety, adding, "Hear not me saying these things but the blessed Paul, As oft as ye do eat this bread, whereof the Body is the antitype. Let us see therefore herefrom whose is the death. As oft as ye eat this bread, and drink this Cup, ye declare the Lord's death. Hear yet plainer in what follows, Till He come: who then is he that is to come? They shall see the son of man coming in the clouds of heaven with great glory. And greater yet, the Prophet before the Apostles did more clearly shew Him Who is coming and hath cried proclaiming concerning the Jews, They shall look on Him whom they pierced. Who then is He which was pierced? The Side, belongs the Side to the Body, or to the Godhead?" Petty therefore as I said, is the profit of the Unbloody Sacrifice, because perchance it hath not been, feasible that the Nature of the Godhead too should be consumed along with the Flesh, because we are not in possession of impossibilities, having the Incorporeal by Itself to eat. But you seem to me to forget that it is by no means the Nature of Godhead that lieth upon the holy Tables of the Churches, yet is it the own Body of the Word Begotten of God the Father: and God by Nature and in truth is the Word. Why therefore dost thou confound all things and jumble them without understanding, all but mocking at our Bread Which is out of Heaven and giveth Life to the world, because it is not called Godhead by the voice of the Divines, but rather the Body of Him Who hath become Man for us, that is, of the Word out of God the Father? And why (tell me) dost thou call it the Lord's Body at all, save because thou knowest it to be Divine and God's? for all things serve their Maker.

Yea the things in thy mind are not right, but thou believest Emmanuel to be merely a God-clad man. And then utterly heedless of thoughts and words that belong to piety, thou supposest that the Priest of the Truth, the wise master-builder and teacher of the Gentiles, the truly holy and all-wise Paul will support thee in thy calumniating, bearing away from the straight and most approved path the force of what are rightly and without adulteration said by him.

For "let us see (he says) herefrom whose is the death. Till He come. Who is He Who is coming? they shall look [13] on Him Whom they pierced." He will come therefore Who suffered death humanly, has been raised Divinely, Who ascended too into the Heavens, Who with all state is on the Throne of the Ineffable Godhead and co-sitteth with the Father, the Seraphim standing around, and the Highest Powers, not unknowing of the measure of their subjection to Him; every Authority and Power and Lordship worshipping Him: for to Him shall bend every knee and every tongue shall confess, Lord Jesus, to the glory of God the Father. He shall come (as I said) seen not in our littleness, but rather in most God-befitting glory. Heaven and the Spirits above encompassing Him as their God and King and standing by the Lord of all. If therefore the Word of God the Father be not rather in flesh, or made Man, but a God-clad man with bodily side and who endured the piercing, how is He seen on the Throne of the Supreme Godhead, revealed to us as a new god fourth after the Holy Trinity? hast thou not shuddered at a mere man, devising worship for the creature? are we then holden in the ancient snares? have we then done insult to God and has the holy multitude of the spirits above gone astray with us? if we have been set free from the ancient deceit, refusing as blasphemous to worship the creature, why dost thou casting us again into the old charges, exhibit us man-worshippers? for WE know and believe that the Word out of God the Father assumed flesh and blood: but since He hath remained the Same, i.e., God, He retained the Dignity of His inherent Excellence over all, albeit in flesh as we, yet being no less God, now too than of old, even though He have been made Man, He hath the Heaven His adorer and the earth worshipping Him: for it is written, that the earth is full of Thy praise, Thy Virtue covered the Heavens, O Lord.

But THOU again, of thy over much infatuation, seest not that thus He is in Nature and Glory: for thou saidst, "Who is he who cometh? they shall see the Son of man coming in the clouds of heaven," as though thou fearedst lest any should disbelieve thee saying that He Which cometh is son of man. Thou confirmest the proof thereof with prophetic testimony also. for thou sayest that it is written, They shall look on Him Whom they pierced. And yet mightier for proof as thou supposedst, most foolishly adding, "Who then is it (he says) that is pierced? the Side: belongs the Side to body or to the Godhead?" If there were any who say that the Word of God have not been made as we, but came among those on earth in bare Godhead, i.e., in semblance and as it were in shadow, as some of the unholy heretics thought good to think, you would have had some plea for such like framing of words; not passing the bound of what was meet: but since the preaching of the truth says clearly and manifestly that the Word of God was made Flesh and was called as we son of man too and suffered for us in the flesh and will also so come as He went up into Heaven, according to the Angel's voice too: whom (tell me) dost thou opposing, and whose opinion cutting off as unlearned and of no account, dost thou strive to shew us that HE Who cometh is a man with bodily side which has been pierced through with the spear?

But thine aim (as I said) is to bring in privily to us Emmanuel as a God-clad man and not rather God made Man, for the Word of God has been made Man. And this faith goes along with the holy and Divine Scriptures and the aim of the Apostolic and Evangelic Tradition tends to this same thing. But THOU again art talking big in another way too: for thou pretendest to be finding fault with those who mingle into one essence, the nature of the flesh and of the Godhead (albeit there is no one as I deem who mingles them up or mixes them one with other), and sayest,

"Why [14], as we were just now hearing, when both are according to thee mingled, does our Lord, delivering to the disciples the force of the Mystery, thus say, He took bread and gave thanks and gave to His disciples saying, Take, eat all of you for this is My Body. Why said He not, This is My Godhead Which is being broken for you? and again giving the cup of the Mysteries, He said not, This is My Godhead Which is being poured forth for you, but This is My Blood which is being shed for you for the remission of sins."

§7. That it is therefore an exceeding folly to want to oppose oneself to those who are not at all, and to no purpose to march forth, taking for contradiction that which no one (I suppose) cared either to think or say, how is it not manifest to all? for if one chose to contend that the ox is not by nature an horse, nor yet man an horse, whereas no one would even endure to think or say this;----how would he not be laughed at and besides a vain talker, beating the air and fighting against things uncertain and devising for himself sweat and toil against what was not there? For I say that something confessed ought first to be laid down, in order that then in duo order ours may be ranged against it.

But let us come to this: for if there be any who should dare to say the Word out of God had been transformed into the nature of the body, one might very reasonably object to him, that He on giving His Body did not rather say, Take eat this is My Godhead which is being broken for you, and, this is not My Blood but rather My Godhead which is being poured forth for you. But since the Word being God made His own the Body born of a woman, without undergoing any alteration or turning, how must not He who saith no untruth say, Take eat this is My Body? for being Life as God, He rendered it Life and Life-giving.

Having therefore opened your eyes but a little to the Truth, you will I suppose charge, yourself against yourself, your superfluity of language, on all sides stuttering and unlearnedly arraying against the Doctrines of piety this thy counterfeit and joyless discourse.

Footnotes:

1. "Thus is there One God, the Holy-Trinity by sameness of Nature speeding unto one Godhead, even though in the giving of Names and conceived of in Proper Existence only, It fitly admit the number Three." Thes. cap. 32 pp. 311 fin. 312. " He shall glorify Me, for He shall receive of Mine and shall tell it unto you; for being the Spirit of Truth He will enlighten them in whom He is, and will lead them unto the apprehension of the Truth. And this we say, not as severing into diversity and making wholly separate, either the Father from the Son, or the Son from the Father, nor yet the Holy Ghost from the Father and the Son, but (since One Godhead truly is, and is thus preached as viewed in the Holy and Consubstantial Trinity), defining the Acts belonging to Each and which seem to be attributed to Them severally, to be the Will and Operation of the Whole Godhead. For the Divine and Unsevered Nature will work through Itself, in no divided way, so far as pertains to the one count of Godhead, although Each hath Personal Existence : for the Father is What He is, and the Son likewise, and the Holy Ghost." On S. John vi. 45 p. 402 O. T. add in S. Johannem p. 784 a. S. Cyril further speaks of the Incarnation as the act of the Whole Holy Trinity. "But He says that He was Incarnate by the Father, although Solomon says, Wisdom builded her an house: and the blessed Gabriel attributeth the creation of the Divine Body to the Operation of the Spirit, when he was speaking with the holy Virgin (for The Holy Ghost, he says, shall come upon thee, and the Power of the most Highest shall overshadow thee)

that thou mayest again understand, that the Godhead being by Nature One, conceived of both in the Father and the Son and in the Holy Ghost, not severally will Each in-work as to ought of things that are, but whatever is said to be done by One, this is wholly the work of the whole Divine Nature." Ib. on vi. 57 pp. 424, 425 O. T.

2. The Word was made flesh and tabernacled in (or among) us. The Easterns in their great dread of Apollinarianism, suspected S. Cyril of pressing S. John's earlier words (sarx egeneto) to mean, was turned into flesh (see p. 44 note e): Nestorius on his side would seem to have rested his, 'the Divine Nature not enduring change into flesh but inhabitation in man' (pp. 28, 30) in part on the words, tabernacled in us. S. Cyril gives two most carefully-weighed expositions of the verse at pp. 4, 5 and 35.

3. Thus the MS., omitting the intermediate part, ver. 32 and most of 33. Omissions of this sort are not uncommon, even in good MSS., while the frequent citation of these verses by S. Cyril, together with the sense, shew that the omission is a slip of some transcriber. The omission seems to indicate that as in other places so here too S. Cyril read from Heaven in verse 33 also and so that the omission took place through the eye of the scribe wandering from the words from heaven in verse 32 to those same words in verse 33.

4. There appears to be an omission here; the Roman editors conjecture that to hagionpneuma may be to be supplied.

5. "Following the faith of the holy Fathers we say that the SON was in God-befitting and Ineffable way truly begotten out of the Essence of God the Father, and that He is conceived of in His Proper Hypostasis, yet is united in Identity of Essence with Him Who begat Him, and is in Him and hath again the Father in Himself. And we confess that He is Light out of Light, God out of God by Nature, Equal in glory and in work, Impress and Radiance and in all Equal, in nought minished. For thus, the Holy Ghost being counted besides, the Holy and Consubstantial Trinity is united in One Nature of Godhead." Ep. 1 to Monks p. 6 b.

6. This is given by Mercator with the heading, Also from the second volume quire 2 as though against the Arians and Macedonians, p. 118 Bal.

7. I have construed this from a Syriac extract in one of Severus' Epistles, which supplies the words, confess and the Same, God made Man, and gives rightly as instead of the et of the present Greek text. Severus' ms. omits the words just above after the Union, and very likely rightly.

8. Marius Mercator gives a Latin translation of this, citing it as "in another treatise in the fifth quire of the book, On the passage of Holy Scripture where it says, If thou shalt have remembered that thy brother hath ought against thee." Op. p. 115 Baluz. It occurs also in a fuller form among the passages cited before the Council of Ephesus, ib. pp 209, 210. and by S. Cyril in his Defence of his 11th chapter against the Eastern Bishops, pp. 192 e 193 a b.

9. [he says]. I have supplied this to fill up the sense from S. Cyril's fuller citations against the Eastern bishops.

10. S. Cyril means that if not God the Word have been sent but a

mortal body only, to this same must refer the words which follow, He. that eateth Me, he too shall live, must refer to a mortal body only, and one just like ours, so that our food should be no longer the Eucharist but only that.

11. See the same explanation given in S. Cyril's commentary on S. John, ad loc.p. 435 O.T.

12. S. Cyril in his great Letter to the monks which Nestorius had seen (see above p. 20 note 1) and was apparently contradicting had said, " And the Divine-uttering Paul will assure us, saying, But when the fulness of time came God sent forth His Son made of a woman made under the law, in order to redeem them that were under the law, in order that WE might recover the adoption. Who then is He who is sent, made (as he said) under the law and of a woman, save He Who is above laws as God? but since He has been called man, made under the Law too, in order to be in all things likened to His brethren?" Ep. 1 to the monks, p. 13 b. And in his 16th Paschal homily, "For as the Divine-uttering Paul writes, God sent forth His Son made of a woman made under the law. For we do not say that the Word of God came down into a man born through woman, in just the same way as He was in the Prophets; but rather we shall crown with right approval John's voice clearly and truly saying, And the Word was made flesh and tabernacled among us. And we shall conceive that the Word has been made flesh, participating in flesh and blood; and this in like way with those who are in blood and flesh, ourselves." p. 227 d e. Nestorius' objection to the idea of Sent anyhow referring to God the Word appears in his objections on pp. 48, 51, 52, 84 as well as in the present section. To it we owe S. Cyril's magnificent teaching here of the Blessings given us in and by the Holy Eucharist: for to the verse specially in controversy, S. John vi. 57, Nestorius adds the preceding ver. 56, with a view to the argument he draws from the word flesh, and S. Cyril in replying gives the full teaching of the Catholic Church on the subject both of the Eucharist, and of the sending. S. Cyril meets Nestorius' teaching not only here but (on the Holy Eucharist) in his great Letter (,3 Epistles p. 65 and chapter 11, p. 69) and the Explanation of chapter 11, p. 156 c d. But in his defence of his chapter 11 against the attack of the Eastern Bishops, S. Cyril cites in full this passage of Nestorius and (after alluding to the present treatise in the words that He has already made a long treatise in answer to Nestorius) proceeds, "What it is he wants to understand, in saying that it is not God the Word Incarnate and made Man that has been sent, but putting severally and apart (as he says) 'the visible,' I cannot say, yea rather his sophism is now evident, for he undoes the plan of the union in order that Christ's Body may be found to be a common body, no longer in truth the 'proper Body of Him who is mighty to quicken all things.'

"For petty confessedly to God the Word are all human things, but since He deigned for our sakes to endure the emptiness that is the salvation of the world, even though He be said to have been sent to preach remission to captives and recovery of sight to the blind, He is glorified rather as enduring the abasement of the Economy with flesh, and no one of those who are wont to think aright will (I suppose) find fault because He lowered Himself for our sakes in our condition.

"Does he not therefore by affirming that 'the visible,' to whom alone he hath allotted the fact of being sent, is some other son and christ than the Word out of God, exhibit our mystery as cannibalism, in unholy wise bringing round the mind of believers to feeble notions and essaying to subject to human reasonings what are apprehended by unquestioning faith alone? for not because the Nature of the Godhead is not eaten, will one therefore say that the holy Body of Christ is common: but it is needful to know (as we said before) that it is the Proper Body of the Word which quickeneth all things, and since it is the Body of Life it is also life-giving, for through It does the SON infuse life into our mortal bodies and undoes the mastery of death: and the HOLY SPIRIT of Christ quickeneth us in equal wise; for it is the Spirit that quickeneth, according to the Saviour's own voice." Def. cap. 11 adv. orient. p. 193 b c d e. So again in S. Cyril's Letter to the Emperor de recta fide (which Nestorius is very likely to have seen though probably not sent so soon as this) S. Cyril cites the text and says, "Yet how is it not true to say that the flesh hath come not out of heaven, but was out of the Virgin according to the Scriptures? yet is not the Word eaten, but He is seen in thousand ways gathering both into One [uniting] the properties of the natures by an economic coming together (sumbasin)" p. 35 d e. When S. Cyril republished this treatise in a revised form, he concluded this extract, " gathering both into One and as it were immingling (anakirnas) the properties of the natures." p. 708 a. In his treatise to the Empresses (Eudocia the Emperor's wife and his sister Pulcheria who had been Empress in her Brother's minority), written at the same time as the treatise to the Emperor, S.Cyril says, " As the Living Father sent Me both I live because of the Father and he that eateth Me he too shall live because of Me. I would gladly ask them who distinguish into two christs, the One, Who I pray is He Who has been sent by God the Father and Who both lives because of Him and is on that account Life-giving? If therefore it is the Word who is out of Him, bare and by Himself, how is He eaten by us in order that we may live because of Him (for unembodied is the Godhead by Nature)? but if they say that he that hath been sent is man alone and by himself, how is he life-giving because he lives because of the Father? albeit how are not all we that are on earth among the living, God the Father quickening us, if it is true that in Him we live and move and are? Since therefore we all of us live because of the Father, how (I pray) is the body of one man alone life-giving on this account and those of the rest have not rather the same operation, seeing that we all (as I said) both are and live because of the Father? what then do we say to this? The Word of God appearing in human form has been called Sent (apostle) (for He was sent to preach remission to captives and recovery of sight to the blind), but He lives because of the Father for He was begotten out of the Living Father: for it must needs, it must needs that the SON born of God the Father

Living and Life be full surely Life by Nature. But since He made His own the body which was taken out of the holy Virgin, He rendered it Life-giving and with reason, for it is the Body of the Life which quickeneth all things. Hence we may not sever into two sons the One Son and Christ and Lord; since He is the Same, Life as out of the Father, Life and Living; Lifegiving through His own Body too, as GOD made as we and Incarnate." de recta fide to the Empresses § 40 p. 177 abed. In the Thesaurus S. Cyril speaks of sending in reference to either the Eternal Generation or the temporal Birth for our sakes (compare S. Aug. on S. John hom. 21 fin. pp. 338 sq. O.T. with homm. 36 40, pp. 507, 545 O.T.) " The SON says that He has been sent by the Father, either [either is supplied from MSS.] after the mode of obedience and Incarnation (for He emptied Himself taking servant's form and became obedient unto death), or as out of the sun the light that is born and emitted from forth it, or out of the fire its heat, indivisibly and inseparably permeating to its participator." Thes. cap. 32 p. 325. In his comm. on S.John, S. Cyril takes sent as belonging to the Incarnation, p. 424 O.T. The very Rev. John Burgon B.D. Dean of Chichester, very kindly sent me from his laboriously constructed Indices of the New Testament citations of the Greek Fathers, a list of the citations in S. Cyril's extant writings of S. John vi. 57. It is probable that Nestorius' allusion to S. Cyril's interpretation of sent, belongs not to any comment on this verse but to the meaning as given in his great Letter to the Monks; which letter Nestorius elsewhere contradicts.

13. Here the part between They shall see and They shall look appears to have been omitted by a not infrequent carelessness of the Scribe in letting his eye wander from the one word to the same word just below. For the sequel refers to these omitted words They shall see the Son of Man coming in the clouds and indicates that their omission was accidental, not intentional.

14. This passage occurs in Mercator, in the middle of a long piece which he gives with the heading, Also in the sixth quire of the same on Judas, against the heretics (p. 110 Bal.). The portion preceding this is given below,p.171. The extract concludes, "Sever the nature but connect the union : confess Christ Son of God, yet a two-fold son, man and God, in order that the suffering may be allotted to the human nature, the undoing of the suffering which was wrought on the man who suffered, may belong to the Godhead alone."

Cyril of Alexandria, Five Tomes Against Nestorius - Book 5

TOME V
[Translated by P.E. Pusey]

Jewish disbelief in Christ followed by some Christian teachers. The SON GOD by Nature gave His own body to death to free us, albeit His Godhead might not suffer. "Glory before the world was," can be no man's glory but that of GOD. Father most strictly God the FATHER though He permit such relations to us. 'Crucified out of weakness,' yet, Lord of glory. 'Servant's form.' 'Not Mine own will.' The forsaking on the Cross. He raised His own Body. S. Thomas' confession. Nicene Fathers. Testimony of GOD and man to the SON.

THE Divine-uttering Paul glories in the Sufferings of Christ and says, one while, But to me be it not that I should glory save in the Cross of Christ through Whom the world has been crucified to me and I to the world, another while again, For I am not ashamed of the Gospel, for it is the power of God unto salvation unto every one that believeth, to the Jew first and to the Greek. And thus did the Spirit-clad deem right both himself to think and besides to teach others, for he hath written not without purpose, but that he might persuade us to be zealous for the rightness of the faith that was in him, choosing to delight us in the Sufferings of Christ. But some are ashamed of the Cross and impiously rising up against them that have been made teachers of all below the sun, by reason that they choose to think contrarily, they (wretched ones!) all but smile at Christ's sufferings and and are ashamed of the Gospel, sick with the Jewish unlearning and in no way inferior to them in infatuation. For the Saviour's Cross hath become to them an offence: and verily they beholding the Prince of Life, the fulfilment of the Law, affixed to the wood, they were wagging at Him their impious heads, not believing that God is of a truth made Man and come down unto emptiness, but supposing rather that He was simply a man as we, and they said, putting forth as out of the evil treasure of their heart evil things, Thou That destroyest the temple and buildest it in three days save Thyself; if Thou be the Son of God, come down from the Cross: and again, He saved others, Himself He cannot save, if He be the king of Israel, let Him now come down from the Cross and we will believe on Him. For they thought not, as I said just now, that He was God by Nature, nor yet in truth Son of God the Father but rather that He was bragging and daring to allot to Himself the glory of the Godhead. Hence they used to say, one while, For a good work we stone Thee not, but for blasphemy, because THOU being a man makest Thyself God; another while they brought Him to Pilate and besought that He should be crucified, and when he demanded that they should tell the reason of their awkwardness towards Him, they straightway began to accuse Him saying that He made Himself the Son of God. But lo now too, not at the hands of them of

Israel nor yet from the multitude of the Pharisees, but at their hands who seem to be Christians and are ranked among teachers and them whose lot is the Divine Priesthood, doth He manifestly suffer equal case. For He is disbelieved to be both God by Nature, and One and Alone and Verily Son of God the Father, and the plea of their ill-counsel as to this very thing, that He chose to suffer death in the flesh, albeit for this cause He descended unto emptiness economically, in order that suffering for us in the flesh, He might bring to nought the mastery of death, as being Himself by Nature Life and sprung of Life, God the Father. For the nature of man was sick of decay, in its firstfruits and original root, i. e., Adam. For since it offended through its disobedience its Law-giver and God and That brought it forth unto being, straightway it was accursed and liable to death, and death hath reigned from Adam unto Moses, the doom for this extending over the whole seed and race that is from him. For as sprung from corruptible root, corruptible are WE too, and abide (wretched!) holden in the meshes of death. But when the Creator planned good things concerning us and willed to transelement the nature of man, decay being taken away, unto what it was at the beginning, He adorned a new root (so to speak) for us, which endured not to be overmastered by death, the One Lord Jesus the Christ, that is, God the Word out of His Essence made man as we, made of a woman. For we do not say that just a man is God-bearing, but that the Word out of God has been of a truth Its very Self united to flesh, in order, having laid down His Life for us, and given to death His own Body for our sakes economically, and then shewn it superior to corruption through the Resurrection from the dead, to give pledge to all who believe on Him that He will raise up us too, and make us superior to the bonds of death, and little heedful of the nets of decay.

Hence I deem it is that the Divine-uttering Paul too, makes a matter of much speech and marvel, the love towards us of God the Father. For he said thus, What shall we say therefore to these things? if God be for us, who is against us? He that spared not His own Son but gave Him up for us all, how shall He not with Him too freely give us all things [1]? albeit exceeding many are the sons by grace and of adoption (for we too have been called gods and all are sons of the Most High), but One and Alone is He Who is so by Nature and is His Own, that is, God the Word Who is out of Him even when He was made Flesh. For thus do we say that He has been given even for all, as Himself too somewhere saith, For God so loved the world that He gave His Only-Begotten Son that whosoever believeth in Him should not perish, but have eternal life. Only-Begotten therefore is He Who was given, for He Alone sprung from the Essence of God the Father, the Word both out of Him and in Him: but since He hath, been made Man, therefore do we make our faith in Him declaring His death after the Flesh and confessing His Resurrection, knowing that the Same is both Son before the ages and Man economically in the last times and that He suffered in the flesh for our sakes and hath risen from the dead.

But (I know not how) the advocate of the Jews' unlearning is indignant at our words, for he said again,

"That therefore the divine Scripture puts, Son, of the birth from the Virgin, Mother of Christ, we have shewn. Hear of His death also, whether God is any where put, so as we might bring in a passible God: Being enemies, it says, we were reconciled to God through the death of His Son, it said not, Through the death of God the Word."

§1. True is it, according as it is written, There is a righteous man that perisheth in his righteousness: for that whoso nature is to hurt, putting on sometimes the shew of being helpful, turns aside from what is right, even the well stablished mind. For he thinks he is pious in no slight degree, essaying to confirm what is confessed by all, therefore saying, In His own Nature the Word out of God the Father is as God beyond sufferings and superior to death ; for how should Life die? Yet he not a whit the less too offends against the doctrines of the Church, wholly unrecking of the economy with flesh of the Only-Begotten, and in no wise considering the depth of the mystery.

If it were under examination by us, what were the Nature of the Word, or we had to declare it to them who asked and were desirous of learning it; it would I suppose be of a surety meet and necessary, hastening to go through every wise and true thought, to shew that It is unapproachable by death and utterly removed from sufferings. But since the mode of the Incarnation gives Him, so far as pertains to the plan of the Economy, even though He choose to die in the flesh, to suffer nought in His own Nature, why bereavest thou us of our fairest boasts? for thou heard'st Him say, The Good Shepherd layeth down His Life for His sheep. Hence even though He be said to suffer, we know that He is Impassible as God, we say that He hath suffered death economically in His own Flesh, in order that treading it and risen in that He is Life and Life-giving, He might transelement unto incorruption that which is tyrannized over by death, i. e., the body: and so unto us too spreadeth the might of the achievement, extending unto the whole race. And verily the Divine-uttering Paul saith, I through the Law died to the law that I might live unto God, I am crucified with Christ, I live, no longer I, but Christ liveth in me, and wherein I now live, I live in faith, in the flesh [2] of the Son of God Who loved me and gave Himself for me. I do not frustrate the grace of God. For no longer do we live our own life but rather that in Christ, and true is it that One died for all that they who live should no more live unto themselves but to Him which died for them and rose. For before that the Only-Begotten Word of God beamed on us, mastered by unlearning and darkness and having the yoke of sin and impiously ascribing worship to the creature rather than our Creator and Maker and practising unblamed every kind of baseness, we wretched abode in severance [from Him], in mind hostile to Him, but we have been reconciled through the death of His Son, as it is written.

But THOU again hast made but slight account of the truth, and putting forth unto us thy speech unbridled unto vapidness , sayest that the world has been reconciled to God, not through the Only-Begotten, i. e. the Word That sprang of the Father; and hearing, the death of His Son, and investigating subtilly as thou supposest, the words of the Divine, thou fearedst not to say, "He said not, Through the death of God the Word." Then how (tell me) were such a word wise, yea rather, how were it not replete with utter distraction? for how were it meet (tell me) to set forth the Life as subject to death; and to the Nature Which quickeneth all things to lay a charge of decay, how were it not wholly distraught and would it not be, and that with reason, a charge of blasphemy reaching unto the very extreme? By no means therefore does the mind of the saints go along with thy subtilties herein, or rather thy idle words: for it knows, it knows that the Word of God suffered in the flesh for our sakes, and through the death of His own Body hath called the world unto reconciliation with the Father Which is in Heaven. And verily when making His discourse with one of the holy disciples He somewhere said, I am the Way and the Truth and the Life and no man cometh unto the Father but by Me: but Truth and Life and Way, who else may be, save the Word which sprang of God, even though He have been made as we, by taking servant's form?

And that through Him we have been manifested partakers of the Divine Nature and, we who once were far, have been made nigh, united participatively through Him to the FATHER and besides to one another in one faith and unity of soul by reason of being made participant of One Spirit; Himself will give assurance saying unto God the Father in Heaven, Not for these alone do I ask but for them also which believe on Me through their word, that they all may be one, as THOU Father art in Me and I in Thee, that they also may be one in us, that the world may believe that THOU sentest Me, and I. the glory which Thou hast given Me, have given them, that they may be one even as WE are one, both I in them, and THOU in Me that they may be perfected into one. Understand therefore how Himself is of Nature in His own Father but is set forth a Mediator and Reconciler through being made as we: He is in us, both through His own Flesh Which quickeneth us in spirit and through partaking of His holiness, I mean again through the Holy Ghost. And He asketh as glory from the Father to make His own Nature manifest unto us, that It is both Life-giving and superior to corruption as God. And verily He said again, I glorified Thee on the earth by perfecting the work which Thou hast given Me to do, and now do Thou glorify Me, o Father, with Thyself with the glory which I had before the world was, with Thee. And a perfected work are WE, in Him first overcoming decay and treading on the might of death, for He lived anew from the dead, having all in Himself.

But haply bearing off to other ideas what has been said, thou sayest that not of God the Word ought these things to be understood, but removing from Him and putting apart by himself him that is born of the holy Virgin as another son, thou affirmest that him it is whom such things befit and art zealous to teach others also to think and say with thee: and wilt (I suppose) surely say that the Only-Begotten Word of God being Lord of glory, would not as though lacking glory, have sought it from the Father. Hear therefore from us too, If thou sayest that the Only-Begotten Son Who is out of God by Nature is not He Who here asketh glory from the Father; who was it who said, Glorify Me with the glory which I had before the world was, with Thee? How then (tell me) was he that is of the holy Virgin, conceived of according to thee as man separately, before the world? will it not pertain to the Creator of the ages, to have a being elder than the world and Co-eternal with the Father? no one will doubt it of those who are accustomed to think aright. When therefore He emptied Himself receiving servant's form, then, then, desirous to mount up unto the glory inherent in Him by Nature and along with the Flesh which was united to Him, in fit season does He say, Do THOU Father glorify Me with Thyself with the glory that I had before the world was with Thee; that the world may believe that THOU sentest Me, and I, the glory which Thou hast given Me, have given them, that they may be one as WE are One, I in them, and THOU in Me that they may be perfected into one. Through Him therefore have we had the reconciliation, for thus hath He perfected the work which the Father hath given Him for consummation. And the supporter of my words will I make again the most holy Paul who thus wrote to those who have been called out of the Gentiles, But now in Christ Jesus YE who sometime were far off were made nigh in the Blood of Christ: for He is our Peace, Who made both one and undid the middle wall of partition, having abolished in His Flesh the enmity, the law of commandments in ordinances, for to make in Himself of twain one new man, making peace; and that He might reconcile both unto God in one body through the cross, having slain the enmity therein, and came and preached peace to you which were afar off and to them that were nigh, and again elsewhere too, Justified therefore by faith, we have peace with God through our Lord Jesus Christ. Therefore we have been reconciled to God the Father through the death of His Son, who brought to nought or slew the enmity in His Flesh, according to the faith of the sacred scriptures.

But thyself art undoing the words of the economy and deignest not to confess that the Word of God hath suffered in the flesh for our sakes, making use of certain unskilful loquacity: for thou sayest that Son is a name common to the Word Which sprang of God and to ourselves. Then having made God the Word, through Whom we have been saved, no worker of the good things that have been wrought to us-ward, thou wilt be evidently caught allotting the things wherein He is glorified to one as we, conceived of as other than He and apart, and thou supposest that community of name will suffice full well for demonstration of what thou saidst and unrightly thoughtest; not considering that even though with things which obtain by nature the being ought, certain other of things that be, be said to be co-named, one must not therefore thrust away the things that are by nature, ever putting their properties about those which are by adoption or imitation. But we must (I deem) ever test the natures of things done and allot them to whomsoever they rightly pertain. As for example, the Father is named and is in truth God, and from Him is every fatherhood both in heaven and upon earth named, as it is written, yet are there with us other fathers too both fleshly and spiritual. If therefore ought of things most God-befitting be said of God the Father, will it belong to those too who by adoption obtain the same title with Him, and will the identity of name thrust Him away from the things which in the highest degree befit Him alone? yet how is it not evident to all that it is both absurd and discordant that any of ours should be minded thus to think and say? Why then dost thou ever talking to us of community of name, dishonour the by Nature and truly Son, putting Him forth and rendering Him alien from kindly deeds to usward? albeit thou oughtest to gather into union what thou blushest not utterly to sever, and [oughtest] to deem one with His own Flesh the Word that is out of God the Father: for thus wilt thou free thyself from much toil, and deeming aright wilt at length be praised. And thou wilt in no wise say that the Godhead of the Only-Begotten is passible, but wilt with us confess that He is Life and Life-giving by Nature and moreover beyond all suffering; next that the flesh suffering which was united to Him, He by the grace of God, as it is written, tasted death for every man, that having shewn His own Temple superior to him who had conquered all that are on the earth, He might be called the firstfruits of them that slept and the firstborn from the dead: transmitting to us too the grace, that being One and Only Son, both before the Incarnation and after it He might yet be called Saviour and Redeemer of all: and freeing (as I said) from sin all who believe on Him, might become peace to them that are afar and to the near, reconciling through Himself to God the Father them who of old worshipped the creature and through sin were at enmity with the All-good God.

But severing again into a pair of sons the One Lord Jesus Christ, he says after this wise:

"Hear their other testimony also; for had they known, they would not have crucified the Lord of glory. Lo he says the Lord of glory, he calls not so the manhood but the Godhead. But this belongs to those who pluck asunder the accurate connection, for when thou sayest, This is not Lord, but the other is, THOU makest Christ a mere man. What then dost thou say, o heretic in clerical form [3]? is the man too Lord or not? if then he be Lord, the things said agree; if he be not Lord, do not THOU making Christ a mere man, fasten the reproach of it on me." Then he says, "Hear we the blessed Paul openly crying out who He is who is crucified. Hear then most plainly the voice, For (says he) He was crucified out of weakness, yet He liveth out of the Power of God. If He were crucified out of weakness, who was it who was weak, heretic? God the Word?"

§2. He is carried away unto absurd thoughts and unto a reprobate mind, in no wise understanding the force of the mystery, as seems to me, but rather every way following his own devices and haply afraid, lest he should be caught either thinking or saying ought that pertains to Tightness or truth. For he arrays against himself, as he supposes, the words of the orthodox, but is caught again putting those things which no one of those who are wont to walk aright as to the Faith, would even so much as endure another saying. For we say that He which was crucified is Lord of glory, and He is so of a truth: yet acknowledging that the Word of God is inseverable and one with the flesh united, to Him having a reasonable soul, we say that He it is Who offered Himself, as it were the Immaculate Offering and most sweet-smelling Sacrifice of His Own Body, to God the Father, and nailed to the wood the handwriting that was against us. And one may hear Him say by the mouth of David, Sacrifice and offering Thou wouldest not but a Body preparedst Thou Me, whole burnt sacrifices and for sin Thou tookest no pleasure in: then said I, Lo I come (in the volume of the book it has been written of Me) to do Thy Will, o God. The commandment according to the Law now availing nought, and perfecting nothing, and God the Father holding the sacrifices through blood unacceptable;----He says that a Body has been prepared for Himself, in order that giving it a Ransom for the salvation and life of all, He might redeem all, from both death and decay and yet more from sins.

We say then that the very Word out of God the Father chose even to suffer for us in the flesh, according to the Scriptures: thus hath the most holy Paul instructed us, Who being in the Form of God held not the being Equal with God a thing to seize, but emptied Himself taking servant's form, made in likeness of man and found in fashion as a man, He humbled Himself and became obedient unto death, the death of the cross, wherefore God also highly exalted Him. View now how He That is in the Form of God the Father as God, the Impress of His Person and in no wise falling short, being and being conceived of in

Equality in everything, hath emptied Himself and brought Himself down of His own will unto lowliness.

What then (tell me) will be the mode of the emptying, how again has He been abased receiving servant's form and made obedient unto death, the death of the Cross? is it not clear to all that the High is abased, not that which from itself and of its own nature is in abasement and brought low; that (I suppose) is emptied which is full and in need of nought; receives the servant's form which before it was free by nature, He is found to be man too Who was not so, before He was so found when He was not? Who then is He That was High by Nature and abased Himself unto lowliness? who the full, that He may be conceived of as emptied? who He That is beyond the measures of bondage, that so He may be said to take the bondman's form? who that not being aforetime man as we is said to have been so found? For I suppose that to dare to allot this to one of those as we and to a common man, would be folly and verily replete with the uttermost of all unwit, but it will pertain with all reason to the Supreme Nature.

But the Word of God, of His exceeding Clemency and Kindness towards us, hath offered for us His own Body and having taken the servant's form, hath become obedient to God the Father unto death: and the choice to suffer in the Flesh, He made not a thing to be spurned, albeit by Nature Impassible as God. Yet does this man foolishly blush at His most God-befitting schemes for us, and thinking he honours Him, wrongs Him: for he bears Him away from the suffering, though no one else says that He suffers in His own Nature; and does not perceive that he forbids Him to be confessed Saviour and Redeemer of all, if so be that he is son and lord other than He, separately and apart, through whom we have been saved and redeemed through the precious Cross. And if so be he be simply man, and not rather the Word out of God the Father appearing in human form, let him come, let him shew that he is both in the Form of the Father and in Equality with Him (for He thought not the being equal with God a thing to seize) and moreover that he took the form of the servant as at one time not possessing it, and came to be in emptiness, as possessing fulness in his own nature: for the Divine-uttering Paul says that He Who is in the Form and Equality with God the Father, was made obedient unto Him even to death, the death of the Cross.

Is not then the absurdity of their notions manifest? when blessed Paul calls Him that was crucified Lord of glory, no one will say, 'He is not speaking of the human nature but the Godhead.' For we confess One Christ and Son and Lord of Glory, the Word out of God the Father made man for our sakes and suffering for us in the flesh, according to the Scriptures.

But he in no small measure blaming, as wishing to pluck asunder the accurate connection (as himself says), those who allot to God the Word the name of Lordship and bear it away from the human nature:----he falling into forgetfulness of what he said, is caught plucking asunder into two the One, and little recking of accurate (according to him) connection. For he unlearnedly enquires, "Is the man too lord or not? if then he be lord, the things said harmonize." Hence if according to thy witless enquiry, the Word is Lord by Himself and the man lord, two surely are the lords and sons. The force then of accurate connection will in no wise profit them who have believed that one ought to conceive of One Christ and Son and Lord with the Flesh united to Him. For the Person of Immanuel being put and brought forward, though one should say man, we conceive of the Word out of God the Father having taken the servant's form and say that He is shewn by the measures of emptiness: and if [we say] Only-Begotten God, we believe the Same now Incarnate and made Flesh. But he (as I said) allotting to a man, individual and alone and considered apart from the Word Which is out of the Father, the achievements of the Economy with flesh, says that he too endured the cross for us and affirms that he is the Lord of glory, putting about a mere creature the glories of the Supreme Nature, for he says, "Let us hear the blessed Paul openly exclaiming who he is that is crucified; for verily He was crucified out of weakness but He liveth out of the Power of God; who is weak o heretic, is it God the Word?"

Utterly imparticipate therefore of all weakness is the Word out of God the Father by us believed to be: for He is the Lord of Hosts. But tell me this, art thou afraid to admit the appellation of weakness in respect to Him? why? albeit the Economy with flesh puts Him apart from all blame, even though He be said to suffer ought of what is beside His own Nature and glory: for if being Rich He became poor and was made as we receiving servant's form, even though He should be said to be weak by reason of the human nature, there is nought repugnant, that you should see the Hich poor, the High in low estate, the Lord of Hosts in weakness as we. Marvellous on this account also is the mystery respecting Him. For how is He said also to hunger, albeit Himself the Bread of Life and Who came down from Heaven and giveth Life to the world? how was He wearied with the journey, Who stablisheth the Heavens with His own Spirit?

But thou wilt not endure (it seems) if one say these things of the Only-Begotten Himself, albeit investigating thine own words I find them clearly saying, as of the Person of the Only-Begotten,

"The form of God, I am clad in servant's form: being God the Word, am seen in flesh: Lord of all, am clad for your sakes in person of a poor man: hungering visibly, I supply food to the hungry."

§3. How then, say, didst thou fearing the appellation of weakness and bearing it away from Him, albeit the plan of the economy will it not, say that He hungers visibly, i. e., humanly, yet Divinely supplies food to the hungry? dost thou not say that it is a form of weakness to be in need of food and to be said to hunger as we? but against them who desire to be fault-finders, full strong will the mode of the economy array itself. We must therefore, either bearing Him away from all things that are said humanly and in mean wise, put such passions about a mere man, or considering that He being God has been made as we, confess that He is impassible in respect of the Nature of the Godhead, but say besides that He endured the weakness in our behalf, according to the human nature and after the flesh, I mean. Since, tell me who ask thee again, The Divine-uttering Paul says that He has been crucified out of weakness; but dost thou bear away this thing from God the Word, saying (I suppose) that it is small and ignoble and not worthy of Him? Other therefore than He is he that was crucified, Whom also our Divine instructor calls Lord of glory, saying, For had they known, they would not have crucified the Lord of glory. Hath He, then yet remained Lord of Glory Who put it aside and endured this ignoble and mean suffering? If therefore He hath remained so, neither hath He any loss through being weak. How then fearedst thou to say that the Word of God came to be in this case economically? But if He truly fell from being any longer Lord of glory, and any one affirm that it is so, he will incur the charge of the most utter blasphemy and that with reason: for to Him boweth every knee and every tongue shall confess Lord Jesus Christ, to the glory of God the Father. For over all that is under Heaven extendeth the glory of Christ Who suffered for us in the flesh, as we have full often said. When therefore thou nearest the Spirit-clad saying, He was crucified out of weakness but He liveth of the Power of God, understand it piously: for he says that He hath suffered humanly, albeit He hath a nature utterly beyond passion. And so having, He bare with the weak flesh and having suffered death humanly, He lived again Divinely, Himself quickening His own Temple, as the Might of the Father.

And verily when the time was now at hand in which He must endure the Cross for us, He went away and prayed saying, Father if it he possihle, let this cup pass from Me, but added hereto at the close of His Prayer, Nevertheless not as I will but as THOU. But since He albeit Word and God all-Powerful, has once been held to be in weakness like we, He giving the cause of this most economically, says, The spirit indeed is willing, the flesh weak. Consider therefore how He though Himself letting go nought, nor yet suffering weakness in His own Nature, permitted His Flesh to go after its own laws, and this thing is said to be His, because His Body is His own. Hence the being weak according to the Flesh proved to us that He was Man, the not enduring death and scaring away decay from His own Body that He is God Who knows not to be weak: for He is the Life and Might of the Father. For that the weakness herein unwonted and unwilled by Him [4] , He made voluntary in the good-pleasure of God the Father, to save all under Heaven, Himself will teach saying, For I have come down from Heaven, not to do Mine own Will but the Will of Him That sent Me, that of all which He hath given Me I should lose nothing but should raise it up at the last day.

Yet how, if the will of the Father be good, does the Son say that He has His own Will, a good one surely, and other than this? For if it be not good, how is He any longer believed to be His Image and Impress? how will He be true, saying, I and the Father are One, and, He that hath seen Me hath seen the Father? for not in the not good, would one behold the Good by Nature. But verily the Son being Good hath sprung from a Good Father and is His exact Image in everything. What Will therefore, which He says is His own, does He letting go, say that He hath done that of the Father? He was about by the death of His own Flesh to set free from death those who had become subject thereto, i. e., us. But to die in the Flesh was ignoble, and unwonted (as I said) and repugnant to Him: yet hath He endured this too for our sakes in the Good-pleasure of the Father. For He knew, He knew and that well that a little dishonoured by reason of the sufferings of the Flesh He should save all, transforming them unto what was incomparably better. For if any be in Christ, a new creature, old things are gone by, behold all things have become new, as it is written.

The God-inspired Scriptures therefore proclaim to the world One Christ and Son and Lord and say that He is the Lord of Glory and that He of His own Will bare for our sakes the contumelies of the Jews, and economically endured Death upon the wood, not in order with us to remain dead, but that having undone the might of death which none might withstand, He might bring again to immortality the nature of man: for He was God in Flesh.

But this man again essaying to gather to himself from all quarters occasions of severing into two the One, arrays himself to no purpose against those who exist not at all, and makes accusal of certain as though they spake against the truth and desired to adulterate the plan of the mystery, and says,

"Here [5] I would gladly enquire of the heretics who mix up into one essence the Nature of the Godhead and of the Manhood, who he is here who is by the traitor betrayed to the Jews: for if there have been a mixture of both, both were together holden of the Jews, both God the Word and the nature of the manhood: which is it that endured the slaughter? I am obliged to use meaner words that what I say may be plain to all. To whom (tell me) befell this deed? for if the Nature of the Godhead, how darest thou commingle both? God [6] hath both remained unholden of the Jews and hath not shared with the flesh in its slaughter: whence (tell me) dost thou get in the mixture?

§4. If then there be who say that there has been a commingling of the natures one with another and that they undergo an impossible fusion, and who maintain that the Nature of the Word could suffer change into flesh, or the Flesh united to Him ever pass into Godhead; they have erred from the truth and, out of their right mind, yea rather sick with the veriest distraction, they shall hear from us, Ye do err not knowing the Scriptures nor the Power of God; for steadfast is the Nature of God the Word, nor knows it to suffer a shadow of turning, but participate in flesh and blood and taking part with us in the same, as it is written, He abode the Same. But if every one who is educated in the Holy Scriptures holds it repugnant to so much as hear that any change was wrought in the Only-Begotten, why dost thou admitting as true and really spoken things so disgraceful and condemned by one voice by all and utterly rejected, essay to sever the Indivisible and that after the Union? For if thou wouldest indeed of a truth learn who it is who is by the traitor given up to the Jews, and endured slaughter, thou wilt clearly hear, The One and Only Christ and Son and Lord, that is the Word out of God Who took the servant's form, made man and Incarnate: for He was sold by the traitor to the rulers of the Jews, and was holden humanly, because He was Man too along with abiding God, but Divinely He was convicting the weakness of them who hold Him. And this the Divine-uttering Evangelist John makes manifest to us, thus writing, Judas therefore having received the band and officers from the chief priests and Pharisees cometh thither with torches and lanterns and weapons; Jesus knowing all things that were coming upon Him, went forth and said unto them, Whom seek ye? they answered Him, Jesus of Nazareth. Jesus saith unto them, I am. And Judas which betrayed Him was standing with them. When therefore He said unto them, I am, they went backward and fell to the ground. Hearest thou that He does not let them who have been gathered together by the traitor behave themselves proudly against His Glory? for He offered Himself saying, I am, but they unstrung by the voice alone, went backward.

And that it was no work of their own strength to hold Him, but that in his season and in need He made death for us welcome, He hath proved saying, As a robber came ye forth with swords and staves to take Me? daily did I sit in the Temple teaching, and ye laid no hold on Me, but all this has been done that the Scriptures of the Prophets might be fulfilled. For what He hath of old foretold through the holy Prophets, this hath He fulfilled, abasing Himself unto emptiness Who is above all the creation, and found in fashion as a man Who is in the Form and Equality with the Father.

Why then dost thou, essaying to bring in privily the name of mixture, wrong in the ears of the more simple the marvel of the economy with flesh? for it does not befit thee bitterly and harshly to come forward saying, "Was God the Word holden? did the nature of the Godhead undergo slaughter?" That of no accurate . . . . thou art saying such things, thou wilt know hence and that easily. We say that the holy Martyrs have been perfected, choosing to suffer all things in order that having striven the good strife, finished their course, kept the faith, they might bind on them the crown of true relationship to Christ. If then any were to come forward and ask, When the bodies of the saints were torn by the steel or wasted by fire or again when they first became prisoners, were their souls holden along with their bodies? did they too become the work of fire and sword? albeit we say that they [the souls] were apart from their bodies, enduring nought of such contumelies in their own nature. Will they therefore (tell me) be for this reason imparticipate of the crowns, because they have not suffered the things of the body? But verily the word of truth does not put them apart from suffering, for they suffered the things of their own, not those of others' bodies.

Unlearned then is it to want to ask whether the nature of the Godhead have been betrayed along with the flesh, or whether It were holden in the meshes of the Jews or endured the slaughter also: but it is pious to conceive rather that the Word will surely and entirely make His own the sufferings that have befallen His own Flesh, but abode Impassible as God yet not external to His suffering Body [7]. But he involving in charges of absurdity the things so economically wrought, and again and again saying that the Nature of the Godhead ought not to be said by any to have undergone slaughter, unholily arrays the force of the Mystery about a man by himself, and says that he it is who was crucified and endured death for the life of the world. For I hear him saying in another exposition of his,

"This is he who was encircled in the thorny Crown, this he who saith, My God, My God why forsookest Thou Me? this he who endured a three days' death." [8]

§5. Such things then doth he say, following his own aim, but WE will shew him a wiser and truer Emmanuel, the whole world's Saviour and Redeemer. For the Word, as we have full often said, was made flesh, and making His own, a Body which knew to suffer contumelies and death, He hath given it for us and, as the Divine-uttering Paul saith, endured the cross, despising the shame. For was it not shame and a sort of abashment to Him that hath a Nature All-Strong and Quickening and above suffering, to seem to be crucified out of human weakness and to come to death after the flesh? And verily the Same saith through the voice of Isaiah, My Back I have given to scourges, My Cheeks to blows, My Face turned I not away from the shame of spittings, and again, Therefore was I not confounded, but I set My Face as a firm rock and I know that I shall not be ashamed, for He is near that justifieth Me. For as far as regards the impious multitudes of the Greeks and also of the Jews, the Mystery of Christ is reputed a stumbling block alike and foolishness, for they deride (miserable ones!) the Precious Cross; but the end of the weakness (as it seemed to them) resulted in might of glory most truly God-befitting. For through the Resurrection from the dead it has been testified that He is God and Son of God in truth, as superior to death and decay, and is worshipped by all together with Him Who begat Him.

And hear the sacred Scriptures proclaiming to us this very thing: Thus saith the Lord, Sanctify Him That holdeth light His Soul, Him that is abhorred by the nations, the servants, the rulers: kings shall see Him and princes shall rise up and worship Him. Confess (it said) that He is Holy by Nature as God, Who held cheaply His own Soul, i. e., despised His own life (for He hath laid it down for His sheep, as Good Shepherd): Him Whom the nations vilely esteemed, servants and officers insulted with blows, while the multitudes of the Pharisees impiously outraged Him, Him shall kings see and rise up, Him shall princes worship, as God, that is, who descended into emptiness, in order that suffering in the flesh, He might save all under Heaven. This is He Who for us was encircled with the Thorny Crown, this, not another, He Who as Man is crucified and says, My God My God why forsookest Thou Me? yet who restrains as God the Light of the sun, and makes it night in mid-day that we should not confess Him Man, simply honoured with mere connection (according to thee) with the Word I mean That is out of God, but should believe rather that He is God, in likeness as we, and in servant's form, remembering Him Who saith by a Saint's voice, And I will clothe the Heavens with darkness, and I will make their covering as sackcloth. For He Who speaketh is at hand, and what He of old hath as God foresignified would be, He in due season was fulfilling, crucified as Man. For the Heaven put on darkness, all but a mourning dress, the sun no longer giving the brightness of its rays to them who had durst outrage the Lord and God of all, hath foresignified the darkness which they should have in mind and heart. For the blessed David too sings somewhere of them, Let their eyes be darkened that they see not and bow down their back alway. And the veil too of the Temple was rent, revealing now to those who believe on Him the holy of holies and shewing the most inward parts, the first tabernacle no longer standing, but the way into the holy now made manifest, that is into the holy of holies. For holy confessedly was the Law too, in that it was the furnisher of righteousness, our guide too unto Christ: yet incomparably holier is the life in Christ esteemed, and more excellent and in better case the worship in spirit and in truth than that in shadows and types. Will not such achievements then be God-befitting and above the nature of man? hath not the saving Passion shamed the waving [sword, brought man again into Paradise? for Christ said to the robber who hung with Him, Today shalt thou be with Me in Paradise: beamed He not on them that were in darkness, uttering with authority, Shew yourselves? For He has emptied Hell as God, and loosed from their bonds those who were in it: and He it was Who of old crieth out to the most enduring Job, Camest thou into the springs of the sea? walkedst thou in the tracks of the depth? are the gates of death open to thee in fear [of thee]? did the doorkeepers of hell seeing thee tremble?

Wherefore then blushest thou not allotting things that are yet God-befitting to one as we and to a mere man? For that the Word of God Himself, taking servant's form, participate in flesh and blood, endured to give His own Body to death for our sakes and, being Impassible by Nature, suffered in the Flesh of His own will, the all-wise Paul will give us proof, writing, Giving thanks unto the Father Which made us meet to be partakers of the lot of the saints in light,

Who delivered us from the authority of darkness and translated us into the kingdom of the Son of His Love, in Whom we have redemption, the forgiveness of sins, Who is the Image of the Invisible God, the firstborn of every creature; for in Him were created all things in Heaven and upon earth, visible and invisible, whether thrones or lordships or principalities or authorities, all things were created through Him and unto Him, and He is before all things and in Him all things consist, and He is the Head of the body, the Church, Who is the beginning, the firstborn from the dead, that in all things He might have the preeminence. See now the Priest of His Mysteries said and that very clearly that the Very God the Word, through Whom are all things and in Whom are all things, Who is the Image of the Invisible God; He through Whom were brought into being both the things which are in Heaven and those on earth, the visible and invisible; He Who is before all things, in Whom all things consist; has been given as Head to the Church, and is Himself the firstborn from the dead.

But (you will perhaps say) the Word out of God the Father is by Nature Life; how then or in what way might Life die? well: necessary and useful is your question. Therefore unto the force of the mystery is serviceably taken, that we conceive and say that the ever-living and Life-giving Word of God was made Flesh, i. e., made His own a Body recipient of death, that Himself might be conceived to suffer, because His Very own Body suffered. For thus do we say that He became the firstfruits of them that slept, and the firstborn from the dead: for He is said to have been laid with us in a tomb through His own flesh, Who raiseth the dead, that we too might be co-raised with Him: for this way did He inaugurate for us and for this hath He humbled Himself, abasing Himself unto emptiness and unto manhood with us; albeit the Only-Begotten is God by Nature and beamed from God the Father.

But he thinks (it seems) that they who suppose that these things are so, and who deem aright, have advanced to the goal of the uttermost distraction; and everywhere alleging that we ought to confess the Word out of God the Father to be Impassible, he removes from Him and that utterly the mode of His Economy: and thinks it not meet either to think or say that He suffered for us, albeit the God-inspired Scripture says that He suffered in the Flesh, He both Impassible and Unembodied, because the Body suffered that is His own and united to Him. He says again thus,

"Therefore concerning our first-fruits, blessed Peter telling, and relating the exaltation by the Godhead of the nature that is seen, says, This Jesus God raised up. God did not die, He raised up. Hear, o Apolinarius, the words of Peter, hear with Apolinarius, thou too Arius. This Jesus, he says, God raised up, the visible, him who was seen with the eyes, affixed to the wood, handled by the hands of Thomas, who cried to him, Handle Me, for a spirit hath not flesh and bones as ye see Me have. And by these words the disciple persuaded, and by the handling of the crucified body persuaded of the resurrection, began to glorify the wonder-working God, Glory to Thee [9], my Lord and my God: not addressing as God that which was handled, for not by handling is the Godhead discerned." And after other, "Of this that was handled was Peter too exclaiming, This Jesus God raised up, being therefore by the Right Hand of God exalted. God the Word had no need of an aiding right hand, o Arius." §6. The Son raiseth up the dead and we say that He is superior to death, for we remember Him Who hath openly said, I am the Resurrection and the Life: yet when the Divine-uttering Peter announces to us saying, This Jesus God raised up, we believe that the Word made man is Jesus Himself. How then will one say that He has been raised by the Father and exalted by His Right Hand? for I think that this should be clearly set forth to those who cannot understand, in order that cutting off occasion of stumbling, we may set forth the way of truth straight and most unerring.

    He gave therefore His own Body to death for a little while: for by the grace of God, as Paul saith, He tasted death for every man. Then being Himself the Life-giving Right Hand and Power of God the Father, He rendered it superior to decay and death: and of this He gives us assurance saying to the Jews, Destroy this Temple and in three days I will raise it up. Understand therefore that Himself promises to rear His own Temple, albeit God the Father is said to raise it: for the Son is, as I said, the Life-giving Right Hand and Power of the Father. So that even though the Father be said to work the quickening of the Divine Temple, He hath wrought it through the Son, and though the Son again be seen to work it, yet not without the Father in the Spirit. For One is the Nature of Godhead, conceived of in three several Persons, and having Its motion and Operation, spiritual I mean and God-befitting, in regard to all things that are done.

    The body therefore yielded to the laws of its own nature, and admitted the taste of death, the Word united thereto permitting it for profit's sake to suffer this: but was quickened by the Divine power of the Word Personally united to it. We conceive then of Whole Emmanuel, which is interpreted, With us is God, when we hear the Divine-uttering Peter say, This Jesus God raised up; and though thou speak of the visible and affixed to the wood, of "him who was handled by the hands of Thomas," no less do WE conceive of the Word out of God the Father Incarnate, and confess One and the Same Son. For being Invisible by Nature He hath become visible, because His too was the visible Body. And verily the Divine David sings to us, God shall come manifestly, our God and shall not keep silence, and moreover the blessed Habaccuc, God shall come from Teman and the Holy One from the deep-shaded mountain. He being also Impalpable is said to have become palpable by reason of the Body united to Him. And Luke writes, Since many essayed to set forth in order an account of those things which have been most surely believed among us, even as they handed them to us which from the beginning were eye-witnesses and ministers of the Word, and to this the wise John saith, That which was from the beginning, which we have heard, which we have seen with our eyes, which we looked on and our hands handled, of the Word of Life, and the Life was manifested and we have seen and bear witness and declare to you the eternal life which was with the Father and was manifested to us. Yet had He not become palpable and visible, as having for His own a Body which is subject to touch and sight, how had the all-wise disciples been made eye-witnesses of the Word? how had they both seen, and say that they handled the Word of Life, Which was with the Father and was manifested to us? This very Same therefore Which was both palpable and visible, Which was affixed to the wood, Thomas recognized and did rightly confess to be God and Lord: for he said immediately, My Lord and my God. Then said to him our Lord Jesus Christ, Because thou hast seen Me, thou hast believed, blessed they which have not seen and believed. Believed what, tell me? is it not that being God by Nature,

He raised from the dead His own Temple? yet how could there be any doubt of this?

But this good man, all but foolishly ashamed of the words of the disciple, says not, 'He confessed Him that He is both Lord and God, the Firstborn from the dead:' but rather he perverts to his own pleasure the force of the word and says that he "began to glorify the wonder-working God, saying, My Lord and my God," and subjoins, "Not addressing as God that which was handled, for not by the touch is the Godhead discerned."

Blamest thou therefore (tell me) the disciple calling Christ Lord and God? though our argument has but just now shewn that the Only Begotten being by Nature God, Impalpable and Invisible, became palpable and visible. But when thou sayest, "for not by the touch is the Godhead discerned," we again will say, Why dost thou, thrusting aside the Economy discourse of Godhead as though bare? and rushing full speed to forgetfulness that the Impalpable and Unembodied was both Incarnate and made Man, endurest not the God-inspired Scripture naming Him God, because that He had been both handled in flesh and likewise seen of the holy Apostles? But WE, my friend, together with blessed Thomas, crowning with the praises befitting Him, Him That was affixed to the wood, Him That was handled by hands and seen of human eyes, say, My Lord and my God.

But that though a man should say that the Word of God suffered in His own Flesh, he would not be without share in being praise-worthy nor in having chosen to think the truth (for even thus hath He abode Impassible): I will essay to shew again from what thyself hast written or saidst in Church. For thou deemest worthy of praise our holy Fathers, those (I mean) who were in their season gathered together at Nicea, as having formed full well for us an accurate and finished confession of faith: yet thou thinkest not what they do (whence should'st thou?) nor yet fixing thy mind on the doctrines of the truth, dost thou long to go straight, but haltest on both thighs, as it is written: foolishly blaming the lovers of right doctrine, yet holding for truth what liketh thyself, yea rather not even caring to abide in what thyself saidst, for I find thee saying of the holy fathers,

"For since if they had said, We believe in One God the Word, death would have been imputed to the Divine Nature, they admit a common term, Christ Jesus, that they may indicate both Him That died, and him that did not die." And he adds, *"So that if a man should say, Such an one is dead, though the soul is immortal, yet since he said the word which iudicates the two natures, both the mortal body and the immortal soul, the expression is free from risk: for both are called man, both the body and the soul: thus it is therefore that that great band spake of Christ."*

§7. That in naming Christ Jesus, they did not indicate two several sons, having a common name, Christ Jesus, but rather the Word out of God made Man, I think no one that deems aright will gainsay, and I think it superfluous for us to yet array many words on this matter besides what have been already said. Yet if thou be not persuaded by our words to think that though we say that the Word of God hath suffered in the Flesh for our sakes, we hold Him even thus Impassible as God, at least allow to thine own words that they appear to have been rightly framed. For just as he who said man, indicated the soul together with the body although it be of other nature than it; and even though such an one's body were said to be dead, the whole person would reasonably be held to have suffered this, albeit he possess a soul which is not recipient of death: so of Christ too the Saviour of us all. For since the Word out of God the Father (as we have repeatedly said) hath partaken of blood and flesh in like manner as we, and made His own the Body that is of the holy Virgin and has thus been called Son of man too ; for this reason when His Flesh died, the plan of true union attributes the suffering to Him, yet knows that He hath remained apart from suffering because He is both God by Nature and Life. And verily the Divine-uttering Peter setting before us this teaching says of Him somewhere to them that believe on Him, Whom having not seen ye love, on Whom, though now ye see Him. not, yet believing, ye exult with joy unutterable and glorified, receiving the fulfilment of your faith, the salvation of your souls, of which salvation the prophets searched out and examined into, who prophesied of the grace to youward, searching what or what manner of time the Spirit of Christ Which was in them was signifying, when It testified beforehand the sufferings of Christ and the glory that should follow, unto whom it was revealed that not unto themselves but to us they were ministering the things which are now declared unto us through them that preached the Gospel unto us with the Holy Ghost sent down from Heaven: which things the Angels long to look into.

Hearest thou that the Spirit of Christ was in the holy Prophets too, and that they proclaimed beforehand the sufferings of Christ and the glory that should follow? Did they then proclaim to the world as though a mere man were suffering for us? and is this the mystery which through our holy Apostles and Evangelists hath been given in trust, and into these things does he say that the Angels long to look? yet how is not he to be utterly repudiated who essays to shut up the might of the mystery within the limits of the human nature alone? God the Word Himself, Who is in the Form of God the Father, hath emptied Himself taking servant's form and hath undergone birth in the flesh for our sakes, Himself hath suffered for us in His own Flesh, and He lived again as God, having emptied Hades and said to them that were in bonds, Come forth, and to them that were in darkness, Shew yourselves. Why then essayest thou to overturn the so dread and marvellous economy through which we have been both saved and have been brought within all good? for what we gained through it, thou wilt know and that very clearly, since blessed Paul hath thus written, And you that were sometime alienated and enemies n your mind in wicked works, yet now hath He reconciled in the body oj His flesh through death to present you holy and unblameable and unreproveable in His sight if so be ye endure in the Faith. Therefore the faith profits them who will hold it unshaken; how it profits, the all-wise John will assure us saying, Who is he that overcometh the world but he that believeth that Jesus is the Son of God? This is He that came through water and blood, Jesus Christ, not in water only, but in water and blood, and the Spirit is Truth; for three testify, the Spirit, the water and the Blood, and the Three are One. If we receive the witness of men, the witness of God is greater, for this is the witness of God, because He hath witnessed concerning His Son: he that believeth on the Son of God hath the witness in himself, he that believeth not God hath made him a liar, because he believed not the testimony which He hath testified regarding His Son. And how God the Father hath testified to His Son, the Divine-uttering John the Baptist will declare saying. And I knew Him not, but He That sent me to baptize with water, He said to me, Upon Whom thou shalt see the Spirit descending and remaining upon Him, This is He Which baptizeth with the Holy Ghost. And I saw and have testified that This is the Son of God. Our Lord Jesus Christ therefore is witnessed to through the Father's Voice, that He is by Nature and in truth His Son, He is witnessed to no less through the water and the Blood and the Spirit. For by the holy water He purgeth away the sins of them that believe, He quickeneth through His own Blood and connecteth to God them on the earth: and since He is God by Nature He maketh also richly the grant of the Holy Ghost, pouring It forth as His own into the hearts of them who believe, and making them partakers of the Divine Nature, and crowning them with the hope of the good things to come.

We confess therefore One Son, Christ Jesus the Lord, that is, the Word of God made Man and Incarnate and Him crucified and raised from the dead and to come in due time in the Glory of God the Father with the holy Angels; through Him and with Him to God the Father be glory with the Holy Ghost for ever. Amen.

Footnotes:

1. S. Cyril in his first Letter to the Monks comments thus on this text: "Then (tell me) how is He who is forth of the holy virgin called God's own Son? for as the own of a man and so of each animal besides, is that which is born thereof by nature: thus God's own will be conceived and said to be that which is out of His Essence. How then has Christ been called God's own Son, who has also been given by God the Father for the salvation and life of all? for He was delivered because of our transgressions, and Himself bare the sins of many in His Body upon the Tree, according to Prophet's voice. It is evident then, that the fact of the Union, of necessity brought forward, shews that He who is forth of the holy Virgin is God's own Son." Epp. p. 15 a b. see also de recta fide to the Princesses Arcadia and Marina p. 104 a.

2. This transposition is probably a manuscript-error, there is no trace of it in the same citation in Glaph. 227 e, 403 b, de Ad. 408 a, de Recta fide G8 b, []in xii Prophetas 853 d.

3. .... see exactly the same expression at the close of serm. 2 in Mercator, "Si haereticus tibi ex persona ecclesiastica mortuum Deum tuum exprobaverit," p. 69 fin. Bal. It is not clear whom Nestorius is addressing as "heretic" and as having called the Godhead Lord of glory. The learned but uncritical Jesuit, John Garnier (see Tillemont's remarks in notes 71, 73, 74, 91 on S. Cyril of Alexandria, t. xiv. 780, 781, 792 sq. ed. 2) supposes this to be a reply (Marii Merc. opp. ii. pp. 29,30. Par. 1673) to S. Proclus' famous homily on the Incarnation (Migne, Patrol. lxv. 679 sqq.), but I do not see any special mention of this point in S. Proclus' Homily. One would naturally expect S. Cyril to be the person referred to, but besides that S. Cyril immediately after disclaims the expression, a List of references to S. Cyril's extant citations of 1 Cor. ii. 8 (generously furnished me by the Dean of Chichester) do not supply any passage likely to be

referred to by Nestorius. S. Cyril in his work against the Arians cites the text in proof that the Son is not less than the FATHER. "Making discourse of the princes of this world and the folly that is in them, he says, For had they known they would not have crucified the Lord of glory. Hence if the SON Who endured the cross for our sakes is Lord of glory, how is He not God by Nature ? how a creature or made, Who is even hymned by the Seraphin? for they say that full is the heaven and the earth of His Glory, and call Him Lord of Sabaoth: for it is clear that of Him are they saying this if He is Lord of glory, as Paul saith." Thes. cap. 32 p. 272 a. Commenting on the whole passage (1 Cor. ii. 6-8) in reference to Nestorian errors, S. Cyril says, "If the mystery of Christ be God's wisdom, and. it is preached to the world and if He is not truly God according to what somehow pleases some to imagine, and our faith is to Himward ; how is the mystery wise if it bear away them on the earth from the true knowledge of God and render the world worshipper of a man? But it is not so, the mystery IS wise for it brings to God them that have strayed. Christ therefore is God, He that has been crucified is rightly called Lord of glory." de recta fide to the princesses, p. 62 a. "Therefore the blessed Paul himself somewhere says of the rulers of this world, For had they known, they would not have crucified the Lord of glory. He knows then that the Crucified is Lord of glory." de recta fide to the Empresses, § 31 p. 168 b c.

4. See also S. Cyril's commentary on these verses of S. John, book 4 beg. pp 383 sqq. O.T.

5. This is given also by Mercator, among his collection of extracts made by S.Cyril, with the title, Also in the sixth quire of the same, on Judas, against the heretics, p. 116 Bal. Mercator's extract is much ampler, comprising as well the heading of § 7 of book 4 (above p. 153) and a little more.

6. The one Greek MS now extant has kai memeneken ho theos, the Roman Editors conjecture ei memeneke, but Mercator translates, Is therefore the Word of God, Who has no participation in the slaughter of His flesh, capable of being apprehended and led to slaughter by the Jews?

7. " How therefore is Life said to die ? by suffering death in Its own flesh, in order that It may be shewn to be life by quickening it again. For come if in regard even to our own selves the mode of death be searched into, no one who deems aright would say that souls perish along with the bodies that are of earth. I suppose that no living person would hesitate as to this. Yet is what happens called the death of man. Thus you will conceive of as to Emmanuel too. For the Word was in him that is of a woman as in His own Body, and He gave it to death in due time, Himself suffering nought in His proper Nature." Letter 1 to the Monks, Epp. p. 17 d e.

8. Serm. 2 p. 64. Bal. see above p. 69.

9. The words Glory to Thee, seem to be a gloss, they are not in the Latin translation of Nestorius' Homily 2. p. 58 ed. Baluz., nor does S. Cyril cite them in his comment a little below, when citing this portion of Nestorius' words.

Against Diodore of Tarsus and Theodore of Mospuestia

By Cyril of Alexandria

CYRIL FROM HIS TREATISE AGAINST DIODORE BISHOP OF TARSUS [1]

of which the beginning is
Nought shall be ranked before the Truth by them at least who love it and are well skilled in uttering what pertains to it.

1. His words from the treatises against Diodore and Theodore: the beginning of the Treatise.
Nothing is valued before the Truth by them who love it and are skilful in speaking what pertains thereto : yet is it right (I say) that they who are thus minded and are zealous rightly to walk in the holy doctrines of the Church, should both guilelessly give heed to any who think and speak aright and not again, holden by reverence and love, commit themselves to those who write not without blame, in order that they be not blamed as calling evil good and good evil, sweet bitter and bitter sweet, and putting darkness for light, and light for darkness : but accomplishing rather that which is consonant to the Divine law (for Judge, it says, righteous judgement), consonant too to the wise Paul, Be ye wise hankers, prove all things : may accept that which is excellent, and keep far from what is not so. For it is absurd that irrational animals, should be instructed by the laws of nature, to know well what is good for them and what is not so: so that they make their food of those things in the field which have no harm in them, and leave those which do harm; and that WE who have understanding and right reason (for nature is wise and has perfectly the power of well examining each thing) should not rightly and without error examine the force of things written or spoken that we may honour with praise the things which are blameless, and turn aside from all which are unduly spoken and which step outside of the doctrines of the truth.

2. Albeit how ought not one who wanted to shew the difference of the properties, I mean of flesh and Godhead, to advance to this very point by such thoughts and words as were meet? For not the same as regards the quality which is inherent in each of the things named, are Body and the Unembodied, the flesh taken of human lump and the Word which beamed forth from the Essence of God the Father. Yet we must not therefore sever into two christs and sons the One Lord J ESUS C HRIST.

3. But that we say that the Flesh of the Lord has been ensouled with reasonable soul, has been full often told by us, and now too no less do we affirm that it is no otherwise.

4. Let Diodore hear now from us too, If you say that He is flesh whom you call a Nazarene or an assumed man, shew thyself to us apart from all disguise and mask, tell (I pray) clearly what you deem good to think, and do not, simply speaking of flesh without soul, attempt to carry away the hearers. Since WE ourselves say that according to the plan of proper nature, the flesh will surely

be of other nature than the Word which sprang out of God the Father, yet hath it become His by Union which may not be plucked asunder.

5. He is rather One and the Same Son, so as to be conceived of as both out of the Essence of God the Father Divinely and out of us humanly, or out of the seed of David. He was called a Prophet as Moses. And we do not disbelieve the title, seeing that we know the might of the Economy with flesh. Not Himself was the Temple nor yet in His own Nature in that He is conceived of as God did He admit the undoing of it: yet was that His own which was undone, just as of each of us his body is his own.

6. Hence His is Divinely the Essence which is before the worlds, His in like wise and not another's that in the last times He should be born in the flesh. For the birth from the holy Virgin was found to the Word, not a way to His Being but unto His manifestation with flesh: and He is in no wise mortal out of mortals but rather Life as out of Life the FATHER.

Yet hath the Body mortal out of mortals and subject unto death become the own of Life, in order that through it contending with death and raised from the dead He might reform unto incorruption and prove superior to death that which has been mastered of death, as regards its own nature: for death falling on the body of Life, became impotent.

7. For that the Word of God endures not to suffer a shadow of turning, nor yet does the flesh letting go what it is, change into the Nature of the Word united to It, every one of them who think aright will (I suppose) say.

8. For withdrawing some little (if you please) the investigation from the person of Christ the Saviour of us all, when we examine one of the things which has been named, as to its nature, itself by itself, one and other in all respects is the bondman's form and the Lord's, or human and Divine, lamb and High Priest, Maker and made.

9. But haply you will say, 'Hath not then in Him dwelt all the fulness of the Godhead bodily?' This too is true and one will not deny what has been written; yet we say that not in another's body do we conceive that the Godhead of the Son hath dwelt, but rather as in His own Temple : just as the soul of man too, being other than [2] the flesh yet together with the flesh makes up the person of a single man, as Peter or Paul.

Yet Christ is conceived of as above this too : for we say that not the Word of God became to the body in place of a soul, as some most absurdly imagine[3]; but we affirm rather that His holy and spotless Body has been ensouled with reasonable soul.

10. All-Perfect confessedly and without increase is the Word of God (for He has been begotten out of the Perfect Father, Wisdom out of Wisdom and Might out of Might), but since Unchangeableness by Nature is His, in nothing wronged by being in a Temple, He hath remained the Same, i. e., []All-Perfect and Wisdom and Might. And the flesh ripening advanced by degrees according to the law of its nature, the Word united to it made a declaration by little and little of His own Wisdom, keeping pace so to say with the increase and advance of His Body and one not inharmonious with the size of His stature. Thus He was regarded by them who saw Him, as being gradually advanced to the successive attainment of the above-named things.

11. Hence He hath partaken like us in blood and flesh, in order that in His own flesh combating with death and bringing it to nought, He might achieve incorruption for our mortal bodies and stay the law that rages in our members

from its tyranny over us. For it was not possible in any other way to mingle life with death, except He had used a mortal Body; neither could the sting of natural pleasures have been blunted in us too, except that which was taken from our lump had been made the own body of the Word.

12. Not soulless, excellent sir, do we say that the flesh forth of the seed of David, united to God the Word is, nor yet will any imagine, if he have a mind not corrupted, that He was to the holy Temple instead of mind and soul [4]; yet we are not accustomed to call man, that which is forth of the seed of David, son apart and separate [5].

13. Yet, wise sir, would I say, soul and body combine unto a man's birth and the one does not precede the other : but God the Word, albeit He was before all worlds as God, was pleased in the latter times to be united to flesh having a reasonable soul, and to be born man, yet keep even so the glory that was His own: for He spurned not the preeminence over all which is inherent in Him, but is worshipped even thus as One and Only Son by us and by the holy angels.

14. The [6] same from his discourse against Diodore beginning, We set nothing before the truth.

For he who is minded to conceive aright, when one names Him who is of the seed of David, understands at once the Word which sprang from God the Father, Who was Incarnate and made in our likeness: but thou sayest that he was the dwelling-place of the Word, surpassing indeed the holy Prophets and in more exalted place, not that He is God of God even though He was made flesh, in incomparable divergence exalted above our human condition ; but that when he was formed, the Word came to him, crowning him with surpassing grace and putting in him Its own Wisdom and Glory, in order that he might become partaker of God and not be himself conceived of as God, the Only-Begotten Word of God, because He was pleased to take our likeness and to be of the seed of Divine David.

15. [7] Holy and without sin is the body of Christ our God and Saviour, and in this respect is incorruptible from the womb, and herein He hath ever no participation or likeness with us, because He was made like unto us in everything except sin, and in like manner with us did He take part in blood and flesh, as said the Apostle in his Discourse.

against the wicked Diodore wrote thus,

Excellent sir, (say I) thou art belching forth foolish words and sick with much absurdity : for from Mary was the Holy Body, yet at the beginning of its formation or subsistence in the womb, was it holy as being the body of Christ, and there is not an instant in which it was not His, [8] but was rather simple flesh, as thou saidst, and in equality with other flesh.

16. the [9] wise Cyril finding fault with this craftiness writes thus against Diodore,

Fearing therefore lest we should downright say Man openly, in his craft he calls Him flesh: else why in the world is it that we do not say that the flesh is the Son of God, but rather call it the flesh of Him Who is in truth and by Nature Son? in order that we may conceive of and say One Christ and Son and Lord.

17. wrote against Diodore thus,

Let him know then that the body which was born at Bethlehem, even though in its natural qualities it is not the same, so to say, with the Word which is from forth God the Father, yet is His and does not belong to another son apart from Him, seeing that the Word Incarnate and made Man is conceived of as One Son and Christ and Lord.

and after this he again adds these too,

Since we too say that in regard of its own property the flesh is of a truth of other nature than the Word Which was born from the Father, yet is it His own in Union inseverable : just as also the Word Which sprang from the Essence of God the Father, will be called seed of Abraham after the flesh, the Economy calling Him thereto and in no wise injuring Him, in regard to His being what He is, for being God by Nature He became of a truth Son of man too, and He is Son of God the Father, not alien nor falsely so called, but He it is Who ineffably and incomprehensibly begat Him of Himself, even though He be not conceived of apart from flesh after the Union [10].

and again after a little,

Hence, even though no one call Him seed of David, Who proceeded forth of the Essence of God the Father, as neither does one so call the Only-Begotten, yet the force of the Union which is without confusion and without change, undoes severance. And again, because neither is the Only-Begotten in regard of His natural quality flesh nor again the Word flesh, he severs them not aright, putting them as though one and another and confessing two sons, to whom he gives barely the connection of affection.

Or haply there are some (I ween) who rave because they do not bring the flesh by change to the nature of the Word, nor yet again bring down the Word unto Consubstantiality with the flesh united thereto.

and after more,

Yet is it wholly unreasonable that thou durst blame them who hold the right faith and art not ashamed to withstand them who confess the Union without confusion; and thou art wholly jumbling up everything and demonstrating that the flesh is of other nature, I mean in respect of God the Word : and if one confess this with thee, keeping clear of the unlearning of the Synousiasts, thou forthwith severest the One into two.

18. and as S. Cyril in his book against Diodore, blaming such falsehood, writes,

If He be full surely a prophet as thou affirmest and confidently sayest, Who received the gift of the SPIRIT, and foretold the things to come, and again ministered the SPIRIT, and it appears to thee not right that the Word Who is forth of God the Father should be called a prophet; who is it that received the gift of the SPIRIT and ministered the revelation of the things to come? Perchance thou sayest, He that is of the seed of David, or as thou callest him, The man of Nazareth. He is then a prophet and nothing else, and just a little exalted above our condition : for He is in no wise Equal, I mean in greatness and in glory to God the Word, if the One be the Giver of the Spirit, the other the minister of the gift from the Spirit. And lo how does the God-inspired Scripture call the Holy Ghost the Spirit of Jesus? for they wished (it says) to go into Bithynia and the Spirit of Jesus suffered them not.

19. For so says S. Cyril when writing against Diodore,

That the Word out of God the Father was not by any called Christ or Jesus as long as He was not yet man, is evident: Christ indicates anointing, Jesus clearly came through Angel's voice, and before His conception in the holy Virgin was put upon Him Who was born of her after the flesh.

20. . . . what wise Cyril put forth against Diodore and wrote thus,

DIODORE. "For while the Lord was in the bowels of the Virgin and of her essence, He had not the honour of sonship; but when He was fashioned and became a temple for God the Word, in that He received the Only-Begotten, He took the honour of the name and was participant with Him in the honour."

to these the Saint mighty in the SPIRIT blaming him said,

CYRIL. Therefore according to thee, Emmanuel was not God nor Son at all, but a common man and one as we, but because on His birth the Only-Begotten came to Him, therefore He became too the Temple of God, and was vouchsafed the sonship and the Dignity: undoubtedly therefore He has the honour as something added to Him.

again he brings forward Diodore varying and contradicting himself and writing thus,

DIODORE. "But he who was of the seed of David, as created, had the Word for his God, and when created he became of God the Word : for with us first a temple is prepared, and then He Who dwelleth enters it; in the womb of the Virgin He Who dwelleth fashioned Himself a Temple and removed not from the Temple but filled it with His glory and His Wisdom : nor as in the case of the Prophets, was there ignorance with Him until the Spirit made revelation."

and again he cites him saying the opposite, after this wise,

"For the Godhead did not immediately on his creation or birth, infuse all His Wisdom within him, but by little and little gave it to the body."

against these things therefore, forthwith did he who wisely exposed them, add,

CYRIL. But it is meet before other things to say this: against what he says and wishes to hold, himself advances the contrary; for he affirms that the Godhead of the Son did not as soon as he was born, put all His wisdom within him, albeit he wrote in what is a little above [Diodorus cited by Cyril] "For with us first------but filled it with His glory and His wisdom" (as above).

21. for he wrote against Diodore thus,

CYRIL. But WE, wise sir, believing that so to think is stupidity, say that the Word took flesh of the holy Virgin and proceeded man, and He was not in a man nor is He seen to take upon Him a man; but He is rather One and the Same Son; in order that He maybe conceived to be of the Essence of God the Father Divinely, and of us humanly, that is, of the seed of David.

and again citing Diodore who says,

"The Perfect Likeness of God the Word, the perfect likeness of the bondman whom He took upon Him,"

Cyril says,

In place of, He was made, or was born according to the flesh of a woman and proceeded man, he oftentimes puts the word took and the word received, in order that he may shew that he is a man who has a connection of affection, I mean with God the Word, and that he may not confess with us that He Who is in truth Lord became man.

22. for he cites Diodore wickedly writing thus,
DIODORE. "But how do ye introduce one worship? is it as to the soul and body of kings? for the soul reigns not by itself and the body reigns not by itself, but God the Word was King before flesh; not therefore as to soul and body, so to God the Word and to flesh [is the worship paid]."

against these things again he answering said,
CYRIL. Of diverse kind then is the worship, and hence it is not One worship from us (for this is what thy word bids us) : but where a difference in worship and honour is paid to the things named, and to each is accurately given what befits it, there full surely inequality of power follows : but inequality and difference in power, in regard to less and greater, comes to Two Hypostases and Persons. Union therefore flees away, the depth of the Mystery departs to nothing, for it is not right, he says, that as to the soul and body of kings should worship be paid, albeit how were it not better that this should be the type? for as out of soul and body is one man, albeit the properties of each have great diversity one to another, I mean as to their mode of being (for the soul is other than the body): so will you understand concerning Christ too the Saviour of us all. For the Word Which was made flesh, i. e., was seen in human likeness, is God: in order that He may be confessed to be and may be in truth, God alike and man, One and Onely All-Perfect Son. But he is saying I know not what, in trifling and childish imaginations daring to sport himself against the Truth.

23. thus S. Cyril cites Diodore as writing,
DIODORE. " A prophet shall the Lord God raise up to you out of your brethren, like one. Was the Prophet at all inferior to Moses? was he not Perfect man? Therefore neither is he of Nazareth less than a man, who is of the seed of David. But Perfect God out of Perfect God took perfect man:" and again, "For the Godhead did not, immediately on his formation or birth, put all His Wisdom within him, but by little and little gave it to the body."

to him who blasphemously utters these and such like lies, amid his blame the righteous accuser of the wickedness says,
CYRIL. It results that He is no longer God, but a God-clad man rather and in equal measure with these others, in whom God manifestly dwelt.

24. and he introduces Diodore wickedly saying,
DIODORE. "The [11] Son of God and that not by reason of ought (for He is so by Nature): the flesh is son by reason of the Son."

as to whom he also draws out his speech and says,
CYRIL. And how (tell me) by reason of the Son is the flesh by itself son? or of whom is it son at all? the Son's? and how dost thou not fall from hence, when thou hast brought the absurdity to this point? well then, is it the son of God the Father, in like manner as He too Who is by Nature and truly of His Essence? Two therefore unquestionably sons of God there are: and lo whither goes Paul who says, One God the Father of Whom everything and WE of Him, and One Lord Jesus Christ through Whom everything and WE through Him?

25. Cyril examining as to Emmanuel too, in these against Diodore wrote thus,

CYRIL. But when we are conceiving of the Only-Begotten Word, as united to His flesh, we do not take it as being like a garment nor do we say that He cast it upon Him like cloaks which are external, as though it were alien : but it is rather a demonstration of the declaration that He was made flesh, i. e. man. The Word therefore had a natural presence in the body which was united to Him and is His, just as also the soul of man is his, albeit the nature is alien.

26. and against Diodore thus,

For we who hold the Right and Immaculate Faith, and ever cleave to the Divine Scriptures, and follow the tracks of the Faith of the Fathers, when we hear 'JESUS,' we understand the Only-Begotten Word made Man.

27. seeing that Diodore too who takes occasion and speaks against them who confound the Matures, i.e. who mingle the flesh of the Lord and foolishly say that it changed into the Essence of God the Word, and became the opposite of what it was before, says that they call One Christ two sons, the wise Cyril cries out on him and says,

CYRIL. Therefore let us give the crown to Paul of Samosata too, who more accurately than thou, did contend against the Synousiasts; for that more than thou did he sever the Mystery of the Economy.

28. striving [12] against Diodore, the all-wise Cyril says thus,

He dared clothe in form of Lord, him who (as he says) is man from Mary, who at the beginning no way surpassed us, but hardly was counted worthy of the name and honour of Son and of God, after he had come forth of the womb. Christ then verily is, as I said, two sons and a new god, and has been crowned by God with supernatural honour in some small degree above the creatures, that together with a mere man He might be worshipped who at last gained the glory, i. e., the complement of the Holy Consubstantial Trinity.

29. for [13] S. Cyril writing against Diodore says thus of the definition of a man,

This, my friend, is the definition of human nature which is also called a substance, that it is a rational animal, mortal, recipient of mind and learning.

***

The [14] same Cyril against Diodore,

We have already often said, when we were making our Defence of all the Chapters, that not because the natures came together unto union, must duality be admitted [15]. For as a man although compounded out of reasonable soul and body, is one and is not divided into two and this whole is called an animal rational and mortal, albeit really mortal in one part, rational in the other part: thus too Immanuel, being One, of Godhead and manhood, whereof each is perfect in itself, is the Same God and man, mortal and Immortal, in time and before all ages, Palpable and Impalpable, Visible and Invisible. For had He Immortal in His own Nature taken nothing from mortal nature, i. e. from the seed of Abraham, WE had not been renewed and lifted up to immortality, vain had been our faith and we had still lain in our sins.

The same Cyril against Diodore,

For as, suffering pains in the flesh He yet remained Impassible in the Nature of His own Godhead : so I say that even while He was growing He was All-Perfect. And while His wisdom was believed to be increasing, He was even then the overflowing fountain of wisdom whence all others draw their wisdom.

Footnotes:

1. Diodore, the "pupil (thremma) of the blessed Silvanus" Bishop of Tarsus, the comrade of S. Flavian (afterward Bishop of Antioch) in toils for the Catholics of Antioch in their low estate through Arian oppression, visitor of S.Meletius Bishop of Antioch in his banishment in Armenia through these same Arians, teacher of S.Chrysostom, commentator on most of the Old and New Testament, present at the Second Council where he signed as Bishop of Tarsus, being then at the beginning of an Episcopate of about 13 years, and who died in the Unity of the Church, nevertheless fell into the error of so parting the two Natures in Christ as to speak of His Manhood as though it were a Man apart from the Son of God. S. Athanasius speaks as though he saw the germ of some such error; he says, "And He became man and did not come into man, for this it is necessary to know, lest perchance these irreligious men fall into this notion also, and beguile any into thinking that as in former times the Word was used to come into each of the Saints, so now He sojourned in a man, hallowing him also and manifesting Himself as in the others." against Arians, iii § 30 p. 442 O.T.

Of Diodore's writings little is preserved excepting some few citations in different writings of Severus. Even of S. Cyril's work these few fragments that survive seem almost entirely due to the Monophysite Controversy in the first half of the sixth century. The fragments are mainly preserved either by Severus of Antioch (chiefly in his work against John Grammaticus of Caesarea, but also in other works) and by John of Caesarea himself who appended a vast number of extracts of S. Cyril to his Apology for the Council of Chalcedon. Anastasius, referred to by the learned Cave, under Severus (Viae dux cap. 6 pp. 90, 92, ed. Ingolstadt, 1606) says of this John, "Then John of Caesarea Grammarian and very many more made defences for the synod (of Chalcedon) through truest extracts . . . Severus having looked into the compilations of the Caesarean and some others who compiled in behalf of the synod through very many extracts of Fathers and writers and demonstrations and proofs, first of all straightway wrote against John of Caesarea." Further on, Severus "laid down as a law to them [in Syria Egypt Alexandria and elsewhere] in the same book which is called Philalethes, that the Faith of Chalcedon frittered away 230 citations of holy Fathers in the defence which John of Caesarea made in its behalf." ib. p.96. In the MSS of John's Defence wnich have supplied many of these passages against Diodore and Theodore, they are numbered 181-196, Cave likewise refers to extracts of Severus' work against the Grammarian in the Catena on Old

Testament Canticles edited by Anton. Caraffa. John of Caesarea signs in the fifth general Council as "John by the mercy of God Bishop of Caesarea of Palestine." t. vi. 218 Colet. He had been Bishop but a short time when the Council was called in A.D. 553, and probably, as Severus was dethroned in A.D. 536, the controversy had taken place before John was Bishop, which will account for his being usually styled John of Caesarea. Leontius of Jerusalem however cites at least once, from the Book of the same Severus against the Grammarian John Bishop of Caesarea. Apol. Conc. Chalc. in Gallandi, Bibl. Vett. Patrum xii. 736. The Lateran council similarly, The same Severus against John of holy memory Bishop of Caesarea of Palestine. Conc. vii. 324 Col. John of Caesarea's Defence of the Council of Chalcedon is extant in MS. in syriac (as Cardinal Mai tells us, in Cod. Vat. 140 written in the eighth Century), and in Greek in a late manuscript at Venice and at Cairo. Of the character of Diodore's writings the learned Tillemont who appears most marvellously to have made himself acquainted with every extant writing of every Father, says "We cannot be judges of this great difficulty [whether Diodore's writings were heretical] because we no longer have his writings which would need to be examined with great care, not stopping at culled passages." t. 8. 568 ed. 2. S. Cyril however who had access to them says of him, "One Diodore, being once as they say, an opponent of the SPIRIT, communicated with the Church of the Orthodox. This man having put off, as he deemed, the spot of the Macedonian heresy, fell into another infirmity. For he deemed and wrote that one son by himself is he who is of the seed of David, born of the holy Virgin ; another Son again by Himself the Word out of God the Father. But veiling the wolf under the sheep's fleece, he pretends to say One Christ, allotting the Name to the Word alone begotten out of God the Father, the Only-Begotten Son : and allotting it in the category of a grace, as himself says, he styles him too of the seed of David son, as united (he says) to the in truth Son: united, not as WE hold, but only as regards dignity, sway and equality of honour. His disciple Nestorius became, and darkened by Diodore's books, feigns" &c. Ep. 1 to Succensus 135 d e. Tillemont thinks that what S. Cyril says of Diodore having been a Macedonian, is not to be pressed, t. 8. 566.

    2. kata seems an error for para.

    3. The Apollinarians: see in Tillemont, above p. 44 note col. 1. The extracts from S. Athanasius, speak of the Apollinarian unwillingness to own that our Lord made His own ought of created matter; see the theory that the body was consubstantial with the Godhead, their refusal to worship ought created, to allow that Christ was man. Diodore and Theodore having all this to battle with speak as if, while holding that the manhood is perfect and complete, they disjoined it altogether from God the Son, making it a distinct man and calling it His in some vague way without uniting Godhead and manhood in one. Calling it His in some vague way hindered their seeing that they were really dividing Christ into Two beings, God and man, separate from each other.

Theodoret notwithstanding the powerful influence of these two minds, and his dread of Apollinarianism, enunciates clearly the Union, though with language occasionally vague. Andrew's statements (of Samosata in the same province) are still more clear. S. Athanasius says, " But ye say again, 'WE do not worship a creature.' O void of understanding! why do ye not consider that, made the Lord's Body, it bears away no created worship? for it has been made the Body of the Uncreated Word: Him Whose Body it has been made, to Him do ye offer the worship also." against Apollinarius, lib. i. 6. t. i. 926 c. " For ye essay to say that the flesh is consubstantial with the Godhead." ib. i. 9 t. i. 929 b. " But ye say again, ,If 'Christ be man, He will be a part of the world, and a part of the world cannot save the world.' O thought of deceit and madness of blasphemy, let them say of what Scripture is this rule or sophism of the devil: albeit the Prophet saith...... And a Man was born in her and the Highest Himself founded her. How then does Christ not save the world, made man? seeing that it is manifest that in the nature wherein sin was committed, therein hath had place the abundance of grace. What is abundance of grace? That the Word hath been made man, abiding God; in order that made man too, He may be believed to be God, so that Christ being man is God, because being God He has been made man, and in human form saves the believers." lib. ii. 7 t. i. 945 b c d. "How then do ye say that the Word, Creator of the rational natures, commingling with Himself flesh, was made a rational man? and how without change and turn hath He been made man, if He did not compact the bondman's form so as to be rational? in order that the Word may be without turn, abiding what He was, and being God may be seen on earth, man endowed with reason : for the Lord is a heavenly man [epouranios anthropos , comp. 1 Cor. xv. 48 cited just below, and as the Heavenly One (ho epouranios) such too the heavenly ones], not as exhibiting flesh from out of Heaven but as compacting Heavenly flesh from out of earth: wherefore also as the Heavenly One, such too the heavenly ones by the participation of His holiness. Wherefore He also makes His own the things of His body. But ye say again, 'How did they crucify the Lord of glory?' But they did not crucify the Word as ye say, not so, but they set at nought the Word, affixing to the Cross the Body of the Word. For it was God Who was set at nought," as above p. 303 note g. "Wherefore the Lord said to the Jews, Undo this Temple and in three days I will rear it. As the Prophet saith, Because was delivered unto death His Soul, not the Word Himself: and John says, He laid down His Soul (psuchen) for us. How then did the Jews avail to undo the Temple of God and to part from Him the indissoluble commixture that had taken place of the flesh with the Word (ten aluton sunkrasin tes sarkos pros ton logon genomenen) , if the death of the flesh is as you take it of such sort. For neither would the body have died except it were parted from somewhat. For except there had being undoing of it, there were no death; if death have not befallen, neither hath resurrection. Allow therefore that an undoing and a parting from the body took place, as it is written in the Gospels, He gave up the ghost, and, He bowed His Head and yielded up the ghost; in order that we may see what ghost ye understood was parted from the body, and [so] the dying had place. For ye said, that the Word having commingled with Himself an impersonal flesh (sarka ten anupostaton) exhibited man truly rational and perfect. If therefore the Word withdrew from the body and thus the dying took place, the Jews prevailed against God, dissolving the indissoluble commixture. Neither therefore hath our death had place there, if the death of the body had place, from God being parted from it. And how did the body parted from the Incorruptible God remain in incorruption? the wounding will be that of the Body, the suffering that of the Word. Wherefore ye speak of a suffering God also, uttering things consonant with yourselves, yea rather agreeing with the Arians: for they teach thus. And the Word, according to you, will by the Resurrection be raised : for it is necessary that one take the beginning of the Resurrection from Hades, in order that the Resurrection may be perfect, both the undoing of death and the release of the spirits that are there." ib. 16 t. i. 952 d e 953 a b c d.

4. this being the Apollinarian error with which Diodore had to contend.

5. The first fragment has been preserved to us in a syriac collection rather later than Severus, the remainder so far (except a few words here and there) belong to John of Caesarea's collection, see above p. 321 note a. Those which follow have been chiefly preserved by Severus either in his controversy with the same Bishop John, or in that with his own fellow-heretic Julian of Halicarnassus. The lines which introduce S. Cyril's fragments are Severus', except in one or two cases which have notes as they occur.

6. This fragment is preserved in same collection as 1.

7. This is given by Card. Mai in a latin translation from a treatise of Severus "Questions with the heretics" (Migne t. ix. col. 1451 n. 21). It is extant also in the British Museum MS. add. 14529 fol. 27 v. I had overlooked it when editing the Syriac fragments but was directed to it later by Wright's Catalogue. This and the following paragraph make up but one piece in Mai: but are separate pieces in the London MSS. Card. Mai too gives the latter portion of this as a separate piece from the Philalethes (n. 18 in Migne) as well as in the longer n. 21, from the Questions.

8. Card. Mai citing this from Severus' Philalethes ends it differently, no one will admit so much as an instant of time in which that (flesh) will be common and like other flesh as you my and not rather be the Flesh of the Word (n. 18 in Migne).

9. from the same collection as 1 and 14.

10. Card. Mai has a portion of this (Migne n. 19) cited "from Severus' defence of his Philalethes," and continues his extract, "Thou therefore while thou art admitting His all-but change into flesh soul-less and reason-less, art dividing into two sons the Only One, impiously rejecting the truth that One is the Son.

11. This extract is given more at length by Leontius of Byzantium, who gives it as, from Book 1 against the Synousiasts.

Contra Nest. et Eutch. lib. iii in Gall. xii. 697.

12. This is preserved to us by Severus in a long letter which he wrote to his fellow-heretic Julian of Halicarnassus, in the British Museum add. 17200. Cardinal Mai also preserved a latin translation of it, I do not know whether he procured it from the same work of Severus.

13. In the fragments as edited, this little piece is only given in latin, from Cardinal Mai's collection, but the British Museum MS. Add. 12155 fol. 180 v has it (as pointed out by Wright in his Catalogue) and supplies the concluding words. The same definition is given by S. Cyril in his Thesaurus, cap. 8 fin. p. 66a &c, ad Hermeiam, lib. 2 p. 425 c &c.

14. This and the following are from the latin translation (not always exact) which Cardinal Mai preserved to us: this one is from the defence of Severus for his Philalethes. They have in Migne ix. 1450, 1452 the numbers 20, and 26.

15. i.e. that we must not "divide the the Hypostases into Two," def. chapter 3 against Eastern Bishops, p. 167 a, a-gainst Theodoret, 213 c d e 214 a. def. against Theodoret chapter 4, pp. 217 e, 218, chapter 6, p. 224 a, chapter 12, p. 239 e.

CYRIL OF ALEXANDRIA FROM HIS SECOND BOOK AGAINST THE WORDS OF THEODORE [1]

of which the beginning is
    They who with clear eye of the understanding view closely the holy and God-inspired Scripture [2].

1. [3] He said to His disciples, Call not any teacher on the earth, for one is your Leader, Christ. For He did not, when He was commanding the Apostles this, distinguish His proper Godhead from His visible body, nor when He affirmed that He was Christ did He distinguish Himself from soul and flesh, being thus both God and man, bondman visible and Lord acknowledged, veiling the height of His Godhead with the low estate of the Incarnation, lifting up the low estate of the visible body by the operation of His Godhead.

2. [4] Let not men deceive nor be deceived admitting as "man of the Lord," as they call Him, a man without a mind, but rather our Lord and God: for neither do we sunder the man from the Godhead but we declare Him One and the Same, erst not man but God and Son only and before the ages, unmingled with body and what belong to body; at the end Man too assumed for our salvation, suffering in flesh, Impassible in Godhead, circumscribed in body, uncircumscribed in Godhead, the Same earthly and Heavenly, seen and conceived of, contained in space and boundless, in order that the whole man which fell under sin might be re-formed by the Same, Whole Man and God.

3. For since the Only-Begotten Word of God being Life by Nature was made flesh, the nature of man re-bloomed unto life: for He has become first among all. And for this reason the Life-giving Word of God made His own flesh which was subject to death, in order that manifesting it superior to both death and decay, He might transmit the grace to us too. For as in Adam we were brought down unto death, so in Christ thrusting aside the tyranny of death, are we re-formed unto immortality.

4. The same from the first book against Theodore [5].
    For as out of soul and body are one man, albeit the properties pertaining to each have the vastest possible difference one to another in respect (I mean) of their being such (for the soul is other than the body): thus will it be conceived of also as to Christ the Saviour of us all.

5. S. Cyril from his first book against Theodore from the last quire [6],
    GOD was He Who suffered in the flesh (wise sir), the Lord of Glory, Who by the grace of God tasted death for every man, not in the Nature of His Godhead but in His Proper Body.

6. for this in that too against Theodore of Mopsuestia in the first book wrote S. Cyril,
    CYRIL. But we make use of necessary examples, everywhere keeping undivided the Union and repelling thy severance. The example of the sun

however, none of them who think aright brings to the establishment of union, knowing that we follow the Divine Scriptures, which have it that the Word of God (as we have said) should partake in like wise as we in blood and flesh ensouled with a reasonable soul, and not on the contrary that it is man who by participation and mere affection, is illuminated by the Divine Economy as if from a ray of the sun.

7. and in the first book of those which he wrote against Theodore of Mopsuestia on this wise,

CYRIL. But Jesus Christ is not conceived of alone and by Himself; or again as without flesh and bare of the likeness usward, but rather as the Word of God, incarnate and made man.

8. Cyril therefore treating of the 318 holy Fathers in his first book wrote these things too against Theodore,

Lo with all clearness do the initiators of all under heaven and the champions of the truth, men elect and spirit-clad, tracking the Divine Words and the Tradition of the Saints and Apostles and Evangelists, who were eye-witnesses and ministers of the Word, bid us believe, not in Two sons, but in One Lord Jesus Christ the Son of God, Begotten from forth the Father. The name Christ is indicative of anointing, and that of Jesus was conferred, not on the bare Word, conceived of apart from flesh, but rather when He was born of a woman in the flesh: yet even so do they say that One is the Only-Begotten, Who was begotten by Nature of the Father, and they affirm that He is God and Consubstantial with the Father; saying that through Him were made all things which are in Heaven and upon earth, and in plain terms they confess, that "for us men and for our salvation He came down, and was both made flesh and made man, and suffered and died and rose the third day and ascended into heaven."

9. and see the all-wise Cyril, justly objecting this to Theodore and writing thus,

Chicanery then is the Mystery of Christ and there is nought true therein; but thus he says, that the glory of God was spread upon him, i.e. the appellation of God, as some tint, was anointed on a man like us; we refuse to be man-worshippers, who worship the creature rather than the Creator.

10. S. Cyril from his Book against Theodore of Mopsuestia [7].

For being God by Nature and truly Son of God the Father, He was made in likeness of men and made His own the flesh which is of the holy Virgin and it is the flesh of God and full of God-befitting might: wherefore it is also life-giving and repels infirmities and works the undoing of death.

11. S. Athanasius from his work upon the Incarnation of the Word: Cyril cited it in his books against Theodore [8].

We confess that He is Son of God and God according to the Spirit, Son of Man according to the flesh, not Two Natures to that One Son, One [Nature] worshipped the other unworshipped, but One Nature of God the Word Incarnate [9], worshipped with His flesh with One worship [10]: nor Two Sons, One, Very Son of God and worshipped, the other the man out of Mary not worshipped, made by grace son of God just as men too are.

and reiterating these matters of faith, ... he defines thus [11],

Him anathematizes the holy Catholic Church, obeying the Divine Apostle who says, If any one preach to you beside that ye received let him be accursed.

12. for S. Cyril cites Theodore who was Archbishop of Mopsuestia, in what he wrote against him who wickedly cried out thus [12],

Theodore. "But yea (he says), for as albeit He was of Bethlehem, He was called a Nazarene because of His abidance and growing up there: so [is He called] man [13] too, because He sojourned in man."

and S. Cyril against these things says thus

Silly and childish and old womanish is the speech, for not as from a city one is called citizen or countryman, so by reason of dwelling in a man, is the Word being God called man.

13. as also Theodore Archbishop of Mopsuestia who in his craft had done this, the wise Cyril blaming, in his book against him thus wrote,

CYRIL. But he thinks that he has said something clever, for he affirms that it is right that the body should be honoured, i. e. the man, for he (I suppose) blushes to call it by the appellation of Son, and to call the Word by that of Body. The Union therefore consists in titles, and an assemblage of mere names: but in truth the Mystery is utterly repudiated.

***

The [14] same Cyril against Theodore.

But he with mouth wide open and reins of blasphemy let loose says that Christ's holiness was imperfect, and did not reach its height ere the Spirit in the form of a dove had come down upon Him. [15] Why was He not Perfect? full surely one who is imperfect cannot be without sin, yea one who is believed to be in part holy is thought to be in another part infirm. Besides what is that defect which (as the opponent asserts) the Holy Ghost supplied, that the other part too might be perfect and might break the devil's onset? Yea and not only is He Holy and verily most perfect but also endued with full power who used to heal sorrows and every sort of infirmity.

Cyril of holy memory from the first book of what he wrote against Theodore [16].

THEODORE.

"If any like to call both God the Word Son of God son of David in an improper sense on account of God the Word's temple which is forth of David, let him name him too which is of the seed of David, Son of God; let him so style him by grace not by nature, not ignorant of his natural ancestors, nor perverting order and calling Him Who is Unembodied a body also; and Him that is before the ages forth of God forth of David too, and that He suffered and is Impassible [17]. A body is not incorporeal, what is from below is not from above, what is before the ages is not out of the seed of David, what suffered is not Impassible, nor are those things directed to the same understanding: what belong to the Body are not God's the Word, and what are God's the "Word have not the body as their seat. Let us confess the natures and not deny the economies."

S. CYRIL.

He who says that the economies must not be denied, utterly uproots the mystery of the human nature: for he dares to say that neither was the Only-Begotten Word of God made man, nor did He appear from forth the seed of holy David, but openly introduces to us a pair of sons, a nature uneven and false in its name. For that it is said to be in an improper sense, wholly shews that it is not truly what it is said to be, for it borrows the other's name. Hence if the Word of God be called man in an improper sense, He clearly was not made man. If he who is out of the seed of David is in an improper sense Son and God, he is by nature and in truth neither God nor Son. False then is the name in either case and the fact is really understood to be that each is called what it is not.

From the same book.

THEODORE.

"And it is convenient that they who view aright, should, when we are looking for natural forefathers, call neither God the Word son of David or Abraham but their Maker: nor the body before the ages out of the Father but the seed of Abraham and David born from Mary. And [18 when the consideration is of natural births, neither is God the Word deemed to be Mary's son: for mortal bears what is mortal by nature and a body like itself. God the Word underwent not two births, one before the ages, the other in the last times, but out of the Father was He begotten by Nature, and the temple which was born of Mary He fashioned to Himself out of the very womb."

Then going on a little and something intervening, he said again,

"But when the consideration is of the saving economy, let both God be called man (not because He became so, but because He assumed it), and man God, not as though he had become uncircumscribed nor every where existent, for the body was subject to touch even after the resurrection, and so was taken up into Heaven and so will come as it was taken up."

CYRIL.

Lo plainly and manifestly is he borne against the Divine Scripture, he repudiates the mystery of Christ and as it were chides God the Word Who for us was pleased to suffer emptiness, and seems to grieve that He was made man. For he utterly takes away the Incarnation and lifts himself against the Unspeakable Wisdom, all-but saying in Jewish mode to Christ the Saviour of us all, For a good work we stone Thee not but for blasphemy, that THOU, a man, makest Thyself God. Let him hear Him then saying openly, If therefore I do not the works of My Father believe Me not, if I do though ye believe not Me believe My Works. For while he knows that the Word of God used Divine Might and Power even when He appeared as man, he denies that He is God and says that He rather dwelt in a man, in order that the Word of God might set forth to us a man to be worshipped and who is honoured with the mere name of Godhead; he is convicted therefore of being utterly ignorant of the might of Christ's Mystery.

Theodore from the same book.

" ' [19] But if (he says) it were flesh which was crucified, how does the sun turn away his rays, and darkness and earthquakes overpower the whole earth and were the rocks rent and the dead arose?' What then do they say of the darkness that happened in Egypt in the time of Moses, not for three hours but for three days? what of the other miracles which were wrought through Moses and through Jesus the son of Nave who made the sun stand, which sun under king Ezechias even went back against nature? and of the remains of Eliseus which raised a dead man? For if what things befell in the time of the Cross shew that God the Word suffered, and they allow not that the things were wrought for the sake of a man: the things too which happened in the time of Moses for the sake of Abraham's race and those in the time of Jesus son of Nave and of king Ezechias will not be. But if those miracles were wrought for the sake of the people of the Jews, much more those on the cross for the sake of God the Word's temple."

CYRIL.

The [20] heaven is astonished for this and has quaked exceeding vehemently, saith the Lord. O wickedness past endurance! o tongue that speaks iniquity against God and mind that lifteth up its horn on high! seems it little to thee that the Lord of glory is fixed to the wood? Whom THOU sayest is neither true Son nor God, but WE believe that He is truly Son and God, Creator and Maker of all things. For neither was God the Word Which is out of God the Father man simply but in human form, not suffering translation or change into flesh, but rather united thereto according to the faith of the holy Scriptures. He it is Who suffered in the flesh and hung on the wood, wrought miracles in Egypt, manifesting His glory through the all-wise Moses.

Theodore from the same book.

"Son [21] by grace he who is man out of Mary, by Nature God the Word. But what is by grace is not by nature and what is by nature is not by grace. There are not two sons. Be these enough for the body which is of us, sonship by grace, glory, immortality, whereby it is made the Temple of God the Word; be it not raised above its nature and let not God the Word in place of the thanksgiving due from us be wronged. And what is the wrong? to combine Him with a body and to suppose that He needed a body for perfect sonship. Nor does God the Word Himself please that He should be David's son, but lord; but that the body should be called son of David, He not only does not grudge but even came for this very end." [22]

CYRIL.

Hence since what is by grace is not by nature and what is by nature is not by grace, there are not two sons, according to thy mode of reasoning. He indeed who is son by grace and not by nature is not truly son, it remains that the glory of true Sonship exist in Him Who is so by Nature not by grace, that is, in God the Word Who is forth of God the Father. Driven out therefore (as I said) from being and being called Son of God is Christ Jesus through Whom too we have been saved, declaring His Death and confessing His Resurrection. For the Word of faith which we preach, brings us to that confession. Hence our faith is in a man and not in Him Who is both by Nature and truly Son of God. For if he is true who says that he obtained the sonship by grace, he will be counted among the multitude of sons, i. e., ourselves, to whom the grace that is from above gives the sonship whereto we were called through Jesus Christ Who is forth of the seed of David according to the flesh. And the Divine Evangelist will assure thee, saying, But they who received Him He gave them authority to become the sons of God, to them that believe on His Name. Then how does he who has obtained the rank of sonship given him by another, avail to give us too a grace not his but acquired and from without?

And after a little. The SON gave Himself unto emptying and, Perfect in all things, was pleased to suffer abasement and to undergo birth according to the flesh of a woman, and was called Son of Abraham and David. Thou marvellest not at so comely a plan of the Economy, yea rather thou findest fault with the Mystery: saying that the Incarnation of the Only-Begotten was a wrong, thou chidest the counsel of God the Father, thou criest out too against the Son Himself Who was pleased to suffer emptying for thy sake. When therefore thou hearest Him saying to God the Father in Heaven, Sacrifice and offering Thou wouldest not, whole burnt sacrifices and for sin Thou requiredst not but a Body Thou completedst for Me; then I said, Lo I come (in the volume of the Book it is written of Me) to do Thy will, o God: I delight to do it; you will say that the Son haply thought not aright of His glory. For He chose completion of the Body and that made not for other but for Himself, according to His own words, for He says, A Body Thou completedst for Me. Albeit thou hear Paul saying of God the Word, Therefore because the sons partook of blood and flesh, He too likewise was made partaker of the same; and thus the wise John writes, And the Word was made flesh and tabernacled in us, rise thou up against them crying out, "Be He not, in place of the thanksgiving due from from us, wronged. God the Word was not made flesh, God the Word was not truly partaker of blood and flesh; He was not born as we of a woman after the flesh, He was not called son of David. For this which is both too petty for Him to be called and not according to His Will, how would He have suffered?" But WE, wise sir, are wont to glorify God the Father because He completed a Body for the Son: and we say that the Son Himself truly made flesh, i.e. man, suffered indeed emptying for our sakes, and underwent the low estate of our poverty, yet remained even thus God and Very Son of God the Father. How then did He not please to be called son of David if He were made man and that not against His will?

From the first Book of Cyril of holy memory that Christ is One against Theodore.

For there are, there are who deny their Redeemer and Lord and say that He is not true Son of God the Father Who in the last times of the age endured for our sakes birth of a woman after the flesh; but rather that a new and late god appeared to the earth, having the glory of sonship acquired from without just like us and boasting as it were in honours not his own, so that it is just man-worship and nothing else, and some man is worshipped together with the Holy TRINITY by us and by the holy angels. These things indeed they, exceeding haughty and much-wise in the knowledge of the Divine Scriptures have inserted in their writings, and as the Lord of all says through one of the holy Prophets, He set a snare to corrupt men. For what else than a snare and a stumbling-block, is a tongue uttering perverse things and counter to the sacred Scriptures and shamelessly resisting the Tradition of the Holy Apostles and Evangelists? We must therefore repudiate them who are obnoxious to such evil charges whether they are among the living or not: for from that which injures it is necessary to withdraw, and not to look to person but to what pleases God.

Footnotes:

1. Theodore, the contemporary and, in early days, comrade of S. Chrysostom, brother of Polychronius, Bishop of Apamea, was for about 36 years Bishop of Mopsuestia in Cilicia: he died in 428. John Archbishop of Antioch and Theodoret were therefore at the opening of their Episcopate when Theodore was now in old age. He seems to have been of a gifted family, for Theodoret closes his history (lib. v. 39) with the praise of Polychronius for grace in speech as well as in nobility of life. And Theodore too was a Preacher and writer, of great repute in the Province of Antioch. But he seems to have lacked stability and a well-balanced mind, and thus his controversy in earlier life against the Arians and Apollinarians led him, as well as Diodore whose pupil he was, to speak of the Incarnation as though it were only a condescension of God the Son in connecting with Himself in some way a man who had an already distinct Being. In the next Century, Facundus Bishop of Hermaeum near Carthage who endeavours most strenuously to defend Theodore, has preserved a long extract of Theodore's from a work called, 'Of Apollinarius and his heresy,' in which Theodore says, "Thirty years ago I wrote a book of 15000 lines on the Incarnation of our Lord in which I examined the faults of Arius and Eunomius hereon and also the empty presumption of Apollinarius, through my whole work; so as to pass over (I believe) nothing pertaining either to the stability of Ecclesiastical orthodoxy or to the proof of their impiety. But they . .. especially instructed by Apollinarius the head of this heresy shewed my work to all who thought as they did, if any how they might find valid answers against it. But since no one ventured to take up the gauntlet against the book . . . they wrote certain silly things which I never said and foisted them into my book and shewed them to their friends, sometimes too to our people who of their over-easiness listened eagerly to it all, and offered it as a proof as they imagined of my wickedness. And one of these writings was to say two sons,, (Theodore in Facundus, Def. iii. Capp. x. 1, Gallandi Bibl. Vett. Patr. xi. 770, 771). Nevertheless however much Theodore attempts to shield himself undercover of interpolations, his assertion (see below pp. 347, 355) of One Son and explanation of how he means One convict him of that heresy which John of Antioch, Theodoret and others, though they valued and admired Theodore, escaped.

2. This is the title with which the Venice manuscript of John of Caesarea's compilation introduces these extracts; he calls it second book because that against Diodore was considered the first. Severus however, the fifth Council and others cite this as Book 1.

3. This first extract belongs to Theophilus Archbishop of Alexandria and is taken from the first of those of his Paschal homilies which S. Jerome translated into Latin and thus preserved to us; John of Caesarea says, 'This testimony Cyril took to himself against what was said by Theodore: it belongs to Theophilus bishop of Alexandria.' It is his Homily for the year 401, when

Theophilus was more than half through his 27 years' Episcopate. It is entitled, "To the Bishops of all Egypt." It is chiefly against Origen but the earlier part contains a clear statement of the Incarnation. S. Cyril quotes a little more of it in his de recta fide to the Princesses, p. 52 a b c.

4. From S. Gregory Naz. Ep. 1 to Cledonius against Apollinarius, as John of Caesarea notes: ' Another testimony of the same Cyril in the same book brought forward by him against what is said by Theodore. It is in the first Letter written to Cledonius by the most holy and blessed Gregory bishop of Nazianzum.'

5. The three first of these extracts are taken from the collection of John, Bishop of Caesarea; this one has been preserved to us by a Manuscript in the Library of S. Mark at Venice.

6. from a collection later than Severus; the next four are from Severus.

7. from the same collection as the passage given above, p. 320, see p. 326 note e: Card. Mai also gives it from Severus against Julian of Halicarnassus.

8. These words of preface are taken from a Compilation mentioned in note g: they are in the British Museum MSS., Add. 14532, 14533, 12155.

9. The Greek is mian phusin Theou Logou sesarkomenen, "One Incarnate Nature of the Word," not 'One Nature of the Incarnate Word' which would be the Monophysite heresy, and this expression S. Cyril carefully states and explains in his second letter to Succensus, Epp. pp. 142, 143. Almost the whole passage is given above, the beginning at p. 265 note e, the sequel at p. 41 note e.

10. On this passage, see Preface.

11. The author of the Collection thus introduces the final words of S. Athanasius, see de recta fide to Arcadia and Marina 40 b.

12. This and the next are from Severus against the Catholic John, Bishop of Caesarea.

13. The following passage from S. Athanasius against Apollinarius will illustrate what suggested to Theodore, in opposing Apollinarians, to err thus sorrowfully. S. Athanasius says, "Tell me therefore how ye say that God was made of Nazareth? is it as declaring a beginning of generation of the Godhead, like Paul of Samosata, or denying the generation in the flesh, like Marcion and the rest of the heretics? not walking after the Gospel standard but chusing to speak out of your own? for therefore do ye say that God has been born of a Virgin and not God and man after the Gospel standard: lest, confessing the birth of the flesh ye should say it was a natural birth, speaking truth, but ye say that God was born, and that He exhibited His own flesh in semblance. For God does not shew forth the beginning of His Generation from Nazareth; but God the Word Who existed before the ages, appeared man out of Nazareth, born of Mary the Virgin and of the Holy Ghost [compare 'Man of the Holy Ghost and the Virgin,' in S. Augustine on S. John hom. 111 fin. p. 998 O.T.], in Bethlehem of Judaea of the seed of David and Abraham and Adam, as it is written; taking all from a Virgin whatever from the beginning God moulded and made without sin unto the subsistence of

man." S. Ath. against Apoll. ii. 5. t. i. 943 c d.

14. This piece is supplied in a latin translation by Card. Mai: see Migne ix. 1451. n. 24.

15. See below pp. 358, 359.

16. This and the following extracts are from the collection prepared for the fifth General Council, and read in its fifth collation. It was in preparation for this Council that Facundus Bishop of Hermaeum (quoted above p. 337) had written his work, and no doubt John of Caesarea's vast array of extracts were prepared for the same purpose.

17. Thus far is given by Leontius of Byzantium as Diodore's. After a number of extracts of Theodore, Leontius gives five, which he attributes to Diodore with the title, The same Diodore out of Book 1 against the Synousiasts. This is the fourth of them. (Against Nestorians and Eutychians Book 3 in Gallandi, xii. G97.) Leontius' translation is a different one from that cited before the fifth Council. Gallandi assigns to Leontius the date about A.D. 610, nearly 60 years later than the Council. The fifth Council and Leontius agree in citing the work on (or as Leontius calls it, against) the Incarnation, in fifteen books, & the four books against Apollinarius (Leontius, book 3 ubi supra pp. 695, 696: Conc. vi. 43 &c). The Council further cites yet another treatise: The same from the book against the Synousiasts or Apollinarists, which blessed Cyril put forth and answered (ib. 54, see below p. 345 and note s: so Pope Pelagius II in his Letter to Elias of Aquileia and other bishops in Istria. Conc. vi. 269). Leontius does not (as far as I see) cite this last, but is it a part of the treatise whence Leontius does cite five pieces as Diodore out of book 1 against the Synousiasts? of these five, the first is by Mercator too (p. 350 Bal.) attributed to Diodore (Mercator does not mention what book he extracted it from), the second is at p. 347, the third at p. 344, the fourth here, a piece of the fifth is by S. Cyril (p. 333) attributed to Diodore, while he attributes 2, 3, 4 to Theodore.

18. cited in part by Leontius under the name of Diodore against the Synousiasts (see last note), but in the fourth collation of the Council it stands as, The same Theodore from the passages which S. Cyril answered. t. vi. 57.

19. In these first words Theodore is citing an Apollinarian objection: compare with the passage S. Cyril's words against Nestorins, above pp. 175, 176. This whole passage is cited in the fourth collation of the Council amid other extracts of Theodore with an allusion to this work of S. Cyril in its title, The same from his book against the Synousiasts or Apollinarians which the blessed Cyril both put forward and answered, t. vi. p. 54. ed. Col. S. Cyril's citation of it and reply comes further on in the fifth collation p. 69 Col. and being a startling passage, part of it is cited (as n. 29) in Pope Vigilius' constitutum, Conc. v. 1334.

20. This piece is also preserved in Syriac by Severus, in his treatise against John the Grammarian in the British Museum MS. 12157 fol. 215 with the title, The same from the first Book of what he wrote against Theodore of Mopsuestia fighting against God.

21. This is also extant, in a different translation, in Leontius

Byzant. against Nestorius and Eutyches Book 3, with the title, The same [Dioodore] from the same book [1 against the Synousiasts] . Gallandi, Bibl. Vet. Patrum, xii. 696. see above p. 343 note q. In the fourth collation of the Council it is cited with the title, The same Theodore, what S. Cyril put forth and answered, t. vi. 57 Col. Pope Vigilius likewise has it as n. 45 in his Constitutum, t. v. 1340. For quo, whereby it is made &c, the fourth collation gives quia, for that, Leontius, et quod, and that. The words, 'to suppose that He needs a body for perfect sonship,' belong to the Apollinarian error which Theodore is opposing: the next words are those of Theodore's own error.

22. See statement of Apollinarian errors, below p. 363 note b.

CYRIL OF ALEXANDRIA FROM THE THIRD BOOK AGAINST THEODORE BISHOP OF MOPSUESTIA

which begins

For burdensome, I suppose, are our words.

1. [1] Hear therefore from us too. Understand, O man, the depth of the Mystery, go along the straight way of the aim of the sacred Scriptures. For one thing and another is Godhead and flesh or manhood, as far as regards the plan of their properties. Since [2] how has the Word being God been made as we, albeit abiding what He was? Yet grant Him His flesh by a Union inseverable, bare Him not of the Veil, for thus will you worship One Son, consubstantial with the Father Divinely, the Same consubstantial to us too humanly. To them who chuse thus to think will Christ turn the knowledge of the Mystery Him ward.

2. For the nature of man which was in Christ was both honoured and hallowed. For that in regard to His Being He would neither be in need of Baptism nor of partaking the Holy Ghost, the fact that He is Bestower of the Spirit will be sufficient to prove.

3. S. Cyril in his second Book against Theodore of Mopsuestia,

But I think that this, viz. that of Christ alone the Saviour of all is it said by the God-inspired Scripture that He was born in the flesh, shews that being God He was made in our likeness. I mean something of this sort: For no one receives one who would say either of the all-wise Moses, or of one of the Saints that he was born in the flesh of the Jews, or of a woman: for no one has any other birth, for of flesh is flesh mother. But if Christ be said to be in the flesh of the Jews, i. e., of a woman, the addition of in the flesh has some wise meaning and replete with declarations of things necessary for the hearers. For in order that we may not suppose that the Nature of the Word, that is, His Godhead, had a beginning of being that It was in the flesh and of flesh, the phrase in the flesh must be taken cautiously and in its necessary meaning. For being God by Nature, and Very Son of God the Father, He was made in likeness of men and made His own the flesh which was of the holy Virgin.

4. for he wrote thus in his second book against Theodore,

But I would fain ask him what he says that unity of Person is. For if he says that the Only-Begotten God the Word Incarnate is One Son, One will be the Person of the Son: but if he altogether distinguish and say that One is said to be and is Son in truth, and one by grace, and to the One gives the glory and the appellation of Godhead and the bare name alone of sonship: but to the other that he receives it as from Another and a Superior, and One so exalted and in Excellency, as is God above man, what room will there be for unity of person, a thing that I know not how it is put forth by him?

5. S. Cyril patriarch of Alexandria against Theodore.

Since then 'it has become the own body of the Word which quickeneth all,' it too is quickening: has it not therefore ascended up above the definitions of its nature? for the Word out of God the Father has largely placed in His Body the operation of His quickening might, so that it should have power to quicken the dead and to heal the sick: just as fire approaching a vessel of brass or of other matter, changes it to its own might and working.

The same Cyril from his second book.

The words of Theodore. " What is man that Thou art mindful of him, or the son of man that Thou visitest him? Let us consider then who the man is in regard to whom he is astonished and marvels that the Only-Begotten has deigned to be mindful of and visit. Yet that it is not said of every one, has been shewn above; that it is not of any one you please, this too is certain. To omit all things, let us take the Apostle's witness which is more trustworthy than all [3]. The Apostle therefore writes to the Hebrews telling of Christ and, confirming His Person which was not well received among them, thus says, But a certain one somewhere testified on this wise saying, what is man that Thou art mindful of him, or the son of man that Thou visitest him? Thou loweredst him a little below the angels, with glory and honour Thou crownedst him and didst set him over the works of Thy hands; Thou didst put all things under his feet. And having spoken the testimony he interpreting it proceeded, But in subjecting all things He left nothing not subject: yet we see not at present all things subjected to him. And teaching us who the man is, since it was doubtful in the words put in blessed David, he added, But we see Jesus lowered a little below the angels on account of the suffering of death, crowned with glory and honour. If therefore we are taught out of the Gospels that it was to the Lord that blessed David said all that are in the psalm &c, both that Thou art mindful, and Thou visitest and Thou loweredst and Thou subjectedst; and out of the Apostle learn that it was Jesus of Whom David speaking says both that He is mindful of Him and that He visited Him, yea also that He subjected all things to Him, when He had lowered Him a little below the Angels; cease ye now at last from your shamelessness, knowing what is right. For [4] ye see (O most wicked of men) how vast the difference of natures in that the one is astounded for that He deigns to be mindful of man and to visit him and to make him partaker of the other things whereof He made him partaker; the other on the contrary marvels, that he hath been vouchsafed to be a partaker of so great things above his nature: and the one is marvelled at as bestowing a kindness and giving great things and above the nature of him who obtains it; the other, obtaining the kindness and receiving from Him greater things than he is."

S. CYRIL.

Be ye sober from your wine, may one cry to them who are thus astray. Put, o man, a door and bolt on thy tongue, cease lifting up your horn on high and speaking unrighteousness against God. How long dost thou insult Christ who endures it? Keep in mind what is written by Divine Paul, Thus sinning against the brethren and smiting their weak conscience, ye sin against Christ. And to say something out of the prophetic books, Sodom was justified by thee: thou hast surpassed the talk of the pagans, which they made against Christ, deeming the Cross foolishness, thou hast shewn the charges against Jewish pride to be a nothing. Thou presumest to lower and (as far as pertains to thee) thou draggest down to dishonour Him Who sitteth in the Thrones above and together with

God the Father hath the same seat. For Him Who rose from the dead is it that the most wise Paul says is sitting on the Thrones of Godhead. For he said, We have such an High Priest Who sitteth on the Right Hand of the Throne of Majesty in the highest, Who is above all princedom and power and lordship and every name that is named not only in this world but also in that to come: for to Him every knee boweth and every tongue confesseth that the Lord Jesus Christ is in the glory of God the Father. And who is He Who is in this case as being God? The same again explaineth who is the priest of His Mysteries: for he said that He emptied Himself, was made in likeness of man and found in fashion as a man and abased Himself made obedient unto death, yea the death of the Cross. Every knee therefore of heavenly and earthly and neath the earth bendeth to Him Who bare the Cross: Whom the adversary casting into the mere and alone measures of the human nature, says was accounted worthy of mindfulness and visiting from God the Word, when surely he ought to know and mind that God the Word was not another Son apart and by Himself from Him who is (as he says) man of the seed of David; but God the Word Himself out of God the Father was made as we, i. e. man, did not rather deem worthy of visiting and mindfulness some other than He.

And out of the same book.

THEODORE.

"Will they now cease from their shameless contest? will they give over empty contention blushing before the proof of what has been said? for he said, Bringing many sons unto glory. Lo therefore the Apostle co-numbering in the rank of sonship with the rest the man that was assumed not for that he partakes of sonship in like manner as they, but in regard that he assumed in like manner the grace of sonship, the Godhead alone possessing sonship by Nature [5]. For it is certain that the glory of sonship is in him specially beyond others on account of the Unity that he has with Him. Whence in the very word too that means Son, he too is in like manner included. But they [6] argue with us, If ye say two things perfect, we shall surely be also saying Two sons. But lo he is called son too by himself in the divine Scripture, without the Godhead, co-numbered with the rest of men, and we do not say Two sons. But One Son there rightly is in our confession, seeing that division of natures must needs remain and union of person be kept indissoluble."

CYRIL.

Fie the madness! He knew not the manifold depth of the mystery of Christ who has trusted in words so cold and childish. But that he no wise understandeth the force of the Scripture proposed, but leaveth the right way and goes off again to the wicked aim put forth by himself, we forthwith teach. For that before all things his aim is, to want to prove that a mere man is co-seated with the Father and to be worshipped as God by every creature, himself shall come in as witness. For numbering Him with those who are sons by grace and the multitude of men, he argues that the. Godhead of the Word has alone the glory of true sonship, all but finding fault with Him Who for our sakes was pleased to suffer emptying: or haply even casting his own base madness on the disciple who says, And the Word was made flesh. We must know therefore that although he somewhere says one and not rather two sons, casting out altogether him who (as he says) is of the seed of David from being God and Son, he refers the glory of true sonship to only God the Word Who is forth of God the Father. This is nought else (as I said) than not to take on Him the measure of human nature, but utterly to destroy the Economy whereby we were both saved and have passed from death and sin and have laid down the yoke of the devil's oppression.

Theodore from the same book.

"Let none be deceived by the craft of the questionings. For it were a wicked thing to put down so great a crowd of witnesses (as the Apostle said) and, deceived by cunning questionings, to join the side of the opponents. But what are the questions which they artfully ask? 'Is Mary mother of man or God's mother?' and, 'Is He Who was crucified, God or man?' But of that there has been a clear solution in these things which we have said before in the replies which were made to the questions: nevertheless let that be said even now which one ought to briefly reply in order that no occasion be left them for their cunning. When [7] therefore they ask, 'Is Mary mother of man or God's mother?' let answer be made them, Both; one from the nature of the thing, the other by reference. For she is mother of man by nature, because he was man in the womb of Mary, who also proceeded thence: but mother of God because God was in the man who was born, not circumscribed within him by Nature, but in him in the affection of the will. Hence it is right to reply, Both, but not in like wise. For not as man took in the womb a beginning of his being, did God the Word too, for He was before every creature. Hence it is right that both be said, each according to their proper notion.

"The same answer is to be made if they ask, 'Was God crucified or man?' Both, but not in like wise: for the one was crucified, as both undergoing the Passion and fastened to the wood and holden of the Jews; the other because He was with him after the reason given above."

And forthwith he goes on adding hereto that man having God indwelling him was crucified.

S. CYRIL.

What are you saying, o mighty man? was the holy Virgin mother of God because God was in what was born of her, indwelling in mere good-pleasure of the will? dost thou call that union? then when the Word being God makes His habitation in ourselves too (for He dwells in the souls of the saints through the Holy Ghost), dost thou confess that in like wise ourselves too have union with Him? Where then will any one see the marvel of the mystery of Christ? For so long as God the Word is believed to have been made man as we, truly marvellous is the Mystery and one will wonder at it deservedly and intensely [8]; but if He be said to dwell in a man in mere good-pleasure of the will, the fact of the economy has another plan. For we have been vouchsafed, as I said, grace of this kind, who are resplendent with the faith Him-ward. For no one, I suppose, will say that not of His own will is He within us; rather of His own will, i. e. after His own inherent will had He good-pleasure towards us.

Yet neither do we say that God the Word Who is con-substantial with the Father, has the beginning of His Being from the flesh of the holy Virgin [9] (for with Him was He ever existent), but rather we know that He was made man as we.

Therefore rightly will the holy Virgin be called by us Mother of God rather than mother of man, since surely 'she hath borne Christ according to the flesh.'

And after more. For when this was put forth for explanation, viz. When He bringeth in the First-Begotten into the world, He saith, And let all the Angels of God worship Him,, he writes again thus,

THEODORE.

"Who then is He Who is brought in into the world and commences His reign, wherefrom it results that He is also worshipped by the Angels? For one will not madly say that God the Word was brought in Who made all things when they were not, bestowing on them through His unspeakable might that they should be."

S. CYRIL.

Callest thou it then madness, to chuse to think aright and to keep in mind the true and right and unmixed Faith? since surely one would say and that deservedly that they are words full of impiety which deny that the Only-Begotten Word of God was brought in by God the Father into the world when He was made man. For He Who by Nature and diversity is superior to all, seeing He is their Creator and is Essentially as greatly superior to them, as is the thing made less than its Maker, entered into the world when He was made a part of it [10], in that He appeared man.

And after a little. But I marvel that the opponent should have written that Jesus too would never have been accounted worthy of connection with God the Word had He not first been rendered spotless through the anointing. For first of all he is openly severing and distinguishing, saying outright Two sons: next let him say, when He was (as he terms it) made spotless and attained connection with God the Word, was it from the very womb, or when, in His thirtieth year, He came to the Jordan and sought John's baptism? If He were holy from the womb, how does he say that He was made holy and not rather that He was so? For in that He is said to be made so, it is quite necessary to understand that He was not what He was made. But if He were holy always, and was not so made in time, how does he say that the SPIRIT soared down upon Him and shewed that He was worthy of the connection and added to Him what He lacked? For this too he has put in his other books. For what was it that was at all lacking to Him unto sanctification from the very womb, yea rather and before Birth after the flesh, to Him Who is holy and spotless and sanctifieth the creature? When therefore he says that Jesus would not have been counted worthy of connection with God the Word except He had first been rendered spotless, he is indicting very many accusations against his empty talk. For first of all he unbecomingly says, been counted worthy: next he severs into another son apart Him Who is forth of the seed of David, whom he shamelessly maintains is called JESUS apart by Himself. Further, to say that He was made spotless, as if at one time He were not so, this too has very great blasphemy. For God the Word united from the very womb to His own flesh was One Son and thus also spotless, the Holy of holies, and giving of His fulness the SPIRIT not only to men but also to the rational powers above and in Heaven.

And after a little,

THEODORE.

"Manifoldly and in many modes of old spake God to the fathers in the Prophets, in these last days He spake to us in His Son. For through the Son He spake to us: and it is clear that he is speaking of the man [11] who was assumed. For to which of the Angels ever said He, My Son THOU art, I to day begat thee? None, he says, hath He made partaker of the Son's dignity. For in this that He said, I begat Thee, He gave as it were through it a participation of sonship, yet this which has been said is openly shewn to have nothing at all to do with God the Word."

S. CYRIL.

Verily in his discourses too which he made to them who were to be baptized, the same Theodore again said, "But this testimony we found not out of our ownselves, but were taught it out of the Divine Scripture, seeing that blessed Paul thus saith, Forth of whom is Christ after the flesh Who is God over all, not that He is forth of the Jews and according to the flesh Who is God over all, but he used the one term to point out the human nature, which he knew was of the stock of Israel, the other to shew the Divine Nature which he knew was over all and king of all [12]."

Hear ye deaf and see ye blind, cried aloud one of the saints to them of the blood of Israel: but I think, and deservedly, that this belongs to them who have not, or who will not understand aright the mystery of Christ. For the god of this world hath blinded the understandings of the unbelievers, and they, not having the Divine and intellectual light in heart and mind, have deservedly gone astray. But if some who are somehow or other holden in like diseases, have been enlightened, yea rather even co numbered with the Doctors, what else will one cry to them than this which has been said by God through one of the holy Prophets, For ye are become a snare of a watchtower in your visitation and as nets spread out in a prop [13] which the hunters have pierced through? For they who ought to be of the greatest profit to those under them, they have been a snare and a net and a stumbling block and pitfall of hades. And thus I say marvelling exceedingly and unable to see whereunto tends the opponent's aim. For he confessed in plain terms that God the Father spake to us through the Son, yet says that that Son is the man who was assumed, who has no share with God the Word in regard to what was said. How therefore is not the slander against the blessed Paul, yea rather the accusal of the Truth itself manifest to all? for not thus did the Apostle who has the Holy Ghost understand it. But the opponent is again turning aside right doctrine to his own pleasure.

From the second book of Cyril Bishop of Alexandria that One is Christ against Theodore.

That the ungodly Nestorius desired to follow the doctrines of Theodore, does not acquit him, rather it will thence work a deeper charge against him. For when he might have taken hold of the right words and spotless discourses of the holy Fathers on the Godhead, he thinks fit to prefer a lie to the truth. For he let alone what was theirs, he chose rather to cleave to what was base and to delight him in such perverted words. That this man therefore who hath such aim and madness, should have leapt down hereto, one may I think blame him and deservedly. For ho ought, he ought to have remembered the most holy Paul who clearly writes to us, Be ye wise money-changers, prove all things, hold fast that which is good, keep ye from every kind of evil. Which thing we, won t to do and hastening to imitate assayers of coin, repudiate those base and counterfeit doctrines, and receive full-gladly all which shine forth with the clear beauty of truth. But again let our argument turn the way befitting it and set before it. There have been writ therefore by good Theodore against the heresy of the Arians and Eunomians about twenty books or more; besides others interpreting the Gospel and Apostolic books: toils which none would have wished to find fault with, yea rather would have honoured the zeal with his approval, if soundness of doctrine had been in them [14]. But if one walk outside of the appointed road, and leaving the right way of truth, go a crooked path and wound the hearts of the more simple, casting therein seeds of perverted understanding, then it will not be without damage for them who are over the people to rest herein, but they will have their reward and gain if they withstand [him]. Hence since in these books or writings which we mentioned above of the man spoken of, have been found certain things full of the uttermost impiety, how would it bo congruous to choose to be silent? for he severs the inseverable Christ and, in place of One Son, he honours a duality falling away from truth and as it were tinted with false names. For he says that God the Word Who is forth of God the Father was called man, yet not that He was so made in truth: the man, Him who is of Mary (as he speaks) whom too he in many places cleverly calls flesh, he says was called indeed God and Son of God, not that He is so in truth.

But [15] Paul a workman exceeding wise to bring in the Divine Mysteries sometimes brings in to manifest the Mystery of Christ even things which are said by some in Divine Scripture, of other people. Yet he does not separate them from the persons of whom we know that they were said, nor yet does he transfer all that is theirs [16] to Christ, but sometimes takes even some very little bit, which he can without risk skilfully transfer to his purpose.

Footnotes:

1. Of the extracts of this last book, John of Caesarea supplies the two first, Severus in his Book against him, gives the third, a rather later syriac collection the fourth; the fifth is from a Monophysite treatise against the Nestorians, from a ninth century MS; the remainder was read before the fifth Council, except the last, a small fragment from Facundus.

2. This is also extant in Syriac, in the MS. 12156 fol. 31 v (quoted by Timothy heretical Bishop of Alexandria and the first of the heretical succession, in his "Letter to them of Constantinople against the heretics [Eutychians] who confess not that God the Word is consubstantial with us according to the flesh, Who is consubstantial with His Father in His Godhead, and against them who say Two Natures" i. e. against the Catholics) with the title, Blessed Cyril Archbishop of Alexandria from the second chapter against Theodore. The Manuscript is itself of the sixth century. It commences with a writing of the same Timothy against the Council of Chalcedon.

3. Thus far is given, in a different translation, by Leontius of Byzantium, against the Nestorians and Eutychians, book 3, in Gall. xii. 693, with the title, The same [Theodore the heretic] from the same [book or discourse x.] i. e. of Theodore's book on the Incarnation, which was written in Theodore's earlier life (Tillemont xii. 436) against the Apollinarians and Arians in 15 Books (ib. 445, 446), see above p. 337 note a. Leontius in his prefatory remarks to these citations speaks of this work as hard to get a sight of. "For we hardly and with great toil and with much thought have been able to find his book against the Incarnation: for they watch carefully and take care not to communicate his books to them who are not taught in them." ubi supra, p. 690. This proves that Leontius did not get his citations second-hand.

4. Compare the extract quoted from the interpretation of the eighth psalm, in the fourth collation of the Council, t. vi. 50 Colet, and that from the fourth book against the ungodly Apollinarius, ib. 46; and in Leontius, book 3 against the Nestorians and Eutychians, the above, and one, the same from the fourth book against Apollinarius. Gall. xii. 696.

5. Thus far is cited in the fourth collation of the Council, as from the interpretation of the Epistle to the Hebrews, t. vi. 57 Col., also by Pope Vigilius, t. v. 1341: the whole passage by Leontius of Byzantium, against the Nestorians and Eutychians, with the title, from the same [twelfth] Book, i. e. on the Incarnation. Gall. xii. 694.

6. they, i. e. the Apollinarians, who accused their opponents of holding two sons, see S. Gregory's complaint of it, below p. 363; Theodore's (who was accused of it with real reason), above p. 337, note a and here. The objection itself is stated in S. Athanasius against Apollinarius, 'that two perfects cannot make one whole,' see below p. 363 note b.

7. From here down to, in the affection of the will is cited in the fourth collation (vi. 57 Colet) as from the twelfth book on the Incarnation, and by Pope Vigilius in his Constitution (v. 1340): also by Leontius, as from the fifteenth book, i. e. on (or as Leontius calls it against) the Incarnation. Gall. xii. 695.

8. see above Scholia §§ 19, 20, pp. 208, 209; also de Recta fide to Arcadia and Marina p. 72 c d 122 e.

9. see Nestorius urging that this would follow if the holy Virgin were to be called Mother of God, and S. Cyril's reply in Book 1 § 1 against Nestorius, above pp. 7-10.

10. See above, pp. 52, 92, 189, also p. 324 note c, where S. Athanasius speaks of the great dread on the part of the Apollinarians as to the Incarnate SON being in any way "a part of the world."

11. These few first words are cited by Leontius of Byzantium, Book 3 against the Nestorians and Eutychians, with the title, the same from the same [twelfth book on the Incarnation]. Gall. xii. 694.

12. In the fourth collation of the Council, are seven citations of Theodore from his book to them that are to be baptized, viz, 35, 36, 37, 38, 39, 41, 42 (t. vi. 55 Col.), but none of these are identical with the one here quoted by S. Cyril.

13. statumine. I do not know how the Latin translator got this word, nor what meaning he attached to it. The Hebrew has Tabor, which the LXX. here translate itaburion, and so S. Cyril quotes the verse elsewhere: but he knew its meaning, for in his commentary on the words, he says that it is a very conspicuous mountain in Galilee.

14. I do not know by what error in translation misled, Facundus Bishop of Hermaeum in Africa (in his Defence of the Three Chapters addressed to the Emperor Justinian just before the fifth Council) takes this to be, And these toils no one has dared to blame but to honour with vote of approval the zeal for right doctrines that is in them. Facundus repeats this three times, book iii. § 3, and 5, book viii. § 6. Gall. xi. 692, 696, 753, and in the latter place urges the extract as a reason why S. Cyril

was not the writer of the books against Theodore. Facundus' work being addressed to the Emperor Justinian, would of course be not utterly unknown to the Council; this present extract is introduced in their acts as ordered to be recited because some laid stress on the word 'good Theodore,' as if S. Cyril were praising him, in order that the context might shew if it were so: after the recital, "the holy Synod said, 'The things recited shew that Cyril of religious memory blaming rather Theodore and his wicked writings, not as implying praise, used such words.' " t. vi. 90 Colet.

15. This extract is preserved by the above mentioned Facundus (book iii. § 6 in Gall. xi. 698) who says that the author of the work [against Diodore and Theodore] treats of a section in which the Apostle says to the Hebrews, For not to the Angels hath He subjected the world to come &c.

16. S. Cyril himself who enjoys so much adapting Old Testament events as types of Christ and His Church, says that some things in the history belong to the history itself.

Against Julian
By Cyril of Alexandria

Book 1 Prefatory Address

Address of the blessed Cyril, Archbishop of Alexandria, to the very pious emperor Theodosius, devoted to Christ.

The exceptional success of your holy principate, which deserves fame but discourages praise, your incomparable provision for piety, are the heritage from On High which you echo and which you have preserved, unconquered, from the traits of envy, thanks to a skill in public affairs which you got from your father and also your grandfather, as can clearly been seen in this field. Also I propose to apply to your own person the words of our Saviour, who said: "A city on a hill cannot be hidden"; isn't what is on the heights not always, on the same basis, the same thing as that which is seen?

However what could equal Your Serenity? Nothing in the world, since the glory of your sceptre has reached the supreme limits by illuminating the whole universe with the glow of your perfect administration, while your leniency and your piety towards Christ delight Heaven □ I mean the rational powers which reign in its heights. So great indeed is the admiration that you receive in these two connections that, having here and there equal and rival virtues, you have placed yourself beyond praise in all its forms. The votive offerings that others devote to you, Emperor Theodosius devoted to Christ, are the trophies of victories, crowns, thanksgivings and all other ways of honouring, not without reason, the imperial power.

2. As for us, that destiny has given to sacred service, we had the duty to offer you a work composed with the greatest care to the glory of God: your inclinations, your practice and the authentic wishes of your heart have indeed always carried you to applaud that glory, to hold execrable those who, like drunken men, insult it in one way or another, to put them in the row of your worst enemies, to gratify on the other hand with every kind of favour those who choose to glorify God in thought and word. I would willingly consider these excellent provisions as a proof of holiness, in perfect suitability to the glorious heights which you occupy. In a psalm to Christ the Saviour of the world, David, the inspired prophet exclaimed: "Didn't I hate those who hate you, Lord, and was I not consumed toward your enemies? I made myself hate them with a perfect hatred, they became my own enemies!" These words are fully justified: indeed one can give as a shining proof of his attachment to your person the combat which he ardently carries out against those who chose, I do not know through what blindness, not to love you; in the same way, one could express all the authenticity of his love for Christ by impetuously attacking those who have discredited Christianity, with on the lips, almost like a cry, these words of the Scripture inspired by God: "I am filled with a jealous zeal for the Lord!"

It is necessary for me to say now what kind of work I am offering you here.

3. Forgive me for having resolved to speak not only against a king, but also for the glory of Christ, the great King, who reigns with his Father over the

world; it is with him alone that it is true to say: "Through me kings reign", because he is the "Lord of glory" in heaven and on earth. It necessarily follows that the champions of the divine teachings - us, in fact - given this office by Christ, must oppose to those who intend to defile his glory the arguments able to plead his cause, to appear sound to readers, to be a more useful aid for those whose heart is easily led astray and is inclined to yield to difficulties, and for those on the other hand who are well established in the faith to be a kind of stick able to support them in the strengthening of this faith and to maintain undimmed the tradition of orthodoxy.

However who is it that has entered into war against the glory of Christ? They are legion, those who at various periods have let themselves go at this foolishnes, driven by the perversity of the devil; but none as went far as Julian, who damaged the prestige of the Empire by refusing to recognize Christ, dispenser of royalty and power. Before his accession to the throne, he was counted among the believers: he had even been admitted to Holy Baptism and had studied the Holy Scriptures.

4. But some sinister characters, followers of superstition, entered I do not know how into connections with him and sowed in him the maxims of apostasy; then, allied with Satan in this design, they led him towards the practices of the Greeks and transformed into a servant of impure demons one who had been raised in holy churches and monasteries: "bad company corrupts good upbringing", as the very wise Paul says. However, I affirm that those who wish to preserve a solid thought, and who keep in their spirit, like an invaluable pearl, the tradition of the true faith, do not have to offer to the peddlers of superstition any occasion to insinuate themselves, in any case to speak to them freely. Is it not written: "You will be holy with the holy, irreproachable with the irreproachable, chosen with the chosen, and you will outwit the cheat"? The eloquence with which he was gifted the all-powerful Julian used against our common Saviour Christ; he composed three books against the holy gospels and against the very pure Christian religion, he used them to shake many spirits and to cause them uncommon wrongs. Indeed, the light-minded and easily seduced fall easily into his sights, and constitute a welcome amusement for the demonic powers; but not spirits strengthened in the faith which do not let themselves be disturbed sometimes: they believe that Julian knows the holy and divine Scriptures, since he accumulates in his own works □ without otherwise knowing well what it says!... □ a number of testimonies that he borrows from them.

5. Very many followers of superstition, when they meet Christians, overpower them with any kind of sarcastic remarks, and rely on the works of Julian to attack us, which they proclaim to be of an incomparable effectiveness, adding that there never was a learned man on our side able to refute them, or even show them at fault; also, at the instigation of more than one person, and full of confidence once again in the word of God: "Get under way, and I will open your mouth!", I put myself to the duty of rebutting this Greek eyebrow raised against the glory of Christ, to help to the extent of my abilities those which have been deceived, in order to convict of error and of ignorance of the Scriptures the man who has accused our common Saviour Christ.

I dedicate my work on this subject to Your Greatness devoted to Christ and very august: may God always keep him, guarantee success against his enemies in an inimitable felicity, place the whole universe at his feet, grant to him to transmit his august power to the sons of his sons, with the approval of Christ, by whom and with whom glory to God the Father and to the Holy Ghost, for all the centuries! Amen.

Book 2 (beginning)

1. We thought that it was by no means unjustified, that it was even useful and necessary to say before all what is the chronological sequence of the characters, and also what idea each has of God: therefore we have carried out with much precision the exposition of these details.

We could be reproached for this by saying: "Why then, having undertaken to defend Christian doctrines and taking in mind to oppose a victorious argumentation to the blasphemies of Julian, did you not decide to engage from the start in that way? Why on the contrary have you diverted the energy which began your exposition into a different goal, to launch into genealogies and to undertake a study of Hebraic and Greek doctrines?"

So let us remove the objections that have been made to us about this choice, by affirming that we intentionally directed our matter towards this digression. Indeed, (Julian), following the example of the Babylonian Rhapsaces, doesn't hesitate to utter in unrestrained language his mocking remarks against the glory of God, and after tossing impious vociferations against our holy religion he quotes the wise ones of Greece unceasingly, crowns their condemnable opinions with all possible praise, desperate to attack the crowned teachings of the Church, to smile at the books of Moses and to put in the dock all these holy people; therefore we were fully justified in accumulating, before passing to the refutation, material which enables us to show in a clear way that the works of the greatest of all, Moses, were prior to those of the wise Greeks, and, moreover, that the Christian faith as it has been transmitted, appears incomparably superior to their dogmatic positions. It was thus, and not differently, that next books could avoid too long digressions and avoid appearing to deviate sometimes very far from the the subject. But enough now on this point.

2. It is now necessary to come to (Julian's) own book. We will reproduce his text word for word, and will oppose our own arguments to his lies in the appropriate order, because we realize that it is necessary to firmly neutralize them. But, as I said, from his open mouth without reserve he spreads every kind of calumny against our common Saviour Christ, and pours against him ill-sounding remarks: I will abstain from responding with similar details, and, advising the wise party to ignore that in his words which risks dirtying the spirit by simple contact, I will endeavour to combat this (method of) 'combat', by denouncing on all occasions his habit of scoffing which speaks wrongly and irrelevantly without ever being able to arrive at saying a true thing.

It also should be known that in his first book he handles a great mass of ideas and does not cease turning and turning over the same arguments in every direction; some developments which are found at the beginning of his work, he also advances in the body of the book and at the end: he thus reveals a kind of disorder in the articulation of his discussion, and, fatally, those who want to argue against what he says seem constantly to be repeating themselves instead of finishing them once for all. We will thus divide his text according to an appropriate classification, we will gather his ideas by categories and will face each of them not on several occasions, but only once, the with appropriate explanations and following the rules of the art (of speaking). Thus, at the beginning of his book against us, he says:

JULIAN
It is, I think, expedient to set forth to all mankind the reasons by which I was convinced that the fabrication of the Galilaeans is a fiction of men composed by wickedness. Though it has in it nothing divine, by making full use of that part of the soul which loves fable and is childish and foolish, it has induced men to believe that the monstrous tale is truth.

CYRIL

3. By 'Galilaeans', he means the Holy Apostles, I think, and by a 'fantastic account' the writings of Moses, the predictions of the holy saints and their declarations inspired by God. However, without his knowledge --- let us say rather: not without intervention of the divinity --- he has made this idea the basis of his own superstition!

In fact there are two Galilees, one in Judaea, the other on the borders of the Phoenician country; and it is written indeed in the Gospels about our common Saviour Christ that it is while walking on the edge of the Sea of Galilee, of Lake Tiberias, that he recruited his disciples. However God said by means of one of the holy prophets: "What are you to me, Tyre and Sidon, and you Galilee, entirely populated with foreigners?" In the same way the divine Isaiah exclaims: "Country of Zabulon, land of Nephtalim, and all you others who live by the edge of the sea, Galilee of the Gentiles! The people sitting in shadow saw a great light..."

So in Judaea, one cannot just imagine the presence of Galilaeans, since there are also all the Gentiles there: 'Galilee of the Gentiles', says Isaiah.

It cannot well or clearly be seen which adversaries the book of Julian aims at in all suitability and veracity: is it us, or himself in company with the believers in the stupid superstition that he loves? Because this is also Galilaean! Well indeed, it can't be doubted for one moment that the direction of the expressions employed by Julian agrees with the nonsense of the Greeks.

4. Where indeed to find all such an apparatus of fables, those vain words, this tasteless and irresponsible jumble of fads of every kind, if not among them and them only, who, twisting their subtle inventions, try to give to falsehood the colours of truth? So strong, so widespread among them is the turpitude that the elite of their spirits, the men cracked to philosophize extremely appropriately on the world which surrounded them, have raised loud cries against the undivine transports of their poets, and affirmed openly that they should abandon their charlatanism. In fact, Plato does not approve those poems, i.e. the homeric poems, which display the gods and goddesses convicted of libidinous passions, abused by quite human cupidities, and in addition prone to tears, deploring the death of those of their blood and breaking out like pansies in 'Woe is me!' because they want to save someone from death and are unable to do so, humbling themselves on the contrary before the fates, and yielding to Destiny, apparently more powerful than the Master of the gods, he that they call 'supreme Zeus'!

But I will not delay in saying all that I could still say on this subject; not wanting to appear to allow myself to be diverted from what is suitable, I will return to the point which my subject designates.

5. If there is a plot, it is a plot of the Greeks: it is they who undertook to use the fantastic to guarantee the truth, and not in all simplicity of spirit, but indeed with impious intentions and the satisfaction of wrongdoing! It is they who gathered against the inexpressible glory of all-powerful God this hateful 'fiction', which set up this 'deception', like some trap aimed at simple souls.

They have in effect mislaid the whole earth by pretending that the sky and the elements in general were God. As the very wise Paul writes: "While calling themselves wise, they fell into madness, and altered the glory of imperishable God by giving him the appearance of perishable man, birds, quadrupeds, and animals."

However, to run with his ideas, we will not throw against others the criticisms which he formulated and will indeed let them attack the Holy Apostles, even the very wise Moses himself and the holy prophets; but when he comes to the bar, will he clearly show what is this 'fiction implemented by malice', of what nature is this 'fantastic account' about which he speaks, in what consists the 'fondness for a fable, the puerile side' of the Christian religion! Did Moses write for us tales, when he professed one God by nature and in truth, unbegotten, eternal, imperishable, without quantity, invisible, immutable, imperceptible, God who is life and who gives life, who is science and power, creator, King and Lord of the universe? Did he deviate from the truth, the word of the holy prophets, who stick step by step to the doctrines of Moses? Will we find a teaching different in the holy Apostles? Certainly not!

6. And then, how can he affirm that the beliefs of Galilaeans do not have in them anything divine, that they are in addition hazardous fables, monstrous fictions? Who would refuse to admit that there can nothing better for men than to know clearly and without error the Craftsman and Lord of the world, one in nature and in truth? Our adversaries themselves, I know, would affirm that the most beautiful remarkable part of philosophy is contemplative philosophy: thanks to it, the spirits which their wisdom considers the best even to see go to great pains, and as much as is possible for men to do, to grasp the divine nature. Since he says that he himself is persuaded of this, would he teach us from where and from whom he obtains this certainty? Because finally it is not necessary that he flatters himself to be the only one with knowledge. If he was convinced of it himself, if that is enough for him to show without possible dispute □ as at least he thinks and affirms --- that Christianity is not worth anything, I will not hesitate to say that this is pure drivel in him, and that he just amuses himself to attack us alone! We will not submit ourselves to such a hostile judge! If on the other hand he considers that the declarations of the critics against anyone must be founded in truth and without lies, then, that he does not say that this is just his conviction; he argues with facts!

However it is indeed he himself, and not us, who he must hand over to justice for the invention of fables, and he is extremely likely to be convicted! What he said will persuade some of us: let us let him speak:

JULIAN

7. *Now since I intend to treat of all their first dogmas, as they call them, I wish to say in the first place that if my readers desire to try to refute me they must proceed as if they were in a court of law and not drag in irrelevant matter, or, as the saying is, bring counter-charges until they have defended their own views. For thus it will be better and clearer if, when they wish to censure any views of mine, they undertake that as a separate task, but when they are defending themselves against my censure, they bring no counter-charges.*

CYRIL

So it is necessary for those who you put on trial to be dumb? You require that the defendant be condemned without being able to break silence, and, without saying a word about your arguments, agrees to confirm the charge against himself! However, to refuse us the right to say anything of your theses is the act of a man who fears the controversy and is not unaware of the unpleasant weakness of his position. If our man, in examining the Christian religion, does not approve it on all points and decrees the crown of the supreme honours to the Greek superstition, I admit that he treats both equally; but if he takes pleasure in the speeches which he allows against us and gives the palm to his erroneous designs while opposing to us, as higher than ours, the Greek religion, how can he ask us to keep silence on and not to make any allusion to this religion, when, in our desire to defend the cause of our own beliefs, it is of that subject precisely that we speak?

8. If, renouncing the right to attack what you write, I had adopted the intention to mention only Greek realities, I could affirm: "His book on this subject is acceptable, and remains within the limits of probability"; but when would we defend ourselves, when we make a point of answering each one of its declarations, how does he still have the right to reproach us for our efforts to plead the cause of our religion while exposing the infamous impiety of the Greeks? Colours can be seen more clearly when there is contrast. "The light is seen in darkness", it is written, and in the same way, I believe, the beauty attached to the virtues appears to simple souls only through the ugliness of their opposites. What inclines to me to give to the Good the palm of victory is the hideousness of the Evil: and for this reason (Julian) has indeed reason to fear the arguments of his own camp, and refuses shamefully the right to produce it on the day, going so far as to impose silence on those which he puts on trial in this lawsuit! Here now is how he opposes other objections to us:

JULIAN

9. *It is worth while to recall in a few words whence and how we first arrived at a conception of God; next to compare what is said about the divine among the Hellenes and Hebrews; and finally to enquire of those who are neither Hellenes nor Jews, but belong to the sect of the Galilaeans, why they preferred the belief of the Jews to ours; and what, further, can be the reason why they do not even adhere to the Jewish beliefs but have abandoned them also and followed a way of their own. For they have not accepted a single admirable or important doctrine of those that are held either by us Hellenes or by the Hebrews who derived them from Moses; but from both religions they have gathered what has been engrafted like powers of evil, as it were, on these nations----atheism from the Jewish levity, and a sordid and slovenly way of*

living from our indolence and vulgarity; and they desire that this should be called the noblest worship of the gods.

CYRIL

The same man who poured out his smear against us to the readers, that if they wanted to contradict him, they must "must proceed as if they were in a court of law and not drag in irrelevant matter, or, as the saying is, bring counter-charges" promptly sets himself to compare the views of the Greeks and the Hebrews on the divine! But this technique of comparing and opposing, at what does it aim? What can be Julian's aim, when he brings together the disagreements between the Hebraic or Christian beliefs and the Greek ones?

10. We can't pretend that he is giving up his accusation, and his need to smear, in order to submit himself to the equitable judgement of his readers, so far as to want to take from them the definition of the best and the worst! In his position, it seems, the only way to find partisans for his ideas about the divinity is to abuse the Christian religion by giving it the worst of it in a confrontation with Greek religion. But such a defeat is impossible for those who know the weakness of error and the force of truth. But we must be on our guard: in telling the legislators to impose silence on us, and to prohibit the least remark about his own cause when we speak about ours, he falls victim to his own prohibitions. Since he cross-examines us, and wants to know what on earth made us give up the Greek religion for that of the Hebrews, well then, let's ask him back the same question! "Why have you yourself given up the Christian religion, and run away from the truth to embrace a lie? Why did you stupidly give preference to the most appalling superstition -- I mean that of idol-worshippers -- over a precise and certain teaching, and then think that you decided well when you have in fact drawn on yourself the final infamy? Does he want to know the real reason which made us give the Greek religion in order to hold in honour that of the Hebrews? We will borrow his own words to reply to him. Here's what he actually writes:

JULIAN

11. *Now it is true that the Greeks invented their myths about the gods, incredible and monstrous stories. For they said that Kronos swallowed his children and then vomited them forth; and they even told of lawless unions, how Zeus had intercourse with his mother, and after having a child by her, married his own daughter, or rather did not even marry her, but simply deflowered her and then handed her over in marriage to another. Then too there is the legend that Dionysus was rent asunder and his limbs joined together again.... This is the sort of thing described in the myths of the Greeks!*

CYRIL

What a defense to present! So what's the point of making a lot of noise and pretending to correct us when we have almost kicked out of existence the babbling of the Greeks, so ugly and improbable, and accorded preference to the truth? The divine Moses and after him the chorus of the holy prophets, the Apostles and the Evangelists, they sing the glory of God, one by nature and in truth; they invite us to imitate them by ripping away the myths from ourselves --- all the unbelievable forms and sleazy ideas -- and involving us in a way of life which attracts admiration. Nothing of what they say is invented, nothing in their ideas demands an incredible explanation. It is a fact that our beliefs agree with the preaching of Moses and with those of the holy prophets, and that the direction of the evangelical and apostolic teaching coincides with the ideas of our predecessors: at the proper time we will give some plain proofs of this.

12. But since (Julian) asserts -- on what head I don't know! ... -- that there is nothing serious or useful in our beliefs, well! let him prove it! Surely he isn't going to leave his assertion bare and without proof? Because anyway, how can there NOT be something serious in our beliefs? Don't we find precision and meticulousness in how Christians talk about God and the creation of the world? Don't the holy scriptures supply us with impeccable and irreproachable morality? Moreover, how can we not be struck by this obvious truth, that no other way, to my knowledge, is able to rightly address the supreme philosophy? Whether it is contemplative or even practical, our philosophical reflection can claim every kind of praise, and the followers of Greek wisdom themselves admire it. It is thus not true that "the Hebraic doctrines taught us atheism" -- that's exactly what he wrote! --- what is true to say, is that the Scripture inspired by God has enabled us to condemn Greek ignorance. Moreover atheism is rather more a description of their beliefs, which do not know the God who is one by nature and in truth: how isn't this evidence on both sides? He also claims that "we took with Greek unconcern to a way of dissolute and nonchalant life", by calling our custom to eat of all without prohibition and to abstain from no food the "careless insouciance" of the Greeks. So these people present as the supreme act of piety, and compare it to the perfection of all virtues, the refusal to consume this or that food!

13. Well! how can they make these things the criterion of purity? Everything comes from God; is perforce good which has its Being from kindness, and he that is most holy and pure could not have created anything that would soil us. And in fact what effect could a food have on those who consume it? What sort of stain could it introduce in them? I believe that what we need to condemn is that which is likely to contaminate someone -- and, very generally, the things that can produce such an effect are the things that we must condemn; adulteries, fornications, scandalmongerings, lies, smears, greed, etc. But the Greeks -- who didn't take any notice of vice of this sort, however -- affect temperance at the table, sometimes renouncing this meat or that, without denying themselves any extravagance! Further, they enjoy honouring sovereign Zeus by voluntarily giving themselves the same appetites as his, and they honour the sovereignty of Aphrodite.

Book 3 THE CREATION OF THE WORLD

(Julian) reproaches us for innumerable things, but mainly he has a go at the most wise Moses, by attacking his writings without moderation. He affirms that when composing the book about the creation of the world, everything he said was untrue and that he was satisfied just to gather old fairystories, that he paid no attention to things that seemed to deserve full attention, and finally that he just wrote poor centos, while imagining that he was saying things which were wise and good to hear. Yet Julian is paralysed with amazement before the ideas of the learned Greeks in this field, and, more than very other, he crowns with acclamations and applause the doctrines of Plato.

14. He throws about insults immoderately, but still let's pass over that for the moment! On the other hand, I will try to establish, as much as I can, that he is badly wrong to take up such grand airs in connection with Greek chatterings. It is necessary, I believe, to present afresh, by extracting them from the works of the Greeks, the various doctrines which they have judged good to profess about the creation of the world, and to oppose the cosmogony of Moses to them: the readers will thus see the verbose subtlety and drivel of these thinkers, as well as the pure source of truth which is in the writings of Moses. Plutarch, who had some fame in his own time, speaks thus about the universe in book 2 of his collection of Theories on Nature: "Pythagoras was the first to name the mass of the universe the 'Cosmos', according to the order which rules in it. Thales and those who hold his doctrines profess that the universe is unique; Democritus, Epicurus and his master Metrodorus say that there is an infinity of worlds within infinity, completely by chance; Empedocles that the circle of the sun defines the limits of the cosmos; Seleucus believes in an unlimited universe, while for Diogenes the Whole is infinite, but the universe is limited. The Stoics set out a difference between the Whole and the universe: the Whole is that which includes the infinite vacuum, while the universe is the cosmos without the vacuum - so that the universe and the cosmos are one and the same thing."

15. Later the same author continues thus about the form of the cosmos: "The Stoics believe that it is spherical, others conical, others still ovoid. Epicurus opines that some worlds are spherical, and others of a different shape." On the question of knowing if the universe has or not a soul, Plutarch expresses himself thus, again by giving the theories of the Greek philosophers: "In general all have claimed that the universe has a soul and is governed by providence; but Democritus, Epicurus and those who hold to ideas about the atoms and the vacuum deny it a soul and assert that it is governed not by providence but by an irrational nature. For Aristotle, it is completely excluded that the universe has a soul, reason or thought, or even that it is governed by providence: in fact there are actually celestial regions with these qualities, because they contain spheres endowed with soul and life, while the regions close to the ground are stripped of it; they take part in an established order, but by accident and not by nature." Enough on this chapter. But as these thinkers

had it in mind to work out at the end of it all whether the cosmos was or was not perishable by nature, they also gave their conclusions on this point: Pythagoras and the stoics held that the universe, created by God, was however corruptible insofar as its own nature went; indeed, perceptible by the senses because likewise corporeal, it was nevertheless to be preserved from destruction thanks to providence and to the safeguard exerted by God. For Epicurus, the universe is perishable because it is also subjected to birth, like an animal or a plant. For Xenophanes, it has no birth but is eternal and imperishable. Aristotle regards the sublunary part of the universe as subjected to external influences: it is in these areas that terrestrial things are perishable.

16. Readers, now you have heard and understood what drivel all this is! Opposing their opinions one to another, vociferating this or that, mixed up anyhow, without nuances, self-reflection, just at their pleasure; how can this avoid the impression that they are just guessing at the truth rather than knowing it? Indeed, some prefer just one universe, others a plurality; some of them believe that this universe is subject to creation, but others are opposed totally to this and opine on the contrary that the universe is imperishable and was not created; some say it is governed by a divine providence, others do without providence and allot the harmonious movements of the elements to automatic mechanisms and accidents; some say that the universe has a soul, others deny that it has a soul or a spirit. In short you could imagine that their theories on each detail are just tossed together, like mixed drinks! But our man has put Plato apart from the others, and he especially likes to linger over his doctrines. However I will say at once that Plato and Pythagoras offer more reasonable ideas about God and the cosmos than the others, because they collected their teaching or rather their knowledge during their stays in Egypt, where the very wise Moses is held in great regard, and where his doctrines are held in reverence and admiration. It is however claimed that Plato contradicted himself in his opinions, and that Aristotle, who was his disciple, not chose to adhere to the ideas of his Master, but to attack him thoroughly and to contradict him! Porphyry tells us that in expressing his ideas on the sky, Plato professed that the material part of it was composed of the four elements, the bond between them being a soul. "Also," Porphyry continues, "it is still today of a mixed nature, and it has received its name by misuse of terminology".

17. Porphyry speaks here, I believe, as an etymologist, and affirms that the sky is called 'ouranos' because it is visible [in Greek: ' oratos']: i.e. the sky was so-called because it is 'seen'. Aristotle had a different opinion on this subject ---- and how could he not, since he does not regard the sky as a compound, still less containing four elements, but considers it like a fifth type of body, independent of the first four and without anything in common with them? Plato himself, professes that the world has a soul and that it is a living being endowed with intelligence; he subordinates it to providence. But his disciple, to return to him, did not think so. He rejects completely the idea that the universe has a soul, is intelligent, or is governed by providence. Under one scheme, it is defined as created and corruptible by nature at least; the other treats the idea of birth as ignorant, and says on the contrary that it is imperishable and uncreated. Another divergence: the skilful and illustrious Plato defines three principles of Everything: God, matter and Idea; God is a creator, matter is substance, Idea is the model of any thing created. Aristotle, once again, is opposed to him, without any point of agreement. To start with, he refuses to regard Idea as a

principle, in his thought and writings, and supposes two principles: God and matter. Still let us say that if Plato supports the theory that there are three principles which make up Everything, God, matter and Idea, he also introduces a fourth which he names the 'universal soul'. Moreover, after having said that the matter is uncreated, he claims that it is thereafter subjected to creation; as for the definition of Idea, after having presented it as a substance itself, he starts to battle against his own theories, since he affirms that it exists in the thought of God, and that it thus does not have a separate existence, i.e. subsistence.

18. So which one do we give our approval to, when we seek the truth, when we seek to start along on the irreproachable way from which every error is banished? Which of the thinkers quoted can we declare innocent of the wrong of telling a lie? Which do we reward as not having stumbled in some detail? Or rather how can we grant a right to teach others, to those who have traveled so far from the truth that they disagree not only with each other but even with themselves? The very wise Julian approves and admires this state of affairs! He scoffs at the writings of Moses and, throwing reason aside, he dares to oppose those of Plato to them, while speaking as follows:

JULIAN

At this point of our study, if you please, we will compare the utterance of Plato. Observe then what this philosopher says about the creator, and what words he makes him speak at the time of the generation of the universe, in order that we may compare the cosmogony of Plato with that of Moses. Thus we can perceive who was the better and who more worthy of God, Plato the idolater, or he of whom the Scripture says that God spoke with him face to face:

"*In the beginning God created the heaven and the earth. And the earth was invisible and without form, and darkness was upon the face of the deep. And the spirit of God moved upon the face of the waters. And God said, Let there be light; and there was light. And God saw the light that it was good; and God divided the light from the darkness. And God called the light Day, and the darkness he called Night. And the evening and the morning were the first day. And God said, Let there be a firmament in the midst of the waters. And God called the firmament Heaven. And God said, Let the waters under the heaven be gathered together unto one place, and let the dry land appear; and it was so. And God said, Let the earth bring forth grass for fodder, and the fruit tree yielding fruit. And God said, Let there be lights in the firmament of the heaven that they may be for a light upon the earth. And God set them in the firmament of the heaven to rule over the day and over the night.*"

19. *In all this, you observe, Moses does not say that the deep was created by God, or the darkness or the waters. And yet, after saying concerning light that God ordered it to be, and it was, surely he ought to have gone on to speak of night also, and the deep and the waters. But of them he says not a word to imply that they were not already existing at all, though he often mentions them. Furthermore, he does not mention the birth or creation of the angels or in what manner they were brought into being, but deals only with the heavenly and earthly bodies. It follows that, according to Moses, God is the creator of nothing that is incorporeal, but is only the disposer of matter that already existed. For the words, "And the earth was invisible and without form" can only*

mean that he regards the wet and dry substance as the original matter and that he introduces God as the disposer of this matter.

CYRIL

About Moses there might be many things to say and lengthy expositions made to he who wants to safeguard our reverence for him. He heard God say to him without ambiguity, "I know you out of all humanity, and you have found grace in my eyes!" The manifold virtue that was in him, and the power of the miracles that he worked in Egypt, make a shining demonstration. Indeed he was shown submitted to God almighty, and assisted him in the revolt which He brought about in his servants against the blindness of the Egyptians. What kind of man Plato was, even in the absence of direct testimony, is proclaimed enough by his passage from Athens in Sicily. It is claimed that, not appreciating his flatteries, Dionysius sold him, inflicting on him, as if he wasn't a free man, the most suitable punishment for a slave. But let us give up this argument for a moment, to return to the main subject.

20. The divine Moses does not appear before our eyes as one who composed doubtful stories, nor one who launched himself out on this road from simple ambition. He had in mind primarily to contribute to making lives led better. And in fact he did not attempt to discourse subtly on the nature of the things, by speaking about what the first principles are named, or about the elements which proceed from it; these things are, in my opinion, too obscure, and inaccessible to some minds. His goal was to form the spirits of his contemporaries with the doctrines of the truth: because they were being misled and had taken to worshipping each according to his imagination. Their extreme ignorance made them ignore the one God, God by nature, and to worship his creations. Some thought that the sky was god, others the disc of the sun; there were even some wretched enough to allot the glory of the supreme nature to the moon, the stars, the earth, to plants, to the watery element, birds, or to brute animals! They had come to this, and such a terrible sickness had affected all the inhabitants of the earth, when Moses came to their help and revealed himself as the initiator into knowledge of great value for all. He proclaimed clearly that there exists by nature only one Creator of the universe, and radically distinguished Him from all other realities which He had merely brought into being and existence. Considering what was useful, and as clearly as possible, neglecting every excessively subtle point, he restricted himself to deal only with that which was strictly essential.

21. How was it useful to him to say what is the nature of the waters, and how they were present at the beginning, or to probe the deeps and the nature of the heavens, to detour into the mode of existence of the angels? It would be difficult for anyone to cover such subjects, which I think that no one understands anyway! Would anyone even be able to do it (thanks to a knowledge lent by God, who had been there tell him), or been able to understand a so subtle speech - or rather one so inaccessible to the spirit? In fact, we find among men, at the time when the book of the very wise Moses was written, an ignorance which exceeds even that of the Greeks. That which should have made possible for those people to understand fully the glory of God was lost, it is obvious from the account, in the pit of the deepest stupidity. As the Scripture inspired by God says, the men of that time should have had some idea of the Creator and maker of the universe from the beauty of things

created. But they reached such a degree of wrong thinking that the things that should have led them to the knowledge of the truth shows that they were disposed instead to follow a lie. The very wise Paul bears a witness worthy of trust to this idea by writing, "Ever since the creation of the world, his invisible nature, namely his eternal power and deity, has been clearly perceived in the things that have been made. So they are without excuse; for although they knew God, they did not honour him as God or give thanks to him, but they became futile in their linking and their senseless minds were darkened."

22. This declaration could touch those who invented the vulgar superstitions, coarse and completely unreasonable; the men, for example, to which as I said the book of Moses was addressed. They are revealed as filled up full of stupidity, as we will realize easily by studying the body of doctrines of their successors. Plutarch, an extremely subtle man, wrote on this subject in book I of his collection of Theories on nature:

"See from where they drew their idea of God: unceasingly the sun, the moon and the other stars, following courses which pass under the earth, rise with always the same colors and identical dimensions, at the same places."

And further in the same book:

"The concept of God is defined thus: an intelligent and fiery breath, lacking form but changing at will and making themselves resemble any thing. Men, in the beginning, conceived an idea like this starting from the beauty of the spectacle which they had before their eyes, because no beautiful thing is born randomly and fortuitously; it needs art to create it!"

I will add to this quotation that which Hermes Trismegistes has written To his spirit (that's the title of the book):

"Thus, do you say, God is invisible? What a heap of blasphemies! Who is more visible than Him? If He created, it is so that this is seen in everything. The excellence of God, his virtue, it is to be visible in everything!"

23. We will find agreement on this point from the accuser of our pious religion, Julian! He professes that the knowledge of God is not taught, that man acquires it by himself; here what he writes:

JULIAN

Our first proof that this is not learned, that it is innate to mankind is the devotion to the divine, a general characteristic of mankind, in private life and in public life, in the individual and in the community. In fact we have faith in something divine, however vague. But to give specific details on this something is a difficult thing for anyone, and even those who know it cannot do so fully.

And further:

To this idea, common to all mankind, is added another: we all have a nature so dependent on the heavens and the gods that are seen there that, even if someone imagines a different god to ours, he always assigns him the heavens as his residence: it is not that he banishes him from earth; but he so to speak establishes the King of the All in the heavens as in the most honourable place of all, and conceives of him as overseeing from there the affairs of this world.

CYRIL

So we see how those pagans who can't endure the crasser errors (worthy of charlatans, and if I might say so, of serfs) and who have abandoned the popular way of looking at things, have not been entirely deprived of the true concept of God. They have worked out what must be the superiority of power of Him who can bring so vast and wonderful a creation under the control of harmonious laws.

24. As for the rest under discussion here, they didn't recognise God through his creation. They were lured away, losing all human common sense. Not content just to worship the heavens, the earth, the moon and the others stars, they also installed in sacred enclosures representations (of them) in varied forms. They engraved there the silhouettes, not only of men, but even of unintelligent animals, of birds and other beasts, and they gave these idols the titles of 'gods' and 'saviours'! How can we not admire the wisdom of Moses? He concealed from the men of that time everything that was complicated, deep, difficult to assimilate, in order to reveal to them instead what would enable them to recover sane ideas, and something which had the virtue to put them on the right road to an irreproachable teaching -- I mean a teaching of an all-powerful God. In the same way we would congratulate for very good reasons the schoolmaster who puts himself at the intellectual level of his pupils, in order to lead them by the hand, step by step, towards discovering sacred truths, without putting to them, at the very beginning, any too elaborate ideas, or any very hard to grasp. At the same time we would refuse to recognise Moses as worthy of praise, who acted in the same way? But Julian, if Moses doesn't seem to you to have said anything worth hearing, do you want us to look at the teaching which is dearest to you? Let's see rely as best we can on the meticulous Theogony of Hesiod!

25. This poet indeed pretends to hear the voice of the gods and makes as if he were possessed by the Muses (as if that were a significant or desirable thing!)

> "Tell me (he writes) how at first the gods and the earth were born,
> The rivers, the infinite sea which swells and foams,
> The sparklings stars, and the immense sky over all."

Further, he tells of the birth of chaos and night, without saying how it occurred:

> "First the earth gave birth to the starry sky, its equal,
> Able to entirely cover it..."

After revealing that the sky was the son of the earth, he adds that the latter, married to the sky, gave birth to the seas, then

> "Koeos, Krios, Hyperion, Japet..."

and also Theia, Rheia, Themis and Mnemosyne.

He adds Phoebus to this list, 'golden-crowned', as he calls him, then Tethys. In his opinion, the last of all these children was Kronos. On top of this he piles up a complete hotchpotch of whimsical and incoherent stories.

Perhaps Julian will claim that Hesiod has made up all these fairy-tales as a poet does: in fact maybe he blushes at the fables of Hesiod! But then why did these take some of it from the hierophant Moses, who composed a clear and accurate work, based on real facts? In fact he affirmed that God created the sky and the earth, the sun and the moon, the stars, light, animals which fly and those which swim, various brute beasts, the splendour of vegetation, edible fruit and the grass of the meadows.

26. See how the text of Moses very wisely cuts short the error which the ancients fell into: don't they name the heavens Zeus, the earth Demeter, the sun Apollo, and the moon 'the noisy goddess with the rod of gold', i.e. Artemis? In a word, allotting according to their imagination a share of glory to each creature of God, they adored these creatures as divinities. However the description made by Moses of the creation of the world was clear, easily comprehensible, without anything lacking in its great exactitude. And that's what we're going to have to show. "In the beginning," he writes, "God created the heavens and the earth." So he denies that matter shared with God the time before the beginning, eternity; or that it was uncreated, as some say. He doesn't present something that didn't exist at one time as coinciding with and coexistant with the eternal; he doesn't confuse the temporary, something which was brought into existence with difficulty, with that which is from time immemorial; something that changes to something which is always itself; nor something which is corruptible with that which is incorruptible! On the contrary, he makes creation happen in a moment, the principle that refers to things brought into existence, because starting from nothing it was brought to be what it is according to the divine will. What he certainly does not say, is that matter existed already, had already been invented, and that God limited himself to being its director and workman, giving form to what was amorphous, and only imposing on matter different qualities, dimensions and volumes. On the contrary he says that, thanks to a secret and unutterable power, in the beginning God brought into being what was not and did not exist in any way whatever!

27. As for the way in which he made creation happen, we do not have the means to say. I affirm that it is beyond any way of expression known to us: how indeed could what exceeds understanding be explained? In my opinion, the approach imagined by the supreme Being and the way that leads to an understanding of his enterprise will be always as inaccessible to our human condition as we are by nature lower than this Being himself. When Moses said, "In the beginning, God created the heavens and the earth", understand that he condenses and summarizes in some way all the details in a single word, when he describes the genesis of all creation. Then, he attempts to say somehow how this creation was put in order and how all the things created were assigned the role in life which they have. Moses also states that that God created through the all-powerful Word: in fact his creator-Word of the universe is God himself and proceeds from God by nature. "God said," Moses continues, "Let there be a firmament!" and this firmament instantaneously becomes real by the operation of the Word, and God gives it the name of 'heaven'. "God said: Let the dry land appear!" and the waters gather in a single body. God said moreover: 'Let the sun be!' and it was; and so for the moon, the stars, the day, the terrestrial and aquatic animals, and the birds. But by nature the elements themselves cannot draw from their own resources the possibility of escaping corruption, on the contrary, they need the hand of He that maintains them in good condition: this

is the sense of the words of Moses: "the breath of God was moving over the waters." Indeed the breath of God vivifies anything, because He is life also by nature, as He proceeds from the life of the Father; everything needs Him, and there is no other means for anything to obtain existence in order to be what it is.

28. So contemplate, as I have just said, the firmament firmly established by the Word and the firm ground emerging after the gathering of the waters in a single body; contemplate the green earth full of grass and trees, and the vital forces included in them which makes possible for them to conceal their transitory nature with the virtue of eternity, to last and remain; see the luminaries of the firmament, created by God only for the purpose of lighting what is on earth, to mark the moments of time, the days, the years! Moses adds that the earth accepted the order to give rise to the brute animals, the Creator on his side distributing to each its form, size and conditions of existence. And when everything in the world had finally been created, when nothing for lacking to supply the needs of man, then, and only then, did the Creator begin to think of the way in which He was going to realise man himself. Because the creation of man, unlike the other creative acts, could not be improvised. The supreme being, in the conception of some and actually, is just grandeur and perfection -- some even say that it is the loss of any spirit, any language, any admiration: however He decided to form the animal in His own image, as much as could be made. Also, having every reason to ensure that this, which must be in His image and resemblance, namely man, did not appear weak, contemptible or different enough from the other animals, He chose to create him only after serious reflection.

29. However, it will be said without inaccuracy, that nothing could escape the divine spirit, since He knows everything indeed before it is born; why then did God reflect, even though He knew in advance the nature of man? The incomparable Moses, as I said, affirms that it was in conformity with the divine economy that man was to some extent honoured by the deliberation of the Creator; he shows that his creation was not done quite simply, might one say, not just like any other: everything happens as if God had taken a particular care of this action. The expression is undoubtedly forced --- but I grant that it appears quite sensible; we affirm that the man is most important of the animals, and was made to resemble He that created him. The irresistible will of God brought into existence the whole of creation: it is not difficult, I think, to convince ourselves of this, even if we only read what Julian's Masters of Superstition wrote. All of them believed that it was right to think and say that everything was somehow created by God, spiritual realities or physical realities, invisible things or visible things. They were unanimous in confessing that everything is in the hands of the King and Lord of the universe; Plato even ascribes these words to him:

"Gods of the gods, works of which I am the Creator and the Father..."
[Extract from the Timaeus; see ch. 33 below].

But we have already quoted the Greeks on this point, and I want to avoid repetition. I will however mention the words of Hermes Trismegistus in his book To Asclepius.

30. This says: "Osiris exclaimed: Then, O very great Good Genius, how did all the earth appear? And the great Good Genius answered: According to a

preconceived plan and, as I said, by draining; the body of water received from the Lord the order to draw itself together, the whole earth appeared, muddy and shaken by tremors; the sun then began to shine, spreading its heat without pause, and made the earth dry, which stood within water, surrounded by water." Another passage reads: "the Creator and Lord of the universe shouted: Let the earth be, let a firmament appear! and all at once the earth was, the first element of creation. " So much for the earth; about the sun Hermes speaks as follows: "Osiris said: Thrice great Good Genius, from where did this large sun appear? and the other answered: Osiris, do you wish us to relate the birth of the sun, the way in which it appeared? It appeared by the providence of the supreme Master! The creation of the sun by the supreme Master was done by the operation of his holy and creative Word." In a similar way, Hermes writes in book I of his Detailed Commentary to Tat: "the Lord of the universe shouted at once by his holy, spiritual and creative Word: Let the sun be! and, at the very moment he said it, the fire which proceeds from an ascended nature --- I understand by this, the unmixed fire, the brightest, most effective and fertile that may be --- was attracted to Nature thanks to the breath which animated it, and was gathered by his care towards the high parts, far from water."

31. Everything was created on the orders of God and by the operation of the creative Word: that, man must think, and it is in conformity with the truth to say it. But how, and by what means it was so, God alone knows! God distributes to each thing created this or that type of being according to His good pleasure. He determines the mode of existence of each. To be convinced of this, it is only necessary to listen to Moses: "Let there be a firmament! and it was so", and again: "Let the waters gather in one place and let the dry ground appear!" Such formulas determine the exact nature of each thing which is brought into being. However, once again, Hermes Trismegistus the Greek raises the subject; he puts into his work God saying to the creatures:

"I will impose to you as an obligation, you who are subject to me, this commandment which was given to you by my Word; make it your law!"

Indeed, as I have just said it, the Creator allotted a natural law to each creature, and those appear, at the discretion of God, to have received some arbitrary type of existence, or to have not received it. This would be the direct and sincere way to present things, but Julian is dazzled beyond reason by the views of Plato and writes:

JULIAN
Now hear what Plato says about the universe : *"Now the whole heaven or the universe,----or whatever other name would be most acceptable to it, so let it be named by us,----did it exist eternally, having no beginning, or did it come into being, and had some beginning? It has come into being, because it can be seen and handled and has a body.*

All such things are things we can touch, and such things can be understood by thought based on using our senses."

And further on

"So, according to reason and probability, we must say that this universe is an animal possessing a soul and intelligence, and in very truth, it owes its beginning to the providence of God."

CYRIL

32. We see then clearly what he -- who, for Julian is the "divine and very wise Plato" -- says: the whole world -- his words -- is submitted to begin sometime, to have a beginning. It can be handled, seen, and has a body, and can be understood by thought based on using our senses, and was created by the providence of God! Julian depends entirely on Platonic tricks of speech, and he spins crowns of praise unceasingly to Plato. But he was mistaken just like Plato; none of his ideas is beyond criticism, and it could be said that he turns around with any wind. We'll go without delay and highlight an example, thanks to a new quotation of his, here:

JULIAN

Let us compare one thing with another, and no more: what kind of creation does the God of Moses do, what kind that of Plato? "God said: Let us create man in our image and our resemblance; and to have dominion over the fish of the sea, the birds of the sky, the animals, and of all the earth, and all the animals which walk on the earth. And God created man, He created him in the image of God; male and female He created them, and God blesses them, saying: Grow and multiply, fill up the ground, bring it under control, rule over the fish of the sea, the birds of the sky, over all the beasts and all the earth."

33. Listen now to the speech which Plato gives to the Creator of the universe: "Gods of the gods, the works of which I am the Creator and Father will be indissoluble as long as it be my will; because if all that was made can be unmake, to want to unmake what was well arranged and which is in good condition is the deed of the malicious!

Also, since you were created, let you be neither immortal nor very indestructible: however, you will not be destroyed, you will not fall under the blow of a mortal destiny, since your lot is to depend on my will, a bond stronger and more sovereign still than those which bound you to your birth. However learn the instructions that I give you. There remain still three mortal races to be created; as long as they do not exist, the heavens will be imperfect, because it will not contain all the races of living beings. However, if I created them myself and communicated life to them, they would be like gods; so in order that they are just mortals and that this All is truly the All, devote yourselves according to your nature to the creation of living beings, by imitating my power as I showed it at the time of your creation. And, those of them whom it is advisable for them to bear the same name as the immortals, which is called 'divine' and which guides those among them who always agree to obey justice, and to you others, I will give you the seed and the principle. For the remainder, mixing the mortal with the immortal, manufacture and generate living beings, give them food to make them grow, and at their death receive them back again!"

CYRIL

34. So this brave man, full of ardour in his attacks against us, derides the creation of man --- i.e. that which the incomparable Moses has revealed --- and regards as negligible the idea that human nature is created with the image and resemblance of God! But what sensible person would disagree that this is one of those ideas which best constitute an embellishment? Is there anything better than to say that we are marked with the divine image? And don't we affirm that the divine substance is that which is most elevated, most sublime in the refulgence of its inexpressible glory, that this truly constitutes the whole of the forms and beauties of virtue? Who would not be struck with the obviousness of what I have just said? So why does Julian sneer at such exceptional realities? Why does he deride that right to dominate the universe with which the thinking and reasoning animal, the one most similar to God of all those which populate the earth, i.e. man, was honoured? Moreover nature itself agrees with the accounts of Moses; but Julian makes no argument from probabilities, and purely and simply denies this view of things, holding only to the words of Plato! He also expresses his admiration, and that in a quite ill-considered way, before the harangue which the philosopher made up, I don't know how, and in which the supreme God is supposed to address himself to created 'divinities' who do not deserve such a name.

35. It is necessary, I think, also to answer him on this point. If Plato is inventing some fiction and, as is the habit of poets, lends to the character of God the words which he considers appropriate to him, he badly missed the mark, and we could sharply scold him for not knowing how to handle a prosopopy appropriately! If on the other hand he claims to have heard the voice of God, then to hell with his drivel! It is impious to claim that God the master of the universe allowed false divinities to share a glory which is his, and his alone, since He said: "I will not give my glory to another, nor my virtues to graven images!" Come! in few words let's oppose the truth to the writings of Plato, as follows. I wish indeed that we could agree that the spiritual powers On High, born of God, were honoured with the name of 'god', since we say that there are in heaven those who bear the names of 'gods' and 'lords'; and besides we ourselves received the honour of such a title, when God spoke thus to us:

"I said: You are gods, and you are all the sons of the Almighty."

But, in this case, there is an explanation which is essential, and this declaration of God on this subject could be well the most obvious proof of his benevolence. In fact, when the Creator of the world had made the thinking and reasonable creature, according to His own image and His own semblance, in His great kindness He honoured it with the name of 'god': and there was nothing wrong with this, since we also are accustomed to giving, say for example to a portrait of a man, this same name of 'man'!

36. Therefore the thinking and reasonable creature, because God holds it in greater regard than those lacking reason and thought, seems to have received in part a higher glory since the denomination of 'god' haloed it with gold; in any case, absolutely no other creature was named 'god'. In fact, like the universe, the sky is not a living being in the true sense of the expression, it is not even endowed with a soul. Even if none of our writers went so far as to guarantee these positions, it would be enough to support them, in the absence of others considered 'sages', to refer to the disciple of Plato in person, Aristotle. This last said, as we have already affirmed, that the universe is in no way endowed with

a soul, nor reason, nor thought. In these cirumstances, the force of truth has prevented Julian from claiming that the universe --- or the Whole, as it could be, to employ the proper term of Plato --- is endowed at all with a soul or even thought, since there are in his camp, as I said, a group of those who touch him more closely on this point than his most resolute contradictors! It is not likely that God gave the mission of creation to gods completely stripped of soul or thought: this arises from the nature of the problem itself, if it is subjected to suitable examination. Who can imagine the Creator of the world entrusting to other divinities the creation of the three races? Would one speak of hesitation on his side, or of total contempt for our destiny? Such attitudes are in my opinion completely foreign to the supreme Essence!

37. Because, if the Creator is good, how could he express hesitation towards some task?

"It was --- Plato also affirms this --- actually a kindness; however a good being does not nourish ill will towards nothing."

As for claiming that God showed scorn, that would amount to allotting vanity and attributing arrogance to Him. However, how could he allow himself to reign over beings whom he judged as unworthy for him to create? Or how is it that he takes pleasure from our worship if he couldn't be bothered to create us in the first place? That He demands that we honour Him, that He requires obedience and understands that human nature is like his in every kind of virtue, it would be the easiest thing in the world for me to bring a thousand veracious testimonies drawn from the inspired Scripture. But as Julian grants especially his confidence to those of his own kind, I recall that Porphyry wrote in book II of his work On Abstinence from animal flesh:

"Let us also therefore sacrifice, but let us sacrifice as appropriate, to God who rules the whole universe, as a sage has said.

No material offerings, no clouds of incense, no formulas of consecration!

Because there is no material body which does not appear from the start impure with respect to the immaterial one. Therefore the word itself, when it passes by words, is inappropriate for God, nor the interior word, when soiled by the evil of the soul: let us adore him through the purity of silence, the purity of thoughts which we form on him!

Thus uniting ourselves to God and assimilating ourselves to him, we must offer to him the holy sacrifice of our intellect, which will be at the same time a hymn to his glory and the path of our safety. However it is in the absence of passions and the contemplation of God that achieves this sacrifice."

38. So God wants us to honour him, and that by the holiness of our life, we will conform ourselves to him on the spiritual level, by engraving his beauty in our souls. But then, tell me Julian, how can he demand this attitude of us, if he has almost abandoned us to other creators, and stripped us of the privilege of being made by him which he gave to all other creatures? What leads him to provide for things here below if they are, as Plato says, given as playthings to other divinities? Because he exercises his providence, and his care and benevolence extend to the smallest things; to learn this we can listen to one who knew God as his father:

"Are not two sparrows sold for an as?
However not one of them will fall to the ground without the consent of our Father."

Perhaps Julian will declare the formula inadmissible because false --- because he contorts himself furiously against God! --- but will this receive a good reception from people of his group, I mean people as deceived as him? Thus Alexander, the disciple of Aristotle, has written in his treatise On Providence:

"To say that God refuses to grant his providence to things here below, is to go resolutely against the concept of God: because one needs a certain ill will and a nature completely perverted not to do good when one can do it; both one and the other ideas are foreign to God, in him is found neither both nor either of them. So it remains that God can and will exercise his providence on the things here below; however it is obvious that he exercises this providence if he can and wishes to do so. Nothing then, among things fortuitous, could in good logic exist without the divine decision and will."

39. Some claim that Plato himself shared this thesis, and it is public knowledge that Zeno of Citium and the Stoics assert it. So from their testimony it results that human things are the object of providence on the part of the Almighty, the single and natural God of the universe. --- "And then, will someone say, what can we conclude from that?" --- well, it is appropriate for a God, exercising of his own wish his providence, not to deprive the human race of his most precious gift, which is to be created by Him, and not to see the job allotted to creators themselves created and which are divine only in name and not by any other measure --- if it is true that it will always be repugnant to the divine glory to allow others the power to create and invite nothing-beings to do it. Because it is impious to claim that the appropriate and privileged character of the divine and unutterable nature can belong naturally to such or such of the creatures which it created. In fact these features are indeed appropriate only to the divine nature and to it alone, and display its glory to a supreme degree. Inaccessible to a creature --- I mentioned this above --- are the exclusive privileges of being single and supreme, and we affirm that one of these privileges is to be able to act as creator and to bring beings from nothing into existence. Under these conditions, how could a nature resulting from birth and creation, destined inevitably for corruption by the same laws which are its being, hold the active role of God?

40. In fact, if to create is regarded as a form of knowledge in God, one cannot present as irrational the gift of the creative capacity made by God to his creature: doesn't it sometimes happen to us that we create things starting from something already made, while using suitable know-how? If on the other hand, as I said, the fact of creating in the way that God does constitutes an ability and capacity pertaining only to an exceptional nature, and exceeds the measure of a creature, why do those people belittle the privilege of the supreme nature, and grant according to their good pleasure to beings created and promised to corruption? After which, persuaded that they have in their heads an idea of genius, they denature instead the words of God, by claiming that the Uncreated

has confided to created beings the power to bring into existence what is specific to him only. --- OK, they say, but then it follows that a thing created by God should be stronger than death and corruption! --- Thus, friends, it is from jealousy towards certain beings that the Creator refused to give them the best part, that on the contrary He condemned them to a worse, one could say, by not being willing to create them! Apparently, He has avoided the fate which prohibited Him from creating mortal beings --- perhaps even He was unaware of this fate completely? If they claim that God was in ignorance, the creature knows more than Him: the creators, they affirm themselves, were perishable beings! If on the other hand, giving up this position, they accept that God knew, how then would a good being refuse to do what he knows to be good? Because in the end it is quite true that the immortal one is preferable to the mortal!

Cyril of Alexandria: Against the Synousiasts
By Cyril of Alexandria

CYRIL OF ALEXANDRIA FROM HIS TREATISE [1] AGAINST THE SYNOUSIASTS [2]

of which the beginning is
A long discourse has already been made by us.

1. A [3] long exposition has already been wrought out by us, who desire to strive for the doctrines of the truth. For it everywhere sets forth One Lord Jesus Christ, Who proceeded forth God the Word out of God the Father Divinely, out of a woman humanly and after the flesh. And let no one say, who has a mind witting how to view each several thing, that I have been borne savagely down on them who have not such faith, seeing that a sort of sorrow sometimes invites hereto, sorrow I mean in regard to them whom we have contradicted. For the fact itself has its proof [4], not an idle excuse. For they [5] indeed are already dead and departing from human affairs, have gone to another life; and it is utter folly in enmity to insult not the living but them who are now dead. Nevertheless since the Truth is dear to the lovers of right doctrine, and it needs befits them to say the truth and to be practised in the power of resisting them who are wont to utter vain things, I thought I ought, seeing that a countless multitude of brethren have suffered no slight harm from what Diodore Bishop of Tarsus and he who was Bishop of Mopsuestia, the most eloquent Theodore, have written of Christ the Lord and Saviour of us all, to say some few things on what they said and to point out to readers the hideousness of the track of both.

2. Since then some stumble and imagine to themselves a change of the Word into blood and flesh, let them be laughed at as beside themselves and let us say to them, Wake up ye drunkards from their wine, and let us examine of what kind is the nature of the flesh, and be ye diligent to think, of what kind again is that of God Who is over all. For unbounded is the interval, and with reason may one say that to venture to compare them at all is not free from responsibility. For the One is by Nature God and Lord of all, Light and Life and Glory and moreover Power, the other is what every body who lives among men knows. When then any affirm that there has taken place a change of the Word into this earthly body, or that the Word being God framed to Himself out of His own Essence, a body of the same nature as our bodies, let them confess first that He ceased to be what He is (He was, as I said, God and Creator, Life and Light, Glory and Power) and let them moreover affirm that to endure the liability to slip that belongs to things generate is nob alien to Him and that to be conversant with a worse condition than that wherein He is, is not untried by Him.

Yet I think one ought to investigate what it is that thrust Him down hereto: was it some necessity and tyranny of passion falling on Him? yet how is it not distraction that any should suppose this so to be? for where is the greater than He and that is able to overpass His Nature? since how is God the Name that is above every name and Lord of Hosts? But it is not necessity (they will haply say) but that a change of His own choice invited Him hereto. But it were impossible that He should suffer this too: for how should the Divine and Untaint Nature make ought that befitted Him not, His choice?

3. But haply they will say in their folly that the Word being God changed into flesh yet not the whole nor altogether: albeit how is it not an evident proof of utter madness, to think and say that these things are so? for first of all to say that not wholly nor yet altogether did He change or undergo turning pertains to those who mete Him and represent Him as quantitied and no longer incorporeal, yea and capable of being conceived of as in space and as become circumscribed. Next how must not the opponents consider this too, that whatever a part of a body subject to the Word suffer, this full surely the whole too will in possibility suffer? (for suffering would not befall one of the parts, unless the nature of the whole body were susceptible of suffering). Hence seeing that the test of their ideas compels us even against our wills to advance to words we would not, beseeching the Word of God to pardon us we say this: that if it is true that He possesseth not the being beyond turning neither is the suffering it impossible to Him, the force of the blasphemy will full surely reach both to the Father Himself and to the Holy Ghost, for Consubstantial is the Holy and untaint Trinity. And then what stability look we for in God as to our own case if He too is weak as we and undergoes commotion unto what is not lawful to say, albeit we heard Him say in plain terms, Behold I am and have not been changed, the Divinely-uttering Psalmist too says that the Heavens are the works of Thy Hands: they shall perish but Thou abidest and all of them shall wax old as a garment and as a covering shalt Thou fold them and they shall be changed, but Thou art the Same and Thy years shall not fail? Consider therefore that he who in spirit speaketh mysteries and is God-taught flings turning to the nature of things generate, saying by way of illustration or demonstration that the heavens shall wax old, and hath reserved Immutability to the God Who is over all, for he hath testified to Him Ever-being and unchangeableness.

And as it has been believed to be impossible that the Nature of the Word should change into what it was not, so can it not be that the generate pass into the nature of Godhead, lest many of Its attributes be seen to be accidents, which if it advanced so far as idea alone would have the charge of blasphemy indelible. For if ought of things generate at all change into the Godhead by Nature, one would not miss of right reasoning if one should chuse to say that It out of things that are not comes into existence and obtains that which is not its, as a sort of material of Its being, and that the body became the substance of incorporeal Essence, tangible and visible of the Invisible and Untangible. And if the Father's Only-Begotten Word is by Nature Life as being of the Father Who is Life, and by change hath admitted unto consubstantiality (as they say) that which, is of the human lump, there is great fear lest we say that He is not unmixed life, for He is not unmingled with what is apt to decay.

In another way too does the opinion of the deceived ones battle with the Economy with flesh: how, we will say. The Lord being God appeared to us that He might destroy the decay which lorded it over us, not that Himself might exhibit His own Nature partaker with decay by immingling with Himself flesh subject to death.

The charge therefore is of equal force, whether one say that the Word of God have been turned into the nature of body or whether that the flesh again is transformed into consubstantiality with God. It is fit therefore that we keep away from both one and other, seeing that it is not without peril to chuse to think beside what one ought to think.

4. That we may believe that even though His holy and all-pure Body be of same nature with our bodies, it is nevertheless august and Divine and far above our measures, as having been made His own, for He hath wrought through it, therefore was it called also bread of life, yea verily it is said both to have come down from Heaven and to give life to the world because of the Word that came down from above and out of Heaven, whose very own too the flesh has been made. Hence Divine it is (as I said), yet may one not surmise if indeed he have a mind well-established and that is versed in skill of dogma, that it has changed into the nature of the Godhead. For to the Nature that is Supreme and above all must be rigidly preserved Simplicity and absence of blending with other and of any appearance of being compounded in what belongs to It or of lacking any addition and coming into fellowship of sameness of nature or consubstantiality with ought unconnatural to It.

For come let us with acute eye of the understanding investigate the idea of the confusers. They say that His Flesh has been changed (I know not how) into consubstantiality with God the Word. Why? or what is it that brings it thereto? For of its own self it has not the impulse that would bring it thereto, and of its natural motions to admit such desires is foreign to it. It remains then to say this, that it was brought hereto by the will of God the Word. Did He then cast away the Economy which He clearly deemed worthy of all account by reason of His inherent Clemency and the Pleasure of His Father? for one may hear Him say clearly through the psalmist's voice, Sacrifice and offering Thou wouldest not, whole burnt-offerings and for sin Thou delightedst not in, but a Body Thou perfectedst Me, then I said, Lo, I come (in the volume of the Book it has been written of Me) to do, O God, Thy Will: I delight to do it. The sacrifices therefore (those I mean according to the Law of Moses) were unwilled by the Father, the Incarnation of the Word or His being made Man, was rather His Choice inasmuch as it brings in the grace that is through faith to those beneath the sky, His Clemency and God-befitting gentleness making a marvellous demonstration of Itself.

What plea will there be for daring to say that He cast off (as I just now said) the august and saving Economy, if so be it be true that He put off from Him the being flesh, having changed it into the Nature of Godhead, albeit the all-wise Paul hath written of His holy Body, For wherein He hath suffered He is able to succour the tempted? But if we take away that wherein He hath suffered, with it surely will go too the means of succour given to us. For the saying that the flesh changed into the Essence of Deity, belongs to those who take from it the being what it is; which if it be admitted to be true, no longer will it be thought or said to be flesh. Since what is the change, if it have remained what it is? What profit therefore is there to our bodies from being partakers of the Mystic and holy offering? or what is the benefit therefrom? for if the Word who is united thereto willed to transform it into His own Nature, why is He found saying to us, I am the bread of Life which came down from Heaven and giveth life to the world and the bread which I will give is My Flesh which I will give for the life of the world, and again, He that eateth My Flesh and drinketh My Blood abideth in Me and I in him?

Hence if the flesh have passed into what it was not, darting up or borne up by the Will of the Word into a position above its own nature, it is time (it seems) that we ourselves too should make after other sort the power of the mystery and follows what pleases him [who thus teaches].

5. Therefore you have the confession of the Incarnation of the Only-Begotten, from which also our faith is True. But if (as our opponents say) the Word united thereto, put off His Flesh, changing it into His own Nature, the change of the Flesh and the confession of our saving Faith will (it seems) come to an end together, and with it surely cease the justification too that is through it, we are yet in our sins, the filth of our old offences is still not cast away.

6. If He have ceased from being as we, i.e. man, together with being also above us Divinely, the foundation of our salvation has been shaken, we unawares returned (it seems) to have to be again lorded over by death and sins. For as when the nethermost foundations of house (it may be) or wall have been shaken, the superincumbent parts too will surely subside with them: thus if the Economy with flesh of the Only-Begotten be not firm, our condition surely has tottered with it and grown weak at last; and how, we will say. For if they say that the Flesh of the Word have been changed into the Nature of the Godhead, there is every need to conceive that He has otherwise departed from His will to be son of man: then how does the all-wise Paul say, For there is one God, One Mediator too of God and men, the Man Christ Jesus Who gave Himself a ransom for us? For He mediates as being the Same, God alike and Man, reconciling us to God the Father through Himself and in Him and conjoining as it were unto union things by their own nature parted unto generic difference by a boundless parting, yet in Christ did they come together unto an union without confusion and that cannot be plucked asunder: for He has been connected Divinely with the Father, and He was connected with us too humanly. Thus is the Man Christ Jesus conceived to be and is our Mediator. But if the Flesh has been really (as he says) cast away by Him, He is gone surely away from mediating between us and His own Father: how therefore do we yet approach Him? who any longer brings us or mediates? For the Divine Paul said that the Mediator is Man: we remember Christ also Himself saying, No man cometh to the Father except through Me. Idle talk therefore and words full of distraction are the inventions of the Synousiasts.

7. The Son of man when He cometh shall He find Faith on the earth [6]? For come let us ask our opponents what sort of faith the Son of man when He comes down out of Heaven would find in them who are on the earth, or how He would have us minded regarding Him: that He has left willing to be son of man, or that He has remained in the likeness usward? though how can one doubt that if it were displeasing to Him to be conceived of as being yet as we are, how were it meet to say, The Son of man when He comes shall He find Faith on the earth, and not rather The Word of God bare and without flesh when He comes, will He find of such sort the faith concerning Him among them on the earth? But since He clearly and manifestly calls Himself Son of man even at the time of His arrival from Heaven, it is I suppose clear that not having changed His Flesh into ought else but rather having it glorified, incorruptible and spotless and adorned with light unapproachable [will He come]: for He will come down

out of Heaven, not in His former low estate (whence should He?) but in the glory of His Father with the Holy Angels.

8. If, His Flesh changed into the Nature of the Godhead, He ceased to be Son of man too, clear would it be to every one henceforth that we too have lost the boast of sonship, as no longer having a First-born among many brethren.

9. He is seen not trans-elementing into the Nature of Godhead that which is unalterably and without confusion flesh, but rather will He rightly be conceived of as adorning it with His own glory and filling it with God-befitting dignities: thus will He be seen in His season by them who are on the whole earth, on His return from Heaven. And verily when having accomplished full well the mystery of the Economy with flesh, He had gone up into Heaven, even though they who saw it had wondered at the thing (for a cloud received Him, as it is written): to them who then marvelled one of the holy Angels addressed him, Men of Galilee why stand ye looking into Heaven? this Man Who was received up from you into Heaven shall thus come again as ye saw Him go into Heaven. Did therefore they who were addressed see the very Word apart from the flesh going up to the Father? or [did they see Him] having cast away the likeness to us and not in a tangible and visible but transfashioned rather into one intangible and invisible? who dares to say this? If He shall so come as He also went up, how is it not true to say that He shall come again embodied and not bare and fleshless Word?

10. The all-wise Paul hath written of Christ, Who shall transfashion the body of our low estate conformed to the body of His glory. Then what will they say to this who say that His flesh changed into the Nature of the Word? will the bodies of the saints too pass by a change into the Nature of Godhead that they too may become conformed to the body of His glory? yet how is this not a frigid speech replete with the uttermost unlearning? for when the flesh is wholly changed (as he says) into the Nature of Godhead, what body will the Word being God use? For somewhat un-embodied is Godhead, and it is true that No one hath ever seen God.

11. But haply they will say that the Flesh did not wholly depart from being what it was, but that it was as it were immingled with God the Word unto a natural oneness. And what do we say to this? First of all, sirs, there is full much difficulty, the reasoning hereon will be weak if ye decide to retain to the Nature of the Word Its unchangeable Being and unalterable Existence (for in no wise will it change unto what it was not): either when it has suffered this It has been shaken from Its God-befitting stability and from the settledness that is inherent in it by Nature, or howsoever one calls it: but I think that it is wise that we should in no wise be able to conceive that ought of things that are could abide in the Nature of the Godhead: for this too is likewise impossible.

Yet if they are well off in examples that can persuade that in commingling and mixture of things mentioned the inherent property of either will be wholly imparticipate of the quality of the other, let them bring forward their examples: for we say that the name corn-mixture will in no wise harm the force of the truth. But if they say that flesh and Word are mixed after the manner of liquids, how do they not know that liquids mixed one with other, say wine and honey, are no longer simply what they were, but are changed into something else by the addition of a quality of a different species?

Hence if they say that the Flesh has been commingled with the Word, there is every need of saying that each of the above-mentioned leaves being what it was, and makes up of both some one intermediate thing, of a different nature full surely from what each was individually and as yet unmingled one with other. Then what results? I would fain ask of our opponents whither matters will proceed, since they say that the Nature of God is henceforth mingled with flesh (for it hath not remained in identity, if their mixture, as has been said, is true). Either therefore they will say that He has this advance for the better, or else a sinking down to the baser, according to reasonable understanding of things. If then they say that He has been displayed superior to Himself, they have given the vote of superiority to the flesh by reason of which He is perceived to have sprung up to the higher: if they say that this was not so but rather that He sank into the worse: the flesh verily did Him too wrong even as it does to ourselves, although we say that He let Himself down to emptiness and entered into the likeness us ward, not in order that Himself might be seen suffering somewhat in His own Nature, but that He might render us who are in flesh and blood superior to flesh and might make us, beyond the measures of human nature, sons of God.

But if as the perverted ones say He have been commingled with flesh, borne aside unto what He was not, how they say that He has not been wronged I cannot conceive [7]; haply He is found to have lost in addition, the very being the Form of the Father, the Likeness and Impress of His Person and to be no longer in equality with Him but rather in a depression and abasement of both Nature and glory.

12. It were therefore nothing hard to add very many discordant things to what have been said; but I think that one ought gladly to withdraw from thoughts tending to absurdity. We must therefore eschew commixture, for thus shall we escape the mischiefs too that come thence. But some other argument (as they say) as to these things finds its way in. For the Divine Paul is found to have written, But if we have also known Christ after the flesh yet now no more do we know Him. Hence if ye know not Christ after the flesh (they say), one must needs say that the flesh changes, so that it is the Nature of the Word Himself: as God is He known [8].

But I suppose one would say straightway to this, 'When therefore he says of us too, But they which are in the flesh cannot please God, but YE are not in the flesh but in the spirit:----does he know that we are bare of flesh and blood? does he utter such things as though to disembodied spirits?' Yet how is it not jugglery to conceive or say this?

In regard to us then he calls by the name of flesh, the unreasonable and not irreprehensible passions of the flesh: but in regard to Christ the Saviour of us all, Who is All-Pure and knows not to transgress (for He did no sin), in other way beseems it that After the flesh be conceived of; for no longer is He in the infirmities of the flesh.

13. He [9] has fasted, He hungered, He waxed weary from long wayfaring, yet more He was crucified and died: He conceded that He should suffer these things, not to the Nature of the Godhead (for the Divine and Supreme Nature is conceived of as beyond suffering) but rather to His own Flesh. But when He rose again having trampled on Death and trans-elemented the nature of man in Himself unto incorruption and life: He is at length seen wholly without share in fleshly infirmity. Therefore with reason does the minister of His mysteries say that no more is He known after the flesh, i. e. in fleshly weakness.

14. Having tasted death in the flesh for our sakes He rose again in His body. And verily, this very thing He had fore-signified to the people of the Jews saying, Undo this Temple and in three days I will raise it, for that has been raised which was dissolved, but we say that the flesh and not the Nature of the Word was dissolved: for that were impossible.

15. Christ therefore Himself the Saviour of us all giving proof to His disciples that He rose from the dead, with flesh and hands and feet and declaring in plain words that He is not a Spirit: how will one doubt that the flesh did not change into the Nature of Godhead, either before the Passion (for He suffered in the flesh of His will) nor when having trampled on death He arose the third day and was thus seen of His disciples?

16. Who of the holy prophets is seen uttering afore things thus hard and impracticable and impossible? who of the holy Apostles or Evangelists spake to them of these things?

No one whatever. Let them therefore, speaking out of their own heart and not out of the mouth of the Lord, as it is written, be ashamed. For WE, whose care is orthodoxy and who makest a special aim zealously to follow the right words of the holy Fathers, not the unbridled mouth and empty-speakings void of understanding of some, will not be minded otherwise than we ought to be minded, but ever going the straight way of the truth and having our mind filled with the holy Scriptures we both say that the Flesh of our LORD was ensouled with reasonable soul and believe that it is Divine and Spotless and glorified and moreover both life-giving and sanctifying, inasmuch as it became the own Flesh of the Word out of God the Father and affirm that it is not (as some have thought fit to think) of a son other than He, nor yet that it is changed into the Nature of Godhead.

17. S. Cyril against Diodore and Theodore in his Book against the Synousiasts wrote thus [10],

But perchance to these things some one will say, 'What then, if when contending with some of the heretics or withstanding them who confuse the Natures [11], they made a discourse grosser than should be?'

I suppose that one would say that if the fault were in a single word, the hearers would forgive what was not far off from what is right. For that in some slight degree they sometimes err even against their will, who apply themselves to subtilty and exactitude of idea, they have some just reason for apology. But if in works thus extensive and in their whole writings so to say, they have attacked the Truth blow upon blow, every where confessing Two sons, what excuse will be sufficient for them?

18. [12] these things too taught S. Cyril in his discourse against those who confuse the Natures, after this sort,

Receiving as a rule of right and undistorted Faith the Holy and God-inspired Scripture we say that when the Only-Begotten Word of God became First-born for us, He ceased not from being what He was and He is called, along with the title of Very God, also Son of Man: and He is not seen to have changed the Nature of the Godhead into flesh, which without change and without confusion was united to Him that He might adorn it with His own Glory: rather we must know that He filled it with God-befitting authority. Thus for a season was He seen of those in all the earth when He came from Heaven.

Footnotes:

1. The opening fragment of this Treatise has been preserved to us by the fifth General Council, those that follow by John Bishop of Caesarea in Palestine, in his Defence of the Council of Chalcedon, of the two last fragments, the former is in Severus' treatise against John, the latter in a later collection. Bishop John heads his citations from S. Cyril: "Divers citations of Cyril Archbishop of Alexandria wherein one may find the difference of the Two Natures proclaimed by him and that God the Word is Impassible and Immortal, the Temple passible and mortal." The ms. containing Bishop John's fifteen citations from this treatise numbers them, 77-90 (91 is a passage from the Glaphyra), while the citations from the 3 books against Diodore and Theodore are numbered 181-190. This led to these fragments being placed first in the edition of S. Cyril's works, following the order of Bishop John's citations. But the present treatise is not purely against the Synousiasts or Apollinarians, though it cites their objections, in something of the same way as S. Athanasius does: but against the Apollinarians with a reference to the previous labours, not free from error, of Diodore and Theodore; see the commencement and the 17th fragment, cited by Severus and the words with which Severus introduces it, below p. 376. See too above p. 335 fragment 27 against Diodore, which may really belong to this book, not to that. I have then no doubt that the present treatise is the one on the Incarnation which Liberatus refers to. He says, "Cyril as reports go, wrote 4 books, three against Diodore and Theodore as authors of Nestorian dogma and another book on the Incarnation, wherein are contained genuine testimonies of old Fathers, i.e., Felix Pope of Rome, Dionysius Bishop of Corinth and the marvellous Gregory called the Wonderworker. And though in the Books the words of Theodore against the Arians are cited yet they maintain that he was Nestorius' master." Liberatus, Breviarium, cap. x. in Gallandi xii. 134. The opening paragraph of this Treatise, "A long discourse has already been made &c", shews that it was written after the books against Diodore and Theodore.

2. S. Athanasius, after having spent all his life in combats and sufferings for the Truth against Arianism, had, in the close of his days, to oppose the mad errors of the Apollinarians or Synousiasts. Their chief errors are stated thus by S. Athanasius in the opening of his first book against Apollinarius; "but these either fancy a change of the Word or suppose that the Economy of the Passion is a semblance; one while saying that the flesh of Christ is Uncreate and heavenly, other while, that it is consubstantial with the Godhead. Next they say that in place of the man that is within in ourselves [i. e. the inner man] there was an heavenly mind in Christ; for He used as an instrument the form which envelopes Him, for it was impossible that He should be Perfect man: for where perfect man is, there too is sin, also that two perfects cannot make one whole." Against Apollinarius lib. i. § 2. t. i. 923. See extracts of his two books against them, above p. 324 note c. S. Athanasius exposes the chief

points of their misbelief more succinctly in his famous Letter to Epictetus, Bishop of Corinth. S. Gregory of Nazianzum, the contemporary of S. Athanasius had to contend with them in his very midst (see Tillemont's life of him, Art. 88 t. 9. pp. 515 sqq. ed. 2) and as Tillemont points out, to bear their accusation that he divided into Two the One Son ("Next they accuse me as though I introduced two natures separated or opposed, and divided the Super-natural and marvellous Union, when I ought either not to do what they accuse me of, or not to accuse them of what they do," second Letter to Cledonius, near the end, t. i. 749 ed. 1609)). Under these circumstances S. Gregory both opposes the Apollinarians, and expresses himself with that accuracy on the Incarnation that his words are cited before the Council of Ephesus as contradicting Nestorius' teaching. He says, "If any suppose that Mary is not mother of God, he is external to the Godhead. If any say that He passed through the Virgin as through a channel, and not that He has been formed in her Divinely alike and humanly, Divinely because without a man, humanly because by the law of bringing forth, he likewise is godless. If any say that the man was formed, that God then entered Him he is condemned; for no Generation of God would this be, but a shunning of birth. If any introduce two sons, one Him who is out of God the Father, the other him who is forth of his mother and not One and the same, may he fall away from the sonship which is promised to them that believe aright. [This will illustrate the strenuous efforts which Diodore Theodore and Nestorius made to persuade themselves that they were not really saying two sons.] For two natures are God and man, as also soul and body, not two sons nor two gods. For neither are there with us two men, even though Paul so spoke of the inner part of man and the outward. And to speak briefly, one thing and other (allo men kai allo) are that whereof the Saviour is, seeing that the invisible is not the same as the visible, and the apart from time with the subject to time, not one and other (allos de kai allos), not so; for Both are One in commixture (hen te sunkrasei), God made-man, man-made-God, or however we are to call it. I say 'one thing and other' in contrast to how it is in the T RINITY: for there it is One and Other (allos kai allos) that we confound not the Persons, it is not one thing and other (allo de kai allo), for in the Godhead the Three are One and the same Thing." first Letter to Cledonius t. i. 738 d 739 a b cited in the council of Ephesus among the authorities which Peter priest of Alexandria and protonotary read out of a collection that he had. S. Cyril, as having drunk in and made his own the teaching of the Fathers which were before him in all his writings speaks expressly of One Christ, and that by Union, the Word remaining Word and the Flesh flesh: see the citation from the seventh Paschal homily (A.D. 420) p. 227 note m, and again p. 233 note z; in the latter place S. Cyril guards against Apollinarian error, in the former against both that, and the parting into Two the Incarnate S ON, which the Apollinarians charged their opponents with doing.

3. From the fifth Collation of the fifth General Council, after S.

Cyril's Letters to John of Antioch, Acacius of Melitine, and the Emperor (t. vi. 101 Col.). I had overlooked it but it is pointed out by the indefatigable Tillemont.

4. I have adopted from the margin of the Concilia the reading convictionem which they give as the reading of the Paris Manuscript, i.e. Biblioth. Imperial. Lat. 16832, formerly belonging to Notre Dame: the Beauvais manuscript also agrees with it.

5. i.e. Diodore and Theodore

6. See this text commented on by S. Cyril at the end of his Treatise de recta fide to the Princesses Arcadia and Marina, and again near the close of his Treatise on the same subject, to the Empresses, § 42, p. 178 d e.

7. Thus I have translated, emending ... from Cardinal Mai's translation of the syriac version.

8. There seems to be some error here in the greek words as preserved to us by these two late MSS. ...Card. Mai's latin version from the syriac is here not close enough to help.

9. It will be observed that this fragment carries on the subject of the previous one: probably only a few lines intervened between them.

10. From Severus against the Catholic Bishop of Caesarea.

11. the Apollinarians.

12. from the collection referred to above, p.326 note e and elsewhere.